YOUR
CHILD'S
HEALTH

YOUR CHILD'S HEALTH

A Pediatric Guide for Parents

Barton D. Schmitt, M.D., F.A.A.P.

Director of Consultative Services, The Children's Hospital of Denver
Professor of Pediatrics, University of Colorado School of Medicine

BANTAM BOOKS

TORONTO · NEW YORK · LONDON · SYDNEY · AUCKLAND

YOUR CHILD'S HEALTH: A PEDIATRIC GUIDE FOR PARENTS
A Bantam Book / September 1987

Library of Congress Cataloging-in-Publication Data

Schmitt, Barton D., 1937–
    Your child's health.

    Includes index.
    1. Pediatrics—Popular works.   2. Children—Diseases—
Treatment.   3. Children—Health and hygiene.   I. Title.
RJ61.S365   1987   618.92   87-47687
ISBN 0-553-34400-5

Published simultaneously in the United States and Canada

PRINTED IN CANADA

WC   0 9 8 7 6 5 4

This book is dedicated to the inner strength of families:
To my parents for believing in me.
To Mary for her love and encouragement.
And to Dave, Elaine, Becky, and Mike for everything they
taught me about fractured femurs, sea urchins, wolf spiders,
pill-swallowing phobia, hypothermia, and having fun.

CONTENTS

Foreword xv
Introduction xvii
Acknowledgments xxi
The Reader's Responsibility xxiii

I. EMERGENCIES

Emergency Telephone Calls 3
Emergency Transportation 4
Emergency Symptoms 5
Resuscitation (Mouth-to-Mouth Breathing) 8
Choking 9
Allergic Reaction, Severe 12
Bites, Animal or Human 13
Bites, Marine Animal 16
Bites, Snake 19
Bites, Spider or Scorpion 21
Bleeding, Severe 24
Bleeding, Minor—See Trauma, Skin
Breathing Difficulty, Severe 26
Burns, Chemical 28
Burns, Thermal 28
Coma 31
Convulsions with Fever 31
Convulsions without Fever 33
Delirium 35
Drowning 36
Electric Shock or Lightning Injury 37
Eye, Chemical In 38
Eye, Foreign Body In 39
Fracture—See Trauma, Bone and Joint
Heat Reactions 41
Poisoning 42

II. TRAUMA

Bone and Joint   49
Ear   52
Eye   53
Finger and Toe   54
Genital   57
Head   58
Mouth   61
Nose   63
Skin   64
Tailbone   69
Teeth   69
Tetanus Booster Following Trauma   71
Suture Removal   71

III. NEW BABY CARE

NORMAL NEWBORNS

First Days in the Hospital: Getting Acquainted   75
First Weeks at Home: Getting Help   79
The Normal Newborn's Behavior   83
The Normal Newborn's Appearance   84
Newborn Rashes and Birthmarks   88
Newborn Skin Care and Bathing   91
Circumcision, Pros and Cons   93
Circumcision Care and Problems   94
Foreskin Care and Problems   96
Breast-feeding   97
Formula-feeding   102
Weaning   106
Solid (Strained) Foods   110
A Healthy Diet   112
Tooth Decay Prevention   117
Normal Growth   119
Normal Development   121
Crying Baby (Colic)   124
Prevention of Sleep Problems   127
Thumbsucking and Pacifiers   132
Sibling Rivalry   136
Accident Prevention   139
Newborn Equipment and Supplies   142
Shoes   147

NEWBORN PROBLEMS

The Sick Newborn: Subtle Symptoms   149
The Sick Infant: Judging the Severity of Illness   150
Cradle Cap   151
Diaper Rash   152
Jaundice of the Newborn   154
Spitting Up (Regurgitation)   156
Tear Duct, Blocked   158
Teething—See Mouth and Throat
Thrush   159
Tongue-Tie   161
Umbilical Cord, Bleeding   162
Umbilical Cord, Delayed Separation   162
Umbilical Cord, Oozing   163
Umbilical Hernia   164

MEDICINES AND IMMUNIZATIONS

Medicines: General Instructions   167
Medicines: Helping Children Swallow Them   169
First Aid Kit   172
Home Medicine Chest   173
Immunization Schedule   175
Immunization Reactions   177

IV. BEHAVIOR PROBLEMS

Crying Baby (Colic)—See Normal Newborns
Night Awakening in Older Infants   181
Sleep Problems, Prevention of—See Normal Newborns
Sibling Rivalry—See Normal Newborns
Thumbsucking and Pacifiers—See Normal Newborns
Bedtime Refusal   187
Breath-Holding Spells   190
Discipline Basics   192
The Timeout Technique   204
The Terrible Twos and Temper Tantrums   208
Discipline Problem Solving   214
Poor Eaters, Poor Appetites   235
Overweight   240
Masturbation in Preschoolers   246
Stuttering   248
Tics (Twitches)   251
Toilet Training   253
Toilet Training Resistance   257

Bed-wetting (Enuresis)   261
Television: Reducing the Negative Impact   267
The Working Mother: Juggling Children, Home, and Career   271
Divorce's Impact on Children   280
Schoolwork Responsibility   283
Short Attention Span   288
School Refusal or Phobia   293
Adolescents: Dealing with Normal Rebellion   297

V. COMMON ILLNESSES

GENERAL SYMPTOMS OF ILLNESS

Fever   305
Decreased Appetite with Illness   312
Increased Sleep with Illness   313
Contagious Diseases and Incubation Periods   314
Frequent Infections   317
The Prevention of Infections   320

BRAIN

Altitude Sickness   323
Breath-Holding Spells—See Behavior Problems
Coma—See Emergencies
Convulsions—See Emergencies
Delirium—See Emergencies
Dizziness   325
Fainting   326
Headache   327
Injury, Head—See Trauma
Motion Sickness   329
Soft Spot, Bulging   330

SKIN: WIDESPREAD PINK OR RED RASHES

Rashes, Unknown Cause (Widespread)   331
Itching, Unknown Cause (Widespread)   332
Ampicillin Rash   334
Chicken Pox (Varicella)   335
Dry Skin   338
Eczema (Atopic Dermatitis)   339
Fifth Disease (Erythema Infectiosum)   342
Heat Rash (Miliaria)   343
Hives (Urticaria)   344
Measles (Rubeola)   346
Measles Vaccine Rash   348

Purple Spots 348
Roseola (Roseola Infantum) 349
Rubella (German Measles) 350
Scarlet Fever 351

SKIN: LOCALIZED PINK OR RED RASHES

Rashes, Unknown Cause (Localized) 353
Itching, Unknown·Cause (Localized) 355
Acne 356
Athlete's Foot (Tinea Pedis) 359
Bites, Insect 361
Boils (Abscesses) 365
Cradle Cap—See Newborn Problems
Diaper Rash—See Newborn Problems
Hand, Foot, and Mouth Disease 368
Impetigo (Infected Sores) 369
Jock Itch 372
Lice (Pediculosis) 373
Newborn Rashes and Birthmarks—See Normal Newborns
Poison Ivy 375
Ringworm (Tinea Corporis) 377
Shingles 378
Sores 380
Tinea Versicolor 380

SKIN: CONDITIONS WITHOUT A RASH

Blisters, Foot or Hand 383
Bluish Lips (Cyanosis) 384
Burns, Chemical—See Emergencies
Burns, Thermal—See Emergencies
Calluses, Corns, and Bunions 384
Cracked Skin 386
Dandruff 386
Fingernail Infection (Paronychia) 387
Foreign Body in Skin (Slivers) 389
Freckles 390
Frostbite 391
Hair Loss 392
Injury (Bruises, Cuts, Puncture Wounds, and Scrapes)
   —See Trauma
Jaundice 392
Lymph Nodes, (or Glands) Swollen 393
Moles (Nevi) 395
Pale Skin 396

Pimples   397
Sunburn   398
Sweating, Excessive   402
Toenail, Ingrown   403
Warts   404
Wound Infections   406

EYES
Allergies of the Eyes   409
Chemical in Eye—See Emergencies
Foreign Body in Eye—See Emergencies
Injury—See Trauma
Itchy Eye   411
Red or Pinkeye (Conjunctivitis)   411
Swelling of Eyelid   413
Stye   414
Tear Duct, Blocked—See Newborn Problems
Yellow Discharge   416

EARS
Earache   419
Ear Congestion   421
Ear Discharge   422
Earwax, Packed   423
Foreign Body in Ear   425
Injury—See Trauma
Itchy Ear   425
Mumps   427
Pierced Ear Infections   429
Pulling at Ear   431
Swimmer's Ear (Otitis Externa)   432

NOSE
Colds   435
Foreign Body, Nose   441
Hay Fever (Allergic Rhinitis)   442
Injury—See Trauma
Nosebleed   445
Sinus Congestion   447

MOUTH AND THROAT
Bad Breath (Halitosis)   451
Canker Sores (Mouth Ulcers)   452

Cold Sores (Fever Blisters)   454
Geographic Tongue   455
Injury, Mouth—See Trauma
Injury, Teeth—See Trauma
Lip, Swollen   456
Sore Throat (Pharyngitis)   457
Swallowing Difficulty (Dysphagia)   459
Teething   460
Thrush—See Newborn Problems
Tongue-Tie—See Newborn Problems
Tonsil and Adenoid Surgery   461
Toothache   464

LUNGS (RESPIRATORY)
Allergic Reaction, Severe—See Emergencies
Breathing Difficulty, Severe—See Emergencies
Breathing, Noisy   467
Chest Pain   468
Choking—See Emergencies
Congestion, Respiratory   469
Cough   469
Croup (Croupy Cough and Stridor)   474
Hoarseness   477
Influenza   478
Wheezing   480

ABDOMEN (GASTROINTESTINAL)
Abdominal Pain   481
Ampicillin Diarrhea   483
Constipation   483
Diarrhea   488
Foreign Body, Swallowed   493
Gas, Excessive   494
Hiccups   496
Nausea   497
Pinworms   497
Spitting Up (Regurgitation)—See Newborn Problems
Stools, Blood in   499
Stools, Unusual Color of   501
Umbilical Hernia—See Newborn Problems
Vomiting   502
Vomiting of Blood   505

BLADDER (URINARY)

Bed-wetting (Enuresis)—See Behavior Problems
Toilet Training—See Behavior Problems
Urination, Pain with (Dysuria)   407
Urine, Blood in   510
Urine, Strong Odor   510

GENITALS

Circumcision, Pros and Cons—See Normal Newborns
Circumcision Care and Problems—See Normal Newborns
Foreskin Care and Problems—See Normal Newborns
Foreign Body, Vagina   513
Injury—See Trauma
Menstrual Cramps (Dysmenorrhea)   514
Swelling, Groin or Scrotum   516
Vaginal Irritation   517

BONES AND JOINTS

Backache, Acute   521
Shoes—See Normal Newborns
Injury, Bone and Joint—See Trauma
Injury, Finger and Toe—See Trauma
Injury, Tailbone—See Trauma
Limb Pain   523
Limp   525
Neck Pain, Acute   525

VI. GLOSSARY

A GLOSSARY OF CHILDREN'S DISEASES REQUIRING PHYSICIAN CONSULTATION

Index   549

FOREWORD

This clearly written and highly informative book fills a need frequently expressed by parents and physicians for an up-to-date authoritative home guide that may be easily consulted for common pediatric problems and emergencies in infants, children, and adolescents. As first-line health care providers for their children, parents want to know not only *what to do* but also the *facts* on which the advice is based. This book meets these parental expectations foursquare.

The comprehensive coverage of this volume is obviously based on a thoughtful analysis and firsthand acquaintance with the concerns and questions that most often confront parents. Equally impressive is the author's ability, based on considerable experience, to give advice that is eminently practical without being redundant.

Emergencies, of course, present an especially urgent need for accurate and easily understood information. Such advice may be truly lifesaving. Urgent situations are therefore extensively covered in this book, with easy-to-follow directions. There is also advice about what medications to have at hand in the home and how to gain a child's cooperation in taking medicine.

The special section on pediatric symptoms and signs—problems such as fever, sleep disorders, crying, convulsions, skin rashes, and other complaints—spells out what these complaints mean, what the parent can do about them, and when it would be appropriate to consult a physician. Information about a child's eyes, ears, nose, mouth, lungs, abdomen, and other body parts addresses many doubts that parents may have from time to time.

This is the kind of book we have all been looking for: a

handy, dependable guide to the parental management of emergencies, symptoms, and other pediatric problems. Today's parents want to be well-informed about child health generally, and this publication provides that desired knowledge. *Your Child's Health*, in my judgment, is the most useful and authoritative pediatric guidebook currently available for parents.

—MORRIS GREEN, M.D.
   Lesh Professor and Chairman
   Department of Pediatrics
   James Whitcomb Riley Hospital for Children
   Indiana University Medical Center

INTRODUCTION

Dear Parents,

Welcome to the universal joys and challenges of parenthood. These guidelines were written to help you provide better health care for your child. I have emphasized the common illnesses and injuries that befall the majority of children. When possible, I have stressed the healthy life-styles and preventive measures you can take to keep your child well. When appropriate, I have cautioned you about the limitations of surgery and drugs. The table of contents, cross-references in the text, and the index have been carefully organized and interwoven so you can find needed advice quickly. And finally, the topics are covered in depth, so you can find answers to almost all of your questions in one book.

To help you use this book, information relating to each of the topics or diseases is organized in the following way:

SYMPTOMS AND CHARACTERISTICS

- What are the symptoms?
- What does it look like?

Causes

- Is it caused by virus, bacteria, allergy, tension, injury, or some other factor?
- Is it contagious?

Expected Course

- How long will it last?

- How bad will it get?
- What are the possible complications?

GUIDELINES FOR CALLING YOUR CHILD'S PHYSICIAN

- How can you recognize serious symptoms and emergencies?
- Should you call immediately?
- Can you safely wait to call during office hours?
- Can your child safely be treated at home without a call?

HOME CARE RECOMMENDATIONS

- What first aid measures can you take for emergencies?
- For nonemergencies, what can you do to make your child comfortable?
- How can you prevent similar infections or injuries in the future?
- How can you speed recovery?

The desire to be better informed about child rearing and childhood illnesses is universal. These guidelines are meant to supplement the health education provided by your child's physician. Most parents also receive ongoing health advice from friends, relatives, newspapers, magazines, radio, and television. Unfortunately, information from the media or nonprofessionals may be confusing, conflicting, or downright alarming. One of the main purposes of this book is to help bridge the information gap with accurate, up-to-date, and straightforward health facts and advice. *Your Child's Health* is the only book of its kind that has been carefully reviewed by eighteen successful parents and pediatricians. The guidelines for when to call your child's physician have been tested by hundreds of physicians and nurses across the country who use my earlier book, *Pediatric Telephone Advice*.

One sound rule of child rearing is: Don't do anything for your child that he can do for himself (such as feeding or dressing). The same advice can easily be applied to parents with regard to health care decision-making. You are an important member of the health care team. You have innate common sense and you know your child better than anyone else. Observe your child's symptoms. Use this book as your reference and make informed decisions. As your ability to differentiate (triage) between serious and nonserious illnesses increases, so will your confidence. The common illnesses and behavior of childhood will come into perspective as something you can competently manage. Don't underestimate your abilities.

I wish you enjoyable and successful parenting during these exciting years.

—BARTON D. SCHMITT, M.D.
Director of Consultative Services
The Children's Hospital
Professor of Pediatrics
University of Colorado School of Medicine
Denver, Colorado

ACKNOWLEDGMENTS

I am immeasurably indebted to my pediatric and parent reviewers for their close examination of my text for accuracy, safety, objectivity, clarity, and completeness. Their effort was extraordinary and their feedback invaluable. Information sharing and constructive criticism were essential to completing this six-year project.

Pediatric Review Board
John D. Bancroft, M.D., Monroe, Wisconsin
John M. Benbow, M.D., Concord, North Carolina
Daniel D. Broughton, M.D., Rochester, Minnesota
Rosemary D. Casey, M.D., Philadelphia, Pennsylvania
David M. Christopher, M.D., Renton, Washington
Morris Green, M.D., Indianapolis, Indiana
Jessie R. Groothuis, M.D., Denver, Colorado
David L. Kerns, M.D., San Jose, California
Cajsa J. Schumacher, M.D., Albany, New York
Daniel R. Terwelp, M.D., Austin, Texas
Wallace C. White, M.D., Denver, Colorado

Parent Review Board
Elizabeth T. Berk, Concord, Massachusetts
Gayle N. Ebel, Bowmar, Colorado
Nancy Gary, Child Health Associate, Denver, Colorado
Doris L. Klein, Child Life Worker, Denver, Colorado
Carol J. Markley, Bowmar, Colorado
Lynne M. Weaver, Littleton, Colorado
Marjorie S. Wise, Englewood, Colorado

In addition, the following colleagues and close friends provided support and encouragement throughout this project:

Steve Berman, Dick Krugman, Ed Plattner, Steve Poole, and Bob Bruegel. The following specialists graciously reviewed materials relating to their fields: Dr. Ray Wood (ENT), Dr. Royce Hatch (dentistry), and Dr. Marianne Neifert (breast-feeding). Betsy Cenedella and Mary Castle provided excellent copy editing. Toni Burbank and Andrew Zega of Bantam Books carefully steered this manuscript through the publishing process. They also looked after my need to be informed and included. While many typists have contributed to this book, Ceil and Michelle Carter took the complete manuscript through three extensive revisions. And finally, my deep gratitude goes out to the many physicians, nurses, students, and parents who have shared questions and ideas with me over the last twenty years.

THE READER'S RESPONSIBILITY

The contents of this book have been carefully reviewed for accuracy.

If you have any questions as to the correct diagnosis or proper treatment for your child, call your child's physician for help.

If you feel your child's condition has become serious, don't be reluctant to recontact your physician. Trust your intuition; you know your child better than anyone else.

The author and publisher disclaim responsibility for any harmful consequences resulting from the misinterpretation or misapplication of information or advice contained in these guidelines.

YOUR CHILD'S HEALTH

I

EMERGENCIES

EMERGENCIES

EMERGENCY TELEPHONE CALLS

LIFE-THREATENING EMERGENCIES
Dial "0" (Operator) or 911.

In larger cities, this call will dispatch an emergency vehicle staffed by a rescue squad. In smaller towns and counties, the operator will connect you with an emergency ambulance service. The direct number for this service is usually found on the inside front cover of your telephone directory. In areas that use 911, children and the elderly should be taught to dial this number for crises. Increasingly, 911 is being linked to a computer system ("enhanced 911") that can determine the address of the incoming call even if the caller can't speak.

NON-LIFE-THREATENING EMERGENCIES
Call your child's physician.

If you don't have a physician, call the nearest emergency room. Always call in first, rather than simply going to an emergency room. Usually the physician will be able to provide you with critical first aid instructions by phone (e.g., for burns, animal bites, or fractures). Your physician can help you decide whether a rescue squad should be sent out or if it is safe for you to come in. Your physician can also tell you where to take your child for the best emergency care.

POISONING
Call your child's physician or the nearest Poison Control Center. (Each region has a toll-free number.)

HOW TO CUT THROUGH RED TAPE
When you call in, always state assertively, "This is an emergency." Do not let the answering service or receptionist put you on hold before talking with you. If you are put on hold, hang up and call back immediately.

EMERGENCY TRANSPORTATION

MAJOR EMERGENCIES
Call your rescue squad or ambulance service.

Definition of a Major Emergency • Children who need resuscitation en route (for instance, those in coma, with severe breathing difficulty, severe choking, or not breathing) must be looked on as "5-minute emergencies." Other children—with major trauma or possible neck injury—need splinting before transportation.

The Staff of Emergency Vehicles • Emergency vehicles are staffed by EMTs (Emergency Medical Technicians). These people are trained in Basic Life Support: cardiopulmonary resuscitation (CPR), splinting, bandaging, and so on. Paramedics are EMTs with additional training in Advanced Life Support: drawing blood, starting IVs, intubation, recording EKGs, and so on. Training ranges from 300 to 600 hours. EMTs are all certified by the National Association of EMTs, which has 20,000 members. While providing emergency care, they are linked by two-way radio to an emergency room physician at their base hospital.

Rescue Squads versus Ambulance Services • In larger cities, rescue squads are often available through local fire departments. Usually rescue squads can respond more rapidly than ambulances, and their service is free. After the patient's condition has been stabilized, they will often call an ambulance company for transport to the hospital if it is warranted. In general the police do not transport sick people, so don't call them for medical emergencies.

LESS SEVERE EMERGENCIES
Go to the nearest hospital offering emergency services. Try to call your child's physician first.

Definition of Less Severe Emergencies • These concern children who need to be seen as quickly as possible but whose condition is currently stable or at least does not pose a danger of suddenly needing resuscitation. Examples are poisonings, slow bleeding, severe pain, and most seizures. These can be looked on as "20-minute emergencies."

Advantage of Car over an Ambulance • A private car is quicker and less expensive than an ambulance. Another option is to call a taxi.

Driving in to Seek Emergency Care • If you are going by private car, don't leave until you know the exact location of the emergency room you will be going to. It is a good idea to rehearse the drive by the fastest route before an emergency occurs. Keep your sick child in the back seat. Try to have a friend or neighbor accompany you and do the driving. Some parents are too shaken by their child's injury to drive safely.

EMERGENCY SYMPTOMS

All the conditions discussed in this chapter are emergencies. I'm sure you won't overlook or underestimate the importance of a major burn, major bleeding, choking, a convulsion, or coma. The following emergency symptoms, however, are highlighted because they are either difficult to recognize or not considered serious by some parents. If your child has any of the following symptoms, contact your child's physician immediately.

SICK NEWBORN
If your baby is less than one month old and sick in any way, the problem could be serious.

SEVERE LETHARGY
To be tired during an illness is normal, but if your child stares off into space, won't smile, has no interest in playing, is too weak to cry, is floppy, or is hard to awaken, these are serious symptoms.

SEVERE PAIN

If your child cries when you touch him or move him, this can be a symptom of meningitis. Such children also don't want to be held. Constant screaming or the inability to sleep also point to severe pain.

CAN'T WALK

If your child has learned to walk and then loses the ability to stand or walk, the most likely reason is that he or she has a serious injury to the legs or an acute problem with balance. If your child walks bent over, holding his abdomen, he probably has a serious abdominal problem such as appendicitis.

TENDER ABDOMEN

Press on your child's belly while he or she is sitting up in your lap and looking at a book. Normally you should be able to press an inch or so in with your fingers in all parts of the belly without resistance. If he pushes your hand away or screams, this is an important finding. If the belly is also bloated and hard, the condition is even more dangerous. (See ABDOMINAL PAIN, page 481.)

TENDER TESTICLE OR SCROTUM

The sudden onset of pain in the groin area can be due to twisting (torsion) of the testicle. This requires immediate surgery.

LABORED BREATHING

You should assess your child's breathing after cleaning out the nose and when he is not coughing. If your child is working hard at breathing, has tight croup, or has obvious wheezing, he or she needs to be seen immediately. Other signs of respiratory difficulty are a breathing rate of more than 60 breaths per minute, bluish lips, or retractions (pulling in between the ribs). (See BREATHING DIFFICULTY, SEVERE, page 26.)

BLUISH LIPS

Bluish lips or cyanosis can indicate a reduced amount of oxygen in the bloodstream. (See BLUISH LIPS, page 384.)

DROOLING

The sudden onset of drooling, especially associated with difficulty in swallowing, can mean that your child has a serious infection of the tonsils, throat, or epiglottis (top part of the windpipe).

DEHYDRATION

Dehydration means that your child's body fluids are at a low level. Dehydration usually follows severe vomiting and/or diarrhea. Suspect dehydration if your child has not urinated in 8 hours, crying produces no tears, the mouth is dry rather than moist, or the soft spot in the skull is sunken. Dehydration requires immediate fluid replacement by mouth or intravenously.

BULGING SOFT SPOT

If the anterior fontanel is tense and bulging, the brain is under pressure. (See SOFT SPOT, BULGING, page 330.)

STIFF NECK

To test for a stiff neck: With your child lying down, lift his head until the chin touches the middle of the chest. If he is resistant to this, place a toy or other object of interest on his belly so he will have to look down in order to see it. A stiff neck can be an early sign of meningitis.

INJURED NECK

Any injury to the neck, regardless of symptoms, should be discussed with your physician because of the risk of damage to the spinal cord.

PURPLE SPOTS

Purple or blood-red spots on the skin can be a sign of a serious bloodstream infection. Explained bruises don't count. (See PURPLE SPOTS, page 348.)

FEVER OVER 105° F

All the preceding symptoms are stronger indicators of serious illness than is the level of fever. All of them can occur with low fevers as well as high ones. Serious infections become a frequent cause of the fever only when it rises above 105° F.

SUICIDE CONCERNS

Because of the marked increase in suicide attempts in adolescence, parents should be alert to any of the following symptoms: preoccupation with thoughts of death or suicide; themes of death in writing or conversation; abrupt withdrawal from friends and family; abrupt decline in schoolwork; reckless risk-taking behavior; depressed mood. Either call the suicide hotline or your child's physician.

CHILD ABUSE CONCERNS

Call your child's physician or the child abuse hotline if you are afraid you might hurt your child, if someone has injured your child, or if someone has shaken your child. Child abuse has a tendency to escalate, so protect your child by seeking help early. Infants are at the greatest risk for a serious reinjury.

RELATED TOPICS

THE SICK NEWBORN: SUBTLE SYMPTOMS, page 149
THE SICK INFANT: JUDGING THE SEVERITY OF ILLNESS, page 150

RESUSCITATION (Mouth-to-Mouth Breathing)

If your child has stopped breathing or is gasping for breath (e.g., from choking, croup, carbon monoxide poisoning, drowning, or head trauma), you won't have time to read these guidelines. So read them now. And take an approved CPR (cardiopulmonary resuscitation) or first aid course. You can't learn external cardiac massage purely from reading. Fortunately, more than 90 percent of children who stop breathing still have a pulse and heartbeat (unlike heart attack victims) and they need only artificial respiration to revive them. The steps in mouth-to-mouth breathing are as follows:

PREPARATION

Rescue Squad • Have someone call a rescue squad immediately. You're going to need help.

Clear the Mouth • Look for any gum, food, foreign object, or loose orthodontic retainer. If present, remove them with your fingers or a Heimlich maneuver (see CHOKING, *Heimlich Maneuver*, page 10.) If any liquid is in the mouth, remove it by turning your child on one side and using gravity.

Position the Head • With your child lying faceup, put a folded blanket or towel (½ inch to 2 inches thick) directly under the back of your child's head. Do not put anything under the shoulders or neck. This "sniffing," head-forward position opens the airway and closes the esophagus (thereby keeping air out of the stomach). The jaw and chin can also be pulled forward to open the airway more. (Note: Some adolescents and adults may require slight extension of the neck for optimal breathing.)

MOUTH-TO-MOUTH BREATHING

Pinch your child's nostrils closed with one hand and seal the mouth with yours. (In small children, an adult can often seal both the child's nostrils and mouth with his mouth.) Blow air with a steady pressure into your child's lungs until you see the chest rise (the smaller the child, the smaller the volume of your puff). Then remove your mouth and your child will automatically blow the air out without any help. During this time, take a breath and refill your lungs. Repeat this at the following rates:

- Under 2 years old: 20 times per minute (once every 3 seconds)
- 2 to 12 years old: 15 times per minute (once every 4 seconds)
- Over 12 years old: 12 times per minute (once every 5 seconds)

Occasionally, take several quite deep breaths to bring plenty of oxygen into your lungs. (Note: If it is impossible to open the victim's mouth, cover the mouth and give mouth-to-nose breathing.) If 4 or 5 breaths don't move the chest, assume the airway is blocked and perform a Heimlich maneuver 6 to 10 times in rapid succession (see CHOKING, below).

CHOKING

Choking is the coughing spasm and sputtering that follows getting liquids or solids on the vocal cords or into the airway. Most children choke on liquids that go down the wrong way or mucus from sniffing back nasal secretions. The child's cough reflex will clear the windpipe of aspirated liquid within 10 to 30 seconds. Complete blockage occurs when solid food (a piece of hot dog, for instance) or a foreign object becomes lodged in the voice box. (It can also occur with severe croup.) Under these conditions, the child is unable to breath, cry, or speak. The child will be in a state of panic, and if the obstruction isn't relieved in 1 or 2 minutes, the child will pass out and have a convulsion due to lack of oxygen.

FIRST AID FOR CHOKING

Call your child's physician immediately in all cases of choking. If your child passes out, call the rescue squad.

Encourage Coughing • As long as your child is breathing and coughing, do nothing except encourage him to cough the material up by himself. Reassure him that it will come out. The main purpose of your child's cough reflex is to clear the windpipe. Don't offer anything to drink, unless your child is choking on something dry and flaky. In general, fluids just worsen the problem by taking up some of the space needed for the passage of air.

Heimlich Maneuver If Breathing Stops in a Child over 1 Year Old • If your child can't breathe, cough, or make a sound, proceed with high abdominal thrusts. Grasp your child from behind, just below the lower ribs but above the waist, in bear-hug fashion. Make a fist with one hand and fold your other hand over it. Give a sudden upward jerk at a 45-degree angle to try to squeeze all the air out of the chest and pop the lodged object out of the windpipe. Repeat this upward abdominal thrust 6 to 10 times in rapid succession. If your child is too heavy for you to suspend from your arms, lay him on his back on the floor. Put your hands on both sides of the abdomen, just below the ribs, and apply sudden, strong bursts of upward pressure.

Back Blows and Chest Compressions for Children Under 1 Year Old • If your infant is under 1 year old, use back blows *before* applying the Heimlich maneuver. Place him or her facedown in a 60-degree incline over your knees or on your forearm. (You need gravity to help propel the object out.) Deliver 4 hard blows with the heel of your hand between the shoulder blades in rapid succession. If breathing has not resumed, lay your child on the floor and apply 4 rapid chest compressions over the lower breast bone (sternum) using 2 fingers. (These revised first aid measures were recommended by the American Academy of Pediatrics in July, 1986.)

Resuscitation If Your Child Passes Out • The rescue squad should be on its way. Quickly open the mouth and look inside with a light to see if there is an object that can be removed with your fingers or a tweezers (usually there is not). Don't put your fingers into your child's mouth unless you can already see the object and think you can pull it out. Probing blindly can wedge an object deeper into the voice box (larynx). If you know how, begin mouth-to-mouth breathing. (Otherwise, see the guideline on RESUSCITATION, page 8.) Air can usually be forced past the foreign object. If mouth-to-mouth breathing doesn't move the chest, repeat the abdominal thrusts or chest compressions.

PREVENTION OF CHOKING ON FOODS

Choking can be life-threatening, so try to prevent its happening again. Choking on foods kills as many children each year as accidental poisonings.

- Foods that are likely to be aspirated into the lungs are nuts of any kind, sunflower seeds, orange seeds, cherry pits, watermelon seeds, gum, hard candies, popcorn, raw carrot, raw peas, and raw celery. These hard foods should not be given to children under 4 years of age because molars are needed to chew them and knowledge is needed to spit them out.

- The soft foods that most commonly cause fatal choking by completely blocking the windpipe are hot dogs, sausage, grapes, and caramels (especially if the child is in a hurry). These dangerous soft foods must be chopped up before serving.

- Warn babysitters and older siblings not to share these foods with small children.

- In general, teach your child to chew all foods thoroughly before attempting to swallow them.

- An especially dangerous time is the morning after parties when some of these foods may be found on the floor by a toddler. Clean up early.

- Avoid letting infants chew on Styrofoam objects. Because it is so light, small bits of Styrofoam can float into the windpipe during gasping.

- Don't give a young child a toy with small, detachable parts. In 5 minutes you'll find the missing part in the mouth (if you're lucky).

- Remind people of all ages not to run or play sports with gum or other material in their mouths.

ALLERGIC REACTION, SEVERE (ANAPHYLACTIC REACTION)

- Immediate symptoms within 30 minutes
- Wheezing, croupy cough, hoarseness, or difficulty breathing
- Tightness in the chest or throat
- Widespread hives, swelling, or itching
- Previous allergic reaction to the same item is added evidence
- Usually caused by a bee-sting, drug, or food

FIRST AID

Call your physician immediately, even if you're not certain if a severe reaction is in progress. Have your child lie down with the feet elevated to prevent shock.

Epinephrine and Antihistamines • If you have an anaphylactic kit, give an injection of epinephrine (adrenaline) 0.01 ml per kilogram of body weight (a 20-pound child gets 0.1 ml, 40 pounds gets 0.2 ml, 60 pounds gets 0.3 ml, and adults get 0.4 ml). Inject it into the subcutaneous (fat) layer by angling the needle about 45 degrees. Check to see whether you have an antihistamine or cold medication containing antihistamines at home. If you do, give 1 dose immediately by mouth in addition to the epinephrine.

Bee-sting Treatment—For Severe Reactions • If a stinger is still present in the bite, remove it. Do this by scraping it off with a knife or credit card rather than squeezing it. Once a reaction has begun, a tourniquet is not helpful, according to the American College of Emergency Physicians in 1985. Rub the bite for 15 minutes with a cotton ball soaked in a meat tenderizer/water solution while seeking medical care.

Transportation • If you can't reach your physician, call an ambulance or go to the nearest Emergency Room (see EMERGENCY TRANSPORTATION, page 4).

PREVENTION OF SEVERE ALLERGIC REACTIONS

Children with anaphylactic reactions need to be evaluated by an allergist. Since the reactions can be fatal, you should keep emergency kits containing epinephrine preloaded in a syringe at home and in the glove compartment of your car. (These are available by prescription only.)

All these children must carry a card in pocket or purse listing their name, parent's home and work phone numbers, physician's name, physician's phone number, and type of allergy. Ideally, your child should wear a medical identification necklace or bracelet that records the insect or drug allergy. Some can be found in pharmacies. They can also be ordered from Medic Alert Foundation, P.O. Box 1009, Turlock, CA, 95381, or National Identification Company, P.O. Box 9438, Denver, CO, 80223.

BITES, ANIMAL OR HUMAN

The following three types of bites are covered in the next few pages. Go directly to the one that applies to your child.

BITES, WILD ANIMAL
BITES, PET ANIMAL
BITES, HUMAN

BITES, WILD ANIMAL

There are two basic types of wild-animal bites: rabies-prone bites and safe ones.

Rabies-Prone Bites • Rabies is a fatal disease. Bites or scratches from a bat, skunk, raccoon, fox, or large wild animal are especially dangerous. Squirrels occasionally carry rabies. These animals can transmit rabies even if they themselves have no symptoms.

Safe Wild-Animal Bites • Rodents such as mice, rats, gophers, chipmunks, and rabbits fortunately are considered free of rabies. In the Southwest, prairie dogs can carry plague, and people should not handle them. Campers should avoid placing bedrolls over rodent burrows.

CALL YOUR CHILD'S PHYSICIAN IMMEDIATELY IF

• The bite was by a dangerous wild animal.

• The bite penetrated the skin (even a puncture from one tooth).

• You have other urgent questions.

FIRST AID FOR SUSPECTED RABIES CONTACT

Wash the wound immediately with lots of running water and a mild dishwashing detergent for 10 to 15 minutes. This should be followed by 5 minutes of soaking in rubbing alcohol. Although it burns, it can kill the rabies virus. If a wild animal is still on the premises, call the police department immediately. If the animal is captured or dead, avoid all contact with it. Saliva from a rabid animal can cause rabies by getting into a cut. In the future, teach your child to avoid direct contact with any wild animal (even healthy ones).

BITES, PET ANIMAL

Most of these bites are from dogs or cats. Bites from domestic animals such as horses can be handled using these guidelines. Small indoor pets (such as gerbils, hamsters, guinea pigs, and white mice) are at no risk for rabies. Dogs and cats are free of rabies in many metropolitan areas. The main risk in pet bites is serious wound infection, not rabies. Cat bites become infected five times more frequently than dog bites. Puncture wounds are more likely to become infected than cuts. Claw wounds are treated the same as bite wounds, since they are contaminated with saliva.

CALL YOUR CHILD'S PHYSICIAN IMMEDIATELY IF

• The teeth or claws went through the skin (i.e., a puncture wound).

• The skin is split open (i.e., a laceration).

• There are superficial cuts *and* the animal seemed to be sick, the attack was unprovoked, or the animal was a stray.

• There are superficial cuts *and* the animal is one without rabies shots. (Exception: a known, healthy, friendly dog who was teased or became frightened.)

• You have other urgent questions.

HOME CARE FOR PET-ANIMAL BITES

First Aid for Puncture Wound or Laceration (Deep Cut) • Wash the area with a mild dishwashing detergent and running water for 10 minutes before going to the physician's office. Vigorous rinsing is the best protection against wound infection. Also check your child's immunization status for tetanus.

Scrapes and Superficial Cuts • For wounds that don't penetrate the skin, wash the area with lots of water and a mild dishwashing detergent for 5 minutes. You can leave it exposed to the air, or put a dressing on it for 12 hours if it's on an area that easily gets dirty. No antiseptic is necessary.

Observation of the Pet • If there is any possibility of rabies, the pet should be carefully watched for any signs of sickness and isolated from contact with humans for 10 days. If the animal belongs to another family and they are not cooperative, report the incident to the police so they can deal with the problem. Too many pets are left to roam without supervision.

Call Your Child's Physician Later If

• The wound begins to look infected.

• The pain increases after the second day.

• The redness increases after the second day.

PREVENTION OF PET-ANIMAL BITES

• Teach your children not to touch strange animals, break up dogfights, go near a dog that's eating, or touch a sleeping dog.

• Children under 4 years of age should always be supervised around dogs. (German shepherds, Dobermans, St. Bernards, and pit bull terriers are especially dangerous.)

• Babies under 1 year of age should never be left alone with a pet. Some have been attacked or smothered in their cribs, possibly due to the pet's jealousy.

• Protect your pet against rabies by yearly rabies shots. The first shot is normally given when your pet is 3 to 4 months old.

BITES, HUMAN

Most of these bites occur during fights. Sometimes a fist is cut when it strikes a tooth. Human bites are more likely to become infected than any other animal bite. Bites on the hands are at increased risk of complications.

CALL YOUR CHILD'S PHYSICIAN IMMEDIATELY IF

• The teeth went through the skin.

• The skin is split open.

• You have other urgent questions.

HOME CARE FOR HUMAN BITES

First Aid for Puncture Wound or Laceration • Wash the area with a mild dishwashing detergent and running water for 10 minutes before going to the physician's office. Also check your child's immunization status for tetanus.

Scrapes and Superficial Cuts • Wash the area with lots of water and a mild dishwashing detergent for 5 minutes. You can leave it exposed to the air, or put a bandage on it for 12 hours if it's on an area that easily gets dirty. No antiseptic is necessary.

Call Your Child's Physician Later If

• The wound begins to look infected.

• The pain increases after the second day.

• The redness increases after the second day.

BITES, MARINE ANIMAL

The following five types of marine bites are covered in the next few pages. Go directly to the one that applies to your child.

JELLYFISH OR PORTUGUESE MAN-OF-WAR REACTIONS
VENOMOUS FISH REACTIONS (as from stingray, stonefish, scorpion fish, catfish)
CUTS OR LACERATIONS (as from moray eels, sharks, barracudas)
SEA URCHIN STINGS
SHOCKS (e.g., from electric eels)

Clearly, all of these unpleasantries occur in salt water. But the dangers of the deep are a small price to pay for the rejuvenating qualities of an ocean vacation. Go to a beach with lifeguards and observe all warning signs or flags.

JELLYFISH OR PORTUGUESE MAN-OF-WAR REACTIONS

The jellyfish and Portuguese man-of-war have long, stinging tentacles (called nematocysts). Fragments of tentacles washed up on the beach after a storm can still cause serious stings. They produce lines of redness and burning pain. Sometimes they cause generalized symptoms of weakness, dizziness, nausea, and headache. Sea anemones (sea nettle) cause similar local reactions for 24 to 48 hours.

FIRST AID

• Wipe off any stinging tentacles with a thick towel or sand. Be careful to protect your hands, since the stingers can even penetrate gloves. Rinse the wound with sea water.

• Neutralize the venom with the continuous application of alcohol (in any available form) for 30 minutes. Meat tenderizer is a second-choice agent for inactivating the toxin.

• Apply a ½ percent hydrocortisone cream (no prescription needed) 4 times a day for a few days to reduce itching.

CALL A PHYSICIAN IMMEDIATELY IF

• Any generalized symptoms have occurred.

VENOMOUS FISH REACTIONS

These creatures always cause localized pain and redness. They also commonly cause weakness, sweating, fever, vomiting, muscle cramps, paralysis, or even shock. The stinging fish usually have venom in dorsal spines. The stingray has one or more venomous spines on its tail. Because of its powerful strike, the stingray often also causes a laceration.

FIRST AID

Fortunately, the venom of all these fish can be destroyed by heat.

• Rinse the area with lots of sea water to dilute the venom.

• Remove any particles of stingray spine left in the wound.

• Immerse the damaged extremity in water as hot as can be tolerated (but under 120°F) until the pain completely subsides (30 to 90 minutes).

CALL A PHYSICIAN IMMEDIATELY IF

• Any generalized symptoms have developed.

For stingrays:

• The skin is split open.

• The barb needs to be removed.

CUTS OR LACERATIONS, MARINE ANIMAL

Some fish cause a bite mark of varying severity without injecting any venom.

CALL A PHYSICIAN IMMEDIATELY IF

• Bleeding won't stop after 10 minutes of direct pressure.

• The skin is split open.

• A puncture wound is present.

FIRST AID

Wash the area with lots of sea water. Later, wash with soap and water for 10 minutes.

SEA URCHIN STINGS

A sea urchin usually causes localized burning pain if part of a venomous spine breaks off in the skin. If not removed, it may be dissolved by the body or it may persist and cause irritation and swelling (a "foreign-body reaction").

FIRST AID

First, stop the flow of venom by detaching any spine that protrudes from the skin. Neutralize the venom with a meat tenderizer/water solution, alcohol, or vinegar for 30 minutes. (Unfortunately, none of these are of proven benefit.) Then wash the area off carefully with soap and water. If any large fragment of a sea urchin barb remains beneath the skin, try to remove it with a sterile needle and tweezers as you would for a splinter. If purplish discoloration remains after the spine is removed, it's merely due to dye from the spine and is unimportant.

SHOCKS, MARINE ANIMAL

Your child may feel shocked, stunned, or partially paralyzed after contact with an electric eel.

FIRST AID

Reassurance should be offered. Your child will be feeling and acting normal in 20 to 30 minutes. No treatment is necessary except lying down with the feet elevated.

BITES, SNAKE

The following three types of snakebites are covered in the next few pages. Go directly to the one that applies to your child.

SNAKEBITES, POISONOUS
SNAKEBITES, NONPOISONOUS
SNAKEBITES, UNIDENTIFIED

SNAKEBITES, POISONOUS

In the United States the poisonous snakes are rattlers, copperheads, cottonmouths (water moccasins), and coral snakes. Over 90 percent of snakebites occur on the leg. In about 30 percent of poisonous snakebites, luckily, no venom is injected. If the venom was injected (envenomation), the fang marks will begin to burn, hurt, and swell within 5 minutes. Therefore, begin first aid only if these signs develop.

CALL YOUR CHILD'S PHYSICIAN IMMEDIATELY IN ALL CASES

FIRST AID

Transportation • Go to the nearest hospital emergency room as rapidly as possible. The most important part of therapy is antivenin, and it needs to be given within 4 hours. Have your child lie quietly, and carry him or her when necessary to reduce absorption of the venom.

Incision and Suction • If you are more than 30 minutes from the hospital, you are certain the snake was poisonous (except for coral snakes), and the fang marks begin to swell or hurt, take

10 minutes to try to remove some of the venom. Use a knife or razor blade, preferably cleaned with alcohol or a flame. Make a single cut in the long direction of each fang mark (don't make cross incisions), ¼ to ½ inch long and deep enough to go through the skin to the depth of the bite mark (about ⅛ inch). First squeeze out the venom for 1 to 2 minutes. Then try suction with a suction cup or your mouth for at least 5 minutes. After suction, wash the incisions vigorously with soap and water. Suction is not useful after 30 minutes.

Venous Tourniquet for Bites on Arm or Leg • If you are more than 2 hours from the hospital, put a venous tourniquet between the bite and the heart, at least 2 inches above the bite (but not around a joint). Use a wide band such as elastic wrap or a stocking. Make it tight enough to stop blood flow in the veins but not the arteries. If the veins do not stand out, the tourniquet is too loose. If the hand or foot turns white and cold, or the pulse disappears, the tourniquet is too tight and may damage normal tissue. Once applied, the American Red Cross recommends you not release the tourniquet until antivenin is given.

SNAKEBITES, NONPOISONOUS

Most nonpoisonous bites are from garter snakes during attempted capture or from pet snakes. All are harmless.

HOME CARE FOR NONPOISONOUS SNAKEBITES

Treatment • Usually, the small teeth of a snake leave a scrape that doesn't even puncture the skin. Wash it well with soap and water. A bandage isn't necessary. If the skin is punctured, call in for a tetanus booster if your child hasn't had one in over 5 years.

Call Your Child's Physician Later If

• Your child develops any symptoms in the next 6 hours.

SNAKEBITES, UNIDENTIFIED

Sometimes the snake has disappeared by the time the parent has been notified. In other cases, the snake has been killed but is hard to identify. (If your child needs to be seen by a physician, bring the snake with you after you're certain it is dead.) Most bites are from harmless snakes, and you can assume this to be the case unless the bite mark burns or swells within 5 minutes.

CALL YOUR CHILD'S PHYSICIAN IMMEDIATELY IF

• One or two puncture (fang) marks are present.

• The bite area burns or hurts.

• The bite area is swollen.

• Blood blisters or purple spots are present in the bite area.

• Your child is acting sick in any way.

• You have other urgent questions.

HOME CARE FOR UNIDENTIFIED SNAKEBITES

See *Home Care for Nonpoisonous Snakebites,* above.

BITES, SPIDER OR SCORPION

The following five types of bites are covered in the next few pages. Go directly to the one that applies to your child.

SCORPION BITES
SPIDER BITES, BLACK WIDOW
SPIDER BITES, BROWN RECLUSE
SPIDER BITES, NONDANGEROUS
SPIDER BITES, UNIDENTIFIED

SCORPION BITES

Scorpions belong to the same class as spiders—called the arachnids. They are found in desert areas. About twenty different kinds occur in the southwestern United States. Scorpions have a poisonous stinger in the tail. Over 90 percent of scorpion bites are on the hands. Most of the bites cause symptoms similar to those of black widow spiders, namely immediate local pain with slight swelling. In the United States, only one scorpion (*C. sculpturatus*) can cause serious or fatal reactions. It is small (1 to 3 inches), uniformly yellow, and without stripes.

CALL YOUR CHILD'S PHYSICIAN IMMEDIATELY IN ALL CASES

FIRST AID

See *First Aid* for black widow spider bites, below.

SPIDER BITES, BLACK WIDOW

The black widow is a shiny, jet-black spider with long legs and a red (or orange) hourglass-shaped marking on its underside. It is about an inch in length, including the legs. The black widow and brown recluse spiders are the only highly venomous spiders in North America. Black widow bites cause immediate local pain and swelling. Muscle cramps also occur for 6 to 24 hours. They rarely cause death (except in younger children or when the victim is bitten by several spiders).

CALL YOUR CHILD'S PHYSICIAN IMMEDIATELY IN ALL CASES

FIRST AID

Apply an ice cube or ice pack to the bite to reduce the spread of the venom. Then go to the nearest emergency room or wherever your physician directs you. A tourniquet is not helpful. Antivenin is available for severe bites in young children, and other medicines can relieve muscle pain.

SPIDER BITES, BROWN RECLUSE

The brown recluse is brown, has long legs, and has a dark, violin-shaped marking on its head. It is about ½ inch in length, including the legs. Brown recluse spider bites cause delayed local pain and blister formation in 4 to 8 hours. The center of the reaction becomes bluish and depressed (i.e., the opposite of swollen). The skin damage may require grafting. The bites are rarely fatal.

CALL YOUR CHILD'S PHYSICIAN IMMEDIATELY IN ALL CASES

FIRST AID

Wash the bite thoroughly with soap and water. Bring the spider with you if possible. (Brown recluse spiders may be hard to identify.)

SPIDER BITES, NONDANGEROUS

More than fifty types of spiders in the United States can cause local but nondangerous reactions (such as golden garden spiders). The bites are painful and mildly swollen for 1 or 2 days, much like a bee-sting. In fact, spiders are probably responsible for most single, unexplained, tender bites that occur on children during the night. (Mosquito bites, on the other hand, are usually multiple and itchy rather than painful.) Many people are unduly concerned about the tarantula, a black, hairy spider that is 2 to 3 inches long. The tarantula is not dangerous. Its mild venom also causes a local reaction resembling a bee-sting.

HOME CARE FOR NONDANGEROUS SPIDER BITES

Treatment • Wash the bite thoroughly with soap and water. Then rub the area with a cotton ball soaked with a meat tenderizer/water solution for 15 minutes. If meat tenderizer is not available, an ice cube applied to the area often helps.

Call Your Child's Physician Later If

• Muscle spasm occurs in the bite area.

• The bite turns into a blister or purple spot.

• A sore occurs that doesn't heal.

• Other new symptoms occur.

SPIDER BITES, UNIDENTIFIED

Although most of these bites are harmless, an occasional one may be due to a black widow spider.

CALL YOUR CHILD'S PHYSICIAN IMMEDIATELY IF

• The bite area burns or hurts.

• Muscle spasm occurs in the bite area.

• The bite has turned into a blister or purple spot.

• Your child is acting sick.

Try to capture the spider (dead or alive) in a jar and bring it along to the physician's office. Don't bludgeon it beyond recognition.

HOME CARE FOR UNIDENTIFIED SPIDER BITES

Treatment • Wash the bite thoroughly with soap and water.

Call Your Child's Physician Later If

• A sore occurs that doesn't heal.

• Any new symptoms develop, especially muscle spasm in the area of the bite.

PREVENTION OF SPIDER BITES

• Don't work in woodpiles, rock piles, rubbish heaps, or dark corners of outdoor buildings without wearing gloves.

• Spray with insecticides any area where black widow spiders are seen.

BLEEDING, SEVERE

This guideline covers arterial (from an artery) bleeding or major venous (from a vein) bleeding. In arterial bleeding, the blood pumps or spurts from the wound with each heartbeat. In major venous bleeding, the blood just runs out of the wound at a steady rate. The arterial bleeding is bright red compared to the darker red of venous bleeding. Minor bleeding (from capillaries), however, can also be bright red. For minor bleeding, see the guidelines on TRAUMA, SKIN, page 64, or NOSEBLEED, page 445.

FIRST AID FOR ARTERIAL BLEEDING

Prevent Shock • Have your child lie down with the feet elevated 10 to 12 inches to prevent symptoms of shock (low blood pressure). If your child is pale and the hands and feet are cold, shock is imminent.

Apply Direct Pressure • If you know the arterial pressure points, apply strong, direct pressure to the artery between the wound and the heart until help arrives. If you do not know the arterial pressure points, place several sterile dressings or the first clean cloth at hand (towels, sheets, shirts, or handkerchiefs) over the wound and apply direct pressure immediately. The pressure must be forceful and continuous, often applied with the palm of the hand. Act quickly, because the ongoing blood loss can cause shock.

Rescue Squad • Have someone call a rescue squad immediately while you tend to the bleeding. (See EMERGENCY TRANSPORTATION, page 4.)

Arterial Tourniquet • A tourniquet is needed only under the following unusual circumstances: the bleeding is arterial; it is from the arm or leg; it cannot be controlled by direct pressure (as with an amputated or mangled limb); and the patient is located at a significant distance from emergency facilities. A tourniquet should be avoided if at all possible since it can damage the uninjured tissues. In 1985 the American College of Emergency Physicians recommended that once an arterial tourniquet is applied, it should be released for 15 minutes of every hour. During this time, direct pressure must be used to prevent excessive blood loss. Apply a tourniquet as follows:

• If you have a blood pressure cuff, use it as a tourniquet. The second choice is a tight elastic bandage. If these items are unavailable, use a piece of cloth (such as a bandanna or stocking).

• Tie it around the limb above the wound.

• Lay a 4- to 5-inch piece of wood or an eating utensil above the knot and tie the tourniquet again.

• Twist the wooden or metal handle until the tourniquet is tight enough to stop the bleeding.

• Tie the stick in place so it won't unwind before you reach the hospital.

FIRST AID FOR VENOUS BLEEDING

Prevent Shock • Have your child lie down with the feet elevated to prevent symptoms of shock. If your child is pale and the hands and feet are cold, shock is imminent. Act quickly.

Apply Direct Pressure

• Place two or three sterile dressings (or a clean towel or sheet) over the wound immediately.

• Apply direct pressure to the wound for 8 to 10 minutes, using your entire hand. Direct pressure can always stop venous bleeding if it is applied to the right spot.

- Then bandage the dressings tightly in place (an elastic bandage gives excellent compression) and leave them there until arrival at the emergency room.

Seek Emergency Care • Go to the nearest emergency room. Exception: Call for a rescue squad if your child is clearly in shock. (See EMERGENCY TRANSPORTATION, page 4.)

FIRST AID FOR OPEN ABDOMINAL WOUNDS
Cover the wound with a sterile dressing. If a knife or other weapon protrudes from the wound, don't remove it before reaching the hospital. When it is removed, the cut it leaves could bleed uncontrollably. Call a rescue squad (see EMERGENCY TRANSPORTATION, page 4.)

FIRST AID FOR OPEN CHEST WOUNDS
A sucking wound of the chest is one that goes through to the pleural space or lung. It can be recognized by the sound of air being sucked into the chest with each effort to breathe in. This type of wound quickly collapses the lung if it is not treated properly.

First Aid • Seal the opening as quickly as possible. Use several sterile dressings or pieces of clean cloth and lots of adhesive tape or plastic wrap to make it airtight. If possible, apply the seal while your child is breathing out. If one part of the chest bulges out when your child breathes out, there are several broken ribs in that area (flail chest). Have your child lie with the bulging part down, or hold a pillow or towel over it to keep it from bulging. If a knife or other weapon protrudes from the wound, don't remove it before reaching the hospital. When it is removed, the cut it leaves could bleed uncontrollably. Call a rescue squad (see EMERGENCY TRANSPORTATION, page 4).

BREATHING DIFFICULTY, SEVERE

STOPPED BREATHING, PERSISTENT
- Call the rescue squad.

- Begin mouth-to-mouth resuscitation if you know how. (Otherwise, go to the guideline on RESUSCITATION, page 8.)

BREATHING, VERY SLOW AND WEAK

• Call the rescue squad.

STOPPED BREATHING, TRANSIENT; AND NOW NORMAL BREATHING

• Call your child's physician immediately.

• Note: In an infant, prolonged periods without breathing (apnea), especially if accompanied by turning blue or limpness, can be a forerunner of crib death and should always receive a careful medical evaluation. On the other hand, breathing pauses of less than 6 seconds (periodic breathing) in infants from birth to 3 months are normal. Occasionally, normal pauses can last for 15 seconds, but check with your physician.

CHOKING

Turn directly to page 9.

CROUP

Turn directly to page 474.

BREATHING FAST

Labored • Call Your Child's Physician Immediately.

With Wheezing • Call Your Child's Physician Immediately.

With Fever • Normal breathing rates are: 40 per minute (under 1 year of age), 30 per minute (1 to 5 years), and 20 per minute (6 to 12 years). These rates apply to children who are calm or sleeping. The rates normally go up 10 or 20 breaths in children who are upset or crying. With fever, the rate rises by 3 for each degree Fahrenheit of elevation (or by 6 for each degree Centigrade). If the rate is appropriate for the level of fever, all is probably well. If it is considerably higher, call your child's physician immediately.

With Snorting • Clean the nose with warm water drops and a rubber suction bulb. If that doesn't help and the breathing rate remains high, call your child's physician immediately.

RELATED TOPICS

BREATH-HOLDING SPELLS (see page 190)
BREATHING, NOISY (see page 467)

BURNS, CHEMICAL

Chemical burns are external burns from lye, acids, or other tissue-damaging chemicals splashed on the skin. Most of these accidents cause only first-degree burns, which may peel like a sunburn during the following week. A few of the stronger chemicals may cause deep burns.

FIRST AID
Remove contaminated clothing and rinse off the burned part of your child's body with clear water for 20 minutes, using the shower or tub. Don't rub the skin during this rinse. Don't apply any burn ointments because washing them off will cause pain. Also, don't apply butter; it only increases the infection rate. If the burned area is large, cover it loosely with a wet clean sheet.

CALL YOUR CHILD'S PHYSICIAN IMMEDIATELY
Call in all cases, after carrying out first aid instructions. The physician will probably need to examine your child if there are any blisters, facial burns, or extensive burns.

RELATED TOPICS
EYE, CHEMICAL IN (see page 38)
POISONING (see page 42)

BURNS, THERMAL

Most of these burns are from hot water or hot drinks. A few are from hot ovens, stoves, electric or kerosene space heaters, exhaust pipes, grease, hair-curling irons, clothes irons, heating grates, and cigarettes. Usually the burn is first degree (reddened skin without blisters) or second degree (with blisters). Neither of these leave any scars. Second-degree burns take up to 3 weeks to heal. A third-degree burn is deep and leaves pain-free areas of black (leathery) or white skin. During healing it usually needs a skin graft to prevent bad scarring if it is larger than a quarter.

FIRST AID FOR THERMAL BURNS

Immediately (don't take time to remove clothing) put the burned part in cold tap water or pour cold water over it for 10 minutes. If you are outside, the nearest garden hose will do. If the burn is small, massage it with an ice cube. This will lessen the depth of the burn and relieve pain. Don't apply any butter or ointments. If the burned area is large, cover it loosely with a wet clean sheet (a dry sheet may stick to the burn). You can also use plastic wrap. The covering will keep it clean and reduce pain.

CALL YOUR CHILD'S PHYSICIAN IMMEDIATELY IF

- More than 2 blisters are present.

- The burn is on the face, neck, hands, feet, or genitals.

- Areas of charred or white skin are present.

- An extremely hot substance caused the burn.

- It was an electrical burn.

- An explosion caused the burn.

- You have other urgent questions.

HOME CARE FOR THERMAL BURNS

Treatment • Wash the area gently with a liquid dishwashing detergent twice a day. Don't open any blisters—the outer skin still protects the burn from infection. For pain, apply cold compresses and take aspirin every 4 hours for at least 24 hours. Do not apply any butter or burn ointments, and do not cover the burn. These only delay the healing and are painful to remove.

Call Your Child's Physician Later If

- Any blisters break open.

- The burn starts to look infected.

- Tenderness or redness increases after day 2.

- The burn hasn't healed after 10 days.

- You feel your child is getting worse.

PREVENTION
Think about how you can prevent similar accidents in the future.

- Never drink anything hot (such as coffee, tea, or cocoa) while holding a young baby. The baby will grab for it, spill it, and probably get burned.

- Once your child can walk, keep hot substances away from the edge of the table or stove (such as a pan of boiling water, a coffee pot, or an iron). The burn from the crockpot left too close to a counter edge can cause scarring for life.

- Don't let a young child touch the faucet handles in a bathtub. He or she may turn on the hot water and be scalded.

- Lower your hot-water heater setting to 130°F or to the "low medium" setting. Higher settings can cause burns in 1 second.

- Use cool humidifiers, not hot vaporizers.

- Supervise children around fires of any kind.

- Use flame-resistant sleepwear.

- Give up smoking, or at least dispose of used cigarettes conscientiously. Cigarettes are the most common cause of residential fires.

- Keep cigarette lighters away from children. Even a 2-year-old can ignite one by inverting it and pushing it across the floor.

- Install smoke detectors in your home. Check them monthly for proper functioning. More people die from smoke inhalation than from burns.

- Teach your children not to hide if a house fire occurs, but to go outside. Have a fire drill and rehearse it.

- Before placing a child under 1 year old in a car seat, check the seat's temperature. Hot straps or buckles have caused second-degree burns. Whenever you park in direct sunlight, cover the car seat with a towel or sheet.

- Avoid fireworks, or allow older children to use them only with close adult supervision. In addition to burns, fireworks (especially bottle rockets) cause 300 cases of blindness per year.

COMA

A child who is unconscious, cannot be fully awakened, or is very difficult to awaken is in a coma. The causes are many, including drug overdose, poisoning, head injury, encephalitis, and low blood sugar. In all cases, you should contact your child's physician immediately.

CALL A RESCUE SQUAD FOR ASSISTANCE AND TRANSPORTATION FOR A COMATOSE CHILD IF

• Your child can't be awakened at all.

• The head or neck may be injured.

• A severe allergic reaction to a bee-sting or medication is possible.

• Your child is not breathing.

• Breathing is slow or weak.

• Breathing is labored (croup, wheezing, choking, etc.).

• The lips are bluish or dusky.

TAKE YOUR CHILD TO THE NEAREST EMERGENCY ROOM

• In all other cases, if your child is breathing normally.

• If your child starts to vomit, place him on the side or abdomen.

CONVULSIONS WITH FEVER

Febrile (fever-related) convulsions or seizures occur in 4 percent of children and are harmless. The average temperature at which they occur is 104°F, although some occur at lower or higher levels of fever. Everyone has a convulsion threshold. For most children the threshold is 106° or 107°F, so they never have a febrile seizure. The fever itself can be caused by an infection in any part of the body, including a simple cold. Each febrile seizure usually lasts less than 5 minutes without any treatment. Most of these children have just 1 febrile seizure in a lifetime. The other 40 percent of children with febrile seizures have 2 or 3 recurrences over the years. They usually stop occurring by age 5 or 6. While seeing a seizure may be frightening, there is no cause for alarm. The seizure does not cause any brain damage. Occasionally a child will hurt himself during a fall. A few children (5 percent) will go on to have seizures without fever at a later age.

FIRST AID FOR FEBRILE CONVULSIONS

Bringing your child's fever down as quickly as possible will shorten the seizure. Remove or loosen the clothing and apply cold washcloths to the forehead and neck. Sponge the body surface or clothing with cool water (but avoid rubbing alcohol). As the water evaporates, the temperature will fall. Don't put the child in a bathtub, however; that could be dangerous during the seizure. When the seizure is over and your child is awake, give the appropriate dose of acetaminophen. (For dosage, see FEVER, page 305) If your child starts to vomit, place him on his side or abdomen. If breathing becomes noisy, pull the jaw and chin forward by placing two fingers behind the corner of the jaw on each side. In addition, check a watch so you can accurately report how long the seizure lasts.

CALL YOUR CHILD'S PHYSICIAN IMMEDIATELY IF

• The febrile convulsion lasts more than 5 minutes.

• In all other cases, after the seizure has stopped.

If you are told to bring your child to your physician's office, keep the fever down during transport. Dress your child lightly and continue sponging if necessary. (Warning: Prolonged seizures have been caused by bundling up sick infants during a long drive. A seizure lasting more than 20 or 30 minutes can be harmful.)

HOME CARE FOR FEBRILE CONVULSIONS

If your physician decides the seizure can be treated safely at home, the following information may help you.

Oral Fever-Reducing Medicines • If your physician agrees, place your child on acetaminophen at the regular dosage every 4 hours for the next 48 hours (or longer if the fever persists). For dosages, turn to FEVER, page 305. Awaken him or her once during the night for medicine. Let your child sleep as much as he or she wishes.

Fever-Reducing Suppositories • Have some acetaminophen suppositories on hand in case your child ever has another febrile seizure (same dosage as oral medicine). Since your pharmacist keeps these suppositories refrigerated, you will have to ask for them. When your child awakens, you can give the other fever-reducing medicine by mouth.

Call Your Child's Physician Later If

• Another seizure occurs.

• The neck becomes stiff. (Note: The inability to touch the chin to the chest is an early symptom of meningitis.)

• Your child becomes confused or delirious.

• Your child becomes difficult to awaken.

• You feel your child is getting worse.

PREVENTION OF FEBRILE CONVULSIONS

The only way to prevent future febrile convulsions is for your child to take an anticonvulsant medicine on a daily basis. Depending on how severe or frequent your child's seizures are, your physician will decide if anticonvulsants are needed.

RELATED TOPICS

FEVER (see page 305)
DELIRIUM (see page 35)

CONVULSIONS WITHOUT FEVER

During a convulsion (seizure) a child becomes unconscious and falls, the eyes roll upward, the body stiffens, and the arms and legs jerk. Most seizures last less than 5 minutes. Convulsions without fever occur in 0.4 percent of children. If they become recurrent, the child is said to have epilepsy. While the causes are many, the usual one is a small scar in the brain tissue that triggers seizures. Seizures can usually be controlled with special medicines.

FIRST AID FOR CONVULSIONS WITHOUT FEVER

Your child should be left on the floor. Place a blanket or rug under him, and move him only if he is in a dangerous place. Loosen any tight clothing, especially a tight collar. If your child vomits or the secretions in the mouth build up, turn your child on his side or abdomen so the secretions can drain out. If your child's breathing is noisy, pull the chin and jaw forward to open the airway more. (This will automatically bring the tongue forward.)

CALL YOUR CHILD'S PHYSICIAN IMMEDIATELY IF

• The seizure lasts more than 5 minutes.

• It's the first one.

• Seizures are occurring frequently.

HOME CARE FOR CONVULSIONS WITHOUT FEVER

Treatment for Previously Diagnosed Convulsions • After the seizure is over, let your child sleep if he wishes. The brain is temporarily exhausted, and there is no point in trying to keep your child awake. Since recurrent seizures are common, work out a plan with your child's physician in advance. Some will want you to give your child twice the usual dose of anticonvulsants at this time.

Common Mistakes in the Treatment of Convulsions • During the seizure, don't try to restrain your child or stop the seizure movements. Once started, the seizure will run its course no matter what you do. Don't try to resuscitate your child just because breathing stops momentarily. This is common during seizures, and resuscitation is unnecessary. Don't try to force anything into your child's mouth. This is unnecessary and can cut the mouth, injure a tooth, cause vomiting, or result in a serious bite of your finger. Don't try to hold the tongue. While children may rarely bite the tongue during a convulsion, they never "swallow the tongue."

Call Your Child's Physician Later If

• Another seizure occurs.

• Your child stays confused or groggy for more than 2 hours.

DELIRIUM

Delirium is the sudden onset of disorientation (talking crazy), strange behavior (acting "wild"), and visual hallucinations (seeing things that aren't there). Judgment and memory are also impaired. Commonly, the child's confused thinking comes and goes (fluctuates). Children mainly get delirium with fevers over 104°F. It usually goes away once the fever is lowered. Illegal drugs can cause delirium. So can cold and cough medicines, especially if two are given together or one is given in too large a dose. Brief delirium can occur when a child awakens in strange surroundings, as on the first night of a vacation. If your child has no fever and has recently sustained head trauma, see the guideline on HEAD TRAUMA, page 58.

CALL YOUR CHILD'S PHYSICIAN IMMEDIATELY IF

• Your child's temperature is normal or less than 102°F.

• Your child is on any medicine that could cause delirium (like antihistamines).

• Head trauma recently occurred.

• The neck is stiff.

• Your child is also vomiting.

• Before the delirium, your child was acting very sick.

HOME CARE FOR FEBRILE DELIRIUM

Fever-Reducing Therapy • Give your child acetaminophen. Remove the clothing and apply cold washcloths to the forehead and neck. Sponge the body surface with cool water. If your child shivers, raise the water temperature. Don't put your child in the bathtub, however; that could be dangerous. See FEVER for details, page 305.

Delirium Therapy • Keep the lights on in your child's room. Be sure a familiar person stays with your child at all times until he or she feels better. It's best if you reassure your child by touching and talking to him. Tell him where he is, who you are, and that he will feel better soon.

Call Your Child's Physician Later If

• The delirium lasts for over an hour.

• The delirium is still present after you lower the fever below 102°F.

• The delirium clears up but your child develops other symptoms that worry you.

DROWNING

FIRST AID
Have someone call a rescue squad immediately. (See EMERGENCY TRANSPORTATION, page 4.)

Resuscitation • Begin mouth-to-mouth breathing as soon as possible. (Review RESUSCITATION, page 8.) This should be started immediately—in the boat, in a life-preserver, or at the latest when the rescuer reaches shallow water. It should be continued until the child is brought to a medical facility, since children have survived long submersions (especially in cold water).

Neck Injury • If there is any possibility of a neck injury (for example, a diving accident), protect the neck from any bending or twisting. If the child is still in the water, he or she can be helped to float on the surface until a spine board is applied or until several people can remove him while supporting the head and back as a unit.

Vomiting • Vomiting is common because the stomach is usually filled with water in drowning. If vomiting occurs, quickly turn the child on his or her side, or facedown, and try to keep the water from entering the lungs. The lungs are usually free of water because they are protected by spasm of the vocal cords. Avoid pressure on the stomach during resuscitation because it can trigger vomiting.

PREVENTION

* Never leave a child less than 3 years old unattended in the bathtub or a wading pool.

* Never leave children who can't swim well unattended near a swimming pool. (More children drown in backyard swimming pools than at beaches or public pools.)

* Make sure that neighborhood pools are fenced off and the gates are kept locked.

* Try to arrange swimming lessons for your child before age 8. (Children are often ready by age 4.)

* Infant water programs should teach water "fun," not "swimming." Children cannot be made "water safe" before age 3.

* Infant programs that encourage submersion of the head for more than a few seconds should be avoided because some babies swallow enough pool water to cause seizures and brain damage.

* Caution children of all ages to check the depth of the water before diving in and to avoid any diving in the shallow end of a pool.

* Caution children not to overbreathe as a way to stay underwater longer. This practice can lead to passing out underwater.

* Caution the accomplished swimmer to continue to swim with a buddy.

ELECTRIC SHOCK OR LIGHTNING INJURY

Electrocution (death from electricity) usually occurs from contact with high-tension wires that have fallen or which the child has climbed up to. Household current can cause severe electric shock if your child is standing in water at the time contact is made. Electric shock usually stops breathing and the heartbeat. Rapid resuscitation can lead to a full recovery.

FIRST AID

Breaking Contact • If your child is still in contact with a live wire, turn off the electricity or break contact with the wire. Be sure to use a nonconducting object (such as a wooden pole).

Call the Rescue Squad Immediately • (See EMERGENCY TRANSPORTA-
TION, page 4.)

Resuscitation • Begin mouth-to-mouth breathing as soon as possible if breathing has stopped. (Review RESUSCITATION, page
8.) Often external cardiac massage will also be needed. Take
a CPR course in advance.

PREVENTION

• Cover all electrical outlets with plastic safety caps.

• Unplug appliances, such as hair dryers and curling irons,
when not in use.

• Keep electrical cords away from toddlers who might chew on
them. (Note: This accident could burn off part of the lip or the
end of the tongue.)

• Teach your child not to turn on lights or electrical appliances while standing on wet floor or ground.

• Teach your child never to touch an electrical appliance, such
as a hair dryer or radio, while in a bathtub. (Note: This
mistake can result in immediate death.)

• Teach your child to avoid open water, tall trees, high ground,
or metal objects (e.g., a shovel) during thunderstorms. Cars
and houses are safe.

EYE, CHEMICAL IN

Acids (e.g., toilet bowl cleaners) and alkalis (e.g., drain cleaners) splashed into the eye can severely damage the cornea,
the clear part of the eye. However, most chemicals (such as
alcohol or hydrocarbons) just cause temporary stinging and
superficial irritation. All should be treated as emergencies
until your physician or a Poison Control Center expert tells
you otherwise.

FIRST AID FOR CHEMICAL IN EYE
Immediate and thorough irrigation of the eye with tap water
is essential to prevent damage to the cornea. (Do not use
antidotes such as vinegar.) Either hold your child faceup

under a gently running water tap or have your child lie down and continuously pour lukewarm water into the eye from a pitcher or glass. It is very important to hold the eyelid open during this process. For most chemicals, the eye should be irrigated for 5 minutes; for acids, 10 minutes; and for alkalis, 20 minutes. If one eye is not burned, cover it while irrigating the other. Any chemical particles that can't be flushed away should be wiped away with a moistened cotton swab. Call your physician immediately after irrigating the eye.

RELATED TOPIC

For mild irritants like soap or food, see the guideline on EYES, RED OR PINKEYE, page 411.

EYE, FOREIGN BODY IN

The most common objects that get in the eye are an eyelash or a piece of dried mucus (sleep). Particulate matter such as sawdust, sand, dirt, or cinders also can be blown into the eyes. The main symptoms are irritation, pain, and tears. Rubbing the eye can lead to the foreign object's scratching the cornea (clear part). See also EYE, CHEMICAL IN, above.

FIRST AID FOR GLASS FRAGMENTS ON THE EYELIDS

Have your child bend forward and try to get flakes of glass off the skin by blowing on the closed eyelids. A few pieces can often be removed from the eyelids by touching them with a piece of Scotch tape. Pour water over the eyelids and face to get off any remaining glass. Cover the eyes with a wet washcloth and go to your physician's office. The eye should not be rubbed.

CALL YOUR CHILD'S PHYSICIAN IMMEDIATELY IF

• Any particle is stuck to the eyeball (especially the cornea).

• Fluid or blood is coming from the eyeball.

• The object hit the eye at high speed (e.g., a particle from striking metal on metal, or metal on stone).

• The foreign object is sharp.

• You have other urgent questions.

HOME CARE FOR FOREIGN BODY IN EYE

Treatment for Numerous Particles • If there are numerous particles in the eye (such as dirt or sand), clean around the eye with a wet washcloth first. Then have your child try to open and close the eye repeatedly while submerging that side of the face in a pan of water. If your child is too young to cooperate with this, hold him or her faceup under a gently running warm-water tap. The eyelids must be held open during the irrigation and this usually requires the help of another person.

Treatment for Particle in a Corner of the Eye • If the particle is in the corner of the eye, try to get it out with the corner of a clean handkerchief, a moistened cotton swab, or a piece of Scotch tape.

Treatment for Particle under the Lower Lid • If the particle is under the lower eyelid, pull the lower lid out by depressing the cheek, and touch the particle with a moistened cotton swab. If that doesn't work, try pouring water on the speck while holding the lid out.

Treatment for Particle under the Upper Lid • If the particle can't be seen, it's probably under the upper lid, the most common hiding place. Try having your child open and close the eye several times while it is submerged in a pan or bowl of water. If you have an eye cup, use it. If this fails, pull the upper lid out and draw it over the lower lid. This maneuver, and tears, will sometimes dislodge the particle.

Call Your Child's Physician Later If

• This approach does not remove all the foreign material from the eye—i.e., if the sensation of "grittiness" or pain persists.

• The vision does not return to normal after the eye has been allowed to rest for an hour.

• The foreign object has been removed, but tearing and blinking persist for more than 2 hours.

First Aid: While waiting to be seen by the physician, cover the eye with a wet washcloth or bandage it shut to relieve discomfort. If eye movement causes pain, cover both eyes.

HEAT REACTIONS

There are three main reactions to an extremely hot environment. All three are caused by excessive loss of water through sweating. For treatment, select the type of heat reaction that pertains to your child. A rectal temperature is more reliable than an oral temperature for these disorders.

HEATSTROKE OR SUNSTROKE

Hot, flushed skin; high fever (at least 105°F); the absence of sweating; delirium or unconsciousness; and shock (low blood pressure) are present.

HEAT EXHAUSTION

Cold, pale skin; no fever (temperature less than 100°F); sweating; and dizziness, fainting, or weakness are present.

HEAT CRAMPS

Severe cramps in the limbs (especially calf or thigh muscles) and abdomen, with no fever, are present.

FIRST AID FOR HEATSTROKE OR SUNSTROKE

• Call your child's physician immediately.

• Heatstroke can be life-threatening. The high fever is a serious emergency. Cool your child off as rapidly as possible. Move him or her to a cool place. Keep the feet elevated. Place ice packs in the armpits and groin. Sponge your child with cool water (as cold as is tolerable), and fan him. If your child is unconscious, immersion in cold water could be lifesaving. (Note: aspirin or acetaminophen is of no help.)

• If your child is conscious, give as much cold water to drink as he or she can tolerate.

• Call for emergency transportation (see page 4).

FIRST AID FOR HEAT EXHAUSTION

• Call your child's physician immediately.

• Put your child in a cool place. Have him or her lie down with the feet elevated. Cover your child with cold wet towels.

- Give as much cold water to drink as your child can tolerate until he or she feels better.

- Your physician will probably want to examine your child's state of hydration. You can drive in, but keep your child lying down in the back seat during the drive and provide unlimited amounts of water.

HOME CARE FOR HEAT CRAMPS

Heat cramps are the most common reaction to excessive heat. They are never serious. Give your child as much cold water to drink as he can tolerate until he feels better. Your child will not need to be seen by the physician.

PREVENTION OF HEAT REACTIONS

- When your child is working or exercising in a hot environment, have him or her drink extra water. Water is the ideal solution for replacing lost sweat. Very little salt is lost.

- Avoid salt tablets, because they slow down stomach emptying and delay the absorption of fluids.

- Have your child wear lightweight clothing.

- Have your child take 5-minute water breaks every 25 minutes in the shade.

- Athletic coaches recommend that we not exercise vigorously if the temperature exceeds 82°F.

- When using a hot tub, limit exposure to 15 minutes and have a "buddy" system in case a heat reaction suddenly occurs. Hot tubs and saunas should be avoided by people with a fever, or following vigorous exercise when the body needs to release heat.

POISONING

Immediately give your child 1 glass of water or milk to rinse the esophagus of any swallowed chemicals (not necessary for swallowed medicines). Then call your child's physician (or the Poison Control Center) immediately for *all* ingestions. Don't induce vomiting until you are certain it is necessary and safe. About 10 percent of poisoning is with substances that can cause harm if they are vomited. Also, more than 50 percent of ingestions are of poisonous substances taken in a nontoxic amount or of nonpoisonous substances. Always suspect poisoning if your child is 1 to 4 years old and has the abrupt onset of unexplained symptoms (without fever). Be prepared to answer the following questions:

• What was swallowed?

• How much was swallowed? (Estimate the maximal amount.)

• When was it swallowed?

• Does your child have any symptoms? (For COMA or CONVULSIONS, go directly to those guidelines, pages 31–33.)

In the meantime, select from the following three guidelines the one that applies to your child's ingestion.

ACIDS, ALKALIS, OR PETROLEUM PRODUCTS
OTHER POISONOUS SUBSTANCES
PROBABLY HARMLESS SUBSTANCES

Some products have first aid for their ingestion listed on the label.

ACIDS, ALKALIS, OR PETROLEUM PRODUCTS

These include toilet bowl cleaners, drain cleaners, lye, Clinitest tablets, ammonia, bleaches, kerosene, gasoline, benzene, furniture polish, and lighter fluid. If these agents are vomited, additional damage can occur to the esophagus or lungs.

FIRST AID
Don't Induce Vomiting.
Have your child drink 1 to 2 glasses of milk (or water) to wash out the esophagus. Keep your child sitting or standing to protect the esophagus. Don't let your child lie down. Your physician will decide where to see you. Bring with you the container the poison was in.

OTHER POISONOUS SUBSTANCES

Poisonous substances include most drugs, chemicals, and plants. The most dangerous prescription drugs of all (in overdosage) are barbiturates, digitalis products, Lomotil, Darvon, Tofranil, and other trycyclic antidepressants. Very dangerous over-the-counter medicines are iron and aspirin.

FIRST AID
Induce Vomiting.

The best way to cause vomiting is with syrup of ipecac. Give 1 tablespoon (3 teaspoons) to children 1 to 6 years old; 2 tablespoons to those over age 6. For infants under 12 months old, give 2 teaspoons (10 ml). Also, give your child about 6 ounces or more of water or other clear fluid. Keep your child walking about to make the ipecac work faster. If your child hasn't vomited in 20 minutes, gagging with a spoon may help. If not, give a second tablespoon of ipecac. Once vomiting begins, repeat the clear fluids until the vomited material comes back clear. Then rest the stomach and give nothing by mouth for 2 hours. If you do not have ipecac at home, you can probably get some from a neighbor. Otherwise rush your child to a pharmacy and give it there. If no pharmacy or physician is within 30 minutes of your home, give your child 2 tablespoons of a liquid dishwashing detergent, such as Joy, Ivory, or Palmolive. It can induce vomiting almost as well as ipecac. If you can get someone else to drive, take a large mixing bowl or a pail and induce vomiting in the car while driving to your physician. Bring the poison container with you.

PROBABLY HARMLESS SUBSTANCES

Fortunately, most children will ingest nonedible substances that do not produce any serious symptoms. It is unnecessary to induce vomiting for these. Some examples of nontoxic substances are candles, chalk, cosmetics (except hair dye or nail polish remover), crayons, dog or cat food, deodorants, detergents (exception: automatic dishwasher detergent), dirt, soaps, greases, oils, hand lotions, 3 percent hydrogen peroxide, lipstick, perfumes, petroleum jelly, rouge, shampoos, and shaving cream. Some harmless drugs are birth control pills, antacids, laxatives, stool softeners, and vitamins (unless they contain iron). Call your physician to be sure.

PREVENTION OF POISONING   •

You were lucky this time, but it's time to poison-proof the house.

• Remember to keep drugs and chemicals locked up, or out of reach. Review where you keep drain cleaners, furniture polish, drugs, and insecticides, since these are the most common dangerous poisons.

• Also, remember that alcoholic beverages have caused serious poisonings. As little as 3 ounces of hard liquor has been fatal to a 2-year-old child.

• Whenever you or your child are prescribed a new drug, remember to keep the safety cap on and carefully check the dosage before giving it.

• Don't leave drugs on countertops, especially when you are called to the door or telephone.

• Don't leave drugs in a purse, because children often search them for candy or gum. When you have guests, keep purses out of reach of children.

• Learn the names of all your house plants and remove any (e.g., dieffenbachia) that would cause more than vomiting or diarrhea. Teach your child never to put leaves, stems, seeds, or berries from any plant into the mouth.

• Don't store any chemicals in soft-drink bottles.

• Even with good planning, keep some syrup of ipecac (periodically check the expiration date) and the telephone number of the Poison Control Center handy.

II

TRAUMA

TRAUMA

BONE AND JOINT TRAUMA

This guideline covers injuries to bones, joints, and muscles. The legs are more commonly injured than the arms. *Fractures* (broken bones) and *dislocations* (bones out of joint) obviously need treatment by a physician. Stretches and tears of ligaments (*sprains*) are due to sudden twisting injuries and require medical attention unless they are very mild. By contrast, most stretches and tears of muscles (*strains*) are due to overexertion and can be treated at home. Excessive jumping gives muscle pain in the front of the upper leg. Excessive running (especially uphill) gives muscle pain in the front of the lower leg (called shin splints). A *muscle bruise* (called a charley horse) is the most common injury in contact sports and can also be treated at home. *Bone bruises* usually follow direct blows to the bone in exposed areas, like the elbow, hip, or knee, and are usually minor injuries.

Similar Condition • If appropriate, turn directly to the guideline for FINGER AND TOE TRAUMA, page 54.

FIRST AID FOR SUSPECTED FRACTURE OR SEVERE SPRAIN

Suspected Fracture • If you suspect a broken bone, take your child in for a medical exam and an X-ray. Don't let your child put pressure or weight on it. Splint the fracture before moving your child so the fracture edges won't damage blood vessels.

- *Shoulder or arm:* Use a sling made of a triangular piece of cloth to support the forearm at an 80- to 90-degree angle. At a minimum, support the injured part with the other hand.

- *Leg:* After placing a towel between the legs, use the uninjured leg as a splint by binding the thighs and legs together. At a minimum, carry your child and don't permit any weight bearing on the injured leg. Transportation can be by car.

- *Neck:* Protect the neck from any turning or bending. Do not move your child until a neck brace or spine board has been applied. Call a rescue squad for transportation.

Suspected Sprained Ankle or Knee • Treat most sports injuries with R.I.C.E. (rest, ice, compression, and elevation). Apply continuous compression with a wet elastic bandage. Numbness, tingling, or increased pain means the bandage is too tight. Apply crushed ice in a plastic bag for 20 to 30 minutes out of every hour. Ice reduces bleeding, swelling, and pain. Keep the injured ankle or knee elevated and at rest for 24 hours. Transportation can be by car. (Note: Sprains are mainly seen in adults. Under age 12 or 14, suspect a fracture.)

CALL YOUR CHILD'S PHYSICIAN

Immediately If

- Your child is under 6 months old.

- The bone is deformed or crooked.

- Your child won't use an arm normally. (Especially if the injury followed someone's pulling on the arm. This condition of young children is called subluxed radius, a partial dislocation of the elbow.)

- Your child won't bear weight on the legs.

- A severe limp is present.

- The joint nearest the injury can't be moved fully.

- The pain is extreme.

- A "snap" or "pop" was felt at the time of an injury to the knee.

During Office Hours If

- There is a large area of swelling.

- The injured area swelled up within 30 minutes.

- The pain interferes with sleep.
- You have other questions.

HOME CARE FOR BONE AND JOINT TRAUMA

Treatment of a Bruised Muscle or Bone • Apply an ice bag or massage the area with ice for 20 to 30 minutes. Repeat this 3 to 4 times the first day. Give your child aspirin as necessary for severe pain. Aspirin usually gives more relief of muscle and bone pain than acetaminophen does. Have your child rest the injured part as much as possible. The pain usually starts to ease after 48 hours, but there may be some discomfort for 2 weeks. (Note: Water in a Styrofoam cup can be placed in the freezer. After it is frozen, the cup can be peeled away and the piece of ice used for massage.)

Treatment of Strained Muscles • These guidelines apply if several muscles hurt after a strenuous practice, athletic game, or long hike. Massage the sore muscles with ice for 20 to 30 minutes. Repeat this 3 to 4 times the first day. Also give your child aspirin for at least 48 hours. If stiffness persists after 48 hours, have your child soak in a hot bath for 20 minutes and gently massage the sore muscles. If the pain is localized, use a heating pad or hot compresses. Repeat this several times a day until improvement occurs. Have your youngster learn about stretching exercises and return to exercise gradually. Next time, he or she should be in better condition before going full throttle. While no longer prescribed for fever in children or adolescents, aspirin is helpful for muscle and bone pain.

Aspirin Dosage Chart

		AGE (YEARS)				
TYPE	STRENGTH	2–3	4–5	6–8	9–11	12+
Children's aspirin	80 mg. tablets	2	3	4	5–6	8
Adult aspirin	325 mg. tablets	—	—	1	1–1½	2

Call Your Child's Physician Later If

- A limp lasts more than 72 hours.
- The pain is not improving by 72 hours.
- The pain is not gone by 2 weeks.
- Other questions come up.

RELATED TOPIC

For the home care of cuts and scrapes, and guidelines on tetanus boosters, see SKIN TRAUMA, page 64.

EAR TRAUMA

This guideline covers injuries to the outer ear (pinna) or ear canal (the channel that carries sound down to the eardrum). Most external injuries are bruises and scratches. If the ear is severely swollen, a blood clot is present which could permanently damage the ear's shape if it is not treated by a physician. Most bleeding from within the ear canal is from a scratch on the lining caused by a fingernail, cotton swab, or physician's otoscope. These scratches just bleed a few drops and then heal nicely. Long, pointed objects, such as pencils, sticks, straws, or wires, carry the risk of puncturing the eardrum or doing even greater damage.

CALL YOUR CHILD'S PHYSICIAN

Immediately If

- The skin is split open.
- The ear is very swollen.
- A pointed object was inserted into the ear canal (e.g., a pencil, stick, straw, or wire).
- More than 4 drops of blood have come from the ear canal.
- Any clear fluid is draining from the ear canal.
- Walking is unsteady.

During Office Hours If

- The injury caused an earache.
- The hearing is decreased on that side.
- You have other questions.

HOME CARE FOR SUPERFICIAL CUTS AND SCRAPES TO THE EAR

Wash the wound vigorously with soap and water for 5 minutes. Then apply pressure for 10 minutes with a sterile gauze to stop bleeding. Leave the area exposed to the air. (See SKIN TRAUMA, page 64, for more details.)

EYE TRAUMA

This guideline covers injuries to the eye, eyelid, and area around the eye. Brushing against a small twig often causes more damage than collision with a large object like a door. The main concern is if the vision has been damaged. Older children can tell us if their vision is blurred or out of focus. Test them at home by covering each eye in turn and having them look at a distant object. Children under 3 years old usually need to be examined to answer this question.

CALL YOUR CHILD'S PHYSICIAN

Immediately If

- The skin is split open.

- Any cut is present on the eyelid or eyeball.

- The eyes are constantly tearing or blinking.

- Your child keeps the eye covered and won't open it.

- Vision is blurred in either eye.

- Your child has double vision or can't look upward.

- The pupils are unequal in size.

- Blood or clouding is present behind the cornea (clear part).

- An object hit the eye at high speed (such as a tennis ball).

- A sharp object hit the eye (such as a metallic chip).

During Office Hours If

- Your child is less than 3 years old *and* there are any findings of injury (like a black eye or bleeding in the white of the eyeball).

- You have other questions.

HOME CARE FOR EYE TRAUMA

Superficial Cuts or Scrapes • Protect the eye with a clean cloth, then wash the wound vigorously with soap and water for 5 minutes. Then apply pressure for 10 minutes with a sterile gauze to stop bleeding. Leave the area exposed to the air. (See TRAUMA, SKIN, page 64, for more details.)

Swelling or Bruises with Intact Skin • Swelling usually follows injury to the soft tissues or bone around the eye. Apply ice for 30 minutes. Give your child aspirin or acetaminophen if necessary for pain. Don't be surprised if a black eye develops over the next 2 days. A black eye is harmless and needs no special treatment. A subconjunctival hemorrhage (flame-shaped bruise of the sclera or white of the eyeball) also shouldn't cause undue concern. These unsightly bruises do not spread to inside the eye. They generally last for 2 weeks and their disappearance cannot be hurried by any medicine or home remedy.

Call Your Child's Physician Later If

• There are any complaints about vision.

FINGER AND TOE TRAUMA

This guideline covers injuries to the fingers or toes. Usually the blow simply causes a bruise or swelling of the soft tissues and underlying bone (as when a heavy object falls on a toe or when a hand is bumped against a wall). However, if the end of a straightened finger or thumb receives the blow (usually from a ball), the energy is absorbed by the joints' surfaces and the injury occurs there (a jammed finger). For jammed fingers, always check carefully that the end of the finger can be fully straightened. In crush injuries (as from slammed car or screen doors), usually the last digit receives a few cuts. Occasionally the nail is damaged. Rarely is there any fracture of the small underlying bone.

CALL YOUR CHILD'S PHYSICIAN

Immediately If

• The skin is split open.

• Any bleeding won't stop after 10 minutes of direct pressure.

• Blood collects under a nail *and* becomes quite painful.

• The fingernail is badly damaged following a crush injury.

• There is any dirt or grime in the wound that you can't get out.

• A finger joint can't be opened and closed completely.

During Office Hours If

• The finger or toe is quite swollen.

• You have other questions.

HOME CARE FOR FINGER AND TOE TRAUMA

The following topics are covered. Go directly to the part that pertains to your child:

BRUISED FINGER OR TOE
JAMMED FINGER
SMASHED OR CRUSHED FINGERTIP
TORN NAIL
SUPERFICIAL CUTS
SKINNED KNUCKLES
RING CAUGHT ON SWOLLEN FINGER

For puncture wounds, go to the guideline on SKIN TRAUMA, page 64.

Bruised Finger or Toe: Treatment • Soak it in ice water for the next hour; 15 minutes in and 15 minutes out to prevent frostbite. Give your child aspirin or acetaminophen as necessary for the pain. Call your physician later if your child is not using the finger or toe normally after a week.

Jammed Finger: Treatment • Soak the hand in ice water for one hour—15 minutes in and 15 minutes out to prevent frostbite. Give aspirin or acetaminophen as necessary for the pain. The finger will be very sensitive for the next week, so protect it by not using it. A splint often makes a child more prone to bumping into things and is unnecessary. Call your physician later if your child isn't using the finger normally within 2 weeks. If this problem is recurrent, tape the involved fingers (so the painful joints can't bend) before sports for 3 or 4 weeks. To prevent future jammed fingers, have your child build up the small muscles of the fingers by daily squeezing exercises with a hand grip.

Smashed or Crushed Fingertip: Treatment • Before taking care of this yourself, recheck the guidelines for when to consult a physician. Soak the hand in ice water for the next hour; 15 minutes in and 15 minutes out to prevent frostbite. Give your child aspirin or acetaminophen as necessary for the pain. Wash the finger well with a mild dishwashing detergent while soaking it. Trim any small pieces of torn skin with a sterile scissors. If there's a chance of a cut's getting dirty, cover it with a Band-Aid for 24 hours, then soak the Band-Aid off and leave the wound exposed to the air for quicker healing. The injured area will be sensitive for the next week, so protect it from re-injury. Call your physician later if you can't get the wound completely clean, any signs of infection develop, or your child isn't using the finger normally in 1 week.

Torn Nail: Treatment • If the nail is cracked but there are no rough edges, leave it alone. If the nail is almost torn through or there is a large flap of nail, use sterile scissors or nail clippers to cut along the line of the tear. Pieces of nail taped in place will catch on objects. Soak the finger for 20 minutes in cold water. Apply an antibiotic ointment (such as Bacitracin or Betadine) and cover it with a nonsticking gauze. Each day, soak off the pad and soak the finger in a warm salt solution (1 teaspoon of salt to a pint of water) for 20 minutes once a day. On the fourth day, cover it with a loose Band-Aid (antibiotic ointment not needed). On the seventh day, the nailbed should be covered with new skin, and both the soaking and the bandaging can be stopped. A new nail will grow in over the next 1 to 2 months.

Superficial Cuts: Treatment • Wash the wound vigorously with soap and water for 5 minutes. Then apply pressure for 10 minutes with a sterile gauze to stop bleeding. Leave the area exposed to the air.

Skinned Knuckles: Treatment • These wounds are deep scrapes of the upper surfaces of fingers or toes. Wash the wound vigorously for 5 minutes with a mild dishwashing detergent and water. Scrubbing with a sterile gauze may be necessary to get all the dirt out. Flaps of skin (especially if they are dirty) should be cut off with sterile scissors or nail clippers. When clean, apply pressure for 10 minutes with a sterile gauze to stop any bleeding. Cover with nonsticking gauze.

Ring Caught on Swollen Finger: Treatment • Call your physician immediately if the finger has turned blue or numb. In most cases, a high priority is to save the ring. The key to removing the ring is reducing the swelling of the finger. This approach requires patience. At 5-minute intervals, alternate soaking the hand in ice water and holding it (with all the fingers straightened) high in the air. At 30 minutes (after the hand has been elevated for the third time), mineral oil or cooking oil can be applied to the finger. While the hand remains elevated, steady upward pressure can be applied until the ring slides off. If it won't slide off, call your physician before the swelling becomes worse.

GENITAL TRAUMA

This guideline covers injuries to the female or male genital area. Most are bruises (with swelling) or minor cuts that heal rapidly in 3 or 4 days.

CALL YOUR CHILD'S PHYSICIAN IMMEDIATELY IF

• The skin is split open.

• Any external bleeding won't stop after 10 minutes of direct pressure.

• Passing the urine is difficult.

• Blood is in the urine.

• Your child is a female *and* there is any bleeding from inside the vagina.

• Your child is a female *and* the injury was from an object that could have penetrated the vagina.

• Sexual abuse could be the cause.

• You have other urgent questions.

HOME CARE FOR GENITAL TRAUMA

For minor cuts, wash the area vigorously with soap and water for 5 minutes. Then apply pressure for 10 minutes with a sterile gauze to stop bleeding. For swelling, apply ice for the next hour (if tolerated). (See SKIN TRAUMA, page 64, for additional information.) Call your physician later if passing the urine becomes difficult.

HEAD TRAUMA

SYMPTOMS AND CHARACTERISTICS

- History of a blow to the head
- Scalp trauma (cut, scrape, bruise, or swelling)

Cause • Every child sooner or later strikes his head. Falls are especially common when your child is learning to walk.

Expected Course • Most head trauma simply results in a scalp injury. Big lumps can occur with minor injuries because the blood supply to the scalp is so plentiful. For the same reason, small cuts here can bleed profusely. Most bruises occur on the forehead. Sometimes black eyes appear after 3 days because the bruising spreads downward by gravity. Only 1 to 2 percent get a skull fracture. Since the presence of a simple skull fracture neither increases the chances of a complication nor changes the treatment, skull X-rays are rarely helpful and not routinely ordered. Usually there are no associated symptoms except for a headache at the site of impact. Children with concussions need to be examined by a physician, but concussions are uncommon following head trauma. Unless there is temporary unconsciousness, confusion, or amnesia, your child has not had a concussion.

CALL YOUR CHILD'S PHYSICIAN IMMEDIATELY IF

- The skin is split open.
- The accident was a severe one.
- Your child is under 1 year old.
- The crying lasted more than 10 minutes after the injury.

- Your child had a seizure (convulsion).
- Your child was unconscious or confused after the injury.
- Your child can't remember the accident (amnesia).
- A severe headache is present.
- Vomiting has occurred 3 or more times.
- Your child is unusually sleepy and difficult to awaken.
- Speech is slurred.
- Vision is blurred or double.
- Walking is unsteady.
- The arms are weak.
- There is any neck pain.
- Blood or watery fluid is coming from the nose or ears.
- The eyes are crossed.
- There are other symptoms that concern you.

HOME CARE FOR HEAD TRAUMA

Wound Care • If there is a scrape, wash it off with soap and water. Then apply pressure with sterile gauze or a clean cloth for 10 minutes to stop any bleeding. For swelling, apply ice for 1 hour. Although the swelling will go down in 3 to 4 days, the bruise may last for 2 to 4 weeks.

Rest • Encourage your child to lie down and rest until all symptoms have cleared (or at least for 2 hours). After 1 hour has passed, your child can be allowed to sleep. Trying to keep your child awake continuously is unnecessary. Just have him or her sleep nearby so you can periodically check on him.

Diet • Give only clear fluids (ones you can see through) until your child has gone 6 hours without vomiting. Vomiting is common after head injuries and there is no need to have him vomit up his dinner.

Avoid Pain Medicines • Don't give acetaminophen or aspirin, because you need to closely follow your child's reaction to the injury. If the headache is bad enough to need a pain medicine, your child should be checked by a physician. In addition, aspirin increases the bleeding tendency.

Special Precautions and Awakening • Although your child is probably fine, close observation for 48 hours will insure that no serious complication is missed. After 48 hours, however, your child should return to a normal routine and full activity.

Awakening • Awaken your child twice during the night: once at your bedtime and once four hours later. (Awakening him every hour is unnecessary and next to impossible.) Arouse him until he is walking and talking normally. Do this for two nights. If his breathing becomes abnormal or his sleep is otherwise unusual, awaken him to be sure a coma is not developing. If you can't awaken your child, call your physician immediately.

Checking Pupils • This is unnecessary. Some physicians may ask you to check your child's pupils (the black centers of the eyes) to make sure they are equal in size and become smaller when you shine a flashlight on them. Unequal pupils are never seen before other symptoms like confusion and difficult walking. In addition, this test is difficult to perform with uncooperative children or dark-colored irises. In general, pupil checks are only necessary on children with severe head injuries, and they will be hospitalized.

Call Your Child's Physician Later If

• The headache becomes severe.

• Vomiting occurs 3 or more times.

• Your child becomes difficult to awaken or confused.

• Walking or talking becomes difficult.

• Your child's condition worsens in any other way.

PREVENTION OF HEAD TRAUMA

• When driving, place your child in a car safety seat. After the child's weight reaches 40 pounds, use a seat belt. Virtually all states now have child-restraint laws, and with good reason: They reduce injuries by 80 percent and deaths by 90 percent.

• Never leave an infant of any age alone on a high place like a bed, sofa, changing table, or an exam table in the doctor's office. Your baby may unexpectedly roll over for the first time or wiggle off and fall on his head.

- Always keep the side rails up on the crib.

- Don't buy a bunk bed. If you already have one, keep children under age 6 out of the top bunk.

- Don't buy a baby walker. They do not accelerate development and 35 percent of infants using them have an accident requiring emergency care.

- Place a sturdy gate at the top of stairways.

- For doors leading to the basement or outdoors, keep them closed and secure with an extra latch above the child's reach.

- If you live on an upper floor of a building, install window locks or guards.

- Don't leave younger children under the supervision of an aggressive sibling.

- Always supervise your child's outside play until he or she has been taught to cross the street safely (age 4 or 5). Three-year-olds can't be expected to keep promises not to go near the street.

- Don't teach your child how to ride a bicycle until your child is old enough (age 7 or 8) to understand such safety issues as emergency stops and rules about right of way.

- Forbid trampolines. Serious accidents have occurred even with close supervision.

MOUTH TRAUMA

Small cuts and scrapes inside the mouth heal up beautifully in 3 or 4 days—much faster than skin injuries. A tear of the piece of tissue connecting the upper lip to the gum is very common. It can look terrible and bleed profusely until pressure is applied, but it is harmless. Infections of mouth injuries are rare. You'll have difficulty finding where the injury was in a few weeks. Cuts of the tongue and insides of the cheeks are usually due to accidentally biting oneself during eating. Cuts and bruises of the lips are usually due to falls. The potentially serious mouth injuries are those to the tonsil, soft palate, or back of the throat (as from falling with a stick in the mouth).

Prevent these by teaching your child not to run or play with any long object in the mouth. Cuts in the mouth usually don't require suturing except for loose flaps of tissue or gaping wounds of the tongue.

Similar Condition • If appropriate, turn directly to the guideline for TEETH TRAUMA, page 69.

CALL YOUR CHILD'S PHYSICIAN IMMEDIATELY IF

• Any bleeding won't stop after 10 minutes of direct pressure.

• A deep or gaping cut is present.

• The injury is to the back of the throat.

• It resulted from falling down with a stick or other long object in the mouth.

• You have other urgent questions.

HOME CARE FOR MOUTH TRAUMA

Stop Any Bleeding • Stop any bleeding by pressing the bleeding site against the teeth or jaw for 10 minutes. For bleeding from the tongue, squeeze the bleeding site with a sterile gauze or piece of clean cloth. Don't release the pressure until 10 minutes are up.

Pain Relief • The area will probably hurt for 1 or 2 days. Apply a piece of ice or a Popsicle as often as necessary. If there is pain at bedtime, give acetaminophen. Avoid aspirin because it increases the bleeding tendency. For a day or so, offer your child a soft diet. Avoid any salty or citrus foods that might sting. Keep food out of the wound by rinsing the area well with water immediately after meals.

Call Your Child's Physician Later If

• You feel the area is becoming infected. (Keep in mind that any healing wound in the mouth is normally white for several days.)

• Other questions come up.

NOSE TRAUMA

Most blows to the nose result in swelling and bruising without a fracture. Even when a fracture is present, nasal X-rays often show nothing conclusive. The best course of action is to wait until day 4, when the swelling is gone. If the nose then appears to be crooked, you will probably be referred to an ear, nose, and throat surgeon. For mild fractures of the nose, this delayed correction leads to the best cosmetic results because the surgeon can see what he is changing.

CALL YOUR CHILD'S PHYSICIAN IMMEDIATELY IF

• The nose is definitely broken or crooked.

• The skin is split open.

• A nosebleed won't stop after 10 minutes of pinching the nostrils closed.

• Clear fluid is draining continuously from the nose.

• Pain is extreme.

• A swelling of the septum (central dividing wall) is visible inside one nostril.

• Breathing is blocked on one side (when you close the other nostril with your finger).

• You have other urgent questions.

HOME CARE FOR NOSE TRAUMA

Bruises or Swelling • Apply ice to the area for the next hour. Give acetaminophen as necessary for pain. (Aspirin should be avoided, since it can increase the body's bleeding tendency and make nosebleeds worse.)

Superficial Cuts or Abrasions • Wash the area vigorously with soap and water for 5 minutes. Then apply pressure for 10 minutes with a sterile gauze to stop bleeding. Leave the area exposed to the air. To stop bleeding from the nostrils, see the guideline on NOSEBLEED, page 445.

Call Your Child's Physician Later If

• The shape of the nose has not returned to normal in 4 days.

• A yellow discharge, increasing tenderness, fever, or other signs of infection occur.

• Other questions come up.

SKIN TRAUMA

The following four skin injuries are covered. Go directly to the type of injury that pertains to your child.

BRUISES
CUTS AND SCRATCHES
PUNCTURE WOUNDS
SCRAPES (ABRASIONS)

BRUISES

Bleeding into the skin from damaged blood vessels gives a black-and-blue mark. Since the skin is not broken, there is no risk of infection. Bruises usually follow trauma with blunt objects. Unexplained bruises can indicate a bleeding tendency. (Exception: Bruises overlying the shins don't count, since children so commonly bump this area.)

CALL YOUR CHILD'S PHYSICIAN IMMEDIATELY IF

• Bruises are unexplained *and* several in number.

HOME CARE FOR BRUISES

Bruises • Apply ice for 20 to 30 minutes. No other treatment should be necessary. Give acetaminophen for pain. Avoid aspirin, since it may prolong the bleeding. Avoid massage. Bruises clear in 2 to 4 weeks after undergoing yellow, green, and brown color changes.

Blood Blisters • Do not open blisters; it will only increase the possibility of infection. They will dry up and peel off in 1 to 2 weeks.

RELATED TOPIC

Bone and Joint Trauma (see page 49)

CUTS AND SCRATCHES

Most cuts are superficial and extend only partially through the skin. They are caused by sharp objects. The cuts which need sutures are deep, go through the skin to the fat layer, and leave the skin edges separated.

CALL YOUR CHILD'S PHYSICIAN

Immediately If

• Bleeding won't stop after 10 minutes of direct pressure.

• The skin is split open.

• The cut is deep (e.g., you can see bone or tendons).

• There is any dirt in the wound which you can't get out. Note: Lacerations must be sutured within 12 hours of the time of injury, and the infection rate is far lower if they are closed within 2 or 3 hours.

During Office Hours If

• Your child hasn't had a tetanus booster in more than 10 years (5 years for dirty cuts).

HOME CARE FOR CUTS AND SCRATCHES

Treatment • Wash your hands. Then wash the wound vigorously for at least 5 minutes with soap and water. Thorough washing is more important than the type of soap; a mild dishwashing detergent provides more cleansing penetration. Rinse the wound well. Leave it exposed to the air if possible; wounds heal faster without a dressing. If the area is one that will probably get dirty (such as the hands or feet), cover it with a Band-Aid or sterile gauze and adhesive tape for 12 hours. Antiseptic ointments or sprays are unnecessary. Don't use alcohol or Merthiolate on open wounds. They sting and damage the normal tissue. Hydrogen peroxide also is not used, because it can break down normal clots and is a feeble germ-killer.

Common Mistakes • Teach your children that kissing an open wound is dangerous, because the wound will become contaminated by the many germs in the human mouth. Let the scab fall off by itself; picking it off may cause a scar.

Call Your Child's Physician Later If

• The cut looks infected (pus is visible, for instance).

• Pain, redness, or swelling increases after 48 hours.

• The wound doesn't heal within 10 days.

RELATED TOPICS

BITES, ANIMAL OR HUMAN (see page 13)
WOUND INFECTIONS (see page 406)
SUTURE REMOVAL (see page 71)

PUNCTURE WOUNDS

The skin has been completely punctured by an object that is pointed and narrow. The most common puncture wound follows stepping on a nail. The wound is not wide enough to need sutures. Since puncture wounds usually seal over quickly and are not cleansed by any active bleeding, wound infections of all kinds are more common with this type of skin injury. Puncture wounds of the upper eyelid (as from a sharp pencil) are especially dangerous and can result in a brain abscess. A deep infection of the foot can begin with swelling of the top of the foot 1 to 2 weeks after the puncture. Tetanus (lockjaw) can occur if your child is not immunized.

CALL YOUR CHILD'S PHYSICIAN

Immediately If

• A dirty object caused the puncture.

• The skin was quite dirty at the time.

• The object went through a shoe.

• You can see some debris in the wound.

• The tip of the object could have broken off in the wound.

• The puncture is on the head, chest, abdomen, or overlying a joint.

• Your child has never received a tetanus shot.

During Office Hours If

• Your child hasn't had a tetanus booster in more than 5 years.

HOME CARE FOR PUNCTURE WOUNDS

Treatment • Soak the wound in hot water and a mild dishwashing detergent for 15 minutes to promote circulation and cleansing. Cut off any flaps of loose skin. If you can make the wound rebleed, that would be helpful. A Band-Aid on the wound for 12 hours will help keep the opening clean.

Call Your Child's Physician Later If

• The wound looks infected.

• Pain, redness, or swelling increases after 48 hours.

RELATED TOPIC

WOUND INFECTIONS (see page 406)

SCRAPES (ABRASIONS)

An abrasion is an area of superficial skin that has been scraped off during a fall—a "skinned" knee from skidding on gravel, for instance. The mild ones are often called friction burns (such as a rope burn or floor burn).

CALL YOUR CHILD'S PHYSICIAN

Immediately If

• There is any dirt or grime in the wound which you can't get out.

• It was a bicycle-spoke injury.

• It was a washing machine wringer injury.

• It is quite deep.

• It involves a very large area.

During Office Hours If

• Your child hasn't had a tetanus booster in more than 10 years.

HOME CARE FOR SCRAPES

Cleaning the Scrape • First, wash your hands. Then wash the wound vigorously for at least 5 minutes with a mild dishwashing detergent (it provides more cleansing penetration) and warm water. The area will probably need to be scrubbed several times with a wet gauze to get all the dirt out. You may have to remove some dirty particles (e.g., gravel) with a tweezers. If there is tar in the wound, it can often be removed by rubbing it with petroleum jelly, followed by soap and water again. A dishwashing detergent cuts grease much better than bar soap. Pieces of loose skin (especially if they are dirty) should be cut off with a sterile scissors. Rinse the wound well.

Dressing the Scrape • If it is small, leave it exposed to the air. If it is large, cover it with Telfa or another nonsticking dressing. Change this in 12 hours, and after 24 hours leave the wound open; wounds heal faster without a dressing.

Antibiotic Ointment • Antiseptic ointments or sprays in general are unnecessary. However, abrasions overlying the elbow, knee, or hand undergo constant stretch. To prevent cracking and reopening of these, apply an antibiotic ointment 1 or 2 times a day to keep the crust soft. Use Bacitracin or Betadine ointment.

Aspirin Or Acetaminophen • Since abrasions can hurt badly, use acetaminophen or aspirin for the first day. (For dosage, see chart on page 310.)

Call Your Child's Physician Later If

• The scrape looks infected.

• The scrape increases in size or spreads to good skin.

• The scrape doesn't heal within 2 weeks.

RELATED TOPIC

WOUND INFECTIONS (see page 406)

TAILBONE TRAUMA

The tailbone (or coccyx) is the small bone at the lower end of the spine. The tailbone is usually injured during a fall onto a hard surface, such as ice or stairs. The pain is due to bruising of the bone or stretched ligaments. Fractures of the tailbone are rare and they heal fine, so an X-ray is unnecessary for this injury. Tailbone injuries can be diagnosed by finding tenderness of the bone located in the upper part of the groove between the buttocks.

HOME CARE FOR TAILBONE TRAUMA

A bruised tailbone will usually hurt for 3 to 4 weeks. Give your youngster aspirin for 2 or 3 days (for dosage, see chart on page 51). Aspirin usually gives more relief of muscle and bone pain than acetaminophen. Sitting on a large rubber ring or a cushion placed forward on the chair will take pressure off the tailbone. A heating pad may also help. Occasionally bowel movements will cause enough discomfort that 1 or 2 tablespoons of mineral oil will temporarily be needed twice a day. (See also CONSTIPATION, page 483, regarding a nonconstipating diet.)

TEETH TRAUMA

This guideline covers injuries to the teeth (usually the front ones). Often, the only noticeable injury is bleeding from the gums. The tooth has been jarred and perhaps slightly loosened. These minor injuries heal in 3 days. The next most common injury is tooth displacement (usually pushed inward). It usually returns to its normal position within a few weeks without any treatment. Chipped (or fractured) teeth need to be seen by a dentist. Teeth that are knocked out (avulsed) constitute an emergency. Although primary teeth can't successfully be replaced, permanent (second) teeth need to be returned to their sockets in the gumline as soon as possible (by 2 hours at the latest). Ideally, someone at the scene of the accident could rinse off the tooth, replace it in the socket and have the child bite down on a wad of cloth to stabilize it until a dentist is reached.

CALL YOUR CHILD'S DENTIST

(Call your physician only if your dentist can't be reached and you are dealing with an emergency.)

Immediately If

• A tooth has been knocked out. (Bring it with you in a cup with some of your child's saliva.)

• A large piece of tooth has been chipped off.

• A red dot is visible inside a fractured tooth.

• Your child is in extreme pain.

• Any bleeding won't stop after 10 minutes of direct pressure. (For bleeding with missing teeth, have your child chomp down on a piece of gauze.)

During Office Hours If

• A small piece of tooth has been chipped off.

• You can see a fracture line in the tooth.

• The tooth is sensitive to cold fluids.

• The tooth has been pushed out of its usual position.

• The tooth is more than slightly loose.

• You have other questions.

HOME CARE FOR TEETH TRAUMA

Treatment • Apply a piece of ice or a Popsicle to the injured gum area, unless it increases the pain. If it still hurts, give your child some acetaminophen. Avoid aspirin, because it increases the bleeding tendency. If any teeth are loose, put your child on a soft diet for 3 days. If a tooth is out of its normal position, try to reposition it with a little finger pressure. If a tooth is broken and dental care must be delayed, temporarily seal the sensitive area with melted candle wax. A delay of several days, however, may lead to a root-canal infection.

Call Your Child's Dentist Later If

• Any new symptoms develop.

• The tooth becomes sensitive to hot or cold fluids during the next week.

• The tooth becomes a darker color.

TETANUS BOOSTER FOLLOWING TRAUMA

The need for a tetanus booster depends on the type of wound (whether or not it is tetanus-prone) and your child's immunization status. All puncture wounds and all cuts (breaks in the skin) caused by an unclean object pose a risk of tetanus. Cuts from a clean knife, piece of glass, etc., are not tetanus-prone wounds unless they become contaminated afterwards. Neither are minor burns or scrapes, because these injuries are so superficial that they have adequate exposure to air. The tetanus bacteria can multiply only if buried in a wound where no air is present. Most children have scrapes from time to time; tetanus boosters for all of these wounds would be impractical.

CALL YOUR CHILD'S PHYSICIAN DURING OFFICE HOURS FOR

- Any puncture wound or dirty cut in children who have had no tetanus booter in more than 5 years.

- Any wound in patients who have had no tetanus booster in more than 10 years. (All immunized children and adults need a tetanus booster every 10 years.)

The administration of a tetanus booster is not an emergency. It can wait 24 hours without increasing the risk of tetanus. Most physicians give a Td booster at these times to help maintain adequate protection against diphtheria as well.
Cautions: If your child has not been immunized against tetanus and sustains a wound, he needs to be seen immediately. Also, if a wound needs suturing, it should be treated as soon as possible.

SUTURE REMOVAL

The following guidelines can serve as a reminder that sutures are ready for removal at different times, depending on the site of the wound.

AREA	NUMBER OF DAYS
Face	3–4
Neck	5
Scalp	6
Anterior chest or abdomen	7
Arms and back of hands	7
Legs and top of feet	10
Back	12
Palms and soles	14

If any sutures come out early, call your child's physician. In the meantime, reinforce the wound with tape. Stitches removed too late can leave unnecessary skin marks or even scarring.

III

NEW
BABY
CARE

NORMAL NEWBORNS

FIRST DAYS IN THE HOSPITAL: GETTING ACQUAINTED

PRENATAL TASKS

Childbirth-preparation classes are especially important during the first pregnancy. These classes reduce the amount of fear that normal parents harbor about labor. In addition they introduce the parents to the world of hospital obstetrics. If at all possible, both parents-to-be should attend these classes, which ideally (though not essentially) will be taught by a husband-and-wife team. During the prenatal period you will have carefully considered the following five questions:

- Will the father be present at labor and delivery? Most fathers find this a memorable experience, and most mothers are grateful to have their husbands present for emotional support. In general, siblings should not be present at the delivery because some of them become frightened by the birth process.

- What baby equipment will you buy? (See NEWBORN EQUIPMENT AND SUPPLIES, page 142.)

- What will you name your baby? Try to narrow your list down to two male and two female names by the time of delivery.

- Will you breast-feed or bottle-feed? (See BREAST-FEEDING, page 97, and FORMULA-FEEDING, page 102.) In some communities, breast-feeding preparation classes are available.

- If your newborn is a boy, will you have him circumcised? (See CIRCUMCISION, PROS AND CONS, page 93.)

DELIVERY OR BIRTHING-ROOM CONTACT WITH YOUR BABY

Parent-infant bonding is one of the strongest human ties. This bonding gets off to a good start if the mother and father have close contact with their newborn during the first hour of life. After your baby has been dried off and placed in a warm blanket, both parents should have private time with the infant until he or she falls asleep. The period of wakefulness usually lasts from 30 to 60 minutes. Many studies over the past decade have found that early contact (preferably 6 hours during the first day) increases the parents' ability to soothe the baby, increases the likelihood of successful breast-feeding, enhances language development, and maximizes the sense that the baby belongs to the parents. This information underscores the importance of the father's being involved with his baby on the day of birth.

ROOMING-IN WITH YOUR BABY

Most hospitals now have units on the maternity ward where the mother and baby can constantly be together, with backup by the nursing staff. Increasing numbers of hospitals have gone over to this arrangement entirely. Others allow modified rooming-in, in which the baby is with the mother whenever the mother is awake. Rooming-in promotes bonding and a better feeding schedule. In this manner, the mother is quite familiar with her newborn by the time she is discharged. The nursing staff is available to help rather than replace the mother.

FEEDING: GETTING STARTED

Getting breast-feeding off to a good start will help guarantee success. During the first 30 minutes of quiet alert behavior after delivery, many babies will be interested in nursing at the breast. For others, the first real attempt at breast-feeding will occur when the baby awakens from his or her initial sleep, at 3 to 6 hours after delivery. Your baby should nurse for about 5 minutes at each breast, 10 minutes altogether. Ask your nurse for help with correct breast-feeding positioning. Your baby's face and abdomen should be against your body so he doesn't have to turn his head to nurse. Also keep his nose clear of the breast for breathing. Breast-feeding should be repeated on demand, approximately every 2½ hours, including night feedings. Have your infant brought to your room at night to nurse if he or she is not rooming in with you around-the-clock. Supplementary formula should not be offered during the early weeks, because it interferes with sucking and milk production. Supplementary glucose water after breast-feeding is seldom necessary, but it probably does no harm.

Don't expect a full milk supply until your milk "comes in" on the second to fourth day after delivery. A common error during this period of engorgement is failing to compress the areola so that the infant can grasp the nipple correctly. Take advantage of the brief hospital stay to get as much help with breast-feeding as possible before going home.

Healthy formula-fed babies should be offered formula as soon as they display an interest in feeding, which is usually 3 to 6 hours after delivery when they awaken from their first sleep. Bottle-fed babies typically take ½ ounce (15 ml) at the first feeding. By 3 days of age, full-term infants will usually take 2 ounces every 3 to 4 hours.

LEARNING PARENTING SKILLS

During the hospital stay, both parents should take a crash course in caring for their newborn. Many of the skills will be demonstrated by the nursing staff. Some will be reviewed by video tapes or audio tapes. Your child's physician may give you written instruction-sheets on some of these topics. Be certain that someone has taught you how to carry out each of the following tasks before you are discharged:

Feeding your baby (see BREAST-FEEDING, page 97, or FORMULA-FEEDING, page 102)
Soothing your baby with touching or holding when he or she is crying (see CRYING BABY [COLIC], page 124)
Normal skin care and bathing (see page 91)
Cord care (see pages 162–164)
Circumcision care (see page 94)
Foreskin care (see page 96)
Diapering (see DIAPER RASH, page 152)
Taking a temperature (armpit and rectal) and reading a thermometer (see FEVER, page 305)
Using a suction bulb (see under COLDS, page 435)
Using an approved car seat (see ACCIDENT PREVENTION, page 139)
Dealing with siblings (see SIBLING RIVALRY, page 136)

You should also be aware there is nothing out of the ordinary about spitting up, loose bowel movements, bowel-movement straining, and unexplained crying.

NEWBORN TESTS AND TREATMENTS

During your hospital stay, your physician will examine your new baby and answer any questions you might have about your baby's appearance (see THE NORMAL NEWBORN'S APPEARANCE, page 84). He will also review normal newborn behavior (see page 83), and symptoms to look for in the sick newborn (see page 149). During the hospital stay your baby will receive a vitamin K injection, which prevents hemorrhagic disease of the newborn, a condition that otherwise could cause severe bleeding in the first 7 days of life. Antibiotic eyedrops will be placed in each eye within one hour of birth to prevent eye infections with gonorrhea or chlamydia, two germs that can be present in the birth canal without any symptoms. A blood test to screen for metabolic diseases that could cause mental retardation will be performed from a heel stick. Your baby's blood type will be determined only if the mother is blood group O or Rh negative. All of these conditions may go untreated or undetected with a home delivery unless special care is taken.

VISITORS—FRIENDS, RELATIVES, AND CHILDREN

The father is the most important visitor. He should come as often and stay as long as possible. He should hold his baby each day. Many hospitals now allow visits by siblings. Studies show that children who visit their mothers after the birth of a newborn are more responsive to their mother and the new baby than nonvisiting children are. Children should be supervised by parents or a responsible adult during the entire hospital visit. Siblings should not visit if they have an acute illness, a fever, or recent exposure to a contagious disease. Hospital visitors, however, can wear the mother out. People should telephone before they come by. If you are tired, consider temporarily canceling all visits (except from your husband).

DISCHARGE FROM THE HOSPITAL

In our country most normal full-term newborns are discharged from the hospital with their mothers by 48 to 72 hours of age. Early discharge is defined as discharge before 24 hours of age. Some parents desire early discharge because of limited insurance coverage, a need for the mother to be home with siblings, or personal preference. A baby should not be discharged before the temperature, pulse, and respirations have stabilized, the baby has urinated, and two successful feedings have occurred. (In a successful feeding, the baby demonstrates normal sucking, swallowing, and stomach-emptying mechanisms—all necessary for weight gain.) Babies who are discharged early should be seen on the third day of life to check them for weight, jaundice, and general health. The first blood sample for phenylketonuria (PKU) should also be collected at this time. Close medical follow-up is essential for infants who are discharged early.

FIRST WEEKS AT HOME: GETTING HELP

PREVENTING FATIGUE AND EXHAUSTION
For most mothers the first weeks at home with a new baby are often the hardest in their lives. You will probably feel overworked, even overwhelmed. Inadequate sleep will leave you with the feeling of fatigue. Caring for babies can be a lonely and stressful responsibility. You may wonder if you will ever catch up on your rest or work. The solution is asking for help. No one should be expected to care for a young baby alone. Every baby awakens one or more times a night. The way to avoid sleep deprivation is to know the total amount of sleep you need per day and to get that sleep in bits and pieces. Go to bed earlier in the evening. When your baby naps, you must also nap. Your baby doesn't need you hovering over him while he's asleep. If he is sick he will have symptoms. While you are napping, take the telephone off the hook and put up a sign on the door stating MOTHER AND BABY SLEEPING. If your total sleep remains inadequate, hire a babysitter or bring in a relative to allow yourself a good nap. If you don't take care of yourself, you won't be able to take care of your baby.

THE POSTPARTUM BLUES
More than 50 percent of women experience postpartum blues on the third or fourth day after delivery. The symptoms include tearfulness, tiredness, sadness, and the inability to think clearly. The main cause of this temporary reaction is probably the sudden decrease of maternal hormones. Since the symptoms commonly begin on the day the mother comes home from the hospital, the full impact of being totally responsible for a dependent newborn may also be a contributing factor. Many mothers feel let down and guilty about these symptoms,

because they have been led to believe they should be over-joyed with the idea of caring for their newborn. In any event, these symptoms usually clear in 1 to 3 weeks as the hormone levels return to normal and as the mother develops routines and a sense of control over her life.

A good way to overcome the postpartum blues is to discuss openly with your husband or a close friend your feelings of being trapped, your sense that these new responsibilities are insurmountable, and your other concerns. Don't feel you need to put on a "Supermom show" for visitors or to suppress crying. In addition, from the beginning it is important for you to have some time for yourself each day. Also, you need an activity outside of the home at least once a week—going to the beauty parlor, shopping, visiting, or seeing a movie. By the third week, setting aside an evening a week for a "date" with your husband is also most helpful. If you don't feel better by the time your baby is 1 month old, see your physician about the possibility of needing counseling for depression.

HELPERS: RELATIVES, FRIENDS, SITTERS

As already emphasized, everyone needs extra help during the first few weeks alone with a new baby. Ideally, you were able to make arrangements for help before your baby was born. The best person to help (if you get along with her) is usually your mother or mother-in-law. If not, teenagers or adults can come in several times a week to help with housework or look after your baby while you go out or get a nap. If you have other young children, you will need daily help. Clarify that your role is looking after your baby. Your helper's role involves shopping, cooking, housecleaning, and washing clothes and dishes. If your newborn has a medical problem that requires special care, ask for some home visits by a public health nurse.

THE FATHER'S ROLE

The father needs to take time off from work to be with his wife during labor and delivery, as well as on the day she and his child come home from the hospital. If the couple has a relative who will temporarily live in and help, the father can continue to work. However, when the relative leaves, the father can take saved-up vacation time as paternity leave. At a minimum he needs to work shorter hours until his wife and baby have settled in. The age of noninvolvement of the father is a thing of the past. Not only does the mother need the father to help her with household chores, but the baby also needs the father to develop a close relationship with him. Today's fathers get involved with feeding, changing diapers, bathing, putting to bed, reading stories, dressing, disciplining, helping with homework, playing games, and calling the physician when the child is sick. Some fathers avoid interacting with the baby during the first year of life because they are afraid they will hurt their baby or, if the baby cries, that they won't be able to calm the baby. The longer they go without learning these skills, the harder it becomes to change. At a minimum, fathers should hold and comfort their babies at least once a day (something commonly overlooked in our culture).

VISITORS

During the first month at home, only close friends and relatives should be allowed to visit. They should call before they visit to be sure that it is a convenient day. They should not visit if they are sick. To prevent unannounced visitors, the parents can put up a sign stating MOTHER AND BABY SLEEPING. NO VISITORS. PLEASE CALL FIRST. Friends without children may not understand your needs. During visits, it is beneficial if the visitor pays special attention to older siblings (see SIBLING RIVALRY, page 136).

FEEDING: ACHIEVING WEIGHT GAIN

Your main assignments during the early months of life are loving and feeding your baby. All babies lose a few ounces during the first few days after birth. Most bottle-fed babies are back to birth weight by 10 days of age, and breast-fed babies by 14 days of age. Then, infants gain approximately an ounce per day during the early months. If milk is provided liberally, the normal newborn's hunger drive sees to it that enough weight is gained.

Breast-feeding mothers often wonder if their baby is getting enough calories, since they can't see how many ounces the baby takes. Your baby is doing fine if he or she demands to nurse every 2 to 3 hours, appears satisfied after feedings, takes both breasts at each nursing, wets 8 or more diapers each day, and passes 4 or more soft stools per day. Whenever you are worried about your baby's weight gain, take your baby to your physician's office for a weight check. Feeding problems detected early are much easier to remedy than those of longstanding. A special weight check 1 week after birth is a good idea for infants of first-time breast-feeding mothers or those concerned about their milk supply. (See BREAST-FEEDING, page 97, or FORMULA-FEEDING, page 102.)

DEALING WITH CRYING

Crying babies need to be held. They need someone with a soothing voice and a soothing touch. You can't spoil your baby during the early months of life. Overly sensitive babies may need a more gentle kind of touch. For additional help on this subject, see CRYING BABY (COLIC), page 124, or PREVENTION OF SLEEP PROBLEMS, page 127.

TAKING YOUR BABY OUTSIDE

Your baby can be taken outside at any age; just dress for the weather. You already took him outside when you left the hospital, and you will be going outside again when you take him for the two-week checkup. Dress him with as many layers of clothing as an adult would wear for the outside temperature. The most common mistake is overdressing babies in the summertime. (See also SUNBURN, page 398.) In the wintertime, babies need a hat because they often don't have much hair to protect against heat loss. The idea that cold air or winds can cause ear infections or pneumonia is a myth. Camping and crowds should probably be avoided during the first month of life. Also try to avoid close contact with sick people during the first year of life.

THE TWO-WEEK MEDICAL CHECKUP

This checkup is probably the most important medical visit during the first year of life. Any physical condition that was not detectable during the hospital stay will usually have developed symptoms by 2 weeks of age. Your baby's height, weight, and head circumference will tell your child's physician how your child is growing. This is also the time during which your family is under the most stress of adapting to a new baby. Try to develop a habit of jotting down questions about your child's health or behavior at home. Bring this list with you to office visits for discussion with your child's physician. Most physicians welcome the opportunity to address your agenda, especially if your questions are ones not easily answered by reading or talking with other mothers. If at all possible, have your husband join you on these visits to the physician's office. Most physicians prefer to get to know the father during a checkup rather than during the crisis time of an acute illness. If you think your newborn is sick between health supervision visits, be sure to call your physician for help (see THE SICK NEWBORN: SUBTLE SYMPTOMS, page 149).

THE NORMAL NEWBORN'S BEHAVIOR

Some findings in newborns that concern parents are not signs of illness. Most of these harmless reflexes are due to an immature nervous system and will disappear in 2 or 3 months:

- Chin trembling
- Lower lip quivering
- Hiccups
- Irregular breathing. (Normally, if your baby is content, the rate is less than 60 breaths per minute, a pause is less than 6 seconds, and your baby doesn't turn blue.)
- Passing gas (not a temporary behavior). See GAS, EXCESSIVE, page 494.)
- Sleep noise from breathing and moving
- Sneezing
- Spitting up or belching. (See SPITTING UP, page 156, for details.)
- Startle reflex (also called the Moro or embrace reflex) following noise or movement
- Straining with bowel movements
- Throat clearing (or gurgling sounds)
- Trembling of arms and legs during crying. (Note: Jittery babies are common. Convulsions are rare. During convulsions, babies have jerking or blinking of the eyes, rhythmic sucking of the mouth, and they don't cry.)
- Yawning

THE NORMAL NEWBORN'S APPEARANCE

Even after your child's physician assures you that your baby is normal and has all his parts, you may find that he looks a bit odd. He does not have the perfect body you have seen in baby books. Be patient. Most newborns have some peculiar characteristics. Fortunately they are temporary. Your baby will begin to look normal by 1 to 2 weeks of age.

The discussion of these temporary newborn characteristics is arranged by body parts. A few minor congenital defects that are harmless but permanent will also be included (marked by an asterisk). Call your child's physician if you are not sure that what you see on your baby matches what is described on this list.

HEAD

Molding • Molding refers to the long narrow head that results from passage through a tight birth canal. This compression of the head can temporarily hide the fontanel. The head returns to a normal shape in a few days.

Caput • This refers to swelling on top of the head or throughout the scalp that is due to fluid being squeezed into the scalp during the birth process. Caput is present at birth and clears in a few days.

Cephalohematoma • This is a collection of blood on the outer surface of the skull. It is due to friction between the skull and the pelvic bones during the birth process. The lump is usually confined to one side of the head. It first appears on the second day of life and may increase in size for up to 5 days. It doesn't resolve completely until 2 or 3 months of age.

Anterior Fontanel • The "soft spot" is found in the top front part of the skull. It is diamond-shaped and covered by a thick fibrous layer. The purpose of the soft spot is to allow rapid brain growth. The soft spot will normally pulsate with each beat of the heart. It normally closes with bone between 9 and 12 months of age.

EYES

Swollen Eyelids • The eyes may be puffy due to pressure on the face during delivery. They may be puffy and reddened if silver nitrate eyedrops are used. This irritation should clear in 3 days.

Subconjunctival Hemorrhage • A flame-shaped hemorrhage on the white of the eye (sclera) is not uncommon. It's harmless and due to birth trauma. The blood is reabsorbed in 2 to 3 weeks.

Iris Color • The iris generally comes in variations of four colors: blue, green, gray, or brown. The permanent color of the iris is often uncertain until your baby reaches 6 months of age. White babies are usually born with blue-gray eyes. Black babies are usually born with brown-gray eyes. Children who are going to have dark irises often change early (by 2 months of age). Children who are going to have light-colored irises usually change closer to 5 or 6 months of age.

Tear Duct, Blocked • See page 158.

EARS

Folded over • The ears of newborns are commonly soft and floppy. Sometimes one of the edges is folded over. The outer ear will assume normal shape as the cartilage hardens over the next few weeks.

Earpits • About 1 percent of normal children have a small pit or dimple in front of the outer ear. This minor congenital defect is of no importance unless it becomes infected.

NOSE

Flattened • The nose can become misshapen during the birth process. It may be flattened or pushed to one side. It will look normal by 1 week of age.

MOUTH

Sucking Callus (or blister) • Sucking callus occurs in the center of the upper lip and is due to constant friction at this point during bottle- or breast-feeding. It will disappear when your child begins cup feedings. Children may also develop a sucking callus on the thumb or wrist.

Tongue-tie • The normal tongue in newborns has a short, tight band that connects it to the floor of the mouth. This band normally stretches with time, movement, and growth. I have never seen a baby with symptoms from tongue-tie (see page 161).

Epithelial Pearls • Little cysts (containing clear fluid) or shallow white ulcers can ocur along the gumline or on the hard palate. These are due to blockage of normal mucous glands. They disappear by 1 to 2 months of age.

Teeth • The presence of a tooth at birth is a rare event. Approximately 10 percent of them are extra teeth without a root structure. The other 90 percent are prematurely erupted normal teeth. The distinction can be made with an X-ray. The extra teeth must be removed by a dentist. The normal teeth need to be removed only if they become loose (with a danger of choking) or if they cause sores on your baby's tongue.

BREASTS

Breast Engorgement • Swollen breasts are present during the first week of life in many girl and boy babies. They are caused by the passage of female hormones across the mother's placenta. Swollen breasts generally last for 4 to 6 months, but longer in breast-fed and girl babies. One breast may regress in size before the other one by a month or more. Never squeeze the breast because this can cause infection. Be sure to call your child's physician if the swollen breast develops any redness, streaking, or tenderness.

GENITALS, GIRLS

Swollen Labia • The labia minora can be quite swollen in newborns due to the passage of female hormones across the placenta. The swelling will resolve in 2 to 4 weeks.

Hymenal Tags • The hymen can also be swollen due to maternal estrogen and have smooth ½-inch projections of pink tissue. These normal tags occur in 10 percent of newborn girls and slowly shrink over 2 to 4 weeks.

Vaginal Discharge • As the maternal hormones decline in the baby's blood, a clear or white discharge can flow from the vagina during the latter part of the first week of life. Occasionally the discharge will become pink or blood-tinged (false menstruation). This normal discharge should not recur once it stops.

GENITALS, BOYS

Hydrocele • The newborn scrotum can be filled with clear fluid. This fluid is squeezed into the scrotum during the birth process. (See SWELLING, GROIN OR SCROTUM, page 516, for details.)

Undescended Testicle • The testicle is not in the scrotum in about 4 percent of full-term newborns. Many of these testicles gradually descend into the normal position during the following months. By 1 year of age only 0.7 percent of all testicles are undescended. These need to be brought down surgically.

Tight Foreskin • Most uncircumcised babies have a tight foreskin that doesn't allow one to see the head of the penis. This is normal and should not be retracted. (See FORESKIN CARE AND PROBLEMS, page 96, for details.)

Erections • Erections occur commonly in the newborn infant, as they do at all ages. They are usually triggered by a full bladder. Erections demonstrate that the nerves to the penis are normal.

BONES AND JOINTS

Tight Hips • Your child's physician will test how far your child's legs can be spread apart to be certain the hips are not too tight. Bending the upper legs outward until they are horizontal is called 90 degrees. (Less than 50 percent of normal newborn hips permit this much spreading.) As long as the upper legs can be bent outward to 60 degrees and are the same on each side, they are fine. The most common cause of a tight hip is a dislocation.

Tibial Torsion • The lower legs (tibia) normally curve in because of the cross-legged posture that your baby was stuck in while in the womb. If you stand your baby up, you will also notice that the legs are bowed. Both of these curves are normal and will straighten out after your child has been walking for 6 to 12 months.

Feet Turned Up, In, or Out • Feet can turn any which way because of the cramped quarters inside the womb. As long as the feet are flexible and can be easily moved to a normal position, they are normal. The direction of the feet will become more normal between 6 and 12 months of age.

Long Second Toe • The second toe is longer than the great toe by heredity in some ethnic groups that originated along the Mediterranean, especially Egyptians.

"Ingrown" Toenails • Many newborns have soft nails that easily bend and curve. However, they are not truly ingrown because they don't curve into the flesh.

HAIR

Scalp Hair • Most hair at birth is dark-colored. This hair is temporary and begins to shed by 1 month of age. Some babies lose it gradually while the permanent hair is coming in; others lose it rapidly, and temporarily become bald. The permanent hair will appear by 6 months. It may be an entirely different color from the newborn hair.

Body Hair (lanugo) • Lanugo is the fine, downy hair that is sometimes present on the back and shoulders. It is more common in premature infants. It is rubbed off with normal friction by 2 to 4 weeks of age.

SKIN
See NEWBORN RASHES AND BIRTHMARKS, below.

NEWBORN RASHES AND BIRTHMARKS

After the first bath, your newborn will normally have a ruddy complexion due to the extra high count of red blood cells. He can quickly change to a pale- or mottled-blue color if he becomes cold, so keep him warm. During the second week of life, the skin will normally become dry and flaky. In this guideline, the following seven rashes and birthmarks are covered. Save time by going directly to the one that pertains to your baby.

ACNE
DROOLING RASH
ERYTHEMA TOXICUM
FORCEPS OR BIRTH CANAL TRAUMA
MILIA
MONGOLIAN SPOTS
STORK BITES (PINK BIRTHMARKS)

ACNE

More than 30 percent of newborns develop acne of the face—mainly small red bumps. This neonatal acne begins at 3 to 4 weeks of age and lasts until 4 to 6 months of age. The cause appears to be the transfer of maternal hormones just prior to birth. Since it is temporary, no treatment is necessary. Baby oil or ointments make it worse.

DROOLING RASH

Many babies have a rash on the chin or cheeks that comes and goes. This is often due to contact with food and acid that has been spit up from the stomach (especially prolonged contact during sleep). Some of this can be helped by placing an absorbent diaper under your baby's face during naps. Also, rinse the face with water after all feedings.

Other temporary rashes on the face are heat rashes in areas held against the mother's skin during nursing (especially in the summertime). Change your baby's position more frequently and put a cool washcloth on the area. No baby has perfect skin. The babies in advertisements wear makeup.

ERYTHEMA TOXICUM

More than 50 percent of babies get a rash called erythema toxicum on the second or third day of life. The rash is composed of ½-inch to 1-inch red blotches with a small white lump in the center. They look like insect bites, but are not. They can be numerous, keep occurring, be present anywhere on the body surface (except the palms and soles), and look terrible. Their cause is unknown, they are harmless, and they resolve by 2 weeks of age (rarely, 4 weeks).

FORCEPS OR BIRTH CANAL TRAUMA

If your baby's delivery was difficult, a forceps may have been used to help him through the birth canal. The pressure of the forceps on the skin can leave bruises, scrapes, or damaged fat tissue anywhere on the head or face. Skin overlying bony prominences (such as the sides of the skull bone) can become damaged even without a forceps delivery by pressure from the birth canal. Fetal monitors can also cause scrapes and scabs on the scalp. The bruises and scrapes will be noted on day 1 or day 2 and disappear by 1 to 2 weeks. The fat tissue injury (subcutaneous fat necrosis) won't be apparent until day 5 to day 10. A firm coin-shaped lump, attached to the skin and sometimes with an overlying scab, is the usual finding. This lump may take 3 or 4 weeks to resolve. If it becomes tender to the touch, soft in the center, or shows other signs of infection, call your child's physician.

MILIA

Milia are tiny white bumps that occur on the faces of 40 percent of newborn babies. The nose and cheeks are most often involved, but milia are also seen on the forehead and chin. Although they look like pimples, they are not infected. They are blocked-off skin pores and will open up and disappear by 1 to 2 months of age. No ointments or creams should be applied to them.

MONGOLIAN SPOTS

A Mongolian spot is a bluish-green or bluish-gray flat birthmark that is found in over 90 percent of Native American, Oriental, Hispanic, and Black babies. They are also seen in 10 percent of Caucasians, especially those of Mediterranean descent. They occur most commonly over the back and buttocks, although they can be present on any part of the body. They vary greatly in size and shape. They have no relationship to any disease. Most fade away by 2 or 3 years of age, although a trace may persist into adult life.

STORK BITES (PINK BIRTHMARKS)

Flat pink birthmarks (also called capillary hemangiomas or salmon patches) occur over the bridge of the nose, the eyelids, or the back of the neck ("stork bites") in more than 50 percent of newborns. The ones in front are often referred to as "an angel's kiss." All the birthmarks on the bridge of the nose and eyelids clear completely. Those on the eyelids clear by 1 year of age; those on the bridge of the nose may persist for a few additional years. Most birthmarks on the nape of the neck also clear, but 25 percent can persist into adult life. Talk with your child's physician during regular visits about blood-vessel birthmarks that are raised or increasing in size (strawberry hemangiomas). These run a small risk of bleeding with trauma. They persist until 6 to 8 years of age but go away without any treatment.

NEWBORN SKIN CARE AND BATHING

BATHING

Bathe your baby daily in hot weather, once or twice a week in cool weather. Keep the water level below the navel or give sponge baths until 2 days after the cord has fallen off. (Reasons: Sitting in poopy bath water can cause a cord infection. Also submerging the cord may interfere with its drying out and falling off. Getting it a little wet doesn't matter.) Use tap water without soap or use a nondrying soap (such as Dove) sparingly. Don't forget to wash the face; otherwise, chemicals from milk or other foods can build up and cause an irritated rash. Also rinse off the eyelids with clean water. The ear canals don't need cleaning. Putting cotton swabs in them just pushes the earwax back in and leads to blockage and possible hearing problems. The earwax moves outward naturally; just pick off flakes of earwax as they come to the surface. Don't forget to wash the genital area. The male genitals can be washed with either plain water or a mild soap. However, when you wash the inside of the female genital area (the vulva), never use soap. This tissue is very sensitive to any soap. Rinse the area with plain water, wiping from front to back. This practice and the avoidance of any bubble baths before puberty may prevent many urinary tract infections and vaginal irritations. At the end of the bath, rinse your baby well; soap residue can be irritating.

Related Topics

CIRCUMCISION CARE AND PROBLEMS (see page 94)
FORESKIN CARE AND PROBLEMS (see page 96)

CHANGING DIAPERS

After wet diapers are removed, just rinse your baby's bottom off with a wet washcloth. After soiled diapers, rinse the bottom under running warm water. After you finish the rear, cleanse the genital area by wiping front to back with a wet cloth. In boys, carefully clean the scrotum; and in girls, the creases of the vaginal lips (labia).

SHAMPOO

Wash your baby's hair once or twice a week with a special baby shampoo that doesn't sting the eyes. You can use an adult shampoo if you are careful about the eyes. Don't be concerned about hurting the anterior fontanel (soft spot). It is well protected.

Related Topic

CRADLE CAP (see page 151)

LOTIONS, CREAMS, AND OINTMENTS

Newborn skin normally does not require any ointments or creams. Especially avoid the application of any oil, ointment, or greasy substance, since this will almost always block the small sweat glands and lead to pimples and/or a heat rash. If the skin starts to become dry and cracked, use a baby lotion, hand lotion, or moisturizing cream twice a day, just as you would for yourself. For deep cracks (as around the ankles), petroleum jelly is better. Cornstarch powder can be used to prevent rashes in areas of friction (as under the diaper). But avoid talcum powders because of the risk of serious pneumonia if your baby breathes some in.

UMBILICAL CORD

Try to keep the cord dry. Apply rubbing alcohol to the base of the cord (where it attaches to the skin) twice a day (including after the bath) until 1 week after it falls off. Clean underneath the cord with rubbing alcohol and a cotton swab by lifting it and bending it to each side. Air exposure also helps with drying and separation, so keep the diaper folded down below the cord area or use a scissors to cut away a wedge of the diaper in front.

Related Topics

UMBILICAL CORD, DELAYED SEPARATION (see page 162)
UMBILICAL CORD, OOZING (see page 163)

FINGERNAILS

Trim the nails once a week to prevent your baby from scratching himself or others. Do it after a bath when the nails are softened. Use a nail clipper, special baby scissors, or a fine emery board. This job usually takes two people unless you do it while your child is asleep. If you don't hold the finger still, you can cause a nasty cut of the fingertip.

CIRCUMCISION, PROS AND CONS

Circumcision means cutting off the foreskin or ring of tissue that covers the head (glans) of the penis. This surgical procedure is usually performed on newborns. In a 1984 survey, 76 percent of American newborn males were reported circumcised that year. (The rate has declined from 90 percent in 1979.) The following information should help you decide what is best for your son.

CULTURAL ASPECTS

Those of the Jewish and Moslem faiths perform circumcision for religious reasons. Nonreligious circumcision became popular in English-speaking countries between 1920 and 1950, due to misconceptions about diseases it could prevent. It never caught on in Asia, South America, Central America, or most of Europe. Over 80 percent of the world's male population is not circumcised. The circumcision rates have fallen to 1 percent in Britain, 10 percent in New Zealand, and 40 percent in Canada.

PURPOSE OF THE FORESKIN

The presence of the foreskin is not some cosmic error. The foreskin protects the glans against urine, feces, and other types of irritation. Infections of the urinary opening (meatitis) and scarring of the opening (meatal stenosis) virtually never occur in the uncircumcised penis. The foreskin may also serve a sexual function, namely protecting the sensitivity of the glans. (See FORESKIN CARE AND PROBLEMS, page 96, for information on hygiene.)

REASONS FOR CIRCUMCISION

The American Academy of Pediatrics has repeatedly stated since 1971 that "there are no medical indications for routine circumcision of the newborn." According to a recent study, however, circumcision may protect against a 1 percent occurrence of urinary tract infections during the first year of life. Circumcision does not prevent sexually transmitted disease later. While it does protect against cancer of the penis, good hygiene offers equal protection against this rare condition. Another argument for circumcision is "so he will look like other boys in his school," or "like his father." The psychological harm from "being different," however, has never been documented. In the final analysis, nonreligious circumcision is simply cosmetic surgery.

DISADVANTAGES OF CIRCUMCISION

Like any surgical procedure, a circumcision can end in complications (2 or 3 percent). Among these are skin infections, bloodstream infections, bleeding, gangrene, scarring, and various surgical accidents. In a recent study, 1 in 500 newborns suffered a serious side effect. In addition, the procedure itself causes some pain, although this pain can be minimized if physicians use a local anesthetic to block the nerves of the foreskin. Finally, the cost of circumcision in the United States is $70 million each year (at $45 per procedure).

RECOMMENDATIONS

Circumcision for religious purposes will continue. Circumcision for other children is open to question. I would suggest leaving your son's foreskin intact unless you are strongly pro-circumcision. Just because a father was circumcised doesn't mean that this unnecessary procedure must be perpetuated on the son. By the year 2000, most American newborns will probably leave the hospital uncircumcised.

CIRCUMCISION CARE AND PROBLEMS

A circumcision is the removal of part of the normal male foreskin. The incision is initially red and tender; the tenderness should be minimal by the third day. The scab at the incision line comes off in 7 to 10 days. If a Plastibel ring was used, it should fall off by 14 days (10 days on the average). While it cannot fall off too early, don't pull it off, because you may cause bleeding. Any scrapes on the head of the penis may normally heal with yellowish-colored skin if your baby has been jaundiced. This is commonly mistaken for an infection.

CALL YOUR CHILD'S PHYSICIAN

(The following statements apply to recent circumcisions.)

Immediately If

- The urine comes out in dribbles.

- The urine stream is weak.

- The head of the penis is blue or black.

- The incision line has more than a few drops of bleeding.

- The normal skin of the penis becomes red or tender.

- Any pus is present.

- Your baby's armpit temperature is over 99.0 or under 96.5°F.

- Your baby is acting sick.

During Office Hours If

- The circumcision looks abnormal to you.

- The Plastibel ring has been attached for more than 14 days. (Note: It can't fall off too early.)

- You have other questions.

HOME CARE FOR CIRCUMCISION PROBLEMS

Treatment

- Plastibel type. Gently cleanse the area with water 3 times a day or whenever it becomes soiled. Soap is usually unnecessary. Petroleum jelly or Bacitracin antibiotic ointment can be applied to the incision line after cleansings to keep it soft during healing.

- Gomco type (i.e., no plastic ring is present). Remove the dressing (which is usually gauze with petroleum jelly) with warm compresses 48 hours after the circumcision was done. Then care for the area as described for the Plastibel.

Call Your Child's Physician Later If

• It looks infected.

• It bleeds more than a few drops.

• The Plastibel ring does not fall off by day 14.

FORESKIN CARE AND PROBLEMS

The foreskin in uncircumcised boys generally causes no problems. However, with overzealous retraction it can get stuck behind the head of the penis (the glans) and cause severe pain and swelling. Occasionally the space under the foreskin becomes infected. Most of these problems can be prevented if you understand when and how to retract the foreskin.

CALL YOUR CHILD'S PHYSICIAN
Immediately If

• The foreskin is pulled back and stuck behind the head of the penis.

• Your child can't pass any urine.

During Office Hours If

• The foreskin is swollen.

• Any pus is coming out of the end of the foreskin.

• The urine stream is weak or dribbly.

• You have other questions.

NORMAL FORESKIN RETRACTION

In general, retraction is overdone in our country. Some physicians feel that parents should not engage in any attempts at retraction, but this runs the risk of smegma collection and infection. The following suggestions are a modest attempt to assist the natural process and maintain acceptable hygiene.

• At birth, the foreskin is normally attached to the head of the penis (glans) by a layer of cells. Over the following years (usually 5 or 6), it gradually loosens up, a little at a time.

Normal erections during childhood probably cause most of the change by stretching the skin. Full retraction needn't be (and can't be) hurried.

• Gentle retraction can begin at 6 to 12 months of age. It can be done *once a week*, during bathing. Perform retraction by gently pulling the skin on the shaft of the penis back toward the abdomen. This will make the foreskin open up, revealing part of the glans. Each time, the foreskin needs to be retracted only once.

• During retraction, the exposed part of the glans should be cleansed with water and dried carefully. Wipe away any whitish material (smegma) that you find there. Smegma is simply the accumulation of dead skin cells that are normally shed from the glans and lining of the foreskin throughout life. Do not use soap or leave soapy water under the foreskin, because this can cause irritation and swelling. After cleansing, always pull the foreskin forward to its normal position. (Note: a collection of smegma that is seen or felt through the foreskin, but which lies beyond the level to which the foreskin is retractable, should be left alone until normal separation exposes it.)

• Avoid vigorous retraction, because this can cause the foreskin to become stuck behind the head of the penis (paraphimosis). Retraction is excessive if it causes any discomfort or crying.

• By age 4 or 5, your boy should be taught to retract his own foreskin and clean beneath it once a week to prevent poor hygiene and infection. Gentle reminders are necessary in the early years.

• Keep in mind that any degree of foreskin movement is normal as long as the boy has a normal urine stream. There should be no rush to achieve full retraction. Full retraction always occurs by puberty.

BREAST-FEEDING

Babies who are breast-fed have fewer infections (especially diarrhea) and allergies during the first year of life than babies on formula. Breast milk is also inexpensive, sterile, and served at the perfect temperature. Breast-feeding becomes especially convenient when one is traveling with a baby. Overall, breast milk is nature's best food for young babies.

HOW OFTEN TO FEED

Your baby can nurse for the first time in the delivery or recovery room. The second feeding will usually be at 3 to 6 hours of age, after your baby awakens from a deep sleep. Thereafter, babies should be nursed at 2- to 2½-hour intervals during the first month of life (longer is okay at night). If your baby cries and less than two hours have passed, he can be rocked or carried in a front pack. If a feeding is given before 2 hours, usually the stomach still has food in it. Don't confuse the need to suck on a thumb or pacifier with the need to eat. For the mother, waiting more than 2½ hours can lead to swollen breasts (engorgement) which causes discomfort and decreases milk production. Although your baby's appetite will determine feeding intervals, the guidelines for bottle feedings per day (see page 104) generally also apply to breast-feeding after the first month of life.

HOW LONG PER FEEDING

Nurse your baby for 5 minutes on each breast on day 1, for 10 minutes on day 2, and for 15 minutes by day 3. Go to the second breast sooner only if your baby falls asleep before 30 minutes of nursing are finished. Try to alternate which breast you start on each time, since sucking is more vigorous at the start of each feeding. Once your milk supply is established (about 4 weeks), 10 minutes nursing per breast is fine, since your child gets more than 90 percent of the milk in this time.

HOW TO KNOW YOUR BABY IS GETTING ENOUGH BREAST MILK

If your baby has 8 or more wet diapers and 4 or more bowel movements per day, he is receiving a good supply of breast milk. (Caution: After 6 weeks of age, bowel movements may normally be passed once every 3 to 7 days.) In addition, most babies will act satisfied after completing a feeding, rather than crying or acting hungry. Your baby should be back to birth weight by 10 or 14 days of age if breast-feeding is going well. Therefore, the 2-week checkup by your baby's physician is very important. If you are breast-feeding for the first time and are concerned about your milk supply or breast engorgement, bring your baby in for a weight check at 1 week of age. The presence of a letdown reflex is another indicator of success.

THE LETDOWN REFLEX

A letdown reflex is indicated by tingling or milk ejection in the breast just prior to feeding, when your baby cries, or when thinking about feeding. It also occurs in the opposite breast while your baby is nursing. Occasionally, letdown is working well without the usual sensations. Letdown is enhanced by adequate sleep, adequate fluids (extra fluids will not help, but a minimum of 1 glass each time you nurse or 1½ to 2 quarts per day is needed), a relaxed environment, and reduced expectations about housework. If your letdown reflex is not present yet, take extra naps and ask your husband and friends for more help. If your urine production decreases, drink extra fluids. Also consider calling the local chapter of the La Leche League.

SUPPLEMENTAL BOTTLES

It is best not to offer your baby any bottles during the first two weeks when you are trying to establish your milk supply. Lactation depends on frequent and prolonged nursing (at least 8 times per day initially). Supplement only if your baby is not gaining well and at your physician's suggestion. After your baby is 4 weeks of age and nursing is well established, offer your baby a bottle of expressed milk, water, or fruit juice (such as apple juice) once a day so that he or she becomes accustomed to the bottle. In this way you can occasionally leave your baby with a sitter and go out for an afternoon or evening. The sitter can feed your baby with pumped breast milk that has been refrigerated. Also, keep 1 or 2 bottles of expressed breast milk (or ready-to-use formula) handy in case you are unexpectedly delayed and your baby is hungry. If practical, supplement with pumped breast milk rather than commercial formula, since taking formula will cancel some of the advantages that breast milk provides.

EXTRA WATER

Babies do not routinely need extra water, except as a source of fluoride. They should be offered a bottle of water twice a day, however, when they have a fever or the weather is hot and dry.

PUMPING THE BREASTS TO RELIEVE PAIN OR TO COLLECT MILK

Engorgement (severe swelling) of the breasts decreases milk production. To prevent engorgement, nurse your baby more often. Also, compress the areola (area around the nipple) with your fingers before each feeding. For milk release, your baby must be able to grip and suck on at least an inch of the areola as well as the nipple. With every missed feeding, pump the breasts. Also, whenever your breasts hurt and you are unable to feed your baby, pump your breasts—for instance, when your baby starts sleeping through the night. A good breast pump is the Kaneson design (about $20). Pumping can also be done by hand; ask someone to teach you the Marmet technique.

SORE NIPPLES

Clean the sore nipple with water after each feeding to remove milk left on the skin. Do not use soap or alcohol, since they remove natural oils. Apply a lanolin cream, such as Eucerin. Try to keep the nipples dry with loose clothing, air exposure, and soft nursing pads. Start your feedings on the side that is not sore. If one nipple is extremely sore, temporarily limit feedings to 5 minutes on that side and change your baby's feeding position by 90 degrees. Before removing your baby from the breast, slide a finger into the corner of the mouth to break the suction rather than pulling him off while he still has a tight grip on your nipple.

VITAMINS/MINERALS/FLUORIDE FOR THE BABY

Breast milk contains all the necessary vitamins and minerals except vitamin D and fluoride. Dark-skinned babies and all prematures need 400 units of vitamin D each day. Usually you won't find vitamin D as a separate product, so ADC drops will do nicely. (The usual dose is 1 ml per day.) White babies need 400 units of vitamin D twice a week, although 15 minutes of sun exposure twice a week may make this unnecessary.

From 2 weeks to 12 years of age, children need fluoride to prevent dental caries. If the municipal water supply contains fluoride and your baby drinks 4 to 8 ounces of water each day, this should be adequate. Otherwise, fluoride drops or tablets (without vitamins) should be given separately. This is a prescription item that you can obtain from your child's physician (see TOOTH DECAY PREVENTION, page 117, for fluoride dosage). Breast milk contains adequate iron during the first year of life.

VITAMINS FOR THE MOTHER

A nursing mother should take a multivitamin tablet daily. She especially needs 400 units of vitamin D and 1,200 mg of both calcium and phosphorus per day. A quart of milk (or its equivalent in cheese or yogurt) can also meet this requirement.

THE MOTHER'S MEDICATIONS

Almost any drug a breast-feeding mother consumes will be transferred in small amounts into the breast milk. Therefore, try to avoid any drug that is not essential, just as you did during pregnancy. Fortunately, the dose your baby receives via breast milk is much less than he or she would receive if we were prescribing it for the baby. Therefore, side effects are uncommon. Some commonly used drugs that are safe for you to take while nursing are acetaminophen, penicillins, erythromycin, stool softeners, antihistamines, mild sedatives, cough drops, nose drops, eyedrops, and skin creams. Aspirin and sulfa drugs can be taken once your baby is beyond 2 weeks of age *and* not jaundiced. Acceptable drugs should nonetheless be taken immediately following breast-feedings so that their level in the breast milk at the time of the next feeding is low. A high intake of caffeine-containing beverages or herbal teas (or excessive smoking of cigarettes) can cause restlessness, crying, even diarrhea. Excessive alcohol can cause drowsiness. Diarrhea in the baby can also be caused by some laxatives (but not by chocolate). Used in moderation, these products shouldn't cause any symptoms. The effect on the baby of foods in the mother's diet is overrated.

Some of the dangerous drugs that *can* harm your baby are tetracyclines, chloramphenicol, antithyroid drugs, anticancer drugs, or any radioactive substance. Women who must take these drugs should not be breast-feeding. Another group of drugs that should be avoided because they can suppress milk production are ergotamines (for migraine), birth control pills (especially estrogen-containing ones), vitamin B6 (pyridoxine) in large doses, and many antidepressants. Overall, most drugs can be taken while breast-feeding.

BURPING

Burping is optional. While it may decrease spitting up, air in the stomach does not cause pain. If you burp your baby, be sure to wait until he reaches a natural pause in the feeding process. Burping twice during a feeding and for about 1 minute is plenty.

CUP-FEEDING

Introduce your child to a cup at approximately 6 months of age. Total weaning to a cup will probably occur somewhere between 9 and 18 months of age, depending on your baby's individual preference (see WEANING, page 106). Regardless of when you start, weaning should proceed gradually. If you discontinue breast-feeding before 9 months of age, switch to bottle-feeding first. If you stop breast-feeding after 9 months of age, you may be able to go directly to cup-feeding.

CALL YOUR CHILD'S PHYSICIAN DURING OFFICE HOURS IF

- Your baby doesn't seem to be gaining adequately.

- You suspect your baby has a food allergy (which usually causes diarrhea or vomiting).

- You need to take a medicine that was not discussed.

- You have sore nipples that do not respond to the recommendations.

- You have a fever. (Also call your obstetrician.)

FORMULA-FEEDING

COMMERCIAL FORMULAS

For those mothers who decide not to or are unable to breast-feed, commercial infant formulas are an excellent alternative. They closely resemble breast milk (unlike whole cow's milk). Bottle-feeding can provide your child with all the emotional benefits and most of the health benefits of breast-feeding. Bottle-fed babies grow as rapidly and are as happy as breast-fed babies. A special advantage of bottle-feeding is that the father can participate.

Use a commercial formula that is iron-fortified to prevent iron deficiency anemia, as recommended by the Committee on Nutrition, American Academy of Pediatrics. The various brands are almost identical. The concentrated formulas are mixed 1-to-1 with water. If you make 1 bottle at a time, you can use warm water directly from the tap. City water supplies are safe. If you have well water, either boil it for 15 minutes or use distilled water until your child is 6 months of age. The advantages of the concentrated formulas over the ready-to-use ones are: The former are less expensive, fluoride has already been added if the water supply contains it, and the formula doesn't need to be warmed up. The powdered commercial formulas have the advantage of being the least expensive.

HOMEMADE EVAPORATED MILK FORMULAS

Making your own formula from evaporated milk is no longer necessary. This formula needs supplements of vitamins and minerals. It also requires sterilized bottles because it is prepared in a batch. While 30 cents less expensive per quart than liquid commercial formulas, it saves little over powdered commercial formulas. If you must use it in a pinch, mix 13 ounces of evaporated milk with 19 ounces of water and 2 tablespoons of regular sugar (sucrose). Place this mixture in sterilized bottles and keep them refrigerated until use.

COW'S MILK

Whole cow's milk should not be given to babies before 6 months of age because it is difficult to digest and is likely to increase allergies. Better yet, use formula until your baby is 1 year of age. Skim milk or 2 percent milk should not be given to babies before 2 years of age, because the fat content of regular milk (approximately 3.5 percent butterfat) is needed for rapid brain growth. (Note: Powdered milk mixed with water becomes skim milk, but evaporated milk becomes whole milk.) Reconstituted evaporated milk causes far fewer intestinal allergies than whole cow's milk does. The American Academy of Pediatrics recommends that parents not use raw (even though certified) milk for children because of the risk of transmitting serious infectious diseases. Stay with the safety record of pasteurized milk products.

TRAVELING

When traveling, use powdered formula for convenience. Put the required number of scoops in a bottle, add warm tap water, and shake. A more expensive alternative is to use throwaway bottles of ready-to-use formula. This product can be stored at room temperature and avoids problems with contaminated water.

FORMULA TEMPERATURE

In the summertime, most children prefer cold formula. In the wintertime, most prefer warm formula. In spring and fall, let your child decide. If you do warm the formula, to prevent mouth burns, be certain to check the temperature before giving it to your baby. Microwave heating deserves special caution, as high temperatures can be reached quickly.

AMOUNTS AND SCHEDULES

The amount of formula that most babies take per feeding (in ounces) can be calculated by dividing your baby's weight (in pounds) in half. Another way to calculate the ounces per feeding is to add 3 to your baby's age (in months), with a maximum of 8 ounces per feeding at 5 or 6 months of age. The maximal amount per day is 32 ounces. Overfeeding during the first 6 months of life can cause vomiting or diarrhea from overfilling the stomach and intestines. If your baby needs more than 32 ounces and is not overweight, start solids.

If your baby is not hungry at some of the feedings, the feeding interval should be increased. Although the feeding schedule should be flexible, the following guidelines apply to most babies:

From Birth to 1 Month

- 6 to 8 milk feedings per day

- no more than every 2½ hours

- To reduce night feedings, awaken your baby if he naps for more than 3 consecutive hours during the day.

From 1 to 3 Months

- 5 or 6 milk feedings per day

- no more than every 3 hours

From 3 to 6 Months

- 4 or 5 milk feedings per day

- no more than every 4 hours

By 6 Months

- 4 milk feedings a day (solids with 3 of these)

- 4-hour intervals

By 9 Months

- 3 milk feedings a day (solids with all meals)

- 5-hour intervals

- 1 or 2 snacks per day (see SOLID [STRAINED] FOODS, page 110)

LENGTH OF FEEDING

A feeding shouldn't take more than 20 minutes. If it does, you are overfeeding your baby or the nipple is clogged. A clean nipple should drip about 1 drop per second when the bottle of formula is inverted. At the end of each feeding, discard any formula left in the bottle, because it is no longer sterile.

EXTRA WATER

Babies do not routinely need extra water. They should be offered a bottle of water twice a day, however, when they have a fever or the weather is hot and dry.

BURPING

Burping is optional. While it may decrease spitting up, air in the stomach does not cause pain. If you burp your baby, be sure to wait until he reaches a natural pause in the feeding process. Burping 2 times during a feeding and for about 1 minute is plenty. More burping may be needed if your baby is a "spitter" (see SPITTING UP, page 156). To reduce the amount of swallowed air, hold the bottle tipped at an angle that keeps the nipple full of formula.

VITAMINS/IRON/FLUORIDE

Commercial formulas with iron contain all of your baby's vitamin and mineral requirements except for fluoride. In our country, the most common cause of anemia in children under 2 years old is iron deficiency (largely because it's not present in cow's milk). Iron can be provided at 4 months of age by adding iron-fortified cereals to the diet. From 2 weeks to 12 years of age, children need fluoride to prevent dental caries. If the municipal water supply contains fluoride and your baby drinks some water each day, this should be adequate. Otherwise, fluoride drops or tablets (without vitamins) should be given separately. This is a prescription item that can be obtained from your child's physician. Try to give fluoride on an empty stomach because mixing it with milk reduces its absorption to 70 percent. Added vitamins are unnecessary after your child has reached one year of age and is on a regular balanced diet, but continue the fluoride.

CUP FEEDING

Introduce your child to a cup at approximately 4 to 6 months of age. Total weaning to a cup will probably occur somewhere between 9 and 18 months of age, depending on your baby's individual preference (see WEANING, below).

BABY-BOTTLE CARIES: PREVENTION

Sleeping with a bottle of milk, juice, or any sweetened liquid in the mouth can cause severe decay of the newly erupting teeth. The sugar in these drinks is converted to acid by the normal bacteria of the mouth. Since liquids tend to pool in the mouth during sleep, the acid etches the enamel. Prevent this tragedy by not using the bottle as a pacifier. If you cannot discontinue the nighttime bottle or replace it with a pacifier, fill it with water. This approach will prevent tooth decay, although it may not improve sleep problems. Of note, dental decay has also resulted when a mother repeatedly falls asleep with her baby asleep on the breast.

WEANING

The definition of weaning is: replacing the bottle or breast (i.e., nipple feedings) with cup-drinking and solid foods. Weaning occurs easily and smoothly unless the breast or bottle has become overly important to the child. Then we have to deal with weaning refusal.

NORMAL WEANING OR HOW TO PREVENT WEANING PROBLEMS

Children normally initiate weaning between 6 and 12 months of age. Between 12 and 18 months of age the parent often has to initiate it, but the child is receptive. After 18 months of age, weaning is usually resisted because the child has become dependent on the breast or bottle. If your child shows a lack of interest in nipple feedings at any time after 6 months of age, start to phase them out. You can tell that your baby is ready to begin weaning when he or she throws the bottle out of the crib, takes only a few ounces of milk and then stops, chews on the nipple rather than sucking it, refuses the breast, or nurses for only a few minutes, then wants to play. The following steps make early natural weaning at 9 to 12 months most likely:

- Keep milk feedings to 4 times a day or less after your child reaches 6 months of age. (Some breast-fed babies may need 5 feedings per day until 9 months of age.) Even at birth, milk feedings should be kept to 8 times per day or less.

- Once your child is on 4 milk feedings a day, be sure 3 of them are given at mealtime with solids (rather than as part of a prenap-time ritual). Your child can have the fourth feeding prior to going down for the night.

• Hold your child for discomfort and stress rather than nursing him or her. Try to separate simple holding from holding with nursing. You can comfort your child and foster a strong sense of security and trust without nursing every time he or she is upset. If you don't follow this guideline, your child will learn to eat whenever he is upset and you may become an "indispensable mother."

• Don't let the bottle or breast substitute for a pacifier. Learn to recognize the need for nonnutritive sucking when your young baby is not hungry. At these times encourage him to suck on a pacifier or thumb rather than giving him food. Feeding your baby every time he or she needs to suck can lead to obesity.

• Don't let the bottle or breast become a substitute for a transitional (security) object at bedtime. Your child should be able to go to sleep at night without having a breast or bottle in his mouth. He needs to learn how to put himself to sleep. If he doesn't, he will develop sleep problems that require the parents' presence during the night.

• Don't let a bottle become a daytime toy. Don't let your child carry a bottle around as a companion during the day. This habit will keep him or her from engaging in more stimulating activities.

• Don't let your child hold the bottle or take it to bed. Your child should think of the bottle as something that belongs to you; hence, he won't protest giving it up, since it never belonged to him in the first place.

• Offer your child milk in a cup by 6 months of age. For the first few months your child will probably accept the cup only after he or she has had some milk from bottle or breast. However, by 9 months of age your child should be offered some milk from a cup before bottle feedings.

• Help your baby become interested in foods other than milk. Introduce solids by spoon by 4 months of age in bottle-fed babies, and by 6 months in breast-fed. Introduce finger foods by 8 months of age. As soon as your child is able to use finger foods, have him or her sit with the family during mealtime. This custom will stimulate your child to ask for other foods that he sees you eating. Consequently, his or her interest in exclusive milk feedings will diminish.

DELAYED WEANING

When Is Weaning Delayed or Abnormal? • Breast-feeding or bottle-feeding can be considered prolonged after about 18 months of age. However, most children will eventually give up breast-feeding and bottle-feeding on their own by about 3 years of age. Therefore, the older toddler who only occasionally nurses or bottle-feeds doesn't necesssarily need any pressure to change. Delayed weaning should be considered abnormal only if it is causing one or more of the following types of harm: the refusal to eat any solids; anemia; tooth decay or baby-bottle caries; obesity from overeating; daytime withdrawal and lack of interest in play due to carrying a bottle around; frequent awakening at night for refills of a bottle; or the inability to stay with a babysitter because your child is exclusively breast-fed and refuses a bottle. If any of these apply to your baby, proceed to the following section. Otherwise, continue to nipple-feed your baby when he or she wants to (less than 4 times a day) and don't worry about weaning.

How to Eliminate Breast or Bottle Dependency

• Reduce the number of feedings your child receives to 3 or 4 per day. When you cut back on the number of feedings and your child comes to you to be fed, substitute extra holding and attention. Extra love isn't harmful.

• Immediately stop allowing your child to carry a bottle around during the day. This companion bottle can accumulate germs that may lead to vomiting or diarrhea.

• Immediately eliminate any bottle that your child takes to bed. In addition to causing sleep problems, it carries the risk of causing tooth decay.

• Once you have accomplished these changes, you needn't proceed any further unless you wish to eliminate breast- or bottle-feedings completely. However, only initiate weaning if your family is not under stress (such as might be caused by moving), and your child is not in crisis (such as being sick or trying to achieve bladder control). Weaning from the breast or bottle to the cup should always be done gradually. The "cold turkey" or abrupt withholding approach will only make your child angry, clingy, and miserable.

To Completely Eliminate All Breast-feedings

• Begin by decreasing their length. Decrease each feeding by 2 minutes; and every 3 days or so, reduce each feeding by another 2 minutes. Don't be in a hurry.

• Follow each breast-feeding with a cup of formula. If your child refuses formula, offer chocolate milk or some other flavor that appeals to his or her taste.

• Since the breast operates on the principle of supply and demand, the reduced amount of sucking time will reduce the amount of milk production. For breast pain, wear a bra with good support and also take an acetaminophen product as often as necessary. For severe pain from engorgement, express 1 ounce of milk or allow your baby to suck for 20 seconds on each side to relieve the pressure. Remember that complete emptying will increase milk production. Weaning by eliminating one breast-feeding at a time is usually not acceptable, because it leaves the mother with painful breast engorgement.

To Completely Eliminate All Bottle-feeding

• The process should also be a gradual one. Prior to each bottle-feeding offer milk in a cup. The four bottle-feedings should be eliminated in the following order: midday, late afternoon, morning, and finally bedtime. The last feeding of the day is usually the most important one to the child. One feeding can be eliminated every 2 to 4 days depending on your child's reaction. Replace each nipple-feeding with a cup-feeding and extra holding. When it comes time to give up the last bottle of the day, gradually reduce the amount of milk on a daily basis over the course of a week.

After Breast-feeding and Bottle-feeding Have Stopped

• Intermittent requests can be responded to by holding your child. If your child was bottle-fed, you can explain that the bottles have all been given away. You may actually want to have your child help you carry the bottles to a neighbor's house. If your child has previously been breast-fed, it can be explained that the "milk is all gone."

CALL YOUR CHILD'S PHYSICIAN DURING OFFICE HOURS IF

• Your child is over 6 months of age and won't eat any food except milk.

- Your child has tooth decay.
- You think your child has anemia.
- This approach to weaning has not been successful after trying it for 1 month.
- You have other questions or concerns.

SOLID (STRAINED) FOODS

AGE FOR STARTING SOLID FOODS

The best time to begin using a spoon is when your baby can sit with some support and voluntarily move his head to engage in the feeding process—i.e., when he or she is ready. This time is usually between 4 and 6 months of age. From a nutritional standpoint, breast milk and iron-fortified formulas meet all of your baby's needs until 4 to 6 months of age. He or she needs nothing else. Introducing strained foods early just makes feeding more complicated and won't help your baby sleep better. The current recommendation of the American Academy of Pediatrics is that bottle-fed babies not be introduced to solids until 4 months of age and breast-fed babies or allergic babies not until 6 months of age. Waiting also reduces the likelihood of food allergies in your baby. By all means, don't give strained foods in a bottle; wait until your child can accept spoon feedings. An exception to the above guideline is to start solids at 3 months of age if your baby is drinking more than 1 quart of formula per day and remains quite hungry.

TYPES OF SOLID FOODS

Between 4 and 8 months of age, introduce your baby to strained foods and cereals. The order is not very important. While most books recommend starting with cereals, it is often helpful to begin with a fruit (bananas, for instance) so that your baby immediately builds a positive association with the spoon. Giving a little milk first also helps with this transition. When your child is very hungry, he or she is intolerant of trying new substances. After 1 or 2 weeks of fruits, go to cereals, usually starting with rice cereal. The cereals are helpful at this time if your child has no other source of iron. Cereal can be mixed with water, fruit juice, or milk.

Introduce only 1 new food at a time and no more than 3 per week. Since your baby is receiving plenty of protein in the milk, meats can be introduced last.

Between 8 and 12 months of age, introduce your baby to mashed table foods or junior foods (though the latter are probably unnecessary). If you make your own baby foods in a baby-food grinder or electric blender, be sure to add enough water to get a consistency that your baby can easily swallow. For convenient individual portions, these homemade baby foods can be poured into ice cube trays, frozen, removed, and stored in plastic freezer bags.

Avoid sweet foods and desserts in the first year of life, since they may interfere with your baby's willingness to try other new, unsweet foods.

Although there is controversy about them, egg whites, wheat, and orange juice may be more likely to cause allergies than other solids and should be avoided until 1 year of age (especially in infants with allergies).

SPOON-FEEDING

Spoon-feeding can be very messy in the beginning. Use a small baby spoon and a scooped-out bib to catch the dribble. Place food on the middle of the tongue. If it is placed on the front, your child will probably push the food back at you. By 1 year of age most children will want to try to feed themselves. (Until they can handle finger foods well, they are not ready for a spoon.) At this time you need one spoon for your baby and one for yourself. Also, put down newspapers under the high chair to reduce your cleanup time.

FINGER FOODS

Most babies love to feed themselves and gain this added sense of independence. Finger foods can be introduced between 9 and 10 months of age. Since most babies will not be able to feed themselves with a spoon until 15 months of age, finger foods keep them actively involved in the feeding process. Good finger foods are toast, cheese wedges, French fries, pieces of scrambled egg, cooked vegetable strips, slices of canned fruit (peaches, pears, or pineapple), slices of banana, dry cereals, crackers, cookies, and breads.

SNACKS

Once your baby goes to 3 meals a day or 5-hour intervals, small snacks will often be necessary to tide him over to the next meal. Most babies go to this pattern between 6 and 9 months of age. The midmorning and midafternoon snack should be a nutritious, nonmilk food. Fruits and dry cereals are recommended. If your child is not hungry at mealtime, the snacks should be made smaller or eliminated.

TABLE FOODS
Your child should be eating the same meals as you do by approximately 1 year of age. This assumes that your family consumes a well-balanced, low animal-fat diet, and that you carefully dice any foods that would be difficult for your baby to chew. Avoid foods like raw carrots that could be aspirated into the lungs. (See under CHOKING, page 9, for a list of dangerous foods.)

HEATING SOLID FOODS
Overheated foods can cause mouth burns. Be careful. Test them before serving to an infant. Microwaves have the disadvantage of heating from the inside out, leaving some parts of the food hotter than others. The cooler temperature of the container can also be misleading. Stir microwave-heated food to distribute the heat evenly before testing it.

VITAMINS
Added vitamins are unnecessary after your child has reached 1 year of age and is on a regular balanced diet.

A HEALTHY DIET

HEALTH PROBLEMS RELATED TO DIET
In the United States, at least six health conditions have been proven to relate to diet. The first four problems occur in children as well as in adults. The last two primarily occur in adults.

Iron Deficiency Anemia • This type of anemia usually occurs between 6 months and 2 years of age. The main symptoms are fatigue and delayed motor development. Iron deficiency anemia can also cause behavioral symptoms such as restlessness, irritability, and poor attention span.

Overweight • Obesity is one of the most common nutritional problems in our country (see OVERWEIGHT, page 240). Obesity is also one of the most important contributing factors in heart disease, hypertension, and some cancers.

Tooth Decay • Tooth decay is accentuated by the intake of sugars as well as by poor tooth-brushing habits (see TOOTH DECAY PREVENTION, page 117).

Intestinal Symptoms • Poor fiber intake can cause intestinal symptoms such as constipation, abdominal discomfort, appendicitis, gallstones, and some intestinal cancers.

Coronary Artery Disease • An increased intake of animal fats (especially cholesterol) contributes to coronary artery disease. This disease hardly exists in poor countries where the population subsists on low-fat, high-carbohydrate diets. It is also less common among vegetarians.

High Blood Pressure • High blood pressure has been associated with an increased salt intake or a decreased calcium intake in some susceptible individuals. Most individuals, however, get rid of extra salt through their kidneys and don't develop hypertension.

EATING RECOMMENDATIONS FOR STAYING HEALTHY

Learn the Four Food Groups • Food can be divided into four basic groups: Milk products, meats/eggs, grains, and fruits/vegetables.

• Milk products include milk, cheese, yogurt, and ice cream.

• Meats include red meats, poultry, fish, and eggs. Eggs have the highest cholesterol content of any of the commonly eaten foods. The cholesterol in one egg is equivalent to the cholesterol in 14 ounces of beef, 1½ quarts of whole milk, or 1 quart of ice cream.

• Grains include breads, cereals, rice, pasta, and so forth.

• Fruits and vegetables may be consumed as solids or juices.

• A healthy diet should be made up of 20 percent milk, meat, and eggs, and 80 percent vegetables, fruits, and grains. (Fiber is found in grains, fruits, and vegetables.) This is similar to the recommendations that children receive 55 percent of their calories from carbohydrates, 30 percent from fats, and 15 percent from protein.

Eat Three Meals a Day • Breakfast is essential for children. Skipping breakfast can compromise performance at school. For dieters, skipping breakfast usually doesn't lead to weight loss. All meals should contain fruits or vegetables, and grains as well. Meat or milk should be included in two of the meals.

Eating snacks is largely a habit. Snacks are unnecessary for good nutrition but harmless unless your child is overweight. If your child likes snacks (and most children under age 5 do), encourage fruits, vegetables, and grains, but don't give them if it is close to mealtime.

Decrease the Intake of Fat (Meat and Milk Products) • Americans eat excessive amounts of meat and dairy products. Although cholesterol is important for rapid growth, after age 2 it should be consumed in moderation (not eliminated). This improved diet can be achieved in the following way:

• Remember that one serving of meat per day is adequate for normal growth and development. (Don't serve meat more than twice a day.)

• Serve more fish and poultry and fewer red meats, since the latter have the highest cholesterol levels.

• Trim the fat off meats.

• Don't serve bacon, sausages, and other meats that have a high fat content.

• Limit the number of eggs to 3 or 4 per week.

• Use 2 percent milk instead of whole milk (after 2 years of age).

• Decrease milk intake to 2 or 3 cups per day. (Encourage water for satisfying thirst.)

• Use margarine instead of butter.

• Keep in mind that red meats may be hard to give up because of the psychological association they have with building muscle mass and strength (both untrue).

Increase the Intake of Fruits, Vegetables, and Grains • Children should consume at least five servings of fruits and vegetables per day. (In actuality 50 percent of American children eat only one fruit or vegetable per day.)

- Try to serve a fruit at every meal.

- Offer fruits as dessert.

- Start every day with a glass of fruit juice. (Caution: Limit fruit juices to 2 cups per day to prevent diarrhea.)

- Since fruits and vegetables are interchangeable, don't force children to eat vegetables they don't like.

- When making casseroles, increase the amount of vegetables and decrease the amount of meat.

- Serve more soups.

- Encourage more cereals for breakfast.

- Use more whole-grain bread in making sandwiches.

Maintain an Adequate Iron Intake • Throughout our lives we need an adequate amount of iron in our diets to prevent anemia. Everyone should know which foods are good sources of iron. Red meats, fish, and poultry are best. Having one serving per day will provide adequate iron. Although liver is a good source of iron, it contains sixteen times more cholesterol than beef and should be avoided. For those young children who refuse meats in general, low-fat luncheon meats can be provided as a meat source. Adequate iron is also found in iron-enriched cereals, beans of all types, peanut butter, raisins, prune juice, sweet potatoes, spinach, and egg yolks. The iron in these foods is better absorbed if the meal also contains fruit juice or meat.

Avoid Excessive Salt • Salt is not usually harmful for people without high blood pressure. However, we can discourage a taste for excessive salt in infants by not adding it to their foods. The salt shaker can be removed from the dinner table. Other herbs and spices can be used instead of salt. Salty foods such as potato chips and pretzels can be purchased sparingly.

Avoid Excessive Pure Sugars • Sweets are not bad. They just need to be eaten in moderation. Most humans are born with a "sweet tooth." They seek out and enjoy candy, soft drinks, and desserts. The main side effect of eating candy is that it can contribute to tooth decay if the teeth are not brushed afterward. A high intake of sugars ("a sugar binge") can cause a temporary reaction, 2 or 3 hours later, of the jitters, sweating, dizziness, sleepiness, and intense hunger. This reaction is not harmful and can be relieved by eating some food. A love of sweets is not related to obesity (if the total calories per day are normal) or hyperactivity. A high sugar intake has not been correlated with coronary artery disease or cancer.

Eating Before Exercise • The best foods to consume before prolonged exercise are complex carbohydrates. These include bread, pasta (noodles), potatoes, and rice. These should be consumed 3 to 4 hours before the athletic event so they have passed out of the stomach. Water consumption continues to be important right up to the time of participation and every 20 to 30 minutes during the activity. Eating meat does not improve athletic performance.

FOOD MYTHS

Some Americans consider a faulty diet to be the cause of most health problems. If this were true the practice of medicine would become relatively easy. Unfortunately, most diseases do not respond to a change in the diet. The following misleading statements have received some attention in the media.

"Everyone Needs Vitamin Supplements." • In general in our society vitamins are overused (the "once a day" vitamin habit). Vitamins do not improve a child's appetite, prevent infections, or increase pep and energy. Added vitamins are unnecessary once your child has reached 1 year of age, if he consumes a regular balanced diet. Vitamin supplements may be helpful in special situations (for instance, if your child is a picky eater, is dieting, or has a chronic disease). Some vitamins taken in excess (mainly vitamins A and D) can cause symptoms and harm. The danger of overdosage is a good example of "more is not better." Keep in mind that vitamins and minerals are already present in foods.

"Natural Foods Are Better." • Natural or organic foods are those grown without pesticides or artificial fertilizers, and processed without preservatives, food colorings, or food additives. Natural foods have no nutritional advantages. They have no higher level of vitamins or minerals. Foods grown in worn-out soil are no different in food value from those grown in rich soil. Foods grown with chemical fertilizers are just as healthy as foods grown with natural fertilizers. The chemicals used to preserve food do not take away from its nutritional or health value. The main difference between these two types of foods is that natural foods are more costly.

"Junk Foods Are Bad." • Junk foods are an area of great confusion. Some people consider any meal served at a fast-food restaurant to be junk food. In truth these meals usually are balanced and contain foods from all four groups (although they may be heavy on fat and low on fiber). Fast-food meals are fine if they aren't eaten on a daily basis. More commonly, some people define any sweet or dessert as a junk food. They claim that these foods "lack nutritional value" or "contain empty calories." In truth, they contain plenty of calories, mainly as sugars. *Empty calories* is a meaningless term.

As previously stated, sugars are not bad unless consumed in excess. Sugars provide quick energy, and during the day, adolescents and children need some high-energy foods. Parents who try to eliminate desserts and candy from their children's diets create an unnecessary battleground. Trying to prohibit sweets makes a youngster feel different from his peers. The restriction is unattainable and perceived as unfair. A better approach is to decrease the value of dessert by serving one portion at the end of the meal, whether or not your child has eaten the main course. Also, set a good example by not eating sweets for snacks, brushing your teeth regularly, limiting what sweets your family purchases, and serving balanced meals at mealtime.

TOOTH DECAY PREVENTION

Tooth decay causes toothaches, lost teeth, malocclusion, and costly visits to the dentist. With present knowledge, 80 to 90 percent of tooth decay can be prevented.

FLUORIDE

• Fluoride builds strong, decay-resistant enamel. Fluoride is needed from 2 weeks to 12 years of age. Drinking fluoridated water or taking a prescription fluoride supplement is the best protection against tooth decay, reducing cavities by 70 percent.

- If fluoride is consumed in drinking water, a child must take at least 1 pint per day (preferably 1 quart per day by school age).

- If your city's water supply doesn't have fluoride added, ask your physician for a prescription during your next routine visit. The dosage of fluoride is 0.25 mg per day in the first 2 years, 0.5 mg from 2 to 3 years of age, and 1.0 mg over age 3. Try to give fluoride on an empty stomach, because mixing it with milk reduces its absorption to 70 percent.

- Fluoride is safe. Over half of all Americans drink fluoridated water. *Consumers Report* (July/August 1978) states: "The simple truth is that there is no scientific controversy over the safety of fluoridation. The practice is safe, economical and beneficial. The survival of any controversy is one of the major triumphs of quackery over science in our generation."

TOOTH-BRUSHING AND FLOSSING

- Tooth-brushing should begin before 1 year of age.

- Try to brush after each meal, but especially after the last meal or snack of the day.

- Brush the molars (back teeth) extra carefully. Decay usually starts in the pits and crevices of the molars.

- To prevent the mouth bacteria from changing food caught in the teeth into acid, tooth-brushing must occur within the first 5 to 10 minutes after meals.

- Help your child brush the teeth at least until age 6. Most children don't have the coordination or strength to brush their own teeth adequately before then.

- If your child is negative about tooth-brushing, have him brush your teeth first before you brush his.

- A fluoride toothpaste is beneficial. Use a nonfluoridated toothpaste, however, until your child reaches an age (usually 3 years) at which he or she understands not to eat toothpaste. Swallowing toothpaste can increase the body's fluoride to a level where it causes white spots on the teeth (another example of too much of a good thing). People of all ages tend to use too much toothpaste; only a drop the size of a pea is needed.

- If your child is in a setting where he can't brush his teeth, teach him to rinse his mouth with water after meals instead.

- Dental floss is very useful for cleaning between the teeth where a brush can't reach. This should begin when your child's molars start to touch. In the early years, most of the teeth have spaces between them.

DIET

- Prevent baby-bottle caries by not letting your infant sleep with a bottle of milk or juice in the mouth. Once the teeth erupt, if your baby must have a bottle at night, it should contain only water. Preferably you should put your child to bed after he or she has finished with the bottle.

- Discourage prolonged contact with sugar (e.g., hard candy) or any sweets that are sticky (e.g., caramels or raisins).

- Avoid frequent snacks.

- Give sugar-containing foods only with meals.

- Parents worry needlessly about soft drinks. The sugar in these products does not bind to the teeth and is cleared rather rapidly from the mouth.

- Since we can't keep children away from candy completely, try to teach your child to brush after eating candy.

VISITING THE DENTIST AND DENTAL SEALANTS

- The American Dental Association recommends that dental checkups begin at age 3 (sooner for dental symptoms or abnormal-looking teeth). The latest breakthrough in dental research is dental sealing of the pits and fissures of the biting surfaces of the molars. Fluoride does little to prevent decay on these surfaces. A special plastic seal can be applied to the top surfaces of the permanent molars. The seal may protect against decay for a lifetime. Ask your child's dentist about the latest recommendations.

NORMAL GROWTH

Normal growth is one of the best indicators of good health and nutrition. Normal heights and weights, however, are difficult to define. Short parents tend to have short children. Tall parents tend to have tall children. For any given height, an ideal weight can be determined from a growth chart. An infant with failure-to-thrive is one who is underweight for his height. A child with obesity is one who is overweight for his height.

Your child's physician weighs and measures your child on each visit. These numbers are plotted on a standard growth chart. Your child's growth rate over time tells us the most about his physical health. The following facts and figures may answer some of your questions about normal growth.

AVERAGE NEWBORNS (FULL-TERM)
Weight: 7 pounds, 5 ounces (normal range: 6 to 10 pounds)
Length: 20 inches (50 cm) (normal range: 18½ to 21½ inches)
Head circumference: 13.8 inches (35 cm) (normal range: 33 to 37 cm)
A premature baby weighs less than 5½ pounds (2.5 kilograms)

AVERAGE WEIGHTS AT DIFFERENT AGES
5 months: double birthweight
12 months: triple birthweight
2 years: quadruple birthweight
1 to 6 years: Weight in pounds = (age × 5) + 17
7 to 12 years: Weight in pounds = (age × 7) + 5
Remember: 1 pound = 16 ounces; 1 kilogram = 2.2 pounds.

AVERAGE HEIGHTS AT DIFFERENT AGES
12 months: double birth length
13 years: triple birth length
2 to 14 years: Height in inches = (age × 2½) + 30
Remember: 1 foot = 12 inches; 1 inch = 2.5 centimeters

PREDICTING ADULT HEIGHTS

	BOYS		GIRLS	MULTIPLY BY
½ adult height is reached at	27	months	20	2
⅔ adult height is reached at	6	years	5	1.5
¾ adult height is reached at	9	years	7	1.3

Another formula is: adult height (boys) = 1.87 × height at age 3
adult height (girls) = 1.73 × height at age 3

NORMAL DEVELOPMENT

The rapid changes in development occur during the first year of life. Your baby will go from a helpless, unresponsive little bundle to a walking, talking, unique personality. Almost all parents worry if their baby is developing fast enough. Keep in mind that there is a wide variation in normal development. While the average child walks at 12 months of age, the normal range for walking is any time between 9 and 16 months of age. Motor development occurs in an orderly sequence starting with lifting the head, then rolling over, sitting up, crawling, standing, and walking. Although the sequence is predictable and follows the maturation of the spinal cord downward, the rate varies.

Again, for speech development the sequence goes from cooing and gurgling to babbling, to imitating speech sounds, to first words, to using words together. The rate, however, can normally vary considerably. The most reassuring characteristics of normal development are the presence of alert eyes, alert facial expressions, and curiosity about the environment.

STIMULATION: ENCOURAGING NORMAL DEVELOPMENT

From birth on, the main determinant of an infant's social, emotional, and language development is the amount of positive contact he has with his parents. Your role in stimulating your child should be fun for both of you. The following recommendations may be helpful:

• Hold your baby as much as possible. Touching and cuddling is good for your baby. Give him or her lots of eye contact, smiles, and affection at these times. Use feedings to emphasize these warm personal contacts.

• Talk to your baby. Babies enjoy being talked and sung to from birth onward. Babies must first receive language before they are able to express language. You don't need a scriptwriter—just put into words whatever you are thinking and feeling.

• Play with your baby. If this doesn't come easy for you, try to loosen up and rediscover your free spirit. Respond to your baby's attempts to initiate play. Provide your baby with various objects of interest. Toys need not be expensive; for example, mobiles, rattles, spools, pots and pans, and various packages that things come in. Encourage your baby's efforts at discovering how to use his or her hands and mind.

- Read to your baby. Even six-month-olds enjoy looking at pictures in a book. Cut out interesting pictures from old magazines and put them in a scrapbook for your baby. Look at the family photo album. Keep these sessions brief.

- Show your baby the world. Enrich his or her experience. Babies don't need to visit a museum yet. They need a guide to point out the leaves, clouds, stars, and rainbows. Don't forget trains, airplanes, and fire trucks. Help your child describe what he or she is experiencing. These first encounters can be exhilarating and unforgettable.

- Provide your child with social experience with other children by age 2. If he or she is not in daycare, consider starting a play group. Young children can learn wonderful lessons from one another, especially how to get along with other people.

- Avoid formal teaching until age 4 or 5. Some groups in our country have recently overemphasized academic (cognitive) development of young children. Trying to create "superkids" through special lessons, drills, computer programs, and classes has put undue pressure on many young children and may result in "early burnout." Old-fashioned creative play and spontaneous learning are much more beneficial during the early years. If it's not fun, your child won't follow through the way you would like.

SYMPTOMS REQUIRING A DEVELOPMENTAL EVALUATION

The following developmental milestones (reprinted with the permission of William K. Frankenburg, M.D., University of Colorado School of Medicine, 1986) are listed by the age at which 80 to 90 percent of normal children are able to perform them. If your child has reached the listed age (corrected for any prematurity by subtracting the months early from the actual age) and is not able to perform the listed tasks, he or she should be seen by your child's physician for a developmental checkup. While failing one of these items does not mean that your child's development is abnormal, it is a warning sign that deserves attention.

3 months

- When your baby is lying on his back, he can move each of his arms as easily as the other and each of his legs as easily as the other. If your child makes jerky or uncoordinated movements with one or both of his arms or legs, this is abnormal.

• Your child can make sounds such as gurgling, cooing, babbling, or other noises, in addition to crying.

6 months

• Your child plays with his hands by touching them together.

• Your child has rolled over at least two times from stomach to back or from his back to his stomach.

9 months

• When your child is playing and you come up quietly behind him, he turns his head as though he heard you. He responds to quiet sounds or whispers in this manner. (Loud sounds do not count.)

• When you hold your baby under his arms, he tries to stand on his feet and supports some of his weight on his legs.

12 months

• When you hide behind something (or around a corner) and then reappear again, your baby eagerly looks for you to reappear.

• Your baby makes "ma-ma" or "da-da" sounds.

18 months

• Your child uses a regular cup or glass without help and drinks from it without spilling.

• Your child walks all the way across a large room without falling or wobbling from side to side.

24 months

• Your child can say at least three specific words (other than "da-da" and "ma-ma") that mean the same thing each time they are said.

• Your child can take off clothes such as pajamas or pants. (Diapers, hats, and socks do not count.)

36 months

• Your child can name at least one picture when you look at animal books together.

• Your child can throw a ball overhand (not sidearm or under-hand) toward your stomach or chest from a distance of five feet.

4 years

• Your child can pedal a tricycle at least 10 feet forward.

• Your child can play hide-and-seek, or other games where he takes turns and follows rules.

5 years

• Your child can button some of his clothing or his doll's clothes. (Snaps do not count.)

• Your child is comfortable when you leave him with a babysitter. (He does not become overly upset.)

6 years

• Your child can dress himself completely without help.

• Your child can catch a small ball (such as a tennis ball) using only his hands. (Large balls do not count.)

RECOMMENDED READING

Brazelton, T.B., *Infants and Mothers: Differences in Development* (New York: Dell Publishing Co., Inc., 1983).

CRYING BABY (COLIC)

SYMPTOMS AND CHARACTERISTICS OF FUSSY CRYING (COLIC)

• Unexplained crying

• Healthy (no sickness or source of pain)

• Well-fed (not hungry)

• Usually cries 1 to 2 hours at a time

• Cries once or twice per day

• Acts fine (happy and fun-loving) between bouts of crying

• Usually consolable when held and comforted

- Onset under 2 weeks of age

- Resolution by 3 months of age

  If your child's symptoms are different, call your physician for help.

Cause • About 10 percent of babies have colic. No one is sure what causes colic, but it is harmless and tends to occur in babies with a sensitive temperament and a below-average need for sleep. Colic is not the result of bad parenting, so try not to blame yourself. Colic is also not due to excessive gas, so don't bother with extra burping, special nipples, or defoaming agents. Cow's milk allergy may, rarely, cause crying but usually only in combination with diarrhea and/or vomiting. During crying spells, babies normally draw up their legs, tense their abdomen, and turn red in the face. These changes tell us nothing about the causes of the crying.

Expected Course • It spontaneously resolves in 2 to 3 months. Gradually your baby will stop having trouble getting to sleep.

CALL YOUR CHILD'S PHYSICIAN

Immediately If

- It seems to be a painful cry rather than a fussy one.

- The cry has become high-pitched.

- Your baby has been crying constantly for more than 3 hours.

- Your baby is under 2 months old *and* acts sick.

- You are afraid you might hurt your baby.

During Office Hours If

- The crying began after 1 month of age.

- Your baby is over 3 months old.

- Diarrhea, vomiting, or constipation occur with the crying.

- You are exhausted from all this crying.

- Your baby mainly cries when you're trying to sleep.

- You can't find a way to soothe your baby.

- You have other questions.

HOME CARE FOR A CRYING BABY

Carrying the Baby and Other Types of Gentle Motion • When your baby cries, he or she needs to be held by someone. Soothing, gentle motion, and physical contact are the best approaches to helping your baby relax and go to sleep. One can't spoil a baby during the first 4 months. Consider using the following: cuddling your child in a rocking chair, providing skin-on-skin contact in a warm bed, rocking your child in a cradle, or carrying your child in a front-pack or pouch (which leaves your hands free to do other things). Helpful gadgets are a wind-up swing, a stroller (buggy) ride, or a vibrating chair. A recent study showed that carrying babies in a front-pack for 3 hours a day when they weren't crying reduced overall daily crying by 50 percent. Some babies are helped by a pacifier, a warm bath, or massage.

Diet for the Baby • Don't feed your baby every time he or she cries. Being hungry is only one of the reasons babies cry. It takes more than 2 hours for the stomach to empty, so wait at least that long between feedings or you may cause cramps from bloating. If you are breast-feeding, avoid coffee, tea, colas, and other stimulants. If you suspect a cow's milk allergy, try a soy formula for 3 days (or avoid all forms of cow's milk in *your* diet, if you are breast-feeding). If the crying dramatically improves on the new formula, call your child's physician for additional advice.

Sleep for the Baby • Try to keep your child from sleeping excessively during the daytime. If 3 hours have elapsed, gently awaken and play with or feed your baby, depending on his or her needs. This will help to cut down the amount of nighttime wakefulness. Babies sleep better and cry less if placed on their stomachs. This sleeping position is also the safest one until the infant is old enough to turn over (about 4 months). If a baby vomits while sleeping on the back, he could choke.

Rest and Help for the Mother • Avoid fatigue and exhaustion. Get at least one nap a day, in case the night goes badly. You must ask your husband, a friend, or a relative for help with other children and chores. Caring for a colicky baby is a two-person job. Hire a babysitter so you can get out of the house and clear your mind. Talk to someone every day about your mixed feelings. The screaming would upset a saint.

Last Resort for a Crying Baby • If 20 minutes of gentle motion doesn't quiet your baby and he has been fed recently, let him cry himself to sleep. On some days, this is the only answer for a fussy baby. Close the door, go into a different room, turn up the radio, and do something you want to do. Even consider earplugs or earphones. Save your strength for when your baby definitely needs you.

Common Mistakes • If you are breast-feeding, don't stop. If your baby needs extra calories, you can supplement with formula a few times a day. If you are formula-feeding, don't change formulas. Special formulas rarely help colic. The available medicines are ineffective and many (especially those containing phenobarbital) are dangerous for children of this age. The medicines that slow intestinal motion (the anticholinergics) can cause fever or constipation. Inserting a thermometer or suppository into the rectum to "release gas" does nothing except irritate the anal sphincter. Stay with TLC (tender loving care) for a cure.

Call Your Child's Physician Later If

• Your baby seems to be in pain.

• Your baby cries constantly for more than 3 hours.

• You can't find a way to soothe your baby.

PREVENTION OF SLEEP PROBLEMS

Sleep problems are easier to prevent than to cure. If you like 8 hours of uninterrupted sleep and believe that children should abide by the rule that nighttime is for sleeping, then these recommendations will appeal to you. The following guidelines can help you prevent severe colic, trained night feeding, trained night crying, fearful night crying, bedtime temper tantrums and bed-sharing in your child. The information is arranged by age.

NEWBORN NURSERY ADVICE

• Hold your baby for all fussy crying during the first 3 months. All new babies cry some during the day. If your baby cries excessively, the cause is probably colic. A crying baby should always be responded to. Gentle motion and cuddling seems to help the most. Remember, babies can't be spoiled during the first 3 or 4 months of life.

- Carry your baby for at least 3 hours a day when he or she isn't crying. This practice will reduce fussy crying and colic. In cultures where babies are carried almost continually, crying is rarely seen. A recent Montreal study showed that supplemental carrying reduces crying by over 50 percent. While extra carrying did not increase the hours of sleep per day, it did increase the hours of contented awake time per day.

- Don't let your baby sleep for more than 3 consecutive hours during the daytime. Attempt to awaken him gently and entertain him. In this way, the time when your infant sleeps the longest will occur during the night. (Note: Many newborns can sleep 5 consecutive hours.) In general, keep him busy during the day rather than encouraging sleep at this time.

- Don't feed your baby if she cries and less than 2½ hours have passed since the previous feeding (2 hours for breast-fed babies). Crying is the only form of communication little babies have. Crying does not always mean she's hungry. She may be tired, bored, lonely, or overheated. Hold your baby at these times or put her to bed. Don't let feeding become a pacifier. Babies who feed frequently during the day become hungry at frequent intervals during the night.

- Make middle-of-the-night feedings brief and boring. You want your baby to think of nighttime as a special time for sleeping. When he awakens at night for feedings, don't turn on the lights, talk to him, or rock him. Feed him quickly and quietly. Provide extra rocking and playtime during the day. This approach will lead to longer periods of sleep at night.

- Place your baby in the crib, sleepy but awake. This advice is more important than anything else in this guideline. Her last waking memory should be of the crib, not of you or being fed. She must learn to put herself to sleep without you being there. Don't expect her to go to sleep as soon as her head touches the mattress. This presleep period often takes 20 to 30 minutes. You don't have to be present during this time. If she is sleepy, she can go to sleep on her own. If she is crying at bedtime, rocking and gentle words may help to settle her down. But try to place her in the crib before she falls asleep. Naps should be handled in the same way. Eventually, you will be able to teach self-quieting.

- Don't change diapers during the night. Babies can survive until morning with a wet diaper. The exceptions to this rule are soiled diapers at night (which are uncommon) or times when you are treating a bad diaper rash. If you must change your child, use a flashlight, do it quietly, and don't provide any entertainment.

- Don't let your baby sleep in your bed. Once your baby has gained such a privilege, change will be extremely difficult. In addition, a very young infant may fall out of the bed or be hurt by a parent who rolls over upon him. For the first 2 or 3 months, you can keep your baby in a crib next to your bed.

2-WEEK ADVICE

- If breast-feeding, offer pumped breast milk in a bottle once a week so your baby will accept bottle feedings. If several months pass without your ever using a bottle, your baby may strongly refuse its introduction. Then, leaving your baby with sitters becomes difficult. His or her dislike of a bottle may also be prevented by offering water or diluted apple juice once a day in a bottle.

- Choose a late bedtime hour (like 10:00 or 11:00 P.M.) and give the last feeding then. Try to keep your child awake for the 2 hours prior to this bedtime. Regularity of bedtime helps your baby organize his sleep. When your baby begins to sleep more than 8 hours, you can shift the bedtime to an earlier hour.

2-MONTH ADVICE

- Move your baby's crib to a separate room. By 2 months of age at the latest, your baby should be sleeping in a separate room. This arrangement will help keep the parent who is a light sleeper from being awakened by the rustlings and noises that all babies make during the night. It also removes the availability of parents from the visible options of the infant who awakens. If separate rooms are impractical, at least put up a screen or cover a crib railing with a blanket.

- Try to delay middle-of-the-night feedings. At 2 months of age, begin to discourage the 2:00 A.M. feeding by whatever means seem appropriate to you. Obviously, never awaken your baby at night for a feeding except at your bedtime. If he fusses, try to wait 5 minutes to see if he really is hungry at this time. Before preparing a bottle, try holding him briefly to see if that will suffice. If you must feed him, give 1 or 2 ounces less formula than you would during the day. If you are breast-feeding, nurse for a shorter interval at night. As 4 months approach, try nursing on one side at night. Between now and 4 months of age, your baby should be able to give up the middle-of-the-night feeding.

4-MONTH ADVICE

• Discontinue the 2:00 A.M. feeding before it becomes a habit. By 4 months of age, your baby does not need to be fed more than 4 times a day. (5 times a day for breast-fed babies.) If you do not eliminate the night feeding at this time, it will invariably become more difficult to stop with each passing month. If your child cries during the night, don't feed him; just comfort him with a back rub and a few soothing words. Don't turn on the light or lift him out of the crib. Your baby needs to learn that the crib is where he stays at night. Try to leave his room as soon as possible. Some children need a little redirection to achieve a more mature sleep cycle. (Note: Some breast-fed babies may need the introduction of solids during the day to help them go without nursing at nighttime.)

• Don't allow your baby to hold the bottle or take it to bed with her. Babies should have the idea that the bottle belongs to the parents. A bottle in bed leads to middle-of-the-night crying, since your baby will inevitably reach for the bottle and find it empty or on the floor.

6-MONTH ADVICE

• Provide a friendly soft toy as a crib companion or transitional object. Six months is the age when separation anxiety begins. If you haven't already helped your child bond with a teddy bear or "horsey," it's time to do so. This security object will provide comfort when your child awakens during the night.

• Leave the door to your baby's room open. Children with separation anxiety become very fearful when they are in a closed space and are not sure that their parents are still available to them.

• During the day, respond to separation fears with holding and reassurance. The extra physical contact will reduce nighttime fears. This step is especially important for single working mothers.

- Don't put your baby to sleep before she has met the babysitter. If a young infant unexpectedly awakens during the night and is responded to by a babysitter she doesn't know, she will usually become extremely fearful and develop sleep problems that continue for several weeks. If you are using a new sitter, bring him or her over during the day to play with your child or at least 1 hour before your time of departure.

1-YEAR ADVICE

- Establish a pleasant and predictable bedtime ritual. While bedtime rituals can start in the early months, they become very important to the child by 1 year of age. Children need a familiar routine and a pleasant story. Both parents can be involved at bedtime, taking turns with reading stories or making them up. Both parents should kiss and hug the child good-night. Finish the bedtime ritual before your child falls asleep.

- Once put to bed, your child should stay there. Some older infants have bedtime temper tantrums. They may protest about bedtime or even refuse to lie down. You should overlook these protests and leave the room. You can ignore any ongoing questions or demands your child makes and solely enforce the rule that your child can't leave the bedroom. If your child comes out, return him quickly, avoid any conversation, skip the hug and kiss, and hold the bedroom door closed for a few minutes. Consistency will prevail.

- If your child has nightmares or bedtime fears, sit with her briefly and reassure her. In contrast to manipulative behavior, never punish or ignore fears. Everyone has 4 or 5 dreams a night. Some of these are good dreams and some are bad dreams. If nightmares become frequent, the cause is often that your child has watched a violent television show or an R-rated movie.

- Don't worry about noises or movements during your child's sleep. During dreams, children often display face-twitching, fist-clenching, or even eye-rolling. Many people have muscle jerks while dozing off to sleep. Keep in mind how a dog acts as it chases a rabbit during its dream state. Overall, anything short of not breathing is probably normal sleep behavior.

- Don't worry about the amount of sleep your child is getting. Sleep requirements vary greatly among different people and at different ages. The best assurance that your child is getting adequate sleep is that he or she is not fatigued or tired during the day. Naps are important to young children, but keep them less than 2 hours each. Children give up their morning naps between 1½ and 2 years of age and their afternoon naps between 3 and 6 years of age. Some children may choose to substitute a "rest period" for the afternoon nap. If the "rest period" is discontinued before 5 years of age, most children can't stay awake (or "civilized") until their regular bedtime.

- Switch from a crib to a bed at age 2 or 2½. Change sooner if your child learns how to climb out of a crib with the springs at the lowest setting. Climb-proofing a crib can't be done. The next attempt at climbing out could result in a serious head injury. Until you find a bed, keep the crib railing down and place a chair next to the crib so your child can descend safely. Don't buy bunk beds. They have a terrible accident rate with children of all ages. A good first bed is a mattress and box spring placed on the floor without a frame.

THUMBSUCKING AND PACIFIERS

SYMPTOMS AND CHARACTERISTICS

- Sucking on the thumb when not hungry
- Finger sucking or fist sucking in some children
- A security object, such as a blanket, may become part of the ritual
- Mainly occurs when tired, bored, sick, or upset
- Mainly occurs when not using the hands to play
- Occurs in 80 percent of infants
- Onset before birth or by 3 months of age at the latest

Causes • A desire to suck on the breast or bottle is a drive that is essential for survival. In addition, more than 80 percent of babies also do some extra sucking when they are not hungry (called nonnutritive sucking). Many fetuses are observed on ultrasound to suck while still in the uterus. This extra sucking ability probably becomes important if the breast milk supply decreases and the infant needs to suck more minutes per day. Thumbsucking also appears to help with normal comforting and quieting and often increases when breast- or bottle-feedings decrease. It does not point to insecurity or emotional problems in your child.

Expected Outcome • The sucking need is strongest during the first 6 months of life. In a study by Dr. T. Berry Brazelton, only 6 percent of thumbsucking babies continued the habit past 1 year of age and only 3 percent continued beyond the age of 2 years. Most children give up thumbsucking by 4 years of age, except those who become involved in a power struggle in the early years with a parent who interferes with their thumbsucking. These children may become fixated on the thumbsucking and persist in the behavior to underscore their independence. Occasionally it simply persists as a bad habit. Thumbsucking must eventually be dealt with because if continued after the permanent teeth erupt, it can lead to an overbite (buck teeth). Even before age 6, frequent thumbsucking can lead to some minor complications. These include paronychia (fingernail infections), and a swollen abdomen with increased passage of gas (secondary to increased air swallowing). By adolescence, all normal children abandon thumbsucking because of peer pressure.

HOW TO OVERCOME THUMBSUCKING

For Children Less Than 4 Years of Age, distract your child or ignore the thumbsucking • It should be considered normal in this age range. In fact, during the first 6 months of life it can be encouraged as a means of self-comforting. You can completely ignore the thumbsucking unless your child is over 1 year of age and it occurs during a time of day when the child is bored. Then you can distract your child by giving her something to do with her hands without mentioning your concern about the thumbsucking. Occasionally praise your child for not thumbsucking. Until your child reaches an age of reason, any pressure you apply to stop thumbsucking will only lead to refusal and lack of cooperation.

After 4 Years of Age, help your child give up thumbsucking during the day • First get your child's permission and commitment to giving up thumbsucking by showing him what thumbsucking is doing to his body. Show him the gap between his teeth with a mirror. Have him look at the wrinkled rough skin (callus) on his thumb. Appeal to his sense of pride. At this point most children will agree they would like to stop thumbsucking.
  Ask your child if it would be all right if you reminded him

in case he forgets. Do this gently with comments such as "Guess what?" and put an arm around your child as he remembers that he was sucking on his thumb again. Encourage your child to use a visual reminder. Self-reminders include painting a star on the thumb with a Magic Marker, putting a Band-Aid on the thumb, or applying fingernail polish for girls. Your child should put these reminders on himself. If your child finds himself sucking on the thumb, he can initiate a competing exercise such as holding the thumb inside a closed fist for 10 seconds or twirling the thumbs. Praise your child whenever you notice he is not sucking his thumb in situations where he previously did.

After Daytime Control Is Established, help your child give up thumbsucking during sleep • Thumbsucking during naps and nighttime is usually an involuntary process. Your child can be told that although it's not her fault, she can learn to not suck the thumb during sleep by putting something on the thumb to remind her. A glove, sock, splint (thumb guard), or piece of adhesive tape that runs up one side and down the other can be used. Your child should be in charge of putting on whatever material is used to prevent thumbsucking. Help your child look upon this intervention as a clever invention rather than any kind of penalty.

Bitter-tasting medicines • A recent study by Dr. P. C. Friman demonstrated a high success rate in 1 to 3 nights using a bitter-tasting solution called Stop-zit (no prescription necessary). Only use it with your child's permission and after 4 years of age. Don't use it as a punishment. Present it as a reminder that "other kids use." Apply Stop-zit at the following times:

• Before breakfast

• Before bedtime

• Whenever thumbsucking is observed day or night

• Observe your child every 30 minutes after his bedtime until you retire

• After 5 nights without thumbsucking, discontinue the morning Stop-zit

• After 5 more nights without the habit, discontinue the bedtime Stop-zit

• For recurrences, repeat the process

Bring thumbsucking to the attention of your child's dentist at least by 6 years of age • By the time the permanent teeth come in, thumbsucking carries the danger of causing an overbite. Dentists have a variety of approaches to thumbsucking. By the time a child is 7 or 8, dentists can place a bar in the upper mouth that interferes with the ability to suck. This helpful appliance does not cause any pain to your child but can spare you the later economic pain of $2,500 of orthodontic treatment.

PREVENTION

Prolonged thumbsucking can usually be prevented if you avoid pulling your child's thumb out of his mouth at any age. Also, don't comment in your child's presence about your dissatisfaction with the habit. Obviously, scolding, slapping the hand, or other punishments will only make your child dig in his heels about thumbsucking. If you can wait, your child will usually give up the thumbsucking naturally. If you turn it into a showdown, you will lose, since the thumb belongs to your child.

THE PACIFIER'S ROLE IN PREVENTION OF THUMBSUCKING

If your baby is one with increased sucking needs, try to interest him or her in a pacifier. The pacifier has to be introduced in the first month or two of life for it to substitute for the thumb. While the orthodontic type of pacifier is preferred because it prevents tongue-thrusting during sucking, the regular type is fine if your child favors it.

The pacifier has several advantages over thumbsucking. Mainly, its use can be controlled as your child grows older. During the first 6 months give it to your baby whenever he or she wants it. After 6 months of age, it should not be used out of your baby's crib. Therefore, it won't interfere with talking or playing. The pacifier will be needed for special circumstances such as traveling or being admitted to the hospital. By the time your child is 3 years of age, you can usually obtain his or her permission to put the pacifier in an envelope, pretend to "send it to another baby," and end the problem forever. The pacifier also exerts less pressure on the teeth and causes less overbite than the thumb.

Some cautions regarding the pacifier should be observed.

• Avoid using one that comes apart (such as made from the nipple and plastic collar for a bottle) or has a shield smaller than 1½ inches (since this could result in choking).

- Avoid pacifiers with a liquid center. (Some have been found to be contaminated with germs.)

- Avoid coating it with jam or honey, as this may cause dental cavities or even botulism.

- Avoid tying it around the neck. (This could cause strangulation.)

- Try to take it out of the mouth before your baby goes to sleep so it doesn't become essential for going to sleep.

- Finally, don't use the pacifier as something to plug up the mouth of a crying baby. (See CRYING BABY [COLIC], page 124, to review other causes of crying besides hunger and sucking needs.)

CALL YOUR CHILD'S PHYSICIAN DURING OFFICE HOURS IF

- Your child is over 3 years old and sucks the thumb constantly.

- Your child is over 5 years old *and* doesn't stop if peers tease him.

- Your child is over 6 years old *and* does any thumbsucking.

- Your child also has emotional problems.

- The thumbsucking does not improve after trying this approach.

- You have other concerns or questions.

RELATED TOPIC

FINGERNAIL INFECTION (PARONYCHIA) (see page 387)

SIBLING RIVALRY

Sibling rivalry refers here to the natural jealousy of older siblings toward the arrival of a new baby. The peak age for sibling rivalry is 1 to 3 years. Not surprisingly, most children prefer to be the only child during these years. The arrival of a new baby is especially stressful for the firstborn. The jealousy stems from the sibling's viewpoint that the newcomer receives all the attention, visitors, gifts, and special handling. The most common symptom is lots of demands for attention. The sibling wants to be held and carried about, especially when the mother is busy with the newborn. Other symptoms include regressive behavior, such as thumbsucking, wetting, or soiling. Aggressive behavior, such as handling the baby roughly, can also occur. All of these symptoms are normal. While some can be prevented, the remainder can be improved within a few months.

PREVENTION

During Pregnancy

• Prepare the older sibling for the newcomer. Talk about the pregnancy. Have him or her feel your baby's movements.

• Encourage your older child to help you prepare the baby's room.

• Move your older child to a different room or big bed months before the baby's birth. If he or she will be enrolling in a play group or nursery school, arrange for it well in advance of the delivery.

• Praise your older child for mature behavior, like talking, using the toilet, feeding or dressing himself, and playing games.

• Don't make any demands for new skills (such as toilet training) during the months just preceding the delivery. Even if your child appears ready, postpone these changes until your child has made a good adjustment to the new baby.

• Tell your child where she'll go and who will care for her when you go to the hospital.

In the Hospital

• Call your older child daily from the hospital.

• Try to have your older child visit you and the baby in the hospital. Many hospitals are accepting this practice.

• If your older child can't visit you, send him a picture of the new baby.

Coming Home

• When you enter your home, spend your initial moments with the older sibling. Have someone else carry the new baby into the house. Give the sibling a gift "from the new baby."

• From the beginning, refer to your newborn as "our baby."

- Encourage your older child to touch and play with the new baby in your presence. Allow him to hold the baby while sitting in a chair with side arms. Avoid such warnings as "Don't touch the baby." Newborns are not fragile and it is important to show your trust. However, you can't allow your older child to carry the baby until he reaches school age.

- Enlist your older child as a helper. Encourage him to help with baths, dry the baby, get a clean diaper, find a pacifier, or fetch toys. At other times encourage him to feed or bathe a doll as you do the same for the baby. Emphasize how much the baby "likes" the older sibling. Make comments such as: "Look how happy she gets when you play with her," or "You can always make her laugh."

- In addition to making your older child feel included, give him the extra attention he needs. Mainly give several one-minute hugs scattered throughout the day. Also try to provide at least 30 minutes a day of exclusive, uninterrupted time. Hire a babysitter and take your older child outside or look through his baby album with him. Make sure that the father and relatives spend extra time with him during the first month. If he demands to be held while you are feeding or rocking the baby, try to include him. At least try to talk with him when you are busy attending to the baby.

- Ask visitors to give extra notice to the older child. Have your older child unwrap the baby's gifts.

- For regressive behavior such as thumbsucking or clinging, accept these as a temporary need. Do not criticize them.

- For aggressive behavior, intervene promptly and send your child to "time-out" for a few minutes. Don't spank your child at these times, because if you hit her, she will eventually get back at the baby. For the next few weeks don't leave the two of them alone.

- If your child is old enough, encourage her to talk about her mixed feelings about the new arrival.

Spacing Children • The ideal spacing between children is 2 or more years. Children less than 2 years apart tend to have a greater number of negative interactions. Another reason for spacing children is that a separate, special early childhood enhances development. More importantly, spacing children increases the ability of the parents to cope successfully with child rearing. The care of three or more preschoolers can be overwhelming, with all their needs to be fed, toileted, dressed, and entertained.

CALL YOUR CHILD'S PHYSICIAN DURING OFFICE HOURS IF

• Your older child tries to hurt the baby.

• Regressive behavior doesn't improve by 1 month.

ACCIDENT PREVENTION

INFANT SAFETY

During the first 3 years of life, children have little sense of danger or self-preservation. They are totally dependent on adults to look after their safety. They cannot be left unattended on a table or bed; they may roll off it and strike their head. For the same reason, crib railings must always be kept in an upright position. A small child cannot be given toys with small parts, because of the danger that the child may put them in his or her mouth and choke on them. Mattresses should not be covered with pieces of thin plastic, because children may get the plastic caught on the face and be smothered by it. Children cannot be left alone in a bathtub while a parent answers the doorbell, because they could drown. Talcum powder should not be used on them because they may breathe it in and develop severe chemical pneumonia. A pacifier or teething ring should not be tied about the neck because it could catch something and strangle them. And babies should not be left to sleep in a car, because they could develop a life-threatening heatstroke.

Unfortunately this is only a partial list of the accidents that can befall a young infant. Adult supervision and vigilance are essential.

CAR SAFETY SEATS

Why Use One? • The number one killer and crippler of children in the United States is motor vehicle crashes. Approximately 700 children under the age of 5 are killed each year, and about 60,000 are injured. Proper use of car safety seats can reduce traffic fatalities by at least 80 percent. Laws have been passed in all 50 states that require children to be sitting in an approved child passenger safety seat. A baby cannot be protected by being held tightly in a parent's arms. During a 30-mile-per-hour crash, the baby will either be crushed between the parent's body and the dashboard or be ripped from the parent's arms with a force of almost 300 pounds. Riding in a car seat also has the advantage of reducing children's misbehavior, motion sickness, and the accident rate caused by children's distracting the driver.

How to Choose One • Since January 1981, all manufacturers of child safety seats must meet stringent government safety standards, including crash-testing. Look for a seat marked as having met Federal Motor Vehicle Safety Standard 213, with the date of manufacture being 1981 or later. If the seat was manufactured between 1971 and 1981, it may or may not meet the government safety standard. When in doubt, contact the National Highway Traffic Safety Administration hotline, (800) 424-9393, for information. The American Academy of Pediatrics also publishes a yearly updated list of infant/child safety seats. This list can be obtained by writing the American Academy of Pediatrics, Division of Public Education, 141 Northwest Point Boulevard, P.O. Box 927, Elk Grove Village, Illinois 60007.

Car safety seats come in four types. Infant safety seats are rear-facing only and are useful from birth to approximately 20 pounds. Convertible safety seats can be used in both rear- and forward-facing positions. They are useful from birth to approximately 40 pounds. Toddler seats are forward-facing only and are useful from 20 to 43 pounds. Booster seats are forward-facing and are useful from 40 to 60 pounds. Children over 60 pounds can use a conventional seat belt without a booster seat. Whenever possible put the car seat in the back seat, which is much safer than the front seat.

How to Use One • Your child's car safety seat can be a lifesaver. But to protect your child, the seat must be used consistently and properly. Most children accept the use of car seats and seat belts as a routine necessity; however, at various times children need some special attention to keep them well protected. Your attitude toward the use of safety belts and child safety seats is of prime importance. If you treat buckling up as a normal part of living—something to be done automatically—your children generally will follow your lead. To keep your kids safe and happy:

- Always use the safety seat, and use it correctly. Start the use of safety seats on the first ride home from the hospital, and keep on using them for every ride.

- Allow NO exceptions for older kids and adults. Everyone buckles up! If adults ride unprotected, the child quickly decides that safety is just kid stuff.

- Give frequent praise for appropriate behavior in the car.

- Remember that a bored child can become a disruptive one. Keep a supply of favorite soft toys and munchies on hand.

- NEVER let a fussy child out of the car seat or safety belt while the car is in motion. If your child needs a break, STOP the car. Don't reward complaints by allowing your child to ride unprotected. That's a disastrous decision, and one that will make it harder to keep him in the seat on the next ride.

- If a child tries to get out of the seat, stop the car and firmly but calmly explain that the car won't go until he is back in place—buckled in the car seat.

- Make a vinyl seatpad more comfortable in hot weather by covering it with a cloth pad or towel.

- When your child travels in another person's car (such as a babysitter or grandparent) insist that the driver also use the car safety seat.

- For long-distance trips, plan for frequent stops, and try to stop before the children get restless. Cuddle young children and let older children snack and run around for 10 to 15 minutes.

(Reprinted with the permission of the American Academy of Pediatrics, 1986)

ACCIDENT PREVENTION OVERVIEW

The prevention of various accidents is discussed throughout this book, along with the first aid for these same accidents. For details on the prevention of any of the following accidents, turn to the appropriate pages.

BURNS, page 28
CHOKING, page 9
DROWNING, page 36
ELECTRIC SHOCK OR LIGHTNING INJURY, page 37
FALLS (see HEAD TRAUMA, page 58)
HEAT REACTIONS, page 41
POISONING, page 42
SUNBURN, page 398

NEWBORN EQUIPMENT AND SUPPLIES

Before the baby is born, most parents prepare a special room. They buy a layette including clothing, a place to sleep, feeding equipment, bathing equipment, and changing supplies. This preparation is called nesting behavior. The most common mistake parents on a limited budget can make during this time is buying something they don't need at all or buying an expensive (often fancy) version of an essential piece of equipment. Sometimes parents can borrow some of the equipment from friends or relatives. The first list describes essential equipment. It may also come in handy next time you need a shower gift. The second list includes helpful but nonessential items. The final list reviews items that are unnecessary for most families.

ESSENTIAL EQUIPMENT

Car Seat • Child restraint seats are essential for transporting your baby in a car. They are required by law in most states. Consider buying one that is convertible and usable until your child reaches 40 pounds or 4 years of age. During the first 9 or 10 months (until your child weighs about 20 pounds) the car seat faces backward; after that time it is moved to a forward-facing position. While car seats must conform to federal safety standards, they are also ranked by consumer magazines. Many hospitals have a rental program for car seats which can save you money unless you are going to have several children. (See ACCIDENT PREVENTION, page 139, on how to select and use a car seat.)

Crib • Since your baby will spend so much unattended time in the crib, make certain it is a safe one. Federal safety standards require that all cribs built after 1974 have spaces between the crib bars of 2⅜ inches or less. This restriction is to prevent a child from getting the head or body stuck between the bars. If you have an older crib, be sure to check this distance, which is approximately the width of 3 fingers. Also check for any defective crib bars. The mattress should be the same size as the crib so that your baby's head can't get caught in the gap. It should also be waterproof. Bumper pads are unnecessary because infants rarely strike their head on the railings. The pads have the disadvantage of keeping your baby from seeing out of the crib; they are also something to climb on at a later stage. During the first 2 or 3 months of life it may be more convenient to have your baby sleep in a drawer, a cardboard box, or a basket that is well padded with towels or blankets.

Bathtub • Small plastic bathtubs with sponge linings are available. A large plastic dishpan will also suffice for the purpose. A molded sponge lining can be purchased separately. As a compromise, a kitchen sink works well if you are careful about preventing your child from falling against hard edges or turning on the hot water, thereby causing a burn. Until the umbilical cord falls off, keep the water level below the navel. Most children can be bathed in a standard bathtub by 1 year of age.

Bottles and Nipples • If you are feeding your baby formula, you will need about ten 8-ounce bottles. While clear plastic bottles cost twice as much as glass ones, you will be glad you bought the unbreakable type the first time you or your baby drops one. You will also need a corresponding number of nipples. If you prepare more than one bottle at a time, you will need a 1-quart measuring cup and a funnel for mixing a batch of formula.

Diapers • If you can afford it, disposable diapers are usually the most convenient. You are spared the chore of rinsing off diapers or plastic pants. (However, bowel movements should be scraped into a toilet for sanitary purposes.) Disposable diapers are also easy for traveling. If you have an automatic washer and dryer, you may prefer to use cloth diapers. You will need 3 dozen to 6 dozen cloth diapers as well as several pairs of plastic pants. You will also need a diaper pail for storing dirty diapers until wash time. During the first 2 or 3 months of life, when most mothers are exhausted by new baby care, another option is to use a diaper service rather than washing the diapers yourself. A diaper service is considerably less expensive than using disposable diapers.

Pacifier • A pacifier is useful in soothing many babies. To prevent choking, the pacifier's shield should be at least 1½ inches in diameter and the pacifier should be one single piece. Some of the newer ones are made of silicone (instead of rubber), which lasts longer because it doesn't dry out. The orthodontic-shaped pacifiers are accepted by some babies but not by others. (See THUMBSUCKING AND PACIFIERS, page 132, for additional information.)

Nasal Suction Bulb • A suction bulb is essential for helping young babies with breathing difficulties due to sticky or dried nasal secretions. A suction bulb with a blunt tip is more effective than the ones with long tapered tips (which are used for irrigating ears). The best ones on the market have a small clear plastic tip (mucus trap), which can be removed from the rubber suction bulb for cleaning. (See under COLDS, page 435, for proper use.)

Thermometer • A rectal thermometer is most helpful if your baby becomes sick. It can also be used for taking temperatures in the armpit. (See FEVER, page 305, for directions on using.)

Humidifier • A humidifier will be helpful in dry climates or areas with cold winters. The new ultrasonic humidifiers are quieter and have other advantages. Do not buy a vaporizer (a gadget that produces steam) because it can cause burns in children and doesn't deliver humidity at as fast a rate as a humidifier.

Diaper and Bottle Bag • For traveling outside the home with your baby, you will need an all-purpose shoulder bag to carry the items that allow you to feed your baby and change diapers.

Highchair • During the first 6 months of life your baby can be held when he or she is being fed. Once your child can sit unsupported and take solid foods, a highchair is needed. The most important feature is a wide base that prevents tipping. The tray needs to have a good safety latch. The tray should also have adjustable positions to adapt to your infant's growth. A safety strap is critical. Plastic or metal chairs are easier to clean than wooden chairs. Small portable highchairs that attach directly to the tabletop are gaining in popularity. They are convenient, reasonably priced, and appear to have a good safety record.

Food Grinder • The time comes when your baby must make the transition from baby foods to table foods. A baby-food grinder takes the work out of mashing up table foods. It's as effective as a blender, easier to clean, and costs less. Food processors have the advantage of allowing you to make larger quantities faster than in a grinder.

Training Cup • By the time your child is 1 year old, he will want to hold his own cup. Buy a spillproof one with a weighted base, double handles, a lid, and a spout.

Bib • To keep food off your baby's clothes, find a molded plastic bib with an open scoop on the bottom to catch the mess.

Safety Gadgets • Once your child is crawling, you will need electric-outlet safety plugs, cabinet door safety locks, bathtub spout protectors, plastic corner guards for sharp table edges, and so forth.

HELPFUL EQUIPMENT
The following items mainly provide your child with forms of transportation or special places to play. While they all have some advantages, if none of them are available, your child could also be carried and permitted to play on a blanket on the floor.

Changing Table • Diapers need to be changed 10 to 15 times a day. While a bed can be used for changing, performing this task without bending over prevents back strain. An old dining table or buffet can work as well as a special changing table.

Automatic Swing • While swings are entertaining to most babies, they are especially helpful for crying babies. They come in windup-spring, pendulum-driven, or battery-powered models. The latter two have quieter mechanisms. Again, a sturdy base and crossbars are important for safety.

Front-pack or Carrier • Front-packs are great for new babies. They give your child a sense of physical contact and warmth. They allow you freedom to use your hands. Buy one with head support. Carrying a baby in front after 5 or 6 months of age can cause a backache for the parent.

Backpack • Backpacks are useful in carrying babies who are 5 or 6 months old and have good head support. They are an inexpensive way to carry your baby outside when you go shopping, hiking, or walking anywhere. The inner seat is usually adjustable to different levels.

Stroller • Another way to transport a baby who has outgrown the front-pack is in a baby stroller. The most convenient ones are the umbrella type, which fold up. A safety belt is important to keep your baby from standing up and falling.

Infant Seat • An infant seat is a good place to keep a young baby when he or she is not eating or sleeping. Infants prefer this inclined position so they can see what is going on around them. Buy one with a safety strap, but don't substitute it for a car seat. Once children reach 3 to 4 months of age, they can usually tip the infant seat over, so discontinue using it.

Playpen • A playpen is a handy and safe place to leave your baby when you need uninterrupted time to cook a meal or do the wash. Babies like playpens because the slatted or mesh sides afford a good view of the environment. Playpens can be used both indoors and outdoors. As with cribs, the slats should be less than 2⅜ inches apart. The playpens with a fine-weave netting are also acceptable although sometimes older infants can climb out of them. Bottomless playpens are gaining in popularity. Your baby should be introduced to the playpen by 4 months of age so that he or she builds up positive associations with it. It is very difficult to introduce a playpen after a baby has learned to crawl. Avoid stringing any objects on a cord across the playpen, because your baby could become entangled in them and strangle.

Gates • A gate is essential if your house has stairways that your baby must be protected from. A gate is also helpful for keeping a child in a specific room with you and out of the rest of the house, as when you are working in the kitchen. Many rooms can be closed off with doors.

UNNECESSARY EQUIPMENT

Some baby equipment is usually not worth the investment, but your judgment may be different. You can bathe your baby without a special bathinette. Nursery monitors or intercoms will not prevent crib deaths and may interfere with the learning of self-soothing behavior. Baby carriages or buggies generally have been replaced by baby strollers or backpacks.

You can determine if your baby is being fed enough without a baby scale (see BREAST-FEEDING, page 97, and FORMULA-FEEDING, page 102). An infant feeder is a bottle with a nipple on one end and a piston on the other, used to feed young babies strained foods. They are advertised as a "natural" step between bottle- and spoon-feeding. Since babies don't need any food except formula or breast milk until at least 4 months of age (at which time spoon-feeding works quite nicely), this item is unnecessary and can lead to forced feedings.

A few items can be harmful. A jumping harness can come loose from its overhead supports and cause injury to the baby. More than 35 percent of infants who use infant walkers sustain an injury requiring medical attention, including skull fractures, dental injuries, and lacerations. Falling down stairs in a walker has resulted in death, probably because of the high speed that can be attained before impact. Also, walkers don't accelerate motor development. In fact, the ability to crawl may be delayed. Some parents use a walker because their child likes to play or eat in it. If that is the case, take off the wheels and convert it into a small table. Finally, shoes are not needed until your child has to walk outdoors (see SHOES, below).

SHOES

The following information may help you make more rational decisions about buying shoes for your young infant.

SHOES VERSUS BAREFOOT

• The only purpose of shoes is to protect from injury, cold, or burns (from asphalt surfaces). No shoes are needed until your child begins to walk in rough terrain. Children who are walking inside a house or outside on sand or grass do not require shoes.

• Before the age of walking, keep your child's feet warm with booties or socks during the winter.

• Once your child begins to walk, he will prefer to walk barefooted because it gives him a better sense of where his feet are and enables him to use his toes for balance.

TYPES OF SHOES

• When your child finally needs a shoe, buy tennis shoes (sneakers) or some other shoe with a flexible sole, such as moccasins, which allow free movement of the foot. Tennis shoes have the advantage of being comfortable, easy to wash, inexpensive, and good for traction.

- Hand-me-down shoes are fine if they are still in good condition and fit.

- Expensive shoes have no advantage at any age for 99 percent of children. Arches do not "fall." Save your money for something more important.

- Heels are not essential at any age, and they can cause tripping during the first 2 years.

- High-top shoes are not useful, and children who wear them are often teased. Occasionally a toddler will need high-top sneakers because his or her feet continually slip out of low-cut ones.

- Even children with flat feet rarely need a special shoe or heel. Tennis shoes are fine for most of these children.

SHOE SIZE AND FIT

- With a little practice, most parents can determine whether or not a shoe fits. Check proper fit with your child putting weight on the shoes. The length should be approximately ½ inch (an index finger) longer than the big toe. The width should allow you to grasp a small piece of shoe at the widest portion of the foot (the pinch test). The heel area should be snug enough to keep the shoe from flopping up and down during walking. Also, maximum flex should be where the foot flexes and not in the middle of the shoe.

- In young, growing children, shoes commonly become too tight before they wear out.

- During the second and third year of life, shoe size can change three times a year, so check the fit every few months.

- Fluoroscopy should not be used in fitting shoes because of the radiation exposure. Hopefully, all of these machines have been banished from shoe stores.

NEWBORN PROBLEMS

THE SICK NEWBORN: SUBTLE SYMPTOMS

A newborn is a baby less than 1 month old. Newborns mainly eat, sleep, cry a little, and need lots of love and their diapers changed frequently. The symptoms of illness in the early months of life can be subtle. Also, newborns can deteriorate quickly. If newborns are sick at all, it can be serious.

CALL YOUR CHILD'S PHYSICIAN IMMEDIATELY IF

- Your baby is less than 1 month old and sick in any way (e.g., cough, poor color, or diarrhea).

- Your newborn's appetite or suck becomes poor.

- Your newborn sleeps excessively—for instance, past feeding times.

- Your newborn cries excessively. (See also CRYING BABY [COLIC], page 124.)

- Your newborn develops a fever over 99°F (37.2°C) axillary, or over 100°F (37.8°C) rectally.

- Your newborn's temperature drops below 96.5°F (36°C) axillary, or below 97.5°F (36.5°C) rectally. (Note: In general, do not take an infant's temperature unless he feels hot or looks sick.)

- You have other urgent questions.

RELATED TOPIC

THE NORMAL NEWBORN'S BEHAVIOR (see page 83)

THE SICK INFANT: JUDGING THE SEVERITY OF ILLNESS

In the first 2 years of a child's life, most parents feel uncomfortable and inadequate in determining how sick their child is during a cold or other infection. Since these children can't talk, they can't help much with diagnosis. How sick your child looks or acts is much more relevant than the level of fever. Also, some children look much better 30 to 40 minutes after the fever is reduced with medicine.

GUIDELINES TO SEVERE ILLNESS

Call Your Child's Physician Immediately If

- Your child is a newborn (less than 1 month old) with any sign of illness.

- Your child looks or acts very sick.

- Your child cannot be made to smile, or hardly responds.

- Your child refuses to play.

- Your child cries constantly for more than 3 hours.

- The cry becomes high-pitched and strange-sounding.

- The cry becomes a weak whimper or moan.

- Your child cannot sleep for more than 30 minutes at a time.

- Your child cannot be comforted for more than 30 minutes at a time.

- Your child cannot be fully awakened.

- The breathing becomes labored.

- The mouth and lips become bluish.

- The skin becomes grayish.

RELATED TOPICS

CRYING BABY (COLIC) (see page 124)
FEVER (see page 305)
THE SICK NEWBORN: SUBTLE SYMPTOMS (see page 149)

CRADLE CAP

Cradle cap consists of oily, yellow scales and crusts on the scalp. It begins in the first weeks of life and is probably caused by adult hormones that crossed the placenta before birth. Without treatment it can last for months; with treatment it usually is cleared up in a few weeks. Cradle cap is not contagious.

CALL YOUR CHILD'S PHYSICIAN DURING OFFICE HOURS IF

• A weepy, raw rash is present behind the ears.

• The rash has spread beyond the scalp.

• You have other questions.

HOME CARE FOR CRADLE CAP

Antidandruff Shampoo • Buy an antidandruff shampoo (no prescription needed) at the drugstore. Wash your baby's hair with it once a day. While the hair is lathered, massage your baby's scalp with a soft brush or a rough washcloth for 5 minutes. Don't worry about hurting the soft spot. Once the cradle cap has cleared up, use a regular shampoo twice a week.

Softening Thick Crusts • If the scalp is very crusty, put some baby oil or mineral oil on the scalp 1 hour before washing to soften the crust. Wash all the oil off, however, or it may worsen the cradle cap.

Resistant Cases • If the rash is very red and irritated, apply ½ percent hydrocortisone cream (no prescription needed) 3 times a day for 4 days.

Call Your Child's Physician Later If

• The cradle cap lasts more than 2 weeks with treatment.

DIAPER RASH

SYMPTOMS AND CHARACTERISTICS

- Any rash in the skin area covered by a diaper

Causes • Almost all children get diaper rashes. Most of them are due to the prolonged contact with wetness, bacteria, digestive enzymes and ammonia that comes with wearing diapers. The ammonia and other skin irritants are made by the action of bacteria from bowel movements on certain chemicals in the urine. Diaper rashes are less common with cloth diapers than with disposable diapers, which don't let the skin breathe. You don't have to switch diapers, however, to clear up a diaper rash. Diaper rashes are much worse with plastic pants, so avoid them until your baby makes enough urine to soak through the diaper. In societies where diapers aren't worn, babies don't acquire diaper rashes.

Allergies to soaps, detergents, whiteners, and bleaches are very rare, and you needn't worry about these.

Expected Course • With proper treatment these rashes are usually better in 3 days. If they do not respond, a yeast infection (*Candida*) has probably occurred. Suspect this if the rash becomes bright red and raw, covers a large area, and is surrounded by red dots. Your physician will have to prescribe a special cream for yeast.

CALL YOUR CHILD'S PHYSICIAN

Immediately If

- The diaper rash has any big blisters (larger than 1 inch across).
- Your child's face is bright red and tender to the touch.
- Your child is acting very sick.

During Office Hours If

- An unexplained fever (over 100°F) is present.
- The rash causes enough pain to interfere with sleeping.
- The diaper rash is a solid bright-red.
- Pimples, blisters, boils, pus, or yellow crusts are present.

- The rash has spread beyond the diaper area.

- Your child is male and circumcised *and* the end of the penis has a sore or scab (meatal ulcer).

- You have other questions.

HOME CARE FOR DIAPER RASH

Change Diapers Frequently • The key to successful treatment is keeping the area dry and clean so it can heal itself. Check the diaper about every hour, and if it is wet or soiled, change it immediately. Exposure to stools causes most of the skin damage.

Air Exposure and Loose-Fitting Diapers • Leave your baby's bottom exposed to the air as much as possible each day. Practical times are during naps or after bowel movements. Put a towel or diaper under your baby. When the diaper is on, fasten it loosely so that air can circulate between it and the skin. Avoid airtight plastic pants for a few days. Put a towel between you and your baby's bottom instead. If you use disposable diapers, punch holes in them to let the air circulate, and avoid the type with tight leg bands. Sun exposure of 5 to 10 minutes per side per day can be most helpful. Warm air from a hair dryer for 3 minutes on the low setting can also encourage healing.

Nighttime Care of Diaper Rashes • At night use disposable diapers that lock wetness inside the diaper and away from the skin. Avoid plastic pants or conventional disposable diapers at night. Awaken once during the night to change your baby's diaper until the rash is better.

Cleansing the Skin • All you need is warm tap water. A mild soap (like Dove) is needed only after bowel movements to help remove the film of bacteria left on the skin. After using a soap, rinse thoroughly and pat dry. If the diaper rash is quite raw, use lukewarm water soaks in a tub for 15 minutes 3 times a day. Adding 1 or 2 tablespoons of baking soda to the water may help healing. (Note: Running water is far superior to disposable diaper wipes. Disposable wipes should be used only for traveling, but avoid those containing alcohol.)

Creams and Powders • Most babies don't need any cream unless the diaper rash becomes infected with yeast. In addition, unless the hygiene measures outlined above are carried through, no cream has a chance to help the rash. If your baby's skin is dry and cracked, apply a hand lotion or cream after a diaper change. Avoid any ointments (like petroleum jelly). Ointments can cause heat rashes and keep weepy rashes from drying up.

After the diaper rash is healed, cornstarch powder can be used to prevent the shiny pink diaper rash that comes from friction against the diaper. Recent studies show that cornstarch does not encourage yeast infections. Avoid talcum powders because of the risk of serious pneumonia if your baby breathes some in.

Washing Cloth Diapers • If you wash cloth diapers yourself, you will need to use bleach (such as Clorox, Borax, or Purex) to sterilize them. During the regular cycle, use any detergent. Then refill the washer with warm water, add 1 cup of bleach, and run a second cycle. Vinegar is not effective in killing germs.

Call Your Child's Physician Later If

• The rash isn't much better in 3 days.

• Any pimples, blisters, boils, pus, or yellow crusts develop.

• The rash spreads beyond the diaper area.

JAUNDICE OF THE NEWBORN

Jaundice is a yellow color of the skin and the whites of the eyes (the sclera). The yellow coloration is due to increased amounts of a pigment in the body called bilirubin. Bilirubin is produced by the normal breakdown of red blood cells. Bilirubin accumulates if the liver doesn't excrete it into the intestines at a normal rate.

TYPES OF JAUNDICE

Physiological Jaundice • Physiological jaundice occurs in more than 50 percent of babies. An immaturity of the liver leads to a slowdown in the processing of bilirubin. The jaundice first appears at 2 to 4 days of age. It usually disappears by 1 to 2 weeks of age and is harmless.

Breast-Milk Jaundice • Breast-milk jaundice occurs in 1 to 2 percent of breast-fed babies. It is caused by a special substance that mothers may produce in their breast milk. This substance (probably a lipase) interferes with bilirubin excretion. This type of jaundice starts at 4 to 7 days of age, and may last from 3 to 10 weeks normally.

Blood Group Incompatibility (Rh or ABO Problems) • If a baby and mother have different blood types, sometimes the mother produces antibodies that destroy the newborn's red blood cells. This causes a sudden buildup in bilirubin in the baby's blood. This type of jaundice usually begins during the first 24 hours of life. Rh problems formerly caused the most severe form of jaundice but now are preventable with an injection of Rho GAM to the mother within 72 hours after delivery which prevents her forming antibodies that might endanger her subsequent babies.

TREATMENT OF SEVERE JAUNDICE

High levels of bilirubin (usually above 20 milligrams percent) can cause deafness, cerebral palsy, or brain damage in some babies. These complications can be prevented by lowering the bilirubin using phototherapy (blue light that breaks down bilirubin). In many communities, phototherapy can be used in the home. In cases where the bilirubin reaches dangerous levels, an exchange transfusion may be used. This technique replaces the baby's blood with fresh blood. Physiological jaundice does not rise to levels requiring this type of treatment. While the bilirubin level may rise above 20 with breast-milk jaundice, the blood bilirubin level can be reduced before it reaches this level by alternating each breast-feeding with formula-feeding for three or four days. (Talk to your baby's physician for the latest instructions.) Breast-feeding never needs to be permanently discontinued for breast-milk jaundice.

CALL YOUR BABY'S PHYSICIAN DURING OFFICE HOURS IF

- Jaundice is noticed during the first 48 hours of life.

- The jaundice involves the arms or legs.

- The color gets deeper after day 7.

- The jaundice is not gone by day 14.

- Your baby is not gaining weight well.

- Call immediately if your baby also starts to act sick. (See THE SICK NEWBORN: SUBTLE SYMPTOMS, page 149.)

Since newborns are going home earlier than formerly, the parent must be more involved with observations about the degree of jaundice. The amount of yellowness is best judged by viewing your baby unclothed in natural light by a window.

SPITTING UP (REGURGITATION)

SYMPTOMS AND CHARACTERISTICS
Regurgitation is the effortless spitting up of 1 or 2 mouthfuls of stomach contents. It is usually seen shortly after feedings. It occurs mainly in children under 1 year of age and begins in the first week of life. More than half of all children have it to some degree.

Similar Condition • If appropriate, turn directly to the guideline for VOMITING, page 502.

Cause • A lack of closure of the valve at the upper end of the stomach is responsible. This condition is also called gastroesophageal reflux (GER) or chalasia.

Expected Course • It improves with age. By the time your baby has been walking for 3 months, it should be totally cleared up. Many babies are better by 8 to 10 months of age after learning to sit well.

CALL YOUR CHILD'S PHYSICIAN
Immediately If

- Any blood is seen in the spit-up material.
- The spitting up has caused your child to choke or cough repeatedly.

During Office Hours If

- Your baby is not gaining weight normally.
- Your baby is frequently cranky.

- Your baby has been walking for more than 3 months and is still spitting up.

- You have other questions.

HOME CARE FOR SPITTING UP

Smaller Amounts of Food • Overfeeding always makes spitting up worse. If the stomach is filled to capacity, spitting up is more likely. Give your baby smaller amounts (at least 1 ounce less than you have been), especially if he is somewhat overweight. Keep the total feeding time to less than 20 minutes. Your baby doesn't have to finish a bottle. Wait at least 2½ hours between feedings, because it takes that long for the stomach to empty itself. Don't add food to a full stomach. Also, cut back on pacifier time. Constant sucking can pump the stomach up with air.

Burping to Prevent Spitting Up • Burp your baby several times during each feeding. Do it when he pauses and looks around. Don't interrupt his feeding rhythm in order to burp him. Burp each time for less than a minute. Keep in mind that burping is less important than giving smaller feedings.

Avoid Pressure on the Abdomen • Avoid tight diapers and the sitting position. They put added pressure on the stomach. Don't double him up during diaper changes. Don't let people hug him or play vigorously with him right after meals. After meals, try to hold your baby in the upright position using a frontpack or backpack. Avoid infant seats because they increase the contact of stomach acid with the lower esophagus. After your child is over 6 months old, a walker can be helpful for maintaining the upright posture after meals. To make the walker safe, remove the wheels.

Cleaning Up • One of the worst aspects of spitting up cow's milk is the odor. This is caused by the effect of stomach acid on the butterfat. The odor is eliminated if you use a commercial formula, because it contains vegetable oils. To protect carpets from spots, try to confine your baby to areas without rugs, such as the kitchen. Also, don't pick your baby up when you're wearing your best clothes. Milk spots are easily cleaned using soda water or tap water with a pinch of baking soda.

Sleeping Position • To avoid choking, be sure your baby sleeps on his abdomen. Avoid having him lie on his back.

Call Your Child's Physician Later If

• Your baby doesn't seem to improve with this approach. Your physician will probably discuss how to thicken feedings with cereal and how to use a "chalasia or reflux harness" after meals.

TEAR DUCT, BLOCKED

SYMPTOMS AND CHARACTERISTICS

• A continuously watery eye

• Tears run down the face even without crying.

• During crying, the nostril on the blocked side remains dry.

• Onset at birth to 2 months of age.

• The eye is not red and the eyelid is not swollen (unless the soggy tissues become infected).

If your child's symptoms are different, call your physician for help.

Cause • Your child probably has a blocked tear duct (dacryo-stenosis) on one or both sides. This means that the channel that normally carries tears from the eye to the nose is blocked. Although the obstruction of the tear duct is present at birth, the occasional delay in onset of symptoms can be explained by the delay in tear production until the age of 3 or 4 weeks in a few babies.

Expected Course • This is a common condition, and over 90 percent open up by the time the child is 6 months of age.

CALL YOUR CHILD'S PHYSICIAN

Immediately If

• The eyelids are red or swollen.

• A red lump appears at the inner lower corner of the eyelid.

During Office Hours If

- The eyelids are stuck together with pus after naps.

- Lots of yellow discharge is present.

- Your child is over 6 months old.

- You have other questions.

HOME CARE FOR BLOCKED TEAR DUCT

Massage • The main treatment for blocked tear ducts is massage. Always wash your hands carefully before doing this. A little sac where tears collect is located in the inner lower corner of the eye. This sac should be massaged 3 times a day in an attempt to force the fluid downward through the tear duct and into the nose. Start at the inner corner of the eye and stroke downward in a firm manner using a cotton swab or your little finger. In most children a plug of cells and mucus blocks the tear duct, and it can be washed out by the massage process. If the eye becomes infected, it is important to stop this downward massage.

Call Your Child's Physician Later If

- The eye becomes infected.

- Your child reaches 6 months of age and the eye is still watering.

- Other questions come up.

RELATED TOPIC

EYES, YELLOW DISCHARGE (see page 416)

THRUSH

SYMPTOMS AND CHARACTERISTICS

- White, irregularly shaped patches

- Coats the insides of the mouth and sometimes the tongue. (If the only symptom is a uniformly white tongue, it's due to a milk diet, not thrush.)

- Adherent to the mouth (cannot be washed away or wiped off easily like milk curds)

- Your child is bottle-fed or breast-fed

If your child's symptoms are different, call your physician for help.

Cause • Thrush is caused by a yeast (called *Candida*) that grows rapidly on the lining of the mouth if it is abraded by prolonged sucking (as when a baby sleeps with a bottle or pacifier). Broad-spectrum antibiotics also make a child susceptible by eliminating the normal bacteria in the mouth. Thrush is not contagious, since it does not invade normal tissue.

CALL YOUR CHILD'S PHYSICIAN DURING OFFICE HOURS IF

- An unexplained fever (over 100°F) is present.

- You have other questions.

HOME CARE FOR THRUSH

Nystatin Oral Medicine • The drug for clearing up thrush is Nystatin oral suspension. It requires a prescription. Call your physician during office hours with the name and telephone number of your pharmacy. Some physicians will want to examine the child before prescribing. Give 1 ml of Nystatin 4 times a day. Place it in the front of the mouth (it doesn't do any good once it's swallowed). If the thrush isn't responding, rub the Nystatin on the affected areas with a cotton swab or a gauze wrapped on your finger. Apply it after meals, or at least don't feed your baby anything for 30 minutes after application. Keep this up for at least 7 days, or until all thrush has been gone for 3 days. If you are breast-feeding, apply Nystatin to any irritated areas on your nipples. Thrush is not a reason to stop nursing.

Decrease the Sucking Time • If eating and sucking are painful for your child, temporarily use a cup and spoon. In any event, reduce sucking time to no more than 20 minutes per feeding. Eliminate the pacifier temporarily, except when it's really needed for going to sleep. Soak all nipples in water at 130°F (the temperature of most hot tap water) for 15 minutes.

Diaper Rash Associated with Thrush • If your child has an associated diaper rash, assume it is due to yeast. Request Nystatin cream and apply it 4 times a day. (Also see the guideline on DIAPER RASH, page 152.)

Call Your Child's Physician Later If

• Your child refuses to eat.

• The thrush becomes worse on treatment.

• The thrush lasts more than 10 days.

• An unexplained fever (over 100°F) occurs.

TONGUE-TIE

True tongue-tie, or tight tongue, is a very rare condition. The length of the lingual frenum, which is a thin band of tissue under the tongue, varies among individuals. At birth, the tongue is normally short and the band is tight. The tongue grows and the band stretches with use. After 1 year of age any tightness may be considered abnormal only if:

• The tip of the tongue can't be protruded past the teeth or gumline

• The end of the tongue becomes notched when it is protruded

Without these findings, your child's tongue is normal.

TREATMENT FOR TONGUE-TIE

If your child has these findings, mention them during your next health supervision visit. Keep in mind that a tongue with less movement than normal does not cause delay or difficulty with speech or sucking. Clipping of the band under the tongue is rarely done anymore, because it is usually unnecessary and also carries the risk of bleeding, infection, and tight scar tissue. It is never done before 1 year of age.

UMBILICAL CORD, BLEEDING

A few drops of blood at the point of separation of the cord is common. The area may bleed a few times from the friction of the diaper or your baby's normal movements.

HOME CARE
The bleeding usually stops by itself or can easily be stopped by direct pressure with a sterile gauze.

CALL YOUR CHILD'S PHYSICIAN IMMEDIATELY IF
• The tie has come undone and the cord is bleeding.

• Any bleeding spot is the size of a quarter or greater.

• Bleeding doesn't stop after 10 minutes of direct pressure.

• Rebleeding continues for more than 3 days.

UMBILICAL CORD, DELAYED SEPARATION

Although most cords fall off between 10 and 14 days of age, an occasional cord may stay for 3 weeks. Cords can also hang by a strand of tissue for 2 or 3 days. Eventually they all fall off by themselves, so just be patient about it. In the meantime:

HOME CARE
Clean the base of the cord (where it attaches to the skin) with rubbing alcohol twice a day. To do this properly, you must lift the cord stump away from the body surface. Also help the cord dry faster by keeping the diaper folded below it. An easier approach is to cut off a wedge of diaper (if disposable) with a scissors so the cord is uncovered.

Call Your Child's Physician Later If
• The cord is still attached after 3 weeks. (Note: The cord can't fall off too early.)

• You have any other questions.

RELATED TOPIC
If the cord begins to look infected, see UMBILICAL CORD, OOZING, below.

UMBILICAL CORD, OOZING

The umbilicus (navel) is oozing, moist, or may even have some dried pus on the surface. Sometimes the cord has already fallen off; more often it is still attached and contributes to the problem. Your baby probably has a superficial infection of the navel from surface bacteria. It usually can be cleared up fairly quickly. Infection of the umbilicus must be treated with respect because of the risk of spread to the liver or the abdominal cavity.

CALL YOUR CHILD'S PHYSICIAN

Immediately If

• Red streaks develop on the normal skin surrounding the navel.

• Pimples or blisters appear around the navel.

• Lots of drainage is coming out of the navel.

• Your baby's armpit temperature is over 99.0° or under 96.5°F.

• Your baby acts sick.

During Office Hours If

• There is a nubbin of tissue inside the navel that looks abnormal to you.

• You have other questions.

HOME CARE FOR UMBILICAL CORD OOZING

Cleansing the Umbilicus • Six times a day, clean the area with rubbing alcohol for several minutes. Use a cotton swab and be vigorous about it. The umbilical area does not have any sensation, so the alcohol won't sting. If the cord is still present, you must clean underneath it by lifting it and bending it to each side. If the cord has fallen off, you can pour some alcohol into the depression and remove it after 2 or 3 minutes.

It takes that long to kill all the bacteria. Air exposure and dryness help healing, so be sure to keep the diaper folded down below the cord area or cut off a wedge of diaper (if disposable) with a scissors.

Common Mistakes • Do not put talcum powder on the umbilicus; it can cause irritation and tissue reaction (talc granulomas). Ointments should be avoided, because they delay drying and healing.

Call Your Child's Physician Later If

• The infection seems to spread.

• The umbilical area is not completely dry and clean by 48 hours on this treatment.

• Your baby begins to act sick.

RELATED TOPICS

UMBILICAL CORD, BLEEDING (see page 162)
UMBILICAL CORD, DELAYED SEPARATION (see page 162)

UMBILICAL HERNIA

An umbilical hernia is a navel that bulges ("pops out") with crying or straining. The bulge may disappear when your baby is quiet. If you feel the area with your finger, you will find a small round opening in the muscles of the abdominal wall. During pregnancy, the umbilical cord's blood vessels pass through this ring, and normally it closes off after birth. Umbilical hernias are very common. They are not painful and they never break. Most close spontaneously by school age. Half of the persistent ones close by adolescence.

TREATMENT

No treatment is needed unless the hernia persists beyond age 5 or 6. At that age, day (outpatient) surgery can be performed to close the defect if the hernia presents a cosmetic problem or the defect is larger than 2 cm (about 1 inch) across. The smaller ones usually continue to close. Covering them with tape, a coin, or a "belly band" does not speed healing, but can lead to a skin rash or infection. Your child's physician will be glad to check the hernia on regular office visits. The only complication (which occurs in less than 1 percent of cases) is getting a loop of intestine stuck in the opening. If you think this has happened (if, for instance, the hernia becomes hard, tender, and won't go back in), call your child's physician immediately for help.

RELATED TOPIC

SWELLING, GROIN OR SCROTUM (see page 516)

MEDICINES AND IMMUNIZATIONS

MEDICINES: GENERAL INSTRUCTIONS

OVERUSE OF MEDICINES

We are a greatly overmedicated society. Many people believe that there is a drug for every symptom. Some physicians prescribe a drug during every office visit. These habits can convey to our young people that drugs are the answer to life's discomforts. More than $4 billion per year is spent on over-the-counter drugs for fever, colds, and coughs—many of them unnecessary. Drugs for vomiting and diarrhea are largely ineffective, and these symptoms respond best to dietary changes. Remember that mild symptoms do not require any medication, and moderate symptoms often respond to home remedies. Drugs are not essential to recovery from most illnesses. Life is not a drug-deficient state.

VIRAL INFECTIONS AND ANTIBIOTICS

- More than 90 percent of infections are due to viruses (as with colds, coughs, croup, and diarrhea).

- Antibiotics ("wonder drugs") kill bacteria.

- Unfortunately, *antibiotics have no effect on viruses;* they don't even slow viruses down.

- *Repeated use of antibiotics increases the likelihood of an allergic reaction.* The more they are used, the more likely the body will develop an allergy to them. That's why 5 to 10 percent of adults are allergic to penicillin.

- All antibiotics have additional side effects—such as wiping out your normal protective bacteria and replacing them with bacteria resistant to the antibiotic.

- *Antibiotics can neither shorten the source of viral illnesses nor reduce symptoms.*

- Fortunately, the body's antibodies, once produced, can kill viruses.

- Use home remedies or nonprescription medicines for the symptoms of viral illnesses.

COMMON SYMPTOMS AND NONPRESCRIPTION MEDICINES

- When your child is sick, your goal is to make him as comfortable as possible.

- If your child is playing and sleeping normally, nonprescription medicines are not needed.

- Give medicines only for symptoms that are causing discomfort, disrupting sleep, or really bothering your child—coughing spasms, for instance.

- Medicines for symptoms can only partially relieve those symptoms (e.g., a fever will be lowered but not normal).

- Medicines for symptoms do not shorten the course of an illness.

- Nonprescription (over-the-counter) medicines also can have side effects.

GUIDELINES FOR SAFE USE OF MEDICINES

- Most medicines can cause poisoning. Keep them out of reach of children. Keep the child-proof caps on.

- Give the correct amount (dosage) for your child. Read the directions on the label carefully. Measure the dose out exactly. Remember that a 1-teaspoon measuring spoon should hold 5 ml (or 5cc). Tableware teaspoons hold varying amounts and should not be used.

- Give the medicine at the correct time intervals. If you forget a dosage, give it as soon as you remember it, and give the next one at the correct interval following the late dosage. Generally, "4 times a day" does not mean you have to awaken your child, unless he sleeps more than 8 hours.

- If you think your child is having a reaction to the medicine, call your physician before discontinuing it. Drug allergies tend to be overdiagnosed (see AMPICILLIN RASH, page 334). Many drug symptoms, such as nausea or jitteriness, disappear when the dosage is reduced.

- Continue antibiotics until the bottle is empty. Your physician will prescribe the correct amount of antibiotic to kill all the bacteria. Stopping the antibiotic early can result in a flare-up.

- Give symptomatic medicines only when your child is having lots of symptoms (e.g., hacking cough) or is uncomfortable (e.g., fever over 102° or 103°F). These medicines do not need to be given continuously. If you decide to use them continuously, however, be certain to stop them once the symptoms have cleared for more than 12 hours.

- Don't give a prescription medicine to anyone except the person it was prescribed for—not to brothers or sisters, for instance. Some adult medicines are never prescribed for children because of their special side effects on the growing body, such as staining the teeth.

- Don't use outdated medicines. They lose their strength over time and some may be harmful. Most liquid antibiotics are worthless after 4 weeks, so discard them if any is left. Most other medicines are potent for 1 to 4 years. While pills usually last longer than liquid medicines, check the label for an expiration date.

RELATED TOPICS

Giving ear drops—see under EAR, SWIMMER'S, page 432
Giving eye drops—see under EYES, YELLOW DISCHARGE, page 416
Giving nose drops—see under COLDS, page 435

MEDICINES: HELPING CHILDREN SWALLOW THEM

A PREVENTIVE APPROACH
When your child is sick, he may need to take some medicines. For liquid medicines, a plastic syringe is easier to use than a spoon with infants or struggling children. If you have only a spoon, keep a towel handy for spillage.

Approach your child in a matter-of-fact way with an expectation that he will take it without resistance. Some children will respond better to an enthusiastic "Mary Poppins" approach.

Position your child sitting up, and place the contents of the syringe onto the floor of the mouth (next to the tongue). Don't squirt it into the pouch inside the cheek, because it won't go down when your child swallows. You must place the liquid beyond the teeth or gumline. Also, don't squirt it into the back of the throat, because of the danger of its going into the windpipe and causing choking. If you drip the medicine in slowly, you can avoid gagging or choking.

MEDICINES THAT TASTE BAD

Bitter medicines will often lead to refusal unless some of the following preventive steps are taken:

• Have your child suck on ice beforehand to partially numb the mouth.

• Serve the medicine cold to reduce the taste.

• Mix it with a strong fruit juice (such as cranberry juice) or Kool-Aid powder to hide the bad taste.

• Dilute the medicine as much as possible (e.g., 1 dose mixed in 2 glasses of cold apple juice), if you're certain your child can drink it all.

• Mix crushed pills with ice-cream toppings, honey, maple syrup, applesauce, or jelly. Before adding the medicine, have your child practice swallowing the topping alone without chewing it—since chewing would bring out the bad taste of the medicine.

• Have a glass of your child's favorite cold drink ready to rinse his mouth afterward—a sort of "chaser."

• Praise and hug your child for all cooperation.

• The older your child is, the more you can ask for his or her suggestions.

• Some respond to being given complete control of the spoon.

REFUSAL OF LIQUID MEDICINES

Some 1- to 4-year-old children vigorously refuse to take medicines. If the medicine is not essential to recovery (such as most nonprescription medicines), discontinue it. If you are uncertain of the importance of the medicine, call your physician for advice. If the drug is essential (such as most antibiotics), apply the following recommendations:

- Be honest and sympathetic ("I'm sorry it tastes bad").

- Be firm and give a reason ("You have to take it, or you won't get well").

- Don't threaten your child or bargain; take action.

- Immobilize your child. Two people are usually needed. Have your friend position your child on the lap, holding the arms with one hand and the head with the other. You can use one hand to hold the medicine and the other to open your child's mouth. If you are alone, first wrap your child with a sheet. Ask the office nurse to show you how this is done.

- Be sure your child is not lying flat, to prevent choking.

- Open your child's mouth by pushing down the chin or running your finger inside the cheek and pushing down on the lower jaw.

- Insert the syringe between the teeth and drip the medicine onto the back of the tongue.

- Keep the mouth closed until your child swallows. Gravity can help if you have your child in an upright position. However, swallowing can't occur if the head is bent backward.

- Afterward, apologize and review the alternative: "I'm sorry we had to hold you. If you cooperate next time, we won't have to."

- Give your child a hug.

- Forcing your child in this way to take an important medicine will teach him you mean business and will eventually bring cooperation.

- Don't attack self-esteem—for instance, by saying, "You're acting like a baby."

- Don't punish, as with spanking or yelling.

- If your child vomits or spits out the medicine, estimate the amount lost and repeat it.

REFUSAL OF PILLS OR CAPSULES
Some children have difficulty swallowing pills and capsules.

- The easiest approach is to empty out the capsules or to crush the pills. This approach is acceptable unless the product is a slow-release or enteric-coated pill. (Check with your physician if you are uncertain what you can do.)

- Slow-release capsules can be emptied as long as the contents are swallowed without chewing. Since capsules usually contain medicines with a bitter taste, the contents need to be mixed with a sweet food.

- Pills are usually made as a convenient alternative to the liquid form, and they may not taste bad. Pills can be crushed between two spoons. Crushing is made easier by first moistening the pill with a few drops of water and letting it soften for 15 minutes.

- If your child is over 6 years old and unable to swallow pills, he should practice this skill. (Some children can't accomplish pill-swallowing until age 10, however.) Place the pill or capsule far back on the tongue and have your child quickly drink water or Kool-Aid through a straw. If your child concentrates on swallowing the liquid, the pill will follow downstream without a hitch. If pills remain difficult, start with small pieces of candy or ice and progress to M & M's. Try to use substances that will quickly melt if they get stuck. If necessary, first coat them with butter. Use the liquid and straw technique. Once candy pellets are mastered, pills will usually be manageable. For extra confidence, split the pill into halves or quarters.

CALL YOUR CHILD'S PHYSICIAN IF

- Your child vomits the medicine more than once.
- You are unable to get your child to take an essential medicine.

  The next time your physician prescribes a medicine, be sure to mention that your child has this common problem. He may be able to prescribe one that tastes better.

FIRST AID KIT

The first aid kit may be needed at home, on a vacation, or while hiking or camping. Therefore, the contents should be kept in a small box that is portable. Medicines are usually not included.

- Band-Aids
- Sterile gauze pads—both regular and nonstick type
- Adhesive tape, ½-inch wide
- Steristrips or butterfly Band-Aids (for closing minor lacerations)
- Soap—small sample bar
- Alcohol wipes (individually wrapped packets)
- Triangular bandage (for sprained ankle or arm injury)
- Tourniquet (can use the triangular bandage)
- Needle and tweezers (for removing slivers or ticks)
- Razor blade (for poisonous snakebite)
- Papain (meat tenderizer powder for bee-stings)
- Insect repellent
- Sunscreen
- Adrenalin and syringes (optional: needed if family member has a severe bee-sting allergy) (See ALLERGIC REACTION, SEVERE, page 12 for details.)
- Optional medicines for camping: antibiotic ointment, hydrocortisone cream, antihistamines
- Extra supplies for hiking or camping: compass, whistle, flashlight, matches

HOME MEDICINE CHEST

This list of nonprescription drugs and supplies will be sufficient to relieve symptoms in the majority of acute illnesses that affect every family. Since these medicines will not shorten the course of the illnesses, give them only when symptoms are really bothering your child. See the specific guidelines for more details on using these drugs. (*CAUTION:* Keep these medicines locked up and away from children.)

- Acetaminophen: for fever or pain
- Aspirin: for pain only

- Thermometer, rectal and oral types
- Rubber suction bulb: for stuffy, blocked nose, after using warm water nose drops
- Vasoconstrictor nose drops: for severely blocked nose
- Butterscotch hard candies: for sore throat
- Cough drops or corn syrup: for mild coughs
- Dextromethorphan-containing (cough-suppressant) cough syrup: for severe coughs
- Humidifier (cool mist type): for coughs or croup
- Ice bag: for injured muscles, bones, and joints
- Long-acting vasoconstrictor eye drops: for irritated, reddened eyes
- Antibiotic eye drops: for bacterial eye infections with a yellow discharge (Note: This is the only prescription item on this list.)
- Cotton balls: for cleaning infected eyes
- Sunscreen (cream and lip balm)
- Hydrocortisone, ½ percent: for itchy skin conditions such as mosquito bites and poison ivy
- Bacitracin or Betadine ointment: for skin infections
- Acetone (nail polish remover): for removing tape from the skin
- Rubbing alcohol (70 percent isopropyl alcohol): for sterilizing the skin or needles
- Ipecac, syrup of (30 ml bottle): for inducing vomiting in some types of poisoning
- Antihistamine medicine (e.g., Chlortrimeton—4 mg tablets or 2 mg per teaspoon syrup): for hives, hay fever, and eye allergies (optional: needed if family members have allergies)
- Dramamine tablets: for motion sickness (optional: if family member has this condition)
- Gastrointestinal medicines: Vomiting and diarrhea respond best to dietary changes, and the numerous nonprescription medicines that are available are unnecessary or harmful. Acute constipation may occasionally require some milk of magnesia, but most children, again, respond to dietary change.

- Tincture of time: cures the majority of self-limited illnesses

- TLC (tender loving care): makes the time pass more quickly for most symptoms

IMMUNIZATION SCHEDULE

These immunizations protect your child against serious, life-threatening diseases. Check the recommended schedule. If your child's shots are not up-to-date, call your physician for an appointment. Ask for an immunization record card, keep it up-to-date, and bring it with you to health checkups and school enrollment.

IMMUNIZATION SCHEDULE

This is the schedule recommended by the American Academy of Pediatrics. The abbreviations are explained below.

AGE	IMMUNIZATION
2 months	DTP, OPV
4 months	DTP, OPV
6 months	DTP
12 months	TB
15 months	MMR
18 months	DTP, OPV
2 years	H. flu
5 years	DTP, OPV
15 years	Td

Explanation of Abbreviations

DTP: diphtheria, tetanus, pertussis (whooping cough)
H. flu: *Hemophilus influenzae* type b
MMR: measles, mumps, rubella
OPV: oral polio virus (drops, not a shot)
(Note: An OPV at the 6-month visit is optional.)
TB: tuberculosis skin test (tine test)
Td: adult tetanus and diphtheria (Note: Continue Td every 10 years throughout life.)

ALTERED SCHEDULE WITH MEASLES EXPOSURE

The measles vaccine can be given to a child as young as 6 months old during epidemics or if the child is exposed to measles. It will need repeating after 15 months of age. Call your child's physician during office hours for additional information.

TUBERCULOSIS SKIN TESTING

While not an immunization, the tuberculosis skin test is an important part of infectious-disease prevention. Early detection permits treatment and prevents spread of this serious lung disease. The frequency of repeat skin tests depends on the incidence of TB in your community and is a judgment best made by your child's physician.

Read your child's TB test 48 to 72 hours after it was placed. Call your child's physician for bumps at any of the 4 prong marks (not for redness). The test is positive if 2 bumps or more are touching.

SMALLPOX VACCINE

Smallpox has been eradicated from the world and vaccination is no longer necessary. The elimination of polio is our next challenge.

THE NEW VACCINE AGAINST *HEMOPHILUS INFLUENZAE* TYPE B

Hemophilus influenzae is a bacterium that causes several life-threatening diseases (e.g., meningitis, epiglottitis, and pneumonia) in young children. This new vaccine gives better than 90 percent protection against these diseases. The minor side effects of a sore injection site and mild fever occur in only 1.5 percent of children. This vaccine will not be given before 2 years of age because the antibody response is poor. If your child is over 2 years of age, the vaccine can still be helpful if given through age 5—that was the recommendation of the American Academy of Pediatrics' Committee on Infectious Diseases, reported in August 1985. The vaccine does not need to be repeated. Talk with your child's physician about this major advance in pediatrics. The vaccine was released in mid-1985.

IMMUNIZATION REACTIONS

RARE, SERIOUS REACTIONS

These vaccines protect children against terrible, life-threatening diseases. (It is worth noting that without protection, the death rate for tetanus and the paralysis rate for polio are both 50 percent.) The occurrence of all these diseases has been greatly reduced in our country. With these benefits, however, came a small risk of severe complications. (For example, following the polio vaccine, 1 person in 3 million actually gets polio.) During office visits for immunizations, your child's physician will probably provide you with information sheets describing the possible reactions to vaccines. Read these informed consent forms carefully and ask questions. Keep in mind that after careful thought, almost all physicians have decided to immunize themselves and their own children.

COMMON, NONSERIOUS REACTIONS

DTP Vaccine • DTP vaccines commonly produce fever, local tenderness, redness, and swelling for 24 to 48 hours. These symptoms can be treated with acetaminophen and cold compresses applied to the tender area. Call your child's physician immediately if your child cries for more than 3 hours, has a fever over 105°F, or has any other unusual reaction. Also, call during office hours if the redness, swelling, or fever lasts for more than 48 hours. A few children develop a small, painless lump (or nodule) at the injection site 1 to 2 weeks after the shot. This DPT nodule is harmless and disappears in about 2 months. Call your child's physician if it gets larger or becomes tender to the touch.

Measles Vaccine • The measles vaccine can result in a fever and rash about 7 to 10 days following the injection. The symptoms are mild, and no treatment is necessary. For details, see MEASLES VACCINE RASH, page 348.

Polio, Mumps, and Rubella Vaccines • There are no common reactions to polio, mumps, or rubella vaccine. A small percentage of older children have brief joint pain or swelling about 14 days following the rubella vaccine.

Egg Allergy • Children who are allergic to eggs can receive all the routine immunizations except measles. If the reaction to eggs was mild and delayed, the measles vaccine can be given. If the reaction to eggs occurred rapidly (within 2 hours of ingestion) or was severe (e.g., difficulty breathing or swallowing), your child should be skin-tested to determine if the measles vaccine would be safe.

PERTUSSIS VACCINE CONCERNS
The pertussis vaccine scare has made some parents postpone their child's immunizations. Keep in mind that pertussis (whooping cough) is a highly dangerous disease, especially for babies. (For babies with whooping cough disease, the death rate is 1% and the brain damage rate is 0.5%.) The chance of getting whooping cough without the vaccine is 1 in 3,000, whereas the risk of having neurological damage with the vaccine is 1 in 300,000. In addition, this risk for developing pertussis increases as the number of immunized children decreases. The American Academy of Pediatrics has stated clearly that "the risk of suffering and death caused by whooping cough is far greater than the possible side effects of the vaccine." The pertussis vaccine should be withheld initially only in children with epilepsy or serious neurologic disease. If you remain opposed, at least give your child the benefits of the tetanus and diphtheria (Td) vaccine. One false claim blamed pertussis vaccine for some crib deaths. Several studies proved that such an association did not exist.

IV

BEHAVIOR
PROBLEMS

BEHAVIOR PROBLEMS

NIGHT AWAKENING IN OLDER INFANTS

SYMPTOMS AND CHARACTERISTICS

- Your child is 4 to 24 months old. Babies normally awaken at night 1 or more times during the first 4 months of life
- Awakens and cries once or several times per night
- Receives parental attention or food at this time
- Usually occurs every night
- Usually has been present since birth
- Occurs in 10 percent to 15 percent of babies
- You would like to help your baby sleep through the night

  If your child's symptoms are different, call your child's physician for help.

Similar Topic • If colic is suspected, save time by turning directly to the guideline for CRYING BABY (COLIC), page 124.

Causes • The causes of resisting sleep or nighttime crying are many. While all children (especially during the first year of life) awaken several times per night following dreams, most can put themselves back to sleep. The ones who have not learned how to do this will instead cry for a parent. If the parent does too much (for instance, rocking), the infant becomes dependent on the parent for help in returning to sleep.

If the parent plays with the baby at these hours (which is a secondary gain), the child may elect to have such fun and games every night. These infants are "trained night criers" (see ROCKING and PROVIDING ENTERTAINMENT, below). The infants who demand to be fed as well as held are "trained night feeders" (see the first three paragraphs below). After 6 months of age, many infants have their normal separation fears accentuated at bedtime and during the night (see SEPARATION FEARS, below). The last three causes mentioned below can contribute to all three types of sleep problems.

Frequent Daytime Feedings • Some mothers misinterpret *demand feedings* to mean "feed the baby every time he cries." This can lead to feeding every 30 to 60 minutes. The stomach becomes conditioned to being fed small amounts frequently, instead of waiting at least 2 hours between feedings at birth (and at least 4 hours by 4 months of age). This problem usually occurs in breast-fed babies if nursing is provided for any distress and the breast has become a pacifier.

Leaving a Bottle in the Bed • Periodically during the night the child sucks on the bottle. When it becomes empty, he or she awakens fully and cries for a refill. In addition to sleep problems, bottles in bed (unless they contain only water) can lead to severe dental caries—known as "baby-bottle caries"—or ear infections.

Nursing the Baby to Sleep • If the last memory before sleep is sucking, the breast or bottle can become the infant's transitional object. (A transitional object is something that helps a waking child cross over into sleep—a teddy bear, for instance.) When he reawakens, the child may think that he cannot return to sleep without being on the breast.

Rocking the Baby to Sleep • Rocking your baby as part of the bedtime routine is great. However, some mothers continue to rock their infants until they go to sleep, even when they are not crying. Infants who have rarely been placed in their cribs while still awake expect their mothers to appear and help them go back to sleep when they awaken normally during the night. Instead of going back to sleep on their own, they cry. Since they customarily fall asleep away from their cribs, they never learn to associate the crib with sleeping.

Providing Entertainment During the Night • The awakening and crying behavior can become frequent if it leads to major secondary gain, such as being walked, rocked, played with, or enjoying other prolonged contact with the parent. Sleeping in the parents' bed reinforces the problem. Trained night crying can also follow an acute illness (e.g., blocked nasal passages) or a change in the infant's sleep environment (perhaps while traveling) during which the parents temporarily provide increased nighttime attention. Many infants quickly settle back into their previous sleep patterns, but some enjoy the nighttime contact so much that they continue in their demands.

Separation Fears • Separation anxiety normally occurs between 6 months and 2 years of age. It is seen during the day whenever the child loses sight of the mother or is left with a sitter, and these fears are often accentuated at bedtime and during the night. Separation fears can become the main content of nightmares.

Changing Diapers During the Night • Some parents check the baby's diaper during the night. If it is wet, they change it. The infant learns to find wetness uncomfortable, and thereafter cries at night whenever he or she is wet.

Excessive Daytime Naps • A baby can sleep only a certain number of hours a day.

Sleeping in the Same Room • Some babies are noisy sleepers. Also, many parents are light sleepers and respond to these normal baby noises. The father who wants his sleep may also pressure the mother to quiet the baby immediately. In addition, a baby who can see his or her parents has an incentive to continue trying to arouse them.

Expected Course • Most babies from birth to 2 months normally awaken twice a night for feedings. Between 2 and 3 months, most need 1 middle-of-the-night feeding. By 4 months of age, some 90 percent can sleep more than 8 consecutive hours without feeding. The remainder can learn to sleep through the night if the recommendations given below, under HELPING YOUR BABY SLEEP THROUGH THE NIGHT, are implemented. Improvement usually occurs in 2 weeks. The older the child, the harder his habits are to change. Infants over 1 year of age will vigorously protest any change and may cry for hours. Without treatment, however, these children don't start sleeping through the night until 3 or 4 years of age, when busy daytime schedules finally exhaust them.

HELPING YOUR BABY SLEEP THROUGH THE NIGHT

Select the aspects of treatment that correspond with the causes of your baby's sleep problem. If your baby is fed during the night, deal with this first (see TRAINED NIGHT FEEDERS, below). If he or she does not awaken for food, go directly to TRAINED NIGHT CRIERS. If your baby is very fearful, vomits, or cries nonstop for hours, start with FEARFUL NIGHT CRIERS. The last group of recommendations below apply to all three types.

Trained Night Feeders • 1. *Increase daytime feeding intervals to 4 hours or more.* Nighttime feeding intervals cannot be extended if daytime intervals remain short, because the stomach has been conditioned to expect frequent feedings and complains if they are delayed. Gradually postpone feeding times until they are more normal for your child's age. Your goal is 4 meals per day by 4 months of age and 3 meals per day by 6 to 9 months of age. (Note: Many breast-fed babies need to be nursed 5 times per day until 9 months of age. Some need the introduction of solids at 4 months of age to help them sleep through the night.) During the day, the infant's demands for unnecessary feedings can be met with extra holding, attention, and sometimes a pacifier. Once babies go to 3 meals per day and 5-hour intervals, many need midmorning and midafternoon snacks. The snack should be a small amount of a nutritious, nonmilk food. Fruit is recommended.

2. *Discontinue any bottle in bed immediately.* Feed your child at bedtime, but don't let him hold or keep the bottle. If he has increased sucking needs, offer him a pacifier or help him find his thumb. Also encourage attachment to a favorite stuffed animal or blanket as an alternative transitional object.

3. *Phase out night feedings.* Keep in mind that normal babies over 4 months old (and premature babies who have reached 11 pounds) do not need any calories during the night for health reasons. Once the daytime feeding intervals are normal (see step 1), nighttime awakening will probably spontaneously decrease or disappear. In the meantime, when your baby awakens at night and appears hungry, feed her but leave her slightly hungry. For bottle-fed babies, the amount can be decreased by 1 ounce every few nights until your infant no longer has a craving for food at this hour. For breast-fed

babies, just nurse on one side, or use pumped breast milk in a cup or bottle (which allows you to control the amount). The middle-of-the-night feeding shouldn't take more than 20 minutes. If it does, burping or handling is excessive.

Trained Night Criers • For nighttime crying, respond briefly or not at all. When your baby awakens and cries, wait at least 5 minutes before going into the room. Crying is not harmful, and infants cannot get over this problem without some crying. Infants should be taught to use their own resources to get back to sleep when they awaken at night. Remember that all children have 4 or 5 partial awakenings each night. If the crying continues, you can go in, but stay for 1 minute or less. When you go in, act sleepy; whisper, "Shhh, be quiet, everyone's sleeping," add a few reassuring comments, and give your infant some gentle pats. Do not turn on the lights. Do not remove your baby from the crib. If your child is standing in the crib, don't attempt to make him lie down. He can do this himself. Absolutely avoid major secondary gain, such as rocking or playing with your infant, bringing him to your bed, or staying in the room for more than 1 minute. Most young infants will cry for 30 to 60 minutes and then fall asleep. If crying continues, you may recheck your baby every 15 to 20 minutes for 1 minute or less if you feel it is necessary. However, don't stay in the room until your child goes to sleep. This brief contact will not reward your baby sufficiently to perpetuate the demanding behavior.

Some families, for various reasons—such as illness, workload, or visitors—can't tolerate *any* crying at night. Deal with the problem as suggested above, but only during naps and at bedtime for the first 2 weeks. At these times, place your child in the crib awake. Let her learn to go to sleep naturally. (During the middle of the night, you can sit next to the crib or even hold your baby. Don't feed her, however, or play with her, or take her to your bed.) After progress has been made during the day, apply the same corrective measures at night.

Fearful Night Criers • If your child sounds fearful, panics when you leave, cries until he vomits, or you know from past experience that he will cry nonstop for hours, take a different approach. Go in immediately and reassure him. Seeing a parent's face will usually calm him. Stay as long as it takes to calm him, but don't lift him out of the crib. At the most, sit in a chair next to the crib with your hand on your child's body. If you must stay, avoid eye contact, don't talk, and leave the lights out. If your child stands up in the crib, don't make him lie down. If you do, it will turn into a game. Now and then leave for a few minutes to teach your child that separation is tolerable. Do the same thing at naptime and bedtime. For separation fears, a night light (to offset fear of the dark) and leaving the bedroom door open (to offset fear of the parent being gone) are always important.

During the day, respond to fears with lots of hugs and comforting. Young babies may need more time being carried about in a front- or backpack. Also practice separation games like peek-a-boo, hide-and-seek, or chase-me. Children of working mothers especially need calm, unhurried breakfasts and extra cuddling time in the evenings—impossible on some days.

Intervention for All Types of Sleep Problems • 1. *Put your baby to bed awake.* Many trained night feeders and criers have rarely, if ever, been placed in their cribs while still awake. If your baby goes to sleep in your arms occasionally, that's fine. But usually place her in the crib awake for bedtime and all naps. Her last waking memory should be of the crib, not of you or the bottle. She must learn how to put herself to sleep without you being there. This step is crucial. Initially, she will complain—cry—about this new assignment.

2. *Move the crib to another room.* If your baby's crib is in your bedroom, move it to a separate room so you aren't awakened by your baby's normal tossing and turning. Likewise, your breathing and turning can awaken your baby. Do this at least by 2 months of age. If this is impossible, cover one side rail with a blanket so your baby can't see you when he normally awakens.

3. *Eliminate any long daytime naps.* If your baby has napped for over 3 hours, awaken him. If your baby takes 3 naps per day, try to convert him to 2. Also, your baby may not be tired at night because day care staff or babysitters have allowed him to sleep excessively during the day.

4. *Don't change diapers during the night.* Babies can survive until morning with a wet diaper. The exception to this guideline is soiled diapers at night (which are uncommon) or times when you are treating a bad diaper rash. If you must change your child, use a flashlight, do it quietly, and don't provide any entertainment.

CALL YOUR CHILD'S PHYSICIAN DURING OFFICE HOURS IF

- You feel the crying has a physical cause (e.g., an earache).
- Your child acts sick.
- Someone in your family can't tolerate any crying.
- Your infant isn't better after 2 weeks with this approach.
- You want additional information.

RECOMMENDED READING

Joanne Cuthbertson and Susanna Schevill, *Helping Your Child Sleep Through the Night* (New York: Doubleday, 1985).

Richard Ferber, *Solve Your Child's Sleep Problem* (New York: Simon & Schuster, 1985).

Sandy Jones, *Crying Baby, Sleepless Nights* (New York: Warner Books, 1983).

Vicki Lansky, *Getting Your Baby to Sleep* (New York: Bantam Books, 1985).

BEDTIME REFUSAL

SYMPTOMS AND CHARACTERISTICS

- Refusal to go to bed or stay in the bedroom
- Often accompanied by going to sleep while watching TV with the parent or sleeping in the parents' bed
- In a milder form, the child stays in the bedroom but prolongs the bedtime interaction with ongoing questions, unreasonable requests, protests, crying, or temper tantrums
- These children can come out of the bedroom because they no longer sleep in a crib
- Often tired in the morning and have to be awakened

Cause • These are manipulative behaviors, not fears. Your child has found a good way to postpone bedtime and receive all kinds of extra attention. Your child is stalling and taking advantage of your good nature. The child who occasionally comes to the parents' bed if he is frightened or not feeling well should be supported at these times. However, manipulative children try to share the parents' bed all night every night or sneak into their parents' bed during the middle of the night and attempt to spend the rest of the night there.

ENDING BEDTIME REFUSAL

Establish a rule that your child can't leave the bedroom at night • Your child needs to learn to put himself to sleep for naps and at bedtime in his own bed. Do not stay in the room until he lies down or falls asleep. Establish a set bedtime and stick to it. Make it clear that your child is not allowed to leave the bedroom between 8:00 at night and 7:00 in the morning (or whatever sleep time you decide upon). Obviously, this change won't be accomplished without some crying or screaming for a few nights.

If your child has been sleeping with you, tell him "Starting tonight, we sleep in separate beds. You have your room, we have our room. You have your bed, we have our bed. You are too old to sleep with us anymore."

Ignore Verbal Requests • Despite ongoing questions or demands from the bedroom, do not engage in any conversation with your child. All of these requests should have been dealt with during your pre-bedtime ritual. Before you give your last hug and leave your child's bedroom, ask "Do you need anything else?" Then don't return or talk with your child, unless you think he is sick. Some exceptions: If your child says he needs to use the toilet, tell him to take care of it himself. If your child says his covers have fallen off and he is cold, promise him you will cover him up after he goes to sleep. You will usually find him well covered.

Close the Bedroom Door if Your Child Screams • Tell your child that it will be opened again when he stops screaming. If he pounds on the door, you can open it after 1 or 2 minutes, and suggest that he go back to bed. If he does, you can leave the door open. If he doesn't, close the door again. For continued screaming or pounding on the door, reopen it approximately every 15 minutes and tell your child that if he quiets down the door can stay open. Never spend more than 30 seconds reassuring him.

Close the Bedroom Door if Your Child Comes Out • If your child comes out of the bedroom, return him immediately to his bed. During this process, avoid any lectures and skip the hug and kiss. Get good eye contact and remind him again that he cannot leave his bedroom during the night. Warn him that if he comes out again you will need to close the door. If he comes out, close the door for 2 or 3 minutes. If he continues to come out, close it for longer periods of time, up to 10 minutes.

Return Him to His Bed if He Comes into Your Bed at Night • For middle-of-the-night attempts to crawl into your bed, sternly order your child back to his own bed. If he doesn't move, escort him back immediately without any physical contact or pleasant conversation. If you are asleep when your child crawls into your bed, return him as soon as you discover his presence. If he attempts to come out again, temporarily close his door. If you are a deep sleeper, consider using some signaling device that will awaken you if your child enters your bedroom (such as a chair placed against your door or a loud bell attached to your doorknob). Some parents simply lock their bedroom door. Remind your child that it is not polite to interrupt other people's sleep. Tell him that if he awakens at night and can't go back to sleep, he can read or play quietly in his room, but he is not to bother his parents.

Barricade the Bedroom Door if Coming Out Continues • If your child is very determined and continues to come out of the bedroom, consider putting a barricade in front of his door. A helpful device is a half-door that is kept locked throughout the night. A heavy dresser, gate, or plywood plank may also serve this purpose. Then if your child screams at night, you can go to him without taking him out of his bedroom and say, "Everyone is sleeping, I'll see you in the morning." If your child attempts to climb over the barricade, a full door may need to be kept closed until morning with a hook, piece of rope, or chain lock. While you may consider this step extreme, it can be critical for protecting children less than 5 years old who wander through the house at night without an understanding of dangers (such as fire, hot water, knifes, going outside, etc.).

Help the Roommate • If the bedtime screaming wakes up a room-mate, have the well-behaved sibling sleep in a separate room until the nighttime behavior has improved. Tell your child with the sleep problem that his roommate cannot return until he stays in his room quietly for 3 consecutive nights. If you have a small home, have the sibling sleep in your room temporarily; this will be an added incentive for your other child to improve.

Praise Appropriate Sleeping Behavior • Praise your child in the morning if he stayed in his bedroom all night. Tell him that people are happier when they get a good night's sleep.

CALL YOUR CHILD'S PHYSICIAN DURING OFFICE HOURS IF

• Your child is not sleeping well after trying this program for 2 weeks.

• Your child is very frightened.

• Your child has lots of nightmares.

• Your child also has several discipline problems during the day.

• You have other questions or concerns.

BREATH-HOLDING SPELLS

SYMPTOMS AND CHARACTERISTICS

• Onset between 6 months and 2 years of age

• Occur only while child is awake

• Follow a precipitating event, such as falling down, being frustrated, or being frightened

• Crying once or twice

• Holding the breath in expiration until blue around the lips

• Passing out (One third of children also progress to having a few muscle jerks.)

• Breathing normally and fully alert in less than 1 minute

If your child's symptoms are different, call your physician for help.

Cause • Five percent of children have an abnormal reflex that allows them to hold their breath long enough to actually pass out. Holding the breath (when frustrated) and becoming bluish without passing out is so common in young infants, it is not considered abnormal.

Expected Course • The attacks occur from 1 or 2 times a day to 1 or 2 times a month, and are gone by age 4 or 5 years. They are not dangerous. The risk of epilepsy or brain damage is nil.

CALL YOUR CHILD'S PHYSICIAN

Immediately If

• Your child is less than 3 months old.

• Your child turns white instead of bluish.

During Office Hours If

• Your child holds his breath for more than 1 minute (by the clock).

• Any muscle jerks occur during the attack.

• More than 1 spell occurs per week.

• You have other questions.

HOME CARE FOR BREATH-HOLDING SPELLS

Treatment During Attacks • These attacks are harmless and always stop by themselves. Have your child lie flat to increase blood flow to the head. Apply an ice-cold wet washcloth to your child's forehead until he or she starts breathing again. Time the length of a few attacks, using a watch with a second hand. Don't start resuscitation; it's unnecessary. Also, don't put anything in your child's mouth; it could cause choking or vomiting. Above all, don't shake your baby, because it could lead to bleeding in the brain (subdural hematomas).

Treatment After Attacks • Give your child a brief hug and go about your business. A relaxed attitude is best. If you are frightened, don't let your child know it. If your child had a temper tantrum that progressed to a breath-holding spell because she wanted her way over something, don't give in to her after the attack. Breath-holding attacks should not result in any payoff for your child, any more than a temper tantrum should.

Prevention of Breath-Holding Spells • Most attacks from falling down or a sudden fright can't be prevented. Neither can most attacks that are triggered by anger. However, if your child is having daily attacks, he probably has learned to trigger the attacks himself. This happens when parents run to the child and pick him up every time he starts to cry, or when they give him his way as soon as the attack is over. Avoid these responses, and your child won't have an undue number of attacks.

Call Your Child's Physician Later If

• The attacks become more frequent.

• You have other questions about breath holding.

DISCIPLINE BASICS

GOALS OF DISCIPLINE

The first goal of discipline is to protect your child from danger. But the higher goal of discipline is teaching right from wrong. Good discipline gradually changes a self-centered child into a mature adult who is responsible, thoughtful, and respectful of others, assertive without being hostile, and in control of his or her impulses. Discipline means to teach, not to punish. To teach respect for the rights of others, first teach your child about parents' rights. Children need a parent who is "in charge." Begin external controls by 4 months of age when you gradually change from a demand schedule of feeding to fitting your child into your schedule. Children start to develop internal controls (self-control) at 3 or 4 years of age. They continue to need external controls (in gradually decreasing amounts) through adolescence.

Another view of discipline is that limit-setting can prevent spoiling. A spoiled child makes unfair or excessive demands on others, doesn't respond to "no" or "stop," always wants an adult to entertain him, and can't tolerate normal frustrations, such as waiting for something. A spoiled child becomes difficult for the parents to love and unacceptable to the adult world. Such children are usually spoiled because of lenient parents who give in to whining and don't follow through with what they say. In addition, parents of a spoiled child tend to be overly available to their child to the point that he doesn't need to learn how to comfort himself, put himself to sleep, or amuse himself. Such parents want the best for their children and don't realize the consequences.

A misconception about spoiling is that it is caused by holding a baby too much. Holding babies is equivalent to loving them. Most cultures hold their babies much more than we do, but without spoiling them. Closeness is good for people.

HOW TO BEGIN A DISCIPLINE PROGRAM

If your child has several discipline problems or is out of control, start here. If you are reading to learn more about normal discipline, go directly to GUIDELINES FOR SETTING RULES, below.

1. *List any problem behavior.* What do you want to change? Take 3 or 4 days to note and write down your child's inappropriate or annoying behavior traits.
2. *Set priorities on correcting the problem behavior.* Some modes of behavior need immediate attention—for instance, those that might cause harm to your child or others. Some are too annoying or obnoxious to be ignored (such as not going to bed). Some instances of unpleasant behavior (such as negativism) are normal and must be tolerated (see TERRIBLE TWOS, page 208). Some families who have an out-of-control child have too many rules and need to rethink what can be overlooked.
3. *Write house rules concerning the most important kinds of misbehavior* (see GUIDELINES FOR SETTING RULES, below).
4. *Devise a discipline response for each type of misbehavior* (see DISCIPLINE [PUNISHMENT] TECHNIQUES, page 196). All behavior, good and bad, is predominantly shaped by consequences. If the consequence is pleasant (a reward or praise), behavior is more likely to be repeated. If the consequence is unpleasant (a punishment), behavior is less likely to be repeated. Young children usually do not respond to lectures or reminders. The best way to get your child to stop doing something is to take action. The most helpful actions are ignoring the misbehavior, redirecting to appropriate behavior, or putting your child into timeout.
5. *Temporarily discontinue any physical punishment* (see REASONS TO LIMIT OR AVOID PHYSICAL PUNISHMENT, page 200).

Most out-of-control children are already too aggressive. Physical punishment teaches them that aggression is acceptable for solving problems.

6. *Discontinue any yelling.* Yelling and screaming teach your child to yell back, thereby legitimizing shouting matches. They also convey that you are not in charge. Yelling often escalates the disagreement and turns it into a win-lose battle. Your child will respond better in the long run to a pleasant tone of voice and words of diplomacy.

7. *Don't take your child to public places until his or her behavior is under control at home.* Misbehaving children are usually more difficult to control in a shopping mall or supermarket. Leave your child with a babysitter or spouse when you need to go to these places.

8. *Take daily breaks from your child.* Ask your spouse to spell you from supervising your young child, to take over all the discipline for a few hours. If this is impossible, hire a teenager a few times a week to look after your child while you go out. Also make a "date" for a weekly night out with your spouse.

9. *Give your child increased positive feedback* (see GUIDELINES FOR POSITIVE REINFORCEMENT, page 202.) Children respond to discipline from people they feel loved by and want to please. Every child needs daily praise, smiles, and hugs. Give your child this increased attention when he is not demanding it, especially if he is behaving in an adaptive way. When all is quiet in your house, make the rounds and catch your child being good. If your child receives more negative comments and criticisms each day than positive responses, you need to restore an emotionally healthy balance by reducing the rules, reducing the criticism, and increasing the positive contacts. Many experts feel that it takes several positive contacts to counter one negative one.

10. *Protect your child's self-esteem.* Your child's self-esteem is more important than how well disciplined he or she is. Don't discuss his discipline problems and your concerns about him when he is around. Correct your child in a kindly way. Sometimes begin your correction with "I'm sorry I can't let you ———." Don't label your child a "bad girl" or "bad boy." After punishment is over, accept your child back into the family circle, convey that all is forgiven and give him a clean slate.

GUIDELINES FOR SETTING RULES

1. *Begin discipline at about 4 months of age.* Prior to 4 months of age, infants don't need any discipline. Starting at this age, however, parents can begin to clarify their own rights. If your child kicks and wiggles during a diaper change, making the process difficult, you can say firmly, "No, help Mommy change your diaper." By 8 months of age, children need rules for safety purposes.

2. *Express each example of misbehavior with a clearly defined rule or instruction.* Vague descriptions of misbehavior (such as "hyperactive," "irresponsible," or "mean") are not helpful. The younger the child, the more concrete the rule must be. Examples of clear rules are: "Don't push your brother" and "Don't interrupt me on the telephone."

3. *Also state the desired, adaptive, acceptable, or appropriate behavior.* Your child needs to know what is expected of him or her. Examples are: "Play with your brother," "Look at books when I'm on the telephone," or "Walk, don't run." Praise your child at these times. Make your praise specific (e.g., "Thank you for being quiet").

4. *Overlook unimportant or irrelevant misbehavior.* The more rules you have, the less likely your child is to listen. Constant criticism is usually ineffective. Behavior such as swinging the legs, poor table manners, or normal negativism are unimportant during the early years.

5. *Use rules that are fair and attainable.* Rules must be age-appropriate. A child should not be punished for clumsiness when he or she is learning to walk, nor for poor pronunciation when learning to speak. In addition, a child should not be punished for behavior that is part of normal emotional development, such as thumbsucking, separation fears, and toilet training confusion.

6. *Concentrate on two or three rules initially.* The highest priority is given to issues of safety, such as not running into the street. Of equal importance is the prevention of harm to others—parents, other children and adults, or animals. Destructive behavior toward property is of the next importance. Then come all the annoying behavior traits that wear you down.

7. *Avoid trying to change "no-win" behavior through punishment.* This type of misbehavior usually involves a body part. Examples are wetting, soiling, hair-pulling, thumbsucking, body rocking, masturbation, not eating enough, not going to sleep, and refusing to complete schoolwork.

No-win behavior is usually uncontrollable by the parent if the child decides to continue it. The first step in resolving a power struggle is to withdraw from the conflict. Then apply positive reinforcement and praise (see GUIDELINES FOR POSITIVE REINFORCEMENT, page 202).

8. *Apply the rules consistently.* After the parents agree on the rules, it may be helpful to print them out and post them in a conspicuous place in the home.

DISCIPLINE (PUNISHMENT) TECHNIQUES

Techniques by Age

• From birth to 4 months: no discipline necessary

• From 4 to 8 months: mild verbal disapproval

• From 8 to 18 months: structuring the environment, distracting, ignoring, verbal and nonverbal disapproval, manual guidance, and temporary timeout in a playpen

• From 18 months to 3 years: the preceding techniques plus temporary timeout in a chair

• From 3 years to 5 years: the preceding techniques plus temporary timeout in a room, natural consequences, logical consequences, restricting places where the child can misbehave

• From 5 years to adolescence: the preceding techniques plus delay of a privilege, negotiation and family conferences, and "I" messages.

• Adolescence: We can't discipline adolescents the way we discipline preschoolers (and vice versa). By the time your child is an adolescent you should discontinue manual guidance and timeout techniques (see ADOLESCENTS: DEALING WITH NORMAL REBELLION, page 297).

Structuring the Home Environment • The surroundings can be modified so that an object or situation that could potentially cause a problem is eliminated. Examples are: putting breakables out of reach, fencing in a yard, setting up gates, putting locks on a special desk, or locking certain rooms.

Distracting, Redirecting, or Diverting • Distracting a child counteracts one temptation with a different temptation. Distraction is especially helpful with young children when they are in someone else's house, a physician's office, or a store where other options for discipline (such as timeout) would be difficult to employ. It also can be used preventively if you're going to be busy at home with guests, the telephone, or feeding a baby. Most children can be distracted with toys or food. School-age children may need books, games, or other activities to keep their attention.

Ignoring the Misbehavior • Ignoring, or extinction, is a technique that is helpful for eliminating unacceptable behavior that is harmless, such as tantrums, sulking, whining, quarreling, or interrupting. The proper way to ignore is to move away from your child, turn your back, avoid eye contact, and stop any conversation with your child. Ignore any protests or excuses. At times, you may need to leave the area where your child is misbehaving.

Verbal and Nonverbal Disapproval • Mild disapproval is often all that is required to stop a young child's misbehavior. The proper technique is to move close to your child, obtain eye contact, assume a stern facial expression, and give a brief, direct instruction such as "no" or "stop." Your comments can be made in a soft but disapproving tone, since you are close to your child. Also show your child what you want him to do (the adaptive behavior). You may want to underscore your serious intent by pointing or shaking your finger. The most common mistake in using this technique is smiling or laughing.

Manual Guidance (Physical Removal or Delivery) • Manual guidance is the process of moving a child from one place to another against his or her will. Sometimes children must be physically removed, from a place where they are causing trouble, to a timeout chair. Other children must be physically taken to the bed, bath, or car when they refuse to go. The correct technique is guiding your child by the hand or forearm. If he refuses to be led, pick him up from behind and carry him.

Temporary Timeout or Social Isolation • Temporary timeout is the most effective discipline technique available to parents for dealing with misbehaving infants and young children. See THE TIMEOUT TECHNIQUE (page 204) for details. Timeout should be applied briefly, on the order of 1 minute per year of age.

Natural Consequences • Natural consequences are the negative results of your child's own actions. They permit your child to learn from the natural laws of the physical world. Examples are: Coming to dinner late means the food will be cold; not dressing properly for the weather means your child will be cold or wet; not wearing mittens while playing in the snow will lead to cold hands; running on ice will usually lead to falling down; putting sand in the mouth leads to an unpleasant taste; breaking a toy means it's no longer playworthy; and going to bed late means being sleepy in the morning. Although it is very helpful for children to learn from their mistakes, it is important that they not be allowed to engage in behavior that could be harmful, such as playing with matches or running into the street.

Restricting Places Where a Child Can Misbehave • This technique is especially helpful for behavior problems that can't be eliminated. Allowing the misbehavior in your child's room prevents an unnecessary power struggle. Indications include: thumbsucking, nose picking, and masturbation. Roughhousing can be restricted to outdoors. The child's tricycle can be restricted to the basement in the wintertime.

Delay of a Privilege • This technique requires that a less preferable activity be completed before a more preferable one is allowed ("work before play"). Examples are: "After you clean your room, you can go out and play"; "When you finish your homework, you can watch TV"; and "When you have tasted all your foods, you can have your dessert."

Logical Consequences • Logical consequences permit children to learn from the reality of the social order. These consequences should be logically related to the unacceptable behavior. Many logical consequences are simply the temporary removal of a possession or privilege. Examples are: removal of toys or crayons that are mishandled, not replacing a lost toy, not repairing a broken toy, sending your child to school partially dressed if she won't dress herself, having your child clean up milk he has spilled or a floor he has tracked mud on, having your child clean up underwear if she has soiled it, and turning off the TV if siblings are quarreling about it. In addition, TV, telephone, shopping, bicycle, and car privileges can all be temporarily suspended if they are misused. The schoolteacher will provide appropriate logical consequences if your child does not complete homework assignments.

Some mistakes made by parents in the area of providing consequences are depriving children of: basic essentials, such as a meal; of activities with an organized peer group, like a team or scout troop; or of greatly anticipated events, such as going to the circus. The main thrust of logical consequences is to make your child accountable for his or her problems and decisions. It is important for children to learn from experience and not be sheltered from realities.

"I" Messages • When your child misbehaves, preface your correction by telling your child how you feel. Say "I am angry" or "I am upset when you do such and such." This approach tends to cause less negative or defensive reactions than "you" messages. (For details see ADOLESCENTS: DEALING WITH NORMAL REBELLION, page 297.)

Negotiation and Contracts • As children become older they need more communication and discussion with their parents. A parent can initiate such a conversation by stating: "We need to change these things. Where do you want to start?" Family conferences also become helpful (see ADOLESCENTS: DEALING WITH NORMAL REBELLION, page 297).

GUIDELINES FOR IMPLEMENTATION OF PUNISHMENTS

• *Be unambivalent.* Mean what you say. Be stern and tough. You know the rules, so take charge.

• *Correct with love.* Talk to your child the way you would want to be talked to. Avoid yelling or using a disrespectful tone of voice. For example, say, "I'm sorry you left the yard, but now you must stay in the house."

• *Precede punishment by one warning or reminder.* After the rule is clearly understood, this warning is unnecessary and you can punish your child without a warning. Avoid repeated threats of punishment if your child doesn't stop what he is doing.

• *With aggressive behavior, punish your child for clear intent.* Interrupt your child before someone is hurt or damage is done. An example would be that you see your child raising a toy to hit a playmate. Intervene before the friend is injured.

• *Apply punishment immediately.* Delayed punishments are less effective, because young children forget why they are being punished. Punishment should occur close in time to the misdeed and be administered by the adult who witnessed the misbehavior. An exception for children older than 4 or 5 years of age is when they misbehave outside the home, thereby taking advantage of you. You may put check marks on your child's hand with a felt-tip pen to indicate the number of punishments to be meted out when you get home. Punishment might be 5 minutes of timeout or 30 minutes of lost TV time for each check mark.

• *Make a one-sentence comment about the rule* during correction. However, avoid making a long speech.

• *Ignore your child's arguments during correction.* This is the child's way of delaying punishment. Especially under 3 years of age, children mainly understand action, not words.

• *Make the punishment brief.* Toys can be taken out of circulation for no more than 1 or 2 days. Timeout should be on the order of 1 minute per year of age.

• *Keep the punishment in proportion to the misbehavior.* Also try to make the punishment relate to the misbehavior (see LOGICAL CONSEQUENCES, above).

• *Follow the punishment by trust.* Welcome your child back into the family circle and do not comment upon the previous misbehavior or require an apology for it.

• *Direct the punishment against the misbehavior,* not the person. Avoid degrading comments such as "You never do anything right."

• *Don't be surprised* if your child temporarily shows an increased frequency of bad behavior once you start dealing with it consistently. Children who are out of control initially go through a phase of testing their parents before they comply with the new system. This testing usually lasts 2 or 3 days.

REASONS TO LIMIT OR AVOID PHYSICAL PUNISHMENT

The place of physical punishment in discipline is controversial. My personal preference is that parents use little if any corporal punishment. We can raise children to be agreeable, responsible, productive adults without ever spanking them. (I didn't say without ever disciplining them.) All children need discipline on hundreds of occasions but there are alternatives to spanking. A parent can just as readily "clear the air" by sending a child to his or her room. Spanking carries the risk of triggering the unrelated pent-up anger that many adults carry inside them. This anger can start a chain reaction ending in child abuse. Parents who turn to spanking as a last resort for "breaking their child's will" may find that they have underestimated their child's determination. In addition, physical punishment makes aggressive behavior worse. It teaches a child to lash out when he or she is angry. Other forms of discipline are more constructive in that they leave a child with some guilt and the early formation of a conscience.

We might ponder why physical punishment by parents is prohibited by law in Sweden. Physical punishment by school personnel is also illegal in more than twenty countries, including the Scandinavian countries, Japan, Italy, and Israel. (The same holds true for only three of our fifty states.) At this time, however, over 90 percent of American parents use some physical punishment in child rearing, and most of them are not ready to give up this type of power over their children.

If you feel the need occasionally to spank your child, certain guidelines for safe physical punishment can be followed.

- Hit only with an open hand. Hitting your child with any instrument interferes with your ability to measure the amount of force you are applying. Paddles and belts commonly cause bruises, some not intended.

- Hit only on the buttocks, legs, or hands. Hitting a child on the face is demeaning as well as dangerous; in fact, slapping the face is inappropriate at any age.

- One swat is enough to change behavior. Hitting your child more than once is more to relieve your anger than to teach your child anything additional.

- Spanking is inappropriate before your child has learned to walk. An upper age limit of 6 to 8 years makes sense, because negotiation and discussion should be used to resolve most differences with school-age children.

- Physical punishment should not be used more than once per day. The more your child is spanked, the less effect it will have.

- Physical punishment should not be used for aggressive misbehavior such as biting, hitting, or kicking. Physical punishment under such circumstances teaches a child that it is all right for a bigger person to strike a smaller person. Aggressive children need to be taught restraint and self-control. They respond best to timeout and an opportunity to think about the pain they have caused.

• Because of the serious risk of causing blood clots on the brain (subdural hematomas), avoid shaking any young child.

• You will need alternatives to physical discipline. Timeout or brief social isolation is much more civilized and effective. Learn the fine points of implementing it (see THE TIMEOUT TECHNIQUE, page 204).

• Babysitters and teachers should not be allowed to spank other people's children. You may wish to clarify this.

• Never spank your child when you are out of control, scared, or drinking. A few parents can't stop hitting their child once they start. They can't control their rage and need help for themselves, such as from Parents Anonymous groups. They must learn to walk away from their children and never initiate physical punishment.

GUIDELINES FOR POSITIVE REINFORCEMENT OF DESIRED BEHAVIOR

Most parents don't give enough positive reinforcement—especially praise. Don't take good behavior for granted. Watch for behavior you like, then praise your child by saying such things as "I like the way you ———," or "I appreciate ———." When you give positive social reinforcement (positive strokes), move close to your child, look at him or her, smile, and be physically affectionate. Although it takes little time or energy, a parent's attention is the favorite reward of most children.

Social reinforcement should principally be used when your child behaves in an adaptive or desired way. Praise the behavior, not the person. Examples are: sharing toys, demonstrating good manners, doing chores, playing cooperatively, treating the baby gently, petting the dog, being a good sport, cleaning the room, or reading a book. Your child can also be praised for trying, such as trying to use the potty or attempting something difficult, like a puzzle. Positive reinforcement will increase the frequency of desired behavior.

You should try to "catch" your child being good, and comment on it three or more times for every one time you discipline or criticize your child. Although difficult, it can be achieved. Some families with teenagers have increased everybody's ability to pay attention to positives by providing each member with ten thank-you cards, one of which is given to a family member whenever one is helpful to another. This increases everybody's awareness of working cooperatively. Social reinforcers are especially helpful when a child is having a bad day.

Special material reinforcers are usually candy or money. While these tangible reinforcers tend to be overused by many parents, other parents are completely opposed to them. They consider them to be bribes. To my way of thinking, a bribe is when something like candy is given to a child for not doing something bad. This type of misbehavior could be dealt with by isolation or some other form of punishment. When I suggest material reinforcers, they are as incentives rather than bribes. As incentives they are used for increasing the frequency of more responsible behavior. Incentives may be helpful in overcoming inertia when children need to engage in an unpleasant behavior, such as eating less for weight loss. They may be useful in overcoming resistance when children are entrenched in power struggles around "no-win" behaviors (e.g., soiling). These reinforcers should be used for only one problem behavior at a time and when praise alone hasn't worked. They should be phased out and replaced by natural (social) reinforcers as soon as possible.

CALL YOUR CHILD'S PHYSICIAN DURING OFFICE HOURS IF

- The misbehavior is dangerous.
- The instances of misbehavior seem too numerous to count.
- Your child is also having behavior problems at school.
- Your child doesn't have many good points.
- Your child seems depressed.
- The parents can't agree on discipline.
- You can't give up physical punishment. (Note: Call immediately if you are afraid you might hurt your child.)
- The misbehavior does not improve in one month using this approach.

RECOMMENDED READING

Edward R. Christophersen, *Little People: Guidelines for Common Sense Child Rearing* (Lawrence, Kan.: H and H Enterprises, 1977).

Don Dinkmeyer and Gary D. McKay, *The Parent's Handbook: Systematic Training for Effective Parenting* (Circle Pines, Minn.: American Guidance Service, 1982).

Thomas Gordon, *P.E.T.*, *Parent Effectiveness Training* (New York: New American Library, 1975).

Charles E. Schaefer and Howard L. Millman, *How to Help Children with Common Problems* (St. Louis: Mosby Medical Library, 1983).

Jerry Wyckoff and Barbara C. Unell, *Discipline Without Spanking or Shouting* (Deephaven, Minn.: Meadowbrook, 1984).

THE TIMEOUT TECHNIQUE

Timeout is a technique used to interrupt unacceptable behavior by removing your child from the area of trouble and placing your child in a chair or room that is more or less isolated. Timeout has the advantage of providing a cooling-off period to allow both child and parent to regain control of their emotions. It prevents the parent from feeling guilty afterward about excessively punishing the child. A child over age 2 or 3 is given a chance to think about the misbehavior and feel a little remorseful about it. This thinking time is the beginning of the formation of a conscience. For a child less than 2 years of age, timeout mainly establishes who is in charge.

Some parents ask what they should do if timeout doesn't work. That shouldn't happen. There's nothing better than timeout. It's much more effective than threatening, shouting, or spanking your child. If used appropriately and repeatedly, it can change any childhood misbehavior. Timeout is your trump card.

Misbehavior that responds to timeout may be aggressive, harmful, or disruptive behavior that cannot be ignored. Timeout is unnecessary for most temper tantrums. Timeout is not needed until at least 8 months of age, when children begin to crawl. By 6 years of age, it can gradually be replaced with logical consequences. By 10 or 12 years of age, timeout is no longer appropriate or accepted.

CHOOSING A PLACE FOR TIMEOUT

Playpens or Cribs • Playpens or cribs are convenient places for timeout with infants. The playpen is preferable because most infants are frightened if they are not in the same room as their parents. If a crib is used, it should have the spring support positioned at the lowest setting. Once a child is able to climb out of the crib or playpen, it can no longer be used for timeout.

Chairs or Corners • A child can be told to sit in a chair if he or she is cooperative. The chair should be placed in a dull, uneventful setting. The chair can be placed facing toward a corner. Some parents prefer to have their child stand facing the corner. A chair is often a good choice for punishment when the child is in a public place such as a store, restaurant, or swimming pool area.

Rooms • Many parents prefer a room for timeout because it offers more confinement and isolation than a chair. Until 3 years of age, most children become frightened if they are put in a room with a closed door. Other ways to barricade your child in a room without completely closing it off are with a gate, a heavy dresser that blocks the lower part of the door frame, or a plank of plywood that goes halfway up the door and is dropped between some runners. Occasionally a parent with carpentry skills can put a half-door or screen door on the timeout room.

The most convenient room for timeout is the child's bedroom. There are two misconceptions about using the bedroom for timeout: namely that the association with punishment will cause sleep problems, and that the toys and distractions in most bedrooms will interfere with time there being considered a punishment. Both of these concerns are unfounded. When a child is put in the bedroom (assuming it doesn't have a TV or radio), the child initially is upset about being excluded from the mainstream and can't focus on playing. Bathrooms and kitchens are a poor choice for timeout because they contain potentially dangerous objects. Dark closets or basements are poor choices because they can be scary for the child.

Closing or Locking the Bedroom Door • Most children under 3 years of age, when sent to the bedroom, will stay there until they are told they can come out. However, some children with poor self-control will come out just as soon as they are put in. If you cannot devise a barricade, then the door must be closed. You can hold the door closed for the 3 to 5 minutes it takes to complete the timeout period. If you don't want to hold the door, you can put a latch on the door that allows it to be temporarily locked. Your child should not be forgotten and kept in timeout longer than a few minutes.

Other Sites for Timeout • If your child is over age 5 and might damage his room, he can be sent outside to the porch or yard. This is also a good place to send a child who is misbehaving at someone else's home. Sometimes your child can be sent to stand or sit in the hallway. If you are in a public place, use a bench or a rest room for timeout. If your child is outdoors with you and misbehaves, he or she can be requested to stand facing a tree.

Other examples of using timeout are: if you are holding your child when he or she misbehaves (e.g., pulls your hair), the child can be put down. If your child misbehaves with a friend, the friend can be sent home. For older children you may leave the room and say, "That's all I have to say on that subject."

HOW TO ADMINISTER TIMEOUT

How Long • Timeout should be short enough so that your child has many chances to go back to the original situation and learn the acceptable behavior. A good rule of thumb is 1 minute per year of age with a maximum of 5 minutes. A kitchen timer is often helpful and can be set for the required number of minutes in timeout. Place the timer where your child can see or hear it. By age 6 most children can be sent to their room "until you can behave," allowing them to choose how long they stay there. If your child leaves timeout early ("escapes"), he or she should be returned to timeout and the timer reset. If your child must be escorted to timeout (once she has reached an age where she usually goes by herself), the timeout time can be doubled. If your child quickly repeats the misbehavior after being released from timeout, the next punishment should also be for an extended time.

Putting Your Child in Timeout • If your child misbehaves, state the rule briefly and send him or her to the timeout chair or room. If he doesn't go immediately, lead him there with manual guidance or, if necessary, carry him there facing him away from you. Expect your child to cry, protest, or have a tantrum on the way to timeout. Don't lecture or spank on the way. Also, don't answer his pleas.

Keeping Your Child in Timeout • Once children understand timeout, most of them will stay there until the time is up. However, you will have to keep an eye on your child. If she gets up from a chair, put her back quickly without spanking. Reset the timer. If your child comes out of the room, intercept her and reset the timer. Also threaten to close the door if she comes out a second time. If your child is a strong-willed 2- or 3-year-old and you are introducing the timeout approach, you may initially need to hold her in the chair with one hand on her shoulder for the entire 2 minutes. Don't be discouraged; this does teach her that you mean what you say. No one should talk with your child while she is in timeout. In fact, no one should be around her (unless she's the hardheaded kind you need to hold in the chair). Isolation and silence are part of the lesson. If your other children touch the timer or tease the child in timeout, they should also be placed in timeout.

Releasing Your Child from Timeout • Make it clear that you are in charge of when timeout ends. After you place your child in timeout, listen carefully for the timer or keep an eye on your watch. Go to your child and state, "Timeout is over. You can get up now." Then treat your child normally and give him a clean slate. Don't review the rule your child broke. Try to notice some positive behavior on your child's part and praise him for it as soon as possible. If your child repeats the problem behavior, quickly repeat the entire process.

Some parents don't start the timer until their child is completely quiet. If the child yells or cries during timeout, the previous time doesn't count. From my experience, as long as the child remains in timeout, it really doesn't matter whether or not he's quiet. If he's having a temper tantrum in timeout, ignore it. The important thing is that he stay there for a certain time period. Your child will not be able to understand the need for quietness until at least 3 years of age, so don't expect this of him before then.

Dealing with a Child Who Messes up the Timeout Room • Children who are out of control can become destructive of their rooms. They may write on the walls, empty out their drawers, or take their beds apart. Your response can include having your child clean up the mess before she leaves the room or taking any toys out of circulation that have been misused. If your child is older, have her pay for the repair of any damage. Some damage may be prevented by removing any scissors or crayons from your child's room in advance.

Practicing Timeout with Your Child • If you have not used timeout before, go over it with your child in advance. Tell your child it will replace spanking, yelling, and other forms of discipline. Review the kinds of negative behavior that will lead to placement in timeout. Also review the positive behavior that you would prefer. Then pretend with your child that he has broken one of the rules. Take him through the steps of timeout so he will understand your directions when you send him to timeout in the future. Also teach this technique to your babysitter.

THE TERRIBLE TWOS AND TEMPER TANTRUMS

From 18 months to 3 years of age many children are in the "Terrible Twos." Stubbornness, opposition, or outright defiance may principally characterize their behavior. They normally are noisy (not quiet), busy (not still), distractible (not focused), impulsive (not cautious), and negative (not cooperative). No matter how calm and gentle a parent you are, your child will throw some temper tantrums. Your child will say no to many of your reasonable requests. You may feel helpless and at your child's mercy. Not until adolescence will you again be put through such an ordeal.

The Terrible Twos are a normal phase in child development. Your child is not deliberately trying to irritate you. Negativism is a normal step in becoming independent. Temper tantrums are a normal step in becoming more verbal. The children who have the most severe form of the Terrible Twos usually are "difficult" children by temperament. From birth they stand out as infants who resist anything new, react intensely, and are unpredictable in their behavior. Occasionally a parent makes the Terrible Twos worse by being excessively strict or having unreasonable expectations. Fortunately all children pass through this phase into a more cooperative one.

DEALING WITH NORMAL NEGATIVISM

Negativism is a normal phase seen in most children between 18 months and 3 years of age. During this time children respond to many requests (including pleasant ones) negatively. They are stubborn in general. They delight in refusing a suggestion, be it to get dressed or take off their clothes, take a bath or get out of the bathtub, go to bed or get up. As a bonus, the better you handle this phase, the fewer temper tantrums your child will have. Consider the following guidelines for helping your child through this phase.

- *Don't take this normal phase too seriously.* To your child, "No" means "Do I have to?" or "Do you mean it?" This response should not be confused with disrespect. This phase is important for self-determination and identity. Try to look at it with a sense of humor and it may last only 6 to 12 months.

- *Don't punish for saying "No."* Punishment should be for what your child does, not what he or she says. Since you can't eliminate the "No," ignore it.

- *Give your child extra choices.* This is the best way to increase your child's sense of freedom and control, so that he or she will become more cooperative. Examples of choices are letting your child choose between a shower or a bath, choose which book is read, which toys go in the tub, which fruit is eaten for a snack, which clothes or shoes will be worn, which breakfast cereal eaten, which game played, whether inside or outside, in the park or in the yard, and so forth. Even for a task your child doesn't like, he can be given a say in the matter by asking him, "Do you want to do it slow or fast?" or "Do you want me to do it, or you?" The more quickly your child gains a feeling that he is a decision-maker, the more quickly this phase will be over.

- *Don't give your child a choice when there is none.* Safety rules are not open to discussion. Taking a bath, going to bed, or going to daycare also are not things that can be negotiated. Don't ask a question when there's only one answer. When a request such as this must be made, it can be presented in as positive a form as possible ("Let's do this"). Directives ("Do this or else") should be avoided.

- *Give transition time when changing activities.* If your child is having fun and must change to another activity, he or she probably needs a transition time. For example, when playing with trucks as dinnertime approaches, your child needs a 5-minute warning. A kitchen timer sometimes helps a child accept the change. Set the timer and say, "In five minutes, it will be time to stop playing and come to eat dinner."

• *Eliminate excessive rules.* The more rules you have, the less likely it is that your child will be agreeable about them. Eliminate unnecessary expectations and arguing about wearing socks, cleaning one's plate, or sleeping in bed. Help your child feel less controlled by making your positive contacts greater than your negative contacts each day.

• *Avoid responding to your child's requests with excessive "No"s.* Be for your child a model of agreeableness. When your child requests something, if in doubt say "Yes," or at least count to ten before you say "No." If you're going to grant a request, by all means do it right away, before your child whines or begs for it.

DEALING WITH TEMPER TANTRUMS

Temper tantrums are immature ways of expressing anger. There are several types of temper tantrums. Some are for attention; others are to avoid doing something. Try to teach your child that temper tantrums don't work, that you don't change your mind or give in because of them. By 3 years of age, your child can begin to be taught to verbalize his feelings ("You feel angry because ———— "). We need to teach children that anger is normal but that it must be channeled. By school age, temper tantrums should be rare. By adolescence, your teenager can be reminded that blowing up creates a bad impression. Teach your child how to keep temper tantrums in check by counting to ten or pausing long enough to regain control. The following suggestions cover appropriate responses to different types of temper tantrums.

Support for Frustration-Related Temper Tantrums • Children normally have temper tantrums when they are frustrated with themselves. They may be frustrated because they can't put something back together. Young children may be frustrated because their parents cannot understand their speech. Older children may be frustrated with their inability to do their homework. At these times children need encouragement. They need their parents to put an arm around them and say, "I know it's hard, but you'll get better at it." They also need praise when they don't give up.

Temper tantrums also normally increase when children are tired (for instance when they've missed a nap) or exhausted (as during a party), because they are less able to cope with frustrating situations. At these times put your child to bed. Hunger can also contribute to temper tantrums. If you suspect this, give your child a snack. Temper tantrums also increase during sickness. Mood is clearly affected by a child's physical state.

Ignoring Attention-Seeking Temper Tantrums • Young children commonly throw temper tantrums to get their way. They may want something to eat right before dinner, want to go with you rather than be left with the babysitter, want candy, want to empty a desk drawer, or want to go outside in bad weather. As long as the temper tantrum is nonmobile and not too disruptive, you can leave your child alone. Harmless behavior can be ignored.

The procedure for dealing with an attention-seeking temper tantrum includes the following: Before the tantrum, redirect your child if you recognize that a certain event is going to push him over the edge. However, don't give in to your child's demands. During the temper tantrum, ignore it completely. Once a tantrum has started, it rarely can be stopped. Move away, even to a different room; you are thereby removing the child's audience. Don't talk to or try to reason with your child. Don't hold your child during the temper tantrum. And by all means, don't give in to your child's demands. After the tantrum, be friendly and try to return things to normal.

Also, praise your child for controlling his temper, verbally expressing his anger, and being cooperative. Be a good model by not screaming or having adult tantrums.

The following types of temper tantrum can be ignored:

• Crying and screaming to get attention

• Whining to get attention. Whining is usually a subthreshold temper tantrum. Some parents find it helpful to tell their child: "I can't understand you when you are whining. Talk to me when you can talk normally." If the whining becomes nerve-wracking, put your child in a "whining chair." Dealing with whining is important to prevent whiny behavior in adults.

• Minor displays of anger such as slamming a door, sticking out the tongue, or making a face. These harmless releases of anger when your child is overruled should be permitted.

- Temper tantrum with pounding and kicking the floor, wall, or door. The only limitation is if your child is damaging property.

- A temper tantrum with head banging. You can assume your child won't hurt herself, since children don't like pain. If she has such a complete loss of control that she throws herself backward and has caused a bump on the back of her head, as a last resort you can throw a glass of water on her when she starts to have a temper tantrum, and then leave the room. Don't rush to her to try to prevent her falls, since this will lead to more frequent tantrums.

- Temper tantrums with breath-holding. While your child will turn blue and pass out for 30 to 60 seconds, he won't hurt himself (see BREATH-HOLDING SPELLS, page 190).

Manual Guidance for Refusal-Type Temper Tantrums • Your child may have a temper tantrum when you tell him he must do something, such as taking a bath. Assuming you have given fair warning and not asked him suddenly to stop what he is doing, your best response for getting your child to follow through is first, to let your child have a temper tantrum for 2 or 3 minutes. Then take him to the intended destination (in this case, the tub), using manual guidance. Then give him a bath with no frills or fun attached. Say something like "We will take a quick bath tonight." A child shouldn't be able to avoid doing something (like going to bed) by having a temper tantrum.

Timeout for Disruptive Temper Tantrums • Some temper tantrums are too disruptive for the parents to ignore. On such occasions, children need to be sent or taken to their rooms (see THE TIMEOUT TECHNIQUE, page 204). Examples are:

- Clinging to you or following you around. This type of interruption should not be tolerated.

- Hitting you during the temper tantrum. This is no longer a temper tantrum but has become aggressive behavior and should be treated as such.

- Throwing something during a temper tantrum.

- Prolonged screaming or yelling.

- Having a temper tantrum in a public place such as a restaurant or church. The rights of other people need to be protected.

VERBAL TEMPER TANTRUMS OF OLDER CHILDREN

We want children to express their anger through talking. Verbal disagreement (normal arguing) is healthy; so is the expression of feelings. Some talking back to parents is also normal. When a school-age child challenges our decisions in a logical way, we need to listen. As long as your child is reasonable, he or she needs to be heard. However, if a rule is important to the parent (for instance, not paying to see the same movie twice), the parent can cut off the discussion in 3 to 5 minutes by saying something like: "I've heard your side of it, but the rule stands and now leave me to get back to my work." Try to teach your child to argue without screaming, exaggerating, being rude, or swearing.

Arguing by Shouting • If your child screams at you, make a brief statement such as "We don't scream in this house. Either talk in a calm voice or go to your room." Then ignore your child for any further out-of-control comments.

Protests and Excuses • Without being abusive, your child may present outlandish comments in order to postpone his punishment. In young children less than 3 years of age, these stalling tactics can be ended by saying: "For the last time, go to your room." If they don't go, they can be taken there. Other children may try to put their parents on a guilt trip by saying: "Everyone else does it," "You never listen to me," or "You don't love me." Your response can be: "Of course I love you, but that has nothing to do with this," and then your child can be ignored by your walking away.

Threats • Some children say "I hate you." These exaggerated remarks are to get your attention ("show stoppers"). Parents should not take these comments too seriously. You can reply: "Well, I love you anyway, but I don't like the way you're acting." If your child is really angry, you can later explain that people who live together normally have both positive and negative feelings about other family members. You can say: "Sometimes I get angry with you, too, but I still care about you." Other children may threaten to run away; you can calmly state: "That would make me very sad." Most children then drop the subject. An adolescent who threatens to run needs to be taken more seriously.

Rudeness and Insults • Verbal abuse can be defined as making derogatory comments about the parent. These include calling the parent stupid, a liar, or a jerk. The parent should not tolerate such comments. If the young person is allowed to continue this type of behavior, he or she will have difficulty keeping friends or pleasing other adults. You can give an "I" message, such as "I feel very hurt when you say rude things like that," in a nonangry voice. You can then send your child to his or her room, or outside. It's very important that you not retaliate with a similar verbal attack. Try to present a model of objective, constructive disagreement. Don't forget to praise your child when she uses politeness and diplomacy in stating her case.

Swearing • Swearing at someone in anger should not be tolerated. The rule can be "No swearing in this house." For punishment your child can be sent to his room. Minor swearing in frustration (e.g., "Damn") should be tolerated. Under age 4, children usually use profanity as an experiment to see what kind of reaction they will get. At this age the behavior will often disappear if it is ignored completely. Washing a child's mouth out with soap is an overresponse. Of course, the parents must limit their own use of profanity.

DISCIPLINE PROBLEM-SOLVING

These guidelines cover specific types of misbehavior and how to deal with them. Most of these discipline problems can occur in well-adjusted children with self-disciplined parents. Each type of misbehavior includes recommendations on how to phrase the rule, the preferred discipline technique, the adaptive behaviors that should be praised, and the parent behaviors that should be modeled to help your child behave better. Refer to DISCIPLINE BASICS (page 192) or THE TIMEOUT TECHNIQUE (page 204) for details on how to implement the different types of punishment or praise recommended in this guideline. The areas of misbehavior are described in the following order: Safety, Aggression, Siblings or Peers, Pets, Destructive Behavior Toward Property, Public Places, Interrupting Others, Delaying or Ignoring Others, Dressing, Sleep, Eating, Washing and Bathing, and Miscellaneous. Specific recommendations for dealing with negativism and different types of temper tantrums are reviewed in THE TERRIBLE TWOS AND TEMPER TANTRUMS (page 208).

SAFETY MISBEHAVIOR

Runs Out of the House or Yard

The rule: "Don't go outside," or "Don't leave your yard."

Until age 3 or 4 most children can't be trusted to stay in their yards. They may wander off and may be harmed on a street, railroad track, pond, or swimming pool.

Discipline technique: Structure your child's environment so that you do not have to supervise him or her to prevent this misbehavior. Lock the outside doors to keep children inside. Leave them outside alone only if you have a safe, fenced-in yard.

Runs Away from the Parent When Walking

The rule: "Stay on the sidewalk or path when you're walking with me," and "Hold my hand when we cross the street."

Discipline technique: If your child starts to run off, catch him immediately. Make this a very serious matter and tell him sternly: "Never run off again." Don't let your child tease you about this or allow running off to become a game. Say firmly, "That's not funny."

- If your child repeats running off, routinely hold his hand when you go walking.

- If this is unsuccessful, take a children's harness with you when you go walking. The harness can be put on if your child breaks the rule and taken off after approximately 5 minutes. If your child breaks the rule a second time, the harness can be put on for 10 minutes. Using a harness occasionally is harmless.

Praise your child: For staying close to you.
Model: Cross streets carefully.

Plays with Electricity or Gas

The rule: "Never touch that, because you can get hurt."

Examples: Chewing on electrical cords, playing with electrical outlets, or turning the knobs on the stove.

Discipline technique: Give your child strong verbal disapproval. Don't let this behavior become something your child can tease you about. Also, put your child in timeout. Some of these hazards can be eliminated by using safety plugs or rerouting electrical cords. Since chewing on an electrical cord can cause severe burns to the mouth, you may wish to underscore your special concern about this behavior by slapping your child once on the hand.

Lights Matches
The rule: "Don't play with matches. They can start fires."
Discipline technique: Remove all matches from your child's reach. Consider teaching your child how to use matches properly after 8 years of age.
Model: The appropriate use of matches.

Climbs Trees or Fences
The rule: "Don't climb trees or fences, because you can fall and be seriously hurt."
You might specify that your child can climb certain trees after reaching an appropriate age, such as 6.
Discipline technique: Timeout. To help your child through this phase, consider designating a safe place to practice climbing, such as on an old sofa or a jungle gym at the playground.

Unfastens Seat Belts in the Car
The rule: "We don't drive unless everyone is buckled up."
Discipline technique: Immediate timeout. Don't start the car until all passengers have buckled their seat belts. As soon as anyone unbuckles, pull your car off the road into a boring place, such as a parking lot. Read a book until your child puts the seat belt on. Children usually want to go somewhere rather than sit in the car.
Praise your child: For keeping the seat belt buckled.
Model: Buckling yourself in.

Rides Bicycle Unsafely
The rule: "Obey the bicycle safety rules."
Discipline technique: Logical consequences of not being able to use the bike for 2 or 3 days.
Praise your child: For riding a bike safely.
Model: Appropriate use of your bicycle.

AGGRESSION

Hurts Another Child
Examples: Hitting, pinching, scratching, knocking down, hair-pulling, or biting.
The rule: "Don't hit. It hurts. We don't hurt people."

Discipline technique: Timeout is the best punishment for any aggressive or harmful behavior. Stop the behavior at the threatening stage. When it looks as if your child might bite or hurt someone, intervene immediately. Don't wait until the victim is hurt or screams. Also, give sympathy and attention to the victim. If your child's friend is aggressive at your house, timeout can consist of sending the friend home. Suggest alternative behavior such as: "If you're angry, tell me about it or hit your pillow."

Praise your child: For being nice to people, playing with friends, and behaving in a friendly manner toward you.

Model: Self-control and verbal problem-solving. Don't use physical punishment to try to change aggressive behavior. For example, don't bite back, because it teaches your child it's fine to bite if you are bigger.

Two Children Physically Fight with Each Other

Definition: Two children are angry with each other and hitting, kicking, or shoving. This is not wrestling. In wrestling, children are not angry with each other but are practicing their physical skills. Wrestling is fine as long as it's done outside or in a recreation room and the opponents are reasonably well matched.

The rule: "Don't fight with each other, because disagreements can't be settled by hitting."

Discipline technique:

* Intervene at the early shoving stage.

* Separate the children without interrogation.

* Send both to timeout in separate rooms or separate corners. Another option is to send one child outside.

* When appropriate, remove the object of conflict, such as use of the TV.

Refuses to Fight • While you can have a rule against fighting in your home and yard, you can't control what goes on in the neighborhood or school. Some parents teach their children to fight (but fight fair). Another option is to teach your child to say "I don't believe in fighting" and to walk away from aggressors. Although the chance of being seriously hurt in a fight is slim, it can happen. Sometimes it's better to be smart than to be brave. Most disagreements can be settled by words, and most bullies can be ignored. You don't have to teach your child to defend himself or herself physically.

Praise your child: For playing with other children in a friendly way and settling verbal disagreements themselves.

Model: Problem-solving without hitting or yelling. Spouse abuse condones physical fighting among children. Also avoid favoritism, which contributes to sibling fighting.

Spits

The rule: "Don't spit. It doesn't look nice."

Discipline technique: If your child spits on another person, use immediate timeout. If your child spits for attention-seeking purposes, restrict the places where it is permitted (such as in the toilet, sink, or outdoors). If your child spits anywhere else, place him or her in timeout.

Praise your child: For not spitting in situations where he or she previously spit.

Model: Nonspitting behavior in your own life. Take a position against chewing (smokeless) tobacco.

Yells, Threatens, Insults, or Swears (i.e., Verbal Aggression) • See THE TERRIBLE TWOS AND TEMPER TANTRUMS, page 208.

MISBEHAVIOR TOWARD SIBLINGS OR PEERS

Fights Physically • See the guidelines on AGGRESSION, above.

Hurts the Baby • See SIBLING RIVALRY, page 136.

Argues or Quarrels

The rule: "Settle your own arguments, but no hitting or yelling." Children cannot go through life with a referee to resolve their differences. They need to learn how to negotiate with other people. Arguing with siblings and peers provides this experience. When possible, stay out of it as long as it remains a verbal argument.

Discipline technique:

• Ignore the arguing (unless it occurs in public and is annoying other people).

• If necessary go to a part of the house where you can't hear the arguing.

• Try to keep your child from bringing the argument to you for an opinion.

• If you become involved, try briefly to help the children clarify what they are arguing about, but let them arrive at a solution.

Don't try to decide who is to blame or who started it. Listening to children's arguments can be counterproductive because it causes them to exaggerate or lie. Stay with helping them define the area of disagreement.

• If the bickering continues and interferes with your ability to concentrate, go to the children and tell them: "Please settle your differences quietly." If they do not change, send them both outdoors or to timeout in separate rooms. If an object such as a TV is involved in a dispute, turn it off.

Praise your child: For settling disagreements politely.

Model: Constructive arguments. Avoid being disagreeable or ill-tempered.

Avoidance of favoritism: Although sibling rivalry is normal, it can become intense if the parents show obvious favoritism. Try to treat your children as unique and special individuals. Don't compare them. Don't polarize them into "good" ones and "bad" ones. Point out to each child his or her strengths, but try not to dwell on the accomplishments of a brighter or more athletic child in a sibling's presence.

Teases or Calls Names

Examples: Calling a child who is not good in school, "dummy"; one who is not athletic, "clumsy"; or one who has a bedwetting problem, "smelly." These derogatory comments can be harmful to the self-esteem, especially if they are true.

The rule: "Teasing and name-calling are not allowed, because they are unfair and hurt someone's feelings."

Discipline technique: Immediate timeout.

Model: The parent should avoid teasing as well.

Tells on Another ("Tattletale")

Definition: Children report their siblings' or others' misbehavior to get them into trouble—a form of oneupmanship.

The rule: "Don't tell me about your brother's misbehavior unless it's dangerous. It hurts your friendship."

This rule is based on the premise that bad news gets around, and if it's important, you'll hear about it.

Discipline technique: Give verbal disapproval: "I don't want to hear about it." You can also remind your child: "Tattletales don't have friends," and "Brothers are supposed to stand up for each other."

Praise your child: For looking after, standing up for, or telling you something good about the sibling or friend.

Model: Being supportive of others and avoiding gossip.

Takes Toys Away from Others

The rule: "Don't grab toys that other people are playing with."
Discipline technique: Use logical consequences and return the toy immediately to the child who owns it or had it. Never let the aggressive child keep a toy he or she has taken away. If the misbehavior recurs, use timeout.
Praise your child: For asking another child if he or she may use a toy, and also for returning a toy when requested.

Doesn't Share Toys

Premise: Children can't be expected to share toys until 3 or 4 years of age. Generosity has to be the child's decision. But you can plant the idea with statements such as "If you share with other children, they will usually share with you."
Discipline technique: A child should not be punished for not sharing his or her toys. Some problems can be prevented by allowing your child to take only one toy to the playground until she reaches an age where she can share. When she's not playing with her toy, pick it up so that other children won't take possession of it. For toys that belong to the family rather than an individual, temporarily put it away if two children can't take turns with it.
Praise your child: For any sharing. Encourage your child to share.
Model: Sharing in your home. Sharing your food, drink, and possessions with your child. Lending household objects to friends. Mention to your child that this is sharing.

Is a Poor Friend or Poor Sport

Examples: Some children are bossy and dominant with their friends, causing the friends to leave unhappily. Others show off so much that their friends find them boring. Others are poor sports or bad losers and try to change the rules of a game or sport.
Discipline technique: Natural consequences. Peer pressure will eventually shape your child's behavior into what is acceptable in the peer group. In the meantime your child will lose some friends until he or she has learned how to treat other children better. Occasionally ask your child: "What could you do to be a better friend?" Overall, let peers work out these disagreements themselves.
Praise your child: For being courteous, agreeable, and a good sport about losing.
Model: Stop being critical and bossy of your child if this

applies. Don't argue with referees at your child's athletic events.

MISBEHAVIOR TOWARD PETS

Hurts Pets
The rule: "Don't hurt your pet, because animals feel pain and sadness just like people." Sometimes preschoolers are unduly rough with pets because they equate them with toys.
Discipline technique: Verbal disapproval followed by timeout.
Praise your child: For playing gently with a pet.
Model: Gentleness with animals.

Doesn't Feed the Pet
The rule: "Pets must be fed or they will starve."
Discipline technique: Give an "I" message, such as: "I really feel sorry for Charlie when you don't feed him." In addition, help your child come up with a reminder system, such as a small note on his mirror to help him remember to feed the pet. Sometimes delaying a privilege and linking it with the chore can be helpful (e.g., "No dinner for you until Charlie's been fed.").
Praise your child: For feeding the pet in a timely manner.
Model: Feeding your child in a timely manner.

DESTRUCTIVE BEHAVIOR TOWARD PROPERTY

Touches Things That Shouldn't Be Touched
Examples: Stereo, television, plants, breakables, or valuables.
The rule: "Don't touch the stereo, because it is only for grownups. Ask me for help if you want it turned on."
Discipline technique: Mainly restructure the environment. Put away valuable or dangerous objects, use gates, and lock doors to make certain areas off limits. For objects that can't be removed, use clear verbal disapproval. If this fails, use temporary timeout.
Caution: Much of this exploratory behavior is normal and contributes to your child's development. In general, encourage this normal curiosity. Allow exploration of some closets or shelves. For example, give your child a drawer of his own in the kitchen where he can keep some utensils you no longer use. As he becomes older, teach your child to explore objects with his eyes rather than his hands.
Praise your child: For asking you to turn on the television or stereo.

Damages or Destroys Property Deliberately

Imitators: Some children take toys or other objects apart out of curiosity. Sometimes children break something accidentally. Since people are more important than property, these children need sympathy and help with their dilemma, not punishment.

The rule: "Don't break things, because they cost money and/or are hard to fix."

Discipline technique: Timeout. In addition, use logical consequences. If the object belongs to the child, don't replace it. If the object is yours and your child is over age 6, have him or her pay for part of it out of allowance money.

Praise your child: For taking good care of your possessions and his or her own.

Model: Show care in handling other people's belongings.

Jumps on Furniture

The rule: "Don't jump on the furniture or bed, because you might break it or get hurt."

Discipline technique: Redirect your child to some other play—if possible, one that involves jumping.

Praise your child: For playing in the bedroom without jumping on the bed.

Draws on the Walls

The rule: "Don't put any marks on the walls, because it's hard to get them clean."

Discipline technique: Logical consequences of having your child clean up the mess he or she has caused, as well as temporarily removing the privilege of using paints, crayons, or markers.

Praise your child: For drawing on paper.

Steals

Definition: Taking toys, food, or money from parents, friends, or a store.

Goal: Parents should try to teach ownership. Children are not developmentally able to learn the difference between what is "mine" and what is "yours" before age 4 or 5. Prior to that age they consider everything "mine" or that they have "borrowed it." Fortunately, they can't conceal stealing well before this age. Parents must also teach that it is wrong to borrow something without the owner's consent.

The rule: "Don't take things that don't belong to you, because they belong to somebody else who will miss them."

Discipline technique: Logical consequences. Try to detect stealing at an early age. Don't accept fabrications of where your youngster found the new possession. Have your child take the stolen object back to the teacher, storekeeper, friend, or other rightful owner. The embarrassment of doing this with you present often prevents future stealing. If the object has been broken or the food has been consumed, help your child think of ways to earn money to pay the owner back. Give your child opportunities to earn money so he or she has less need to steal. Also try to teach that people can't have everything they want.
Praise your child: For honesty.
Model: Honesty.

Breaks or Throws Toys

The rule: "Don't break toys, because they cost money. Don't throw toys, because you might break something in the house."
Discipline technique: Logical consequences.

- If the toy is not broken, take it out of circulation for 2 days. The toy has to go back into circulation in order to teach proper behavior.

- If the toy is broken, delay the repair for at least 2 days. Teach that things can't be fixed until you have some free time.

- If the toy can't be repaired, either don't replace it or have your child use his or her own money to replace it.

Praise your child: For taking good care of possessions.

MISBEHAVIOR IN PUBLIC PLACES

Touches Objects that Shouldn't Be Touched

Example: Grabs food off the shelves in a grocery store.
The rule: "Don't touch anything without my permission, because everything here belongs to the store and some things can break."
Discipline technique: Mainly, distract your child on arrival by getting her a snack, such as animal cookies.

- Keep her involved by giving her safe foods to carry or having her push the grocery cart.

- If she's sitting in the grocery cart seat, hand her foods to place in the basket.

- Talk with your child as you shop so that she feels involved.

- Avoid taking your 2-year-old to a store with lots of breakables, such as a glass shop.

Praise your child: For helping.

Has a Temper Tantrum in a Public Place
Example: Often, children have temper tantrums when they beg for a toy or candy at the store and are not given it.
The rule: "We buy only food at the grocery store, not toys."
Discipline technique: Ignore your child and remain firm. If your child is having a temper tantrum in a safe place, walk on and he will stand up and follow you. If your child is near breakable objects or is a reckless child, take him outside for timeout. If he is annoying other people (as in a restaurant or church), also take him outside.
Model: No yelling or tantrums in the store.

Runs Away from the Parent in a Store
The rule: "Stay close to me in the store so you won't get lost."
Discipline technique: Timeout. First try putting your child in the grocery cart for 2 or 3 minutes if she doesn't stay near to you. If she won't stay in the grocery cart, take her outside and put her in timeout facing the wall of the building or sitting inside your car while you stand by. Consider buying a harness and bringing it with you to the store. Harness your child only if she wanders off. Remove it every 5 minutes, giving her a chance to prove that she can control herself in a public setting. As a last resort, leave your child at home with a sitter and be sure to tell her before you go to the grocery store that she can't come this time because she didn't stay near to you.
Praise your child: For following you through the store.

INTERRUPTING OTHERS

Demands Constant Entertainment and Attention
Example: Some children demand that their parents play with them all the time. When a parent is reading, watching TV, fixing her hair, or thinking, the child complains of boredom, or sadness, or wants to be picked up. This situation is an example of the invasion of parents' rights, assuming the parent talks to the child and plays with the child at other times. Even parents of 1- and 2-year-olds can reasonably insist on several 15-minute blocks of personal time each day while the child is awake.
The rule: "Don't interrupt me when I'm busy."

Discipline technique: First, redirect your child by stating: "I'm going to read the newspaper now. What are you going to do?" Suggest some toys. If your child keeps talking, say: "I can't listen now. We'll play when I'm done with the newspaper." If your child continues to talk or makes demands, either ignore the child or make temporary use of timeout.

Praise your child: For entertaining himself or herself.

Interrupts the Parent on the Telephone

The rule: "Don't interrupt me when I'm on the telephone, because I can't hear what the other person is saying."

Discipline technique: Redirect your child by giving him or her special toys to play with which you have saved for this situation and keep near the telephone. If your child continues to be disruptive, put the caller on hold (or hang up) and place your child in timeout. Then return to the telephone.

Praise your child: For being quiet and waiting while you are on the telephone. Smile at your child while you are on the telephone.

Prevention: Place most of your telephone calls during your child's nap or after bedtime. Keep calls to less than 5 minutes when your child is awake.

Interrupts Guests

Premise: When your child has friends over, you don't interrupt them. Children don't have the right to interupt their parents' friends. After an initial greeting and some brief attention, your child should not be allowed to crawl on guests or interrupt adult conversations.

The rule: "Don't interrupt me when I'm talking to my friend, because it makes it hard for us to talk."

Discipline technique: For a younger child, distract him with special toys or games. For an older child, tell her she has to find something to do. If your child persists in interrupting, don't feel guilty about sending her to her room or, if it's near bedtime, to bed. Children should be able to take a back seat to guests. Other adults will approve of your insisting on this.

Praise your child: For good behavior when guests are over.

Interrupts Family Conversations with Incessant Talking and Questioning

The rule: "Don't talk when other people are talking. Don't change the topic." Although we like children to talk, they need to wait their turn if someone else is talking.

Discipline technique: Ignore the child who is interrupting and continue your conversation with the other person. If the interruption continues, tell the interrupting child that you will be glad to talk with him when you are finished talking with the other person. Suggest he do something else for now. If he continues to be disruptive, send him to timeout.

Praise your child: For not interrupting and for waiting.

Model: Not interrupting other people and listening carefully when they speak.

DELAYING OR IGNORING OTHERS

Doesn't Come When Called

Example: This condition is also called "parent deafness" or "tuning out the parents." This behavior occurs when children don't want to listen or follow through with a parent's suggestion. A child does not need his hearing tested if the "deafness" only occurs in selected circumstances.

The rule: "Listen to what I say, because I'll only tell you once."

Discipline technique: If you have something important to tell your child, go to her and elicit eye contact before giving your instruction. If she doesn't follow through, use logical consequences, such as cold food for getting to dinner late.

Praise your child: For coming when called.

Model: Discontinue shouting from the other room. Discontinue lectures or commands. Listen carefully to your child and respond promptly. Discontinue repeated reminders.

Doesn't Come Home on Time

The rule: "Come home on time."

Discipline technique: Logical consequences of grounding for one day or having your child come home earlier in the future.

Praise your child: For keeping deadlines.

Model: Being punctual.

Doesn't Get Ready to Go Somewhere on Time

The rule: "Don't be late when we have to go somewhere."

Discipline technique: Give your child some lead time. If the activity is not essential, have your child miss that activity. If the activity is important, use manual guidance to interrupt your child's dawdling.

Praise your child: For being ready on time.

Model: Don't make your child wait for you. Show your child how you get ready in a hurry.

DRESSING MISBEHAVIOR

Doesn't Cooperate When the Parent Tries to Dress the Child or Change a Diaper

The rule: "Hold still when I'm trying to dress you."

Discipline technique: Give your child strong disapproval if she doesn't cooperate while you're getting her dressed. Don't smile, talk to her, or allow this behavior to become a game.

Praise your child: For helping you get her dressed.

Won't Dress Himself Though Able To

Premise: Once a child is old enough to dress himself, the parent should never need to dress him again. Avoid situations where you feel that you are pressured into becoming involved in the dressing process.

The rule: "You're old enough to dress yourself."

Discipline technique: If you're going to stay at home, don't allow your child to watch TV or go outdoors until he is completely dressed. Also, avoid buying clothing which is hard to get on.

Procrastinates Dressing When the Parent Is Trying to Leave

Examples: You need to take your child to school, daycare, the store, or on some other errand. Your child won't dress herself (despite being able to) and eats breakfast slowly.

The rule: "You must be ready to leave the house by eight-thirty each morning, because we can't be late to school."

Discipline technique: Logical consequences.

- Give your child 10 minutes' warning before departure, preferably using a kitchen timer. Encourage your child to "beat the timer."

- If your child is not dressed at departure time and you are driving somewhere, put her clothes and shoes in a bag and take her to the car dressed as she is. If she likes, she can try to get dressed in the car, though that will be difficult with the seat belt on. If your child is going to school, try to get there a few minutes late to provide some additional pressure to speed up on the next morning. If your child misses a school bus, take her to school yourself, but be sure again that she's a few minutes late.

- Provide breakfast in the morning, but if your child is not finished with breakfast at the time of departure, that is her problem.

• Don't nag during the time your child is stalling and dawdling. By all means don't dress your child at the last minute.

Praise your child: For trying to dress herself, completely dressing herself, dressing herself promptly, or being ready to leave for school or other appointments on time.
Model: Dress before breakfast. Show your child how you sometimes dress in a hurry.

Doesn't Dress Appropriately for the Weather
The rule: "It's up to you to dress so that you won't be too hot or too cold. This is today's weather forecast."
Discipline technique: Natural consequences.
Model: Preparedness for weather variation during the day.

SLEEP MISBEHAVIOR

Awakens and Cries • See NIGHT AWAKENING IN OLDER INFANTS, page 181.

Climbs Out of the Crib
Premise: Once a child climbs out of a crib with the springs on the lowest setting, he or she will definitely try to climb out again and eventually will fall and possibly get hurt.
Response: Correct this hazard on the same day your child climbs out. One solution is to put your child's mattress on the floor. Another is to leave your child in the crib with the crib railing down and a chair next to the bed so he or she can easily get out. Eventually you can transfer your child to a floor-level bed.

Won't Take a Nap
The rule: "Don't leave your room during quiet time."
Every day after lunch, you or your child's caretaker can expect him to spend 60 to 90 minutes resting in his room. During this time he may read but not turn on the radio or TV.
Discipline technique: Return your child to his room if he comes out before 60 to 90 minutes is up. If he comes out a second time, close the door temporarily.

Tries to Delay Bedtime
Examples: From the bedroom, your child makes demands for another kiss, hug, story, or drink. He may demand that you come back to tuck in the covers or find his security object. Often he comes out and tries to get permission to stay up

until you go to bed. All of these maneuvers have the intention of delaying bedtime. They are "wants," not "needs."

The rule: "Don't leave your bedroom after I put you to bed at night, because you need your sleep."

Discipline technique: For details, see BEDTIME REFUSAL (page 187).

- Establish a set bedtime and keep to it. Don't let your child change the bedtime hour. Consider using a kitchen timer as a reminder.

- Have a pre-bedtime ritual that is less than 30 minutes before "lights out." Keep the ritual fun, consistent, and calming.

- At the end of your usual bedtime ritual, ask your child: "Is there anything else you need?" Most children will say "No." If your child says "Yes," allow a few reasonable requests. (This doesn't include extra bedtime stories.) Then leave the bedroom. That should be your last conversation with your child for the night.

- If there are any verbal demands or interruptions from the bedroom, ignore them.

- If your child comes out of the room, return him immediately using manual guidance. During this time do not talk to him or give him a second hug and kiss. Warn him that if he comes out again, you'll need to close the door.

- If he does come out again, shut the door for 2 or 3 minutes each time. If holding the door closed is a bother, put a hook on it for these few minutes.

- If these bedtime protests and tantrums awaken another child (roommate), temporarily have the roommate sleep in your bedroom or another room.

Praise your child: For going to bed without protest.

Is Negative at Bedtime

Examples: Your child refuses to put on her pajamas, lie down, close her eyes, or stay in bed.

The rule: "Stay in your bedroom after we put you to bed."

Discipline technique: Natural consequences. Your child will eventually become tired and go to sleep. Your child can't be forced to fall asleep. Insisting on any of the actions mentioned above is unnecessary—it doesn't matter if your child sleeps on the floor in her daytime clothing.

Two Children Play and Talk in the Bedroom After Bedtime

The rule: "After bedtime you have to be quiet so that your mind will be able to go to sleep."

Discipline technique: Logical consequences. For every night that children stay up, fight, play, or make noise, they will be put to bed 15 minutes earlier the following night. If one child in particular tries to keep the other one up, that child can be sent to bed 1 hour earlier.

Praise your children: (On the following morning) for going to sleep without a fuss.

Wanders or Prowls About During the Night

Examples: Some children awaken during the night and move about the house getting into trouble. They may raid the refrigerator or leave it open. They may watch TV, or turn on the stove or water faucet. Unlike sleepwalkers, they are awake.

The rule: "If you wake up during the night, except for going to the bathroom, you have to stay in your room."

Discipline technique: Nighttime restriction to the bedroom. Because of the safety issues, until children are safety-conscious, (namely, at 4 or 5 years of age) they need a barricade to keep them in their bedrooms. This can be a gate, plywood plank, or locked door. A chain lock (hotel lock) can keep your child in the room yet allow him to open the door partially in case he needs to cry out for someone. If your child is one who needs to urinate during the night, a pot can be placed in his room. After 4 years of age most children will stay in their rooms if they awaken early and have been told they're expected to stay and play quietly.

Sleeps with the Parents

The rule: "Stay in your room during the night. Starting tonight we sleep in separate beds. We have our room and you have your room. You have your bed and we have our bed. You are too old to sleep with us anymore." Since many normal children sleep with their parents during the early years, the parents must decide if they want to discourage it.

Discipline technique: If your child crawls into your bed, she should be sternly ordered back to her own bed. If she doesn't move, she can be escorted back immediately without any conversation. If your child usually doesn't awaken you when she crawls into your bed, use a signaling device that will awaken you if your child enters your bedroom (for instance, a chair placed against your door that will fall when it is moved or a loud bell attached to your doorknob). Some parents simply lock their bedroom door. Another approach is to put a barrier in front of your child's bedroom door.

Wants to Choose His or Her Own Bedtime

Assumption: Adolescents should be able to take care of their own sleep requirements before going off to college.

The rule: "Stay up as late as you want, but it's your responsibility to get yourself up in the morning with an alarm clock and to get to school on time. Also, you can't make any noise after the rest of the family has turned in."

Discipline technique: Natural consequences.

EATING MISBEHAVIOR

Doesn't Eat Enough • See POOR EATERS, POOR APPETITES, page 235.

Stands Up in the Highchair

The rule: "Don't stand up in your chair. Stay seated until the meal is over." This is an important safety issue.

Discipline technique: Some children can be confined to their highchair with the safety strap; others can wiggle out of it. Logical consequences of being put down and having the meal end can teach your child not to stand up.

Praise your child: For staying in his chair at future meals.

Plays with Food

Definition: During the early months of learning self-feeding, many children will make a mess of their highchair tray and of themselves. They may also make a mess because they mix their food with hand or spoon. Children should not be punished for this normal behavior.

The rule: "'Don't throw or drop your food. Don't put food on your body. Eat without making a mess."

Discipline technique: When your child throws food, take him out of the highchair and put him in timeout in the playpen for 2 minutes. Then let him return to the table. If he repeats the misbehavior, assume he has had enough to eat and put him down permanently. To deal with some of the normal sloppiness of young eaters, put down newspapers and offer your child small amounts of food at any one time. A dog also comes in handy.

Praise your child: For eating without making a mess.

Eats Too Slowly

Definition: Some of these children are not hungry. Others are being negative. The problem arises when a child has not finished eating but the rest of the family has completed their meal.

The rule: "The meal is over when everyone else is done eating, because we have to clean up."

Discipline technique: Natural consequences. Clear away your child's plate and put her down after a reasonable amount of time. Don't give her any between-meal snacks if she only eats part of her meal. Serve her smaller portions.

Praise your child: For not playing or wasting time during meals.

Eats Too Fast

Definition: Most of these children are in a hurry to go back to their play. They may gulp their food in an unsavory manner.

The rule: "Mealtime lasts for at least ten minutes (or whatever length of time the parents decide on) whether you're done earlier or not. Mealtime is a special time when our family gets together."

Discipline technique: Logical consequences. Children will learn that finishing quickly does not allow them to leave the dinner table sooner.

Praise your child: For eating slowly, chewing food with the mouth closed, and eating with good manners.

Demands Frequent Snacks

Definition: Some children want a snack, fruit juice, or soda pop every 30 minutes. Frequent snacking leads to tooth decay, is disruptive, and can't be continued when the child enters school.

The rule: "Don't ask for a snack until snack time. We only have one snack in the morning and one snack in the afternoon."

Discipline technique: Ignore your child's requests for snacks before snack time. If he persists, send him to timeout.

Takes Food from the Refrigerator or Food Cabinets

The rule: "You're not permitted to open the refrigerator until you're five years old. Ask a grown-up if you need something out of the refrigerator."

Discipline technique: If your child opens the refrigerator without your permission, send her to timeout. Put a stop sign on the refrigerator door as a reminder. If your child gets into food cabinets, also send her to timeout. With a persistent child, you may need to put locks on the doors or move snack foods to higher cabinets.

Leaves the Kitchen a Mess

The rule: "Whoever makes a mess in the kitchen cleans it up."
Discipline technique: Logical consequences. If you find the kitchen messy, call your child to clean it up. If your child is not at home, cancel the snack privilege for the next day. As a reminder, put up a sign: CLEAN UP AFTER YOURSELF, in the kitchen.
Praise your child: For cleaning up the kitchen.
Model: Cleaning up after yourself in the kitchen area.

Messes Up the Rest of the House with Food

The rule: "We only eat in the kitchen."
Discipline technique: Logical consequences. If you find crumbs or dirty dishes outside the kitchen area, call your child to clean it up. If your child starts to walk around the house eating food, send your child back to the kitchen.
Model: Not taking food outside the kitchen.

WASHING AND BATHING MISBEHAVIOR

Procrastinates About Washing, Bathing, or Toothbrushing

The rule: "We wash our hands before meals. We have a clean face and smell good before going places. We brush our teeth after meals and before bed."
Discipline technique: Logical consequences. Your child is not allowed to have his dinner until he has washed his hands. Your child is not allowed to go to school until he is clean, even if this means he will be late for school. You decide whether or not his body or teeth are clean enough, by doing a recheck after your child has had an opportunity to brush his teeth or wash again. For infants, use more distraction (such as storytelling) and enthusiasm to make your child feel positive about the cleaning process.
Praise your child: For spontaneously brushing teeth or washing. Also compliment him on how he looks and smells afterward.
Model: Have good hygiene habits yourself.

Wets or Soils During the Day • See TOILET TRAINING RESISTANCE, page 257.

Smears Fecal Material

Definition: A child in diapers takes fecal material and smears it on the bed, walls, bathroom, and so on. Rather than being deliberate, usually this behavior arises from a chance discovery by a bored child, perhaps one who is left in bed too long. Unlike the parents, the child is usually not repulsed by feces.

The rule: "Don't get any poo-poo on your bed or the walls. Poo-poo is messy. Poo-poo goes in the toilet."

Discipline technique: For fecal smearing, give clear verbal disapproval without yelling or showing anger. Clean up your child without any entertainment or conversation. Then clean the room, with your child's help if possible. Avoid any physical punishment, because if you overrespond to the first few times your child does this, you may initiate a power struggle. If you are also toilet training your child at this time, reduce any pressure about his or her performance.

Prevention: Supervise your child more closely. Don't leave him alone for more than 10 minutes at a time. When he awakens from his nap, lift him out of bed promptly. Leave him some toys in the bed to play with if he awakens early. Put his diapers on tightly so he can't easily get his hands inside.

Praise your child: For telling you when his pants are full and he needs to be changed.

MISCELLANEOUS

Won't Talk When Able To

Definition: Some children point at things, pull on their parents' sleeves, and play dumb rather than talking.

The rule: "If you want something, tell me."

Discipline technique: Ignore your child after stating once: "I don't know what you want unless you tell me."

Praise your child: For talking.

Won't Confess or Apologize

Definition: Children can't be made to confess or apologize. This expectation is too high for many normally stubborn children.

Discipline technique: Rather than turning this into a power struggle, eliminate it as a problem by not asking for apologies or confessions.

Model: Demonstrate that you can sometimes apologize, such as stating: "I'm sorry that I said such and such when I corrected you."

Lies

Premise: Self-protective lies are commonplace. Children usually lie to try to avoid punishment. Hence the saying, "Ask me no questions and I'll tell you no lies." During the first 5 years of life, children have such a rich imagination that often reality and fantasy merge. During these early years, the term *lying* doesn't have much meaning.

The rule: "Don't lie. Tell me the truth."

Discipline technique for occasional lying: Express verbal disapproval with an "I" message, such as "I really feel bad when you lie to me and I hope you tell me the truth next time." Double the amount of time your child has to spend in timeout if she lies compared to the amount of time she has to spend there if she doesn't lie (i.e., 2 minutes per year of age instead of 1). Never punish harshly for lies. One of the most common reasons for frequent lying is a child's attempt to avoid painful punishment.

Discipline technique for frequent lying: For misbehavior with evidence, punish your child based on the facts available. For misbehavior without any evidence, overlook it. Avoid asking your child to testify against himself—to confess. Avoid interrogating, testing, or trying in any way to catch your child in a lie. Excessive lying is almost always due to harsh punishment, frequent punishment, trying to please adults with high expectations, or a parent's preoccupation with lying. Quizzing makes children better liars and gives them a self-image of not being trusted.

Praise your child: For telling the truth.

Model: Being truthful yourself and lying as little as possible (including tactful lies).

POOR EATERS, POOR APPETITES

SYMPTOMS AND CHARACTERISTICS

- You think your child "doesn't eat enough," "is never hungry," "won't eat unless you feed him," or "eats slower than anyone else"

- Your child is between 1 and 5 years of age

- The energy level remains normal

- The growth remains normal
- Your child is not losing weight

Causes • Between 1 and 5 years of age, many children normally gain only 4 or 5 pounds per year, in contrast to the 15 pounds gained during the first year of life. Children in this age range can normally go 3 or 4 months without any weight gain. This normal slowdown in growth results in a reduced need for calories and a normal decline in appetite (called physiological anorexia). Food intake is governed by the appetite center in the brain. Kids eat as much as they need for growth and energy. Any hungry child will eat if food is available. No child will voluntarily starve himself at this age.

The appetite may decrease even further if parents try to force the child to eat more than he needs (even though he is of normal height and weight). They may apply pressure because they fear that decreased eating might cause poor health or a nutritional deficiency—neither of which is true. But forced feedings always decrease the appetite. If the child is going through a normal phase of negativism, the struggle can accelerate.

Two other reasons that parents attempt to force their children to eat are short stature and normal shifting linear growth. The 3 percent of children under the third percentile in height are said to have short stature. The majority of them are well nourished. Feeding them more cannot increase their height—but it can make them fat as well as short. Children with shifting linear growth concern their parents, because their growth rate falls off before 1 year of age. Many children with short parents are born with average height. During the second half of the first year of life, however, they may shift to a lower height percentile (or line on the growth curve) because it corresponds to the height of their parents. Once they get to the new growth channel, they continue to grow along it at a normal rate. They never appear to be underweight during any of this gradual shifting.

Expected Course • Once you allow your child to control his own food intake, the "problem" will disappear in a matter of 2 to 4 weeks. Rest assured, your child's appetite will reach gigantic proportions by adolescence.

IMPROVING POOR APPETITES

Let Your Child Rediscover His Appetite • The most common reason for never appearing hungry is that your child has received enough snacks that he never becomes truly hungry. You have stayed one meal ahead of his appetite. Let your child miss 1 or 2 meals if he chooses and then watch his appetite return. Meal skipping is harmless. The appetite center will protect him.

Never Feed Your Child If He Is Capable of Feeding Himself • The greatest tendency for parents of a child with a poor appetite is to pick up the utensils, load up the spoon, smile, and try to trick or coerce the child into taking it. Once your child is old enough to use a spoon (usually age 12 to 15 months), never again pick it up for him. If your child is hungry, he will feed himself.

Offer Finger Foods • Finger foods can be started at 6 to 8 months of age. They allow your child a major role in self-feeding even if he is not yet able to use a spoon.

Keep Milk Intake Under 16 Ounces Per Day • If your child eats cheese or yogurt, reduce milk by an equivalent amount. Most children in our society receive excessive milk, which fills kids up and dulls the appetite. Milk is a food and contains as many calories as most solid foods.

Limit Snacks to Two Per Day • Offer small-sized snacks of nutritious foods. Provide them only if your child requests them and offer some food choices. If your child is thirsty between meals, offer water to quench the thirst. Keep juice to less than 6 ounces per day. If your child skips the majority of a meal, cancel the next snack. Some of these children do quite well on only 2 meals a day and no snacks.

Serve Small Portions of Food • A child's appetite is decreased by being served more food than he could possibly eat. Serving a small amount (less than you think he will eat) on a large plate leads to a sense of accomplishment. If your child seems to want more, wait for him to ask for seconds.

Consider Giving Your Child Daily Vitamins If Food Intake Is Borderline • Although vitamins are probably unnecessary, they are not harmful in normal dosages and may allow you to relax about your child's eating patterns. However, they won't increase the appetite.

Make Mealtimes Pleasant • Draw your children into the conversation. Tell them what's happened to you today and ask about their day. Talk about fun subjects unrelated to food. Avoid making it a time for criticism or struggle over control.

Avoid Conversation About Eating at Any Time • Don't discuss food intake in your child's presence. Trust the appetite center to look after your child's food needs. Don't provide praise for appropriate eating. Don't give bribes or rewards for meeting your eating expectations. Children should eat for themselves. Occasionally the child can be praised for trying new foods that he does not like the taste or texture of.

Don't Keep Your Child Sitting at the Dinner Table After the Rest of the Family Is Done • This only causes your child to develop unpleasant associations with mealtime.

COMMON MISTAKES

Parents who are worried that their child isn't eating enough can initiate many irrational patterns of feeding. Some awaken the child at night to feed him or her. Some offer the child snacks at 15- or 20-minute intervals throughout the day. Some try to make the child feel guilty by talking about other children in the world who are starving. Others threaten that "If you don't eat what I cook, it means you don't love me." Some parents force the child to sit in the highchair or at the table for long periods of time after the meal has ended. The most common mistake, of course, is picking up a spoon or fork and trying various ways to get food into the child's mouth. Another mistake is cooking special foods for the child. Although the child may eat these, the total calories consumed per day will probably not increase (since it does not need to increase).

PREVENTION

The main way to prevent feeding struggles is by teaching your child how to feed himself or herself from as early an age as possible. You needn't wait until your child is old enough to use a spoon independently. For the young child, you can allow your child to initiate the feeding (by reaching or leaning forward) and to pace the feeding (by turning the head or gesturing). Food should not be placed in the mouth just because it is inadvertently open. The hands should be free and not pinned down during feedings. Do not insist that your child empty the bottle or clean the plate. By the time your child is 6 to 8 months old, finger feeding should be initiated. By 12 months of age your child should start to learn how to use a spoon and should be completely self-feeding by 15 months of age.

RESPECT SPECIFIC FOOD DISLIKES

Children of all ages (and adults) commonly have a few food dislikes. Usually, parents of these children are not concerned about the amount of calories consumed but about their child missing some essential food or nutrient. The complaints are usually about vegetables, a greatly overrated food. Vegetables are in the same food group as fruits and can be entirely replaced by fruits without any harm to the child. There are no essential foods, just essential food groups.

If your child has a few strong food dislikes (for example, something that makes her gag), she should not be served them when they are prepared as part of the family meal. A minimal-amount rule can be put into effect for other food dislikes. For example, the preschool-age child must taste each food, and the parents should trust her word that she has done so. By school age, most children will take 1 bite per year of age (for example, a 7-year-old will eat 7 peas).

An unnecessary area of friction for these children is a ruling that if they don't clean their plates, they are not allowed to have dessert. Since desserts are not harmful, a better approach is to allow your child 1 serving of dessert if she complies with the minimal-amount rule for foods she dislikes.

CALL YOUR CHILD'S PHYSICIAN DURING OFFICE HOURS IF

- Your child has not had a medical checkup in the last year.

- Your child is losing weight.

- Your child has not gained any weight in 6 months.

- Your child has associated symptoms of illness (such as diarrhea or fever).

- Your child gags on or vomits some foods.

- Someone is punishing your child for not eating.

- This approach has not improved mealtimes in your house within 1 month.
- You have other questions or concerns.

RELATED TOPICS

MEDICINES: HELPING CHILDREN SWALLOW THEM (see page 169)
OVERWEIGHT (see below)

OVERWEIGHT

SYMPTOMS AND CHARACTERISTICS

- Your child is overweight in the eye of the beholder
- More than 20 percent over ideal weight for height
- Skin fold thickness of more than 1 inch (25 millimeters)
- Occurs in 25 percent of children
- Also called obesity

Causes • The tendency to be overweight is usually inherited. If one parent is overweight, 50 percent of the children will be overweight. If both parents are overweight, 80 percent of the children will be overweight. If neither parent is overweight, less than 10 percent of the children will be overweight. Heredity alone (without overeating) accounts for most mild obesity.

Moderate obesity is usually due to a combination of heredity, overeating, and underexercising. However, some overeating is normal in our society. People like to eat because it makes them feel good. But only those who have the tendency to be overweight will gain weight. It is therefore not reasonable to blame your child for being overweight. Perhaps 10 percent of overweight adults eat excessively because they are depressed.

Less than 1 percent of obesity has a physical cause. Your physician can easily determine this by a simple physical examination. While obesity is not your child's fault, something can be done about it.

Expected Course • Losing weight is very difficult. Keeping the weight off is also a chore. The best age for losing weight is over 15 years, or whenever appearance becomes critical to your child. The self-motivated teenager can follow a diet and lose weight regardless of what the family eats. The second-best age for helping your child lose weight is before 5 years. At this age, you are still in control of what foods are being served. The younger your child, the more influence you have. However, the diet must be acceptable to your child at any age.

Trying to help your child lose weight between 5 and 15 years of age is like trying to push water uphill. Once children are outside the home, they have access to so many foods that trying to impose a diet is fruitless. In the long run, the most important factor is how easily a particular child gains weight (i.e., genetics).

PREVENTION OF EXCESSIVE WEIGHT GAIN IN INFANTS

A fat baby is not necessarily a healthy baby. On the other hand, only 10 percent of overweight 1-year-olds go on to become overweight adults. The ones who continue to be overweight usually have a family history of obesity in the parents, siblings, or grandparents. Any infant with a strong family tendency toward obesity needs help. Some physicians would wait until such a child showed signs of being overweight before making any alterations in the diet, but prevention is easier than treatment. From the beginning, try to teach your child to stop eating before he or she reaches a point of satiation (i.e., a sense of complete fullness and reluctance to eat another bite). If your family has a problem with easy weight gain, consider the following dietary precautions to help your baby:

• Try to breast-feed. Breast-fed babies tend to be lighter in weight.

• Don't assume that a crying baby is always hungry. Most crying babies want to be held and cuddled. Don't feed your baby every time he or she cries.

• Don't assume a sucking baby is hungry. Your baby may just want a pacifier or help with finding the thumb.

• Don't assume your baby is hungry every time he or she fusses in hot weather. Your baby may be thirsty and just need some water.

- Don't insist your baby finish every bottle. Unless the baby is underweight, he knows how much formula he needs.

- Don't worry if your baby sleeps through a feeding.

- Don't enlarge the hole in the nipple of a baby bottle. This will deliver formula at too fast a rate.

- Limit the frequency of feedings to no more than every 3 hours.

- Avoid solids until 4 months of age (6 months in breast-fed babies).

- Convert to 3 meals a day by 6 months of age.

- Don't insist that children clean their plates or finish a jar of food.

- Don't encourage your child to eat more after she signals she is full.

- Avoid sweets until 12 months of age.

- Don't give your child food to distract her or keep her occupied. Instead, give toys when you need some free time.

- Use praise for good behavior. Use food for rewards only in solving special problems such as toilet training.

- *CAUTION:* Don't put your baby on 2 percent milk or skim milk before 2 years of age. Your baby's rapid brain growth needs the fat content of whole milk.

WEIGHT LOSS IN OLDER CHILDREN AND TEENAGERS

Readiness and Motivation • Children are usually not ready to lose weight until they reach the teenage years. Teenagers can be helped with motivation by joining a weight-loss club such as TOPS, Weight Watchers, or Overeaters Anonymous. Sometimes schools have a special class or gym class for helping with weight loss. Often the school nurse will talk with overweight children both in groups and individually once a week, as well as weigh them. Children are also better motivated if the diet and exercise programs are undertaken by the entire family. Competing with a parent to see who can lose weight faster can be helpful.

Weight loss is not healthy during the rapid growth spurt of the first 2 years of life or early adolescence. During these years any attempt to change weight should try to slow down the rate of gain without actually losing any weight.

Setting Weight-Loss Goals • Pick a realistic target weight, depending on your child's bone structure and degree of obesity. The loss of 1 pound per week is an attainable goal. Your child will have to work quite hard to maintain this rate of weight loss for several weeks. Weigh your child once per week at the most. Daily weighings generate too much false hope or false disappointment. When losing weight becomes a strain, have your child take a few weeks off. During this time, help your child hold his or her weight constant.

Once your child has reached the target weight, the long-range goal is to try to maintain that weight within 5 pounds in either direction. Staying at a particular weight is possible only through a permanent moderation in eating. The tendency to gain weight easily will probably be with your child for a lifetime. It's important for your child to understand this.

Diet: Decreasing Calorie Consumption • Your child should eat 3 well-balanced meals a day and average-sized portions. There are no forbidden foods. Your child can have a serving of anything his family or friends are eating. However, there are forbidden amounts. While your child is reducing, he must leave the table a bit hungry. There's no question about it, dieting is painful. Your child can't eat until he's satiated (full) and hope to lose weight. Shortcuts such as fasting, crash dieting, or diet pills rarely work and may be dangerous. Calorie counting is helpful for some people but it is usually too time-consuming. Consider the following guidelines on what to eat.

• Fluids: Have your child take all milk as skim or 2 percent milk. Limit milk to 16 ounces per day, as it has lots of calories. All other fluid intake should be either water or diet drinks. Encourage drinking 6 glasses of water per day.

• Meals: Encourage average portions. Discourage seconds.

• Desserts: Encourage smaller-than-average portions. Encourage more Jell-O and fresh fruits as desserts. Avoid rich desserts. No seconds.

• Snacks: Limit snacks to 2 or fewer per day. Serve only special low-calorie foods such as raw vegetables (carrot sticks, celery sticks, raw potato sticks, pickles, etc.), raw fruits (apples, oranges, cantaloupe, etc.), popcorn, or diet soft drinks.

• Types of food: Serve fewer fatty foods. Fat has twice as many calories as the same portion of protein or carbohydrate. Trim the fat off meats. Serve more baked, broiled, boiled, or steamed foods (fewer fried foods). Serve more fruits, vegetables, salads, and grains. Unfortunately, no food is a particularly good appetite suppressant.

• Vitamins: Give your child one multivitamin tablet per day while reducing.

Eating tips • In order to counteract the tendency to gain weight, your youngster must be taught eating tips and habits that will last for a lifetime. The following habits can make keeping off pounds easier:

• Discourage skipping any of the 3 basic meals.

• Encourage drinking a glass of water before meals.

• Serve smaller portions. Don't serve adult helpings to children before adolescence.

• Suggest chewing the food slowly.

• Offer second servings only if your child has waited for 10 minutes after finishing the first serving.

• Discourage the need to consume all the food in the serving bowls. Leftovers can be placed in the refrigerator.

• Don't purchase high-calorie snack foods such as potato chips, candy, or regular pop.

• Do purchase and keep available diet soft drinks, fresh fruits, and vegetables.

• Leave only low-calorie snacks out on the counter—fruit, for instance. Put away the cookie jar.

• Store food only in the kitchen. Keep it out of other rooms.

• Offer no more than 2 snacks per day. Discourage your child from continual snacking ("grazing") throughout the day. The number of snacks we eat each day is a matter of habit. A person can learn to go through a day with no snacks without developing symptoms.

• Allow eating in your home only while sitting at the kitchen or dining room table. Discourage eating while watching TV, studying, riding in a car, or shopping in a store. Once eating becomes associated with these events, the body learns to expect it.

- Discourage eating alone.

- Help your child reward herself for hard work or studying with a movie, TV, music, or book, rather than food.

- Put up reminder cards on the refrigerator and bathroom mirror which state: EAT LESS.

Exercise: Increasing Calorie Expenditure • Daily exercise to the point of breathing hard can increase the rate of weight loss as well as the sense of physical well-being. Diet and exercise together are the most effective way to lose weight. As your child loses weight, exercise will become less tiring because he or she will be in better condition and have less weight to move about. Try the following forms of exercise:

- Encourage walking instead of riding in a car.

- Encourage using stairs instead of elevators.

- Encourage learning new sports. Swimming and jogging are the sports that burn the most calories. Your child's school may have an aerobics class.

- Encourage taking the dog for a long walk.

- Encourage spending 30 minutes a day exercising or dancing to records or music on TV.

- Encourage using an exercise bike or Hula Hoop while watching TV.

- Limit TV sitting time to 2 hours or less per day.

Social Activities: Keeping the Mind Off Food • The more outside interests your child participates in, the easier it will be for him or her to lose weight. Spare time fosters nibbling in everyone. Most snacking occurs between 3:00 and 6:00 P.M. Help your child fill after-school time with activities such as music, drama, sports, scouts, or other clubs. A part-time job after school may help. If nothing else, encourage your child to call or visit a friend. An active social life almost always leads to weight reduction.

MASTURBATION IN PRESCHOOLERS

SYMPTOMS AND CHARACTERISTICS

Masturbation is self-stimulation of the genitals for pleasure and self-comfort. Children may rub themselves with a hand or other object. During masturbation, a child usually appears dazed, flushed, and preoccupied. Masturbation is more than the normal inspection of the genitals commonly observed in 2-year-olds during baths. The frequency varies from once a week to several times per day. Masturbation occurs more commonly when a child is sleepy, bored, watching television or under stress.

Cause • Occasional masturbation is a normal behavior of many infants and preschoolers. Up to a third of children in this age group discover masturbation while exploring their bodies. It continues simply because it feels so good. Some children masturbate frequently because they are unhappy about something, such as having their pacifier taken away. Others are reacting to punishment or pressure to stop completely. Masturbation has no medical causes. Irritation in the genital area causes pain or itching; it doesn't cause masturbation.

Expected Course • Once masturbation begins, it will seldom stop completely. It may decrease in frequency if associated power struggles or unhappiness are remedied. By age 5 or 6, most children can learn some discretion and masturbate only privately. Masturbation becomes almost universal at puberty with normal surges in hormones and sexual drive.

Common Misconceptions • Masturbation does not cause any physical injury or harm to the body. It is not abnormal or excessive unless it is deliberately done in public places after age 5 or 6. It does not mean your child will be oversexed, promiscuous, or sexually deviant. Masturbation can cause emotional harm (such as guilt and sexual hangups) only if adults overreact to it and make it seem dirty or wicked.

COMING TO TERMS WITH MASTURBATION IN PRESCHOOLERS

Have Realistic Goals • It is impossible to eliminate masturbation. Accept the fact that your child has learned about it and enjoys it. The only thing a parent can control is where it occurs. A reasonable goal is to permit it in the bedroom. Clarify for your child "It's OK to do that in your bedroom when you're tired." Don't ignore it completely or your child will think he or she can do it freely in any setting, leading to criticism by other adults.

Accept Masturbation at Naptime and Bedtime • Leave your child alone at these times. Stay out of your child's room. Avoid surveillance or checking up. Do not forbid lying on the abdomen and do not ask if your child's hands are between the legs.

If Your Child Masturbates at Home Outside the Bedroom • Intervene as soon as possible. First try to distract your child with a toy, game, or puzzle. Suggest your child run an errand within the house. If that fails, explain to your child: "I know that feels good, and it's okay to do it in your room or the bathroom. But it's not to be done in the rest of the house or when other people are around. It's something we do when we're alone." Eventually this will help children become sensitive to other people's feelings. Often this can't be accomplished readily before age 4 or 5. The younger child may need to be sent to his or her room to masturbate.

If Your Child Masturbates at Daycare or Preschool • Review your approach with your child's teachers and ask that they try to keep their responses consistent with yours. First they should try to distract the child. If that is not effective, they should catch the child's attention with comments such as "We need to have you join us now." Masturbation should be tolerated at school only at nap time.

Increase Physical Contact with Your Child • Some children will masturbate less if they receive extra hugging and cuddling throughout the day. Try to be sure that your child receives at least 1 hour per day of special time together and physical affection from the parents.

Common Mistakes • The most common mistake that parents make is to try to completely eliminate masturbation. This leads to an all-out power struggle which the parents inevitably lose. Parents must also discontinue any physical punishment, yelling, or lecturing about masturbation. They should not label masturbation as bad, dirty, evil, or sinful (the "moral approach"). They should avoid tying the hands or using any kind of restraints. All of these approaches lead only to resistance and, possibly, later sexual inhibitions.

CALL YOUR CHILD'S PHYSICIAN DURING OFFICE HOURS IF

- Your child continues to masturbate when other people are around.
- You're afraid your child has been taught to masturbate by someone.
- Your child tries to masturbate others.
- You feel your child is unhappy.
- You cannot accept any masturbation by your child.
- This approach does not bring improvement within 1 month.
- You have other questions or concerns.

STUTTERING

SYMPTOMS AND CHARACTERISTICS OF STUTTERING

- Also called stammering
- Repeating of sounds, syllables, words, or phrases
- Hesitations and pauses in speech
- The absence of smooth speech flow
- Increases when tired, excited, or stressed
- Fear of talking
- Occurs in boys 4 times more frequently than in girls

SYMPTOMS AND CHARACTERISTICS OF NORMAL DYSFLUENCY AND DYSARTHRIA

Normal dysfluency (nonfluency) is a term used to describe the normal repetition of words or phrases when children are learning to speak between 18 months and 5 years of age. It occurs because the mind is able to form words faster than the tongue can produce them. Normal dysfluency (pseudostuttering) occurs in 90 percent of children, in contrast to true stuttering, which occurs in only 1 percent of children. Normal dysfluency lasts for approximately 2 or 3 months if handled correctly.

Normal dysarthria (mispronunciation) is a term used to describe the abnormal pronunciation of many children as they learn to speak. Sounds are substituted or left out, so the word becomes hard to identify. Approximately 70 percent of children pronounce words clearly from the onset of speech. However, the other 30 percent of children between the ages of 1 and 4 produce many words that are unintelligible to their parents and others. At least 90 percent of them become completely understandable by age 4 and 96 percent by age 5 or 6. Unlike normal dysfluency, normal dysarthria is not a brief phase but instead shows very gradual improvement over several years as development unfolds. The cause is usually genetic. Tongue-tie (see that topic, page 161) plays no role.

Both normal dysfluency and normal dysarthria are part of learning to talk. They go unnoticed by the child. They improve with time rather than become worse, as with true stuttering. They do not cause the child any apprehension. Any parents who think their child is unique in this area should attend a nursery school to hear the wide variation in normal speech of preschoolers.

CAUSES OF TRUE STUTTERING

True stuttering occurs in only 1 percent of children. Although there are some genetic aspects, in most cases stuttering develops when a child with normal dysfluency or dysarthria is pressured to improve and in the process becomes sensitive to his inadequacies. Soon thereafter the child begins to anticipate speaking poorly and struggles to correct it. Tension occurs during speaking. The more the child attempts to control his speech the worse it becomes (a vicious cycle). The repetitions become multiple, rather than single. Temporary stuttering can occur at any age if a person becomes overly critical and fearful of his own speech. Although it is normal for us to be aware of what we are saying, how we are saying it is normally subconscious.

PREVENTION

These recommendations are also useful for helping your child overcome mild stuttering.

Encourage Conversation • Keep the content pleasant and enjoyable. Sit down and talk with your child at least once a day. However, avoid requests for verbal performance or reciting. Make speaking fun.

Don't Correct Your Child's Speech • Avoid any disapproval, such as "Stop that stuttering" or "Think before you speak." Remember that this is your child's normal speech for his age and is not controllable. Avoid attempts to improve your child's grammar, verb tense, or enunciation. Also avoid praise for good speech—which implies that your child's previous speech wasn't up to standard.

Don't Interrupt Your Child's Speech • Give your child ample time to finish what he is saying. Don't complete sentences for him. Don't allow siblings to interrupt one another.

Don't Ask Your Child to Repeat Himself or Start Over • If possible, guess at the message. Try to become a careful listener when your child is speaking. Only if you don't understand a comment and it appears to be an important one should you ask your child to restate it.

Don't Ask Your Child to Practice a Certain Word or Sound • This just makes the child more self-conscious about his speech.

Don't Ask Your Child to Slow Down When He Speaks • Try to convey to your child that you have plenty of time and are not in a hurry. Model a relaxed rate of speech. A rushed type of speech is a temporary phase that can't be changed by orders from the parent.

Don't Label Your Child a Stutterer • Labels tend to become self-fulfilling prophecies. In fact, don't discuss in your child's presence that he or she has any kind of speech problem.

Warn Other Adults Not to Correct Your Child's Speech • The preceding instructions must be shared with babysitters, teachers, relatives, neighbors, and visitors. Don't allow siblings to tease or imitate your child who stutters. If they do so, send them to their room for timeout. Encourage your child to talk about frustrations. If your child becomes quite upset while speaking, say something sympathetic like "That's a hard word." Then ask him about his feelings and help him express them. Reassure him that his speech will become better.

Help Your Child Relax and Feel Accepted in General • Try to increase the hours of fun and play your child has each day. Try to slow down the pace of your family life. Avoid situations that seem to bring on stuttering. If there are any areas in which you have been applying strict discipline, try to back off.

CALL YOUR CHILD'S PHYSICIAN DURING OFFICE HOURS IF

- Your child is over age 5.

- The stuttering is severe.

- Your child has associated facial grimacing or tics.

- Your child has become self-conscious or fearful about his or her speech.

- Your family has a history of stuttering in adulthood.

- Speech is also delayed (no words by 18 months or no sentences by 2½ years).

- Speech is totally unintelligible to others *and* your child is over age 2.

- Speech is more than 50 percent unintelligible to others *and* your child is over age 3.

- Speech is 10 percent unintelligible to others *and* your child is over age 4.

- The stuttering doesn't improve after trying this program for 2 months.

- You have other questions or concerns.

TICS (TWITCHES)

SYMPTOMS AND CHARACTERISTICS

- Rapid, repeated muscle twitches (also called habit spasms)

- Eye-blinking, facial-grimacing, forehead-wrinkling, head-turning, or shoulder-shrugging are most common types

- Tics increase with stress

- Tics decrease with relaxation

- Tics disappear during sleep

- Occur in 20 percent of children

- Occur in boys 3 times more frequently than in girls
- Peak age is 6 to 10 years

Causes • Tics reflect the spilling over of emotional tension. They mean your child is under pressure. They are involuntary, not deliberate.

Tics usually occur in normal, bright, sensitive children. Tics are more severe in children who are shy or overly conscientious. Tics can be accentuated by critical parents who nag, pressure for achievement beyond the child's ability, or draw negative comparisons to siblings.

Expected Outcome • If tics are ignored, they will usually disappear in 2 months to 1 year's time. If extra effort is made to help the child relax, they will usually improve more quickly. Without intervention, most children with tics have spontaneous improvement or clearing at adolescence. Approximately 3 percent of children with tics develop incapacitating tics if they are not handled appropriately.

HOW TO HELP YOUR CHILD WITH TICS

Help Your Child Relax in General • Tics are a barometer of inner tension. Make sure your child has free time and fun time everyday. If he or she is overscheduled with activities, try to lighten the commitments. If your child is unduly self-critical, praise him more and remind him to be a good friend to himself.

Identify and Remove Specific Environmental Stresses • Keep a tic diary. Whenever your child has a flurry of tics, write down the date, time, and the preceding event. From this diary, you should be able to identify some of your child's pressure points. (Note: Your child shouldn't be aware you are keeping this diary.) In any event, reduce the amount of criticism that your child receives about grades, music lessons, sports, keeping his or her room clean, table manners, and so forth. Avoid stimulant medications (such as decongestants), which can lower the threshold for tics.

Ignore Tics When They Occur • When your child is having tics, don't call his or her attention to them. Reminders imply that they are bothering you. If your child becomes worried about the tics, then every time they occur, the child will react with tension rather than acceptance. The tension in turn will trigger more tics (a vicious cycle). Don't allow siblings or others to tease your child about the tics. Be sure that relatives, friends, and teachers also abide by this approach. When tics occur, people should say nothing and back off from any pressure they may be applying.

Don't Talk About Tics When They Are Not Occurring • Stop all family conversation about tics. The less said about them, the less your child will be apprehensive about their occurring. If your child brings up the topic, reassure him that he will regain control over his facial muscles and the tics will go away.

Avoid Any Punishment for Tics • Some parents have the mistaken idea that tics are a bad habit that can be broken. This idea is absolutely false. Also having children practice tic control in front of a mirror usually makes them realize they can't control the tics. Any facial exercises or massage should also be discontinued, because they just draw undue attention to the problem.

CALL YOUR CHILD'S PHYSICIAN DURING OFFICE HOURS IF

- The tics interfere with friendships or schooling.
- The tics involve sounds, words, or profanity.
- The tics involve coughing.
- The tics involve parts of the body other than the head, face, or shoulders.
- The tics become frequent (more than 10 per day).
- The tics have lasted for more than a year.
- The tics are not better after trying this program for 1 month.
- You have other questions or concerns.

TOILET TRAINING

Toilet training can be considered achieved when your child can walk to the potty, undress, urinate or defecate, and pull up his or her pants without any reminder or assistance from anyone. Some children will learn to control their bladders first; others will start with bowel control. Both can be worked on simultaneously. Nighttime bladder control is normally delayed for several years. The gradual type of toilet training discussed here can usually be completed in 2 weeks to 2 months.

TOILET TRAINING READINESS

Don't begin training until your child is clearly ready. Readiness doesn't just happen; readiness includes concepts and skills you can teach your child from 12 months of age onward. Reading some of the special toilet learning books to your child can help (see Mack and Lansky). Most children with normal development can be made ready for toilet training by 24 months of age, many by 18 months. By age 3, your child will probably have trained himself. If the following indications are present, your child is ready.

• Your child understands what "pee, poop, dry, wet, clean, messy, and potty" mean. Teach him the vocabulary.

• Your child understands what the potty is for. Teach this by having your child watch parents, older siblings, and peers use the toilet correctly.

• Your child prefers dry, clean diapers. Change your child frequently.

• Your child likes to be changed. As soon as he is able to walk, teach him to come to you immediately whenever he is wet or dirty to have his diaper changed. Praise him for telling you.

• Your child understands the connection between dry pants and using the potty. "If you go pee-pee in the potty, your pants will stay nice and dry."

• Your child can recognize the sensation of a full bladder and the urge to have a bowel movement—that is, he paces, jumps up and down, holds his genitals, pulls at his pants, squats down, or tells you. Clarify for him: "Your body wants to make some pee or poop."

• Your child has the ability to postpone briefly the urge to go. He may go off by himself and come back wet or soiled, or he wakes up from naps dry.

THE TOILET TRAINING PROCESS

The main approach to training must be encouragement, patience, praise, and making the process fun. Avoid any pressure or punishment. Your child must feel in control of the process.

Buy Supplies

• Potty chair (floor-level type). Having the feet reach the floor during training gives your child leverage for pushing and a sense of security. It also offers the freedom of getting on and off at will. This type is also portable.

• Loose-fitting training pants. Switch from diapers to training pants after your child has been through the basics of readiness and likes sitting on the potty chair. Diapers are too hard for your child to take off alone, and they grant permission to be wet. Once you start using training pants, use diapers only for naps and nighttime. Avoid having your child go bare-bottom, because wet clothing can be an incentive to stay dry.

• Favorite treats (fruit slices, raisins, candy, potato chips, cookies, and the like) for rewards

• Stickers or stars, for rewards

Make the Potty Chair One of Your Child's Favorite Possessions • Several weeks before you plan on beginning toilet training, take your child with you to purchase a potty chair. Narrow it down to two or three models and let your child make the final decision. Make it very clear that this is your child's own special chair. Help your child put his name on it. Allow your child to decorate it or even paint it a different color. Then have your child sit on it fully clothed until he is comfortable with using it as a chair. Have your child use it while watching TV, eating snacks, playing games, or looking at books. Keep it in the room in which your child is currently playing—often the kitchen. Only after your child is clearly friendly toward the potty chair (for at least one week), proceed to step 3 and begin toilet training.

Encourage Practice Runs to the Potty • Take your child out of diapers and into training pants. State in a positive way: "Now we're going to use the potty." Encourage your child to walk to the potty, pull down his pants, and sit there. Your child can then be told: "Try to pee-pee in the potty." If your child is reluctant to cooperate, he can be encouraged to sit on the potty by doing something that is fun— you might read a story, for instance. If your child still wants to get up after 1 minute of encouragement, permit it. *Never* force your child to sit there. *Never* physically hold your child there. Even if your child seems to be enjoying it, end each session after 5 minutes, unless something is happening. Carry this out as many times each day as possible. The best times are 20 minutes after meals, after naps, and whenever your child gives you a signal that looks promising (see TOILET TRAINING READINESS, above).

Praise or Reward Your Child for Cooperation or Any Success

• All cooperation with these practice sessions should be lavishly praised with words: "Johnny is sitting on the potty just like Daddy," perhaps, or "You're trying real hard to make pee-pee in the potty."

• If your child urinates into the potty, he can be rewarded with treats or stickers, as well as praise and hugs. While a sense of accomplishment is enough for some children, others need treats to overcome their negativism.

• The big rewards (like going to the ice-cream store) should obviously be reserved for when your child spontaneously walks over to the potty and uses it, or asks to go there with you and then uses it.

• Once your child uses the potty spontaneously on two or more occasions, you can stop the practice runs. For the following week, continue to praise your child frequently for dryness and using the potty. (Note: Practice runs and reminders should not be used for more than 1 or 2 months.)

• While you're at all this, train your child early in the good habit of rinsing the hands each time he finishes using the toilet.

Change Your Child for Urine or BM Accidents • Change your child as soon as it's convenient, but respond sympathetically. Say something like: "You wanted to pee-pee in the potty, but you made pee-pee in your pants. I know that makes you sad. You like to be dry. You'll get better at this." If you feel a need to be critical, keep it to mild verbal disapproval and use it rarely (e.g., "Big boys don't go pee-pee in their pants," or mention the name of another child whom he likes and who is trained).

Then your child should be changed into dry training pants in as neutral and nonangry a way as possible. Avoid physical punishment, yelling, or scolding. Pressure or force can turn the normally negative child of this age into a completely uncooperative one. Also, keeping your child in wet or soiled pants for punishment is counterproductive.

Review the Following Guideline on Toilet Training Resistance If

- Your child won't sit on the potty or toilet.
- Your child is negative about toilet training.
- You begin to use force or punishment.
- Your child is over 3 years old and not daytime toilet trained.
- This approach isn't working after 2 months.

RECOMMENDED READING

Joanna Cole, *The Parents Book of Toilet Teaching* (New York: Ballantine Books, 1983).

Vicki Lansky, *Toilet Training* (New York: Bantam Books, 1984).

——, *Koko Bear's New Potty* (New York, Bantam Books, 1986).

Alison Mack, *Toilet Learning* (Boston: Little, Brown, 1978).

TOILET TRAINING RESISTANCE

Children who refuse to be toilet trained either wet themselves, soil themselves, or try to hold back their bowel movements (thus becoming constipated). Many of these children also refuse to sit on the toilet or will use the toilet only if a parent brings up the subject and marches them into the bathroom. Any child who is over 2½ years old and not toilet trained after several months of trying can be assumed to be resistant to the process, rather than untrained. Consider how capable your child is at delaying a BM until he or she is off the toilet. More practice runs, such as you used in toilet training, will not help. Your child's control is already impressive. Instead, your child now needs full responsibility and some incentives.

The most common cause of not being toilet trained is that the child was reminded too much. Too much pressure was placed on the child through lectures or nagging. Some of the children have been forced to sit on the toilet against their will, occasionally for long periods of time. A few have been spanked or punished in other ways for not cooperating.

If your child is a daytime wetter or soiler, you can probably help. If your child holds back bowel movements and becomes constipated, medicines will also be needed, so first talk with your child's physician. If your child also has bed-wetting, work on the daytime wetting first, because it will be much easier to change. If your child has small amounts of wetting that occur while trying to pull down underwear or undo a zipper, this is normal and no special intervention is needed. Occasionally a girl will have some leakage of urine because she stands up too quickly after urinating. She simply needs to sit there an extra 10 seconds. Also, some of the children with small smears of stool in their underwear simply need a careful review of how to wipe themselves "until clean."

HELPING THE UNCOOPERATIVE CHILD

Transfer All Responsibility to Your Child • Your child will decide to use the toilet only after he realizes that he has nothing left to resist. Have one last talk with him about this subject. Tell him you realize that you can't help him anymore and that it's up to him what he does with "his pee" and "his poop." Tell him you're sorry you punished him, forced him to sit on the toilet, or reminded him so much. Tell him from now on you won't try to help him, because he doesn't need any help and he's "in charge." Then stop talking about this subject with your child or with others when your child is present. When your child stops receiving so much attention and conversation for nonperformance (not going), he will eventually decide to perform for attention.

Stop All Reminders About Using the Toilet • Let your child decide when she needs to go to the bathroom. He should not be reminded to go to the bathroom, nor asked if he needs to go. Reminders are a form of pressure, and pressure doesn't work. Your child should not be made to sit on the toilet against his will, because this will foster a negative attitude about the whole process. He knows when his rectum needs to be emptied (the defecation urge), when his bladder is full, and where the bathroom is. If your child doesn't respond when he needs to, the best reminder of wetness is urine dripping down the leg, and the best reminder of soiling is the odor.

Give Incentives for Using the Toilet • If your child stays clean and dry, he or she needs plenty of positive reinforcement. This reinforcement should include praise, smiles, and hugs from everyone in the family. This positive response should occur every time your child passes his bowel movement or urine into the toilet. For the child who soils or wets himself on some days and not others, this recognition should occur whenever he is clean for a complete day. Better yet, on successful days a parent should take 20 minutes to play a special game with the child or take him for a walk.

For turning around a resistant child, special incentives (such as jelly beans, chocolates, or pennies) are invaluable—especially under age 5. Take your child to the grocery store to select 2 bags of favorite candies. For using the toilet, err on the side of giving too much (e.g., a handful each time). If you want a breakthrough, make your child "an offer he can't refuse."

Give Stars for Using the Toilet • Get a calendar for your child and post it in a conspicuous location. Place a star on it for every BM or urination into the toilet. This record of progress should be kept until your child has gone 2 weeks without any accidents.

If Your Child Won't Sit on the Toilet, Try to Change His Attitude • First, ask your child if he wants to use the big toilet, the potty chair, or newspaper on the bathroom floor—that is, give him choices. The potty chair is usually the least threatening and gets your child out of the bathroom, which may have some bad associations due to forced sitting. Then try to reestablish a pleasant feeling toward the potty chair. Encourage your child to sit on it for watching TV. If he is trained for urine, have him sit down to urinate. If necessary, give him stars for simply sitting on the potty chair. Once your child seems comfortable with the potty chair, the preceding incentive system will bring results.

Most day wetters have used the toilet sometimes and will improve with this system. Some soilers have *never* used the toilet, and in the beginning will need a pleasant reminder *once a day* when they are clearly holding back. You can state: "Do you know how you can make your tummy feel better? After your tummy gets rid of the poop, it will feel good and probably want some candy." However, don't accompany your child into the bathroom or stand with him by the potty chair. He needs to get the feeling of success that comes from doing it on his own, and then finding you to tell you what he did.

Remind Your Child to Change Clothing If He Wets or Soils Himself • Don't ignore soiled or wet clothes. As soon as your child is noted to be soiled or wet by odor or behavior, remind him to clean himself up immediately. The main role you have in this program is to enforce the rule "You can't walk around wet or with a mess in your pants." Don't expect your child to confess to being wet or soiled, nor ask him a question he will probably answer with a lie. If he is wet, he can probably change into dry clothes by himself. This makes it more boring, which is good. Also have your child rinse the wet underwear in the sink and then hang it on the side of the bathtub to dry. If your child is soiled, he will probably need your help with cleanup, but keep him involved. Have your child rinse the soiled underwear in the toilet. This may be "yucky," which is also good. Then store them until washday in a bucket of water with a lid. Your child may also need a 5-minute soak in the bathtub if he is soiled. If he wets or soils himself when you are out in public places, always have him carry a brown bag with extra clothes in it. If your child has an accident, find a public restroom and put him through his paces.

Don't Punish for Accidents • Respond gently to accidents. Your child should not be criticized or punished. In addition, siblings should not be allowed to tease. Your child should never be put back into diapers. If there is anyone in your family who wants to "crack down" on your youngster, have that person talk to your child's physician, because this kind of pressure will only delay a cure and it could cause secondary emotional problems. Try to keep your family optimistic about this problem. Eventually all children want to be "grown up" and will use the toilet.

Ask the Preschool Staff to Apply the Same Strategy • Children who soil or wet themselves at school need access to the bathroom at school, especially if they are shy. Remind your child it's fine to leave the classroom to go to the bathroom. Send the school a note requesting unlimited privileges to go to the school bathroom anytime your child wants to without raising his hand and also during recess. If the problem is significant, you might also temporarily supply the school with an extra set of clean underwear.

CALL YOUR CHILD'S PHYSICIAN DURING OFFICE HOURS IF

- Your child is over 5 years old.
- Your child is constipated.
- Your child has diarrhea.
- Urinary tract infections occurred previously.
- Passing the urine causes pain or burning.
- The urine stream is weak or dribbly.
- Your child's underwear is constantly damp.
- Your child wets while running to the toilet.
- Your child wets during laughter.
- Your child drinks excessive fluids.
- The symptoms are not improved by 1 month on this program.
- The symptoms are not cleared by three months.

BED-WETTING (ENURESIS)

SYMPTOMS AND CHARACTERISTICS

Enuresis is the involuntary passage of urine during sleep more than once a month. This very common problem occurs in 40 percent of children at age 3, in 30 percent at age 4, in 20 percent at age 5, in 10 percent at age 6, in 7 percent at age 8, in 3 percent at age 12, and in 1 percent by age 18. Therefore, we consider it normal until at least age 6.

Causes • Those children who take the longest to become dry at night have poor bladder control, often because of heredity. The kidneys are normal. In addition, many of these children have small bladders which cannot hold the total night's urine production. Small bladders are a normal variation that run in families. Physical causes are very rare, and your physician can easily detect them. Emotional problems are rarely part of enuresis unless people mishandle it.

Expected Course • Most children with bed-wetting overcome it between ages 6 and 10. If one of the parents was a bed-wetter, the child will probably become dry at the same age the parent did. Even without treatment, all children eventually get over it. Therefore, treatments that might have harmful complications (such as some drugs) should never be used. On the other hand, treatments without side effects can be started as soon as your child has been toilet trained for more than 6 months.

CALL YOUR CHILD'S PHYSICIAN DURING OFFICE HOURS IF

- Passing the urine causes pain or burning.
- The urine stream is weak or dribbly.
- Wetting occurs days as well as nights.
- Your child drinks excessive fluids.
- Your child was previously dry.
- Your child is over 12 years old.
- You have other questions.

HOME CARE FOR ANY AGE CHILD WITH BED-WETTING

Fluid Intake • Discourage fluids during the 2 hours prior to bedtime. Give gentle reminders about this, but don't refuse a few swallows of water if your child says he or she is thirsty.

Daytime Urination • During the daytime, encourage your child to pass urine infrequently to increase bladder size. If your child has daytime frequency, encourage him or her to go less frequently without making an issue out of it. By all means, don't remind your child to use the bathroom. On the other hand, always have your child pass urine at bedtime. The night should start with an empty bladder.

How to Protect the Bed from Urine • Most children wear extra-thick underwear in addition to pajamas. This keeps much of the urine from getting through to the sheets. If your child agrees, disposable diapers will make morning cleanups easier. Large ones, such as Attends by Proctor & Gamble, come in all waist sizes starting at 20 inches. Since the lining of these diapers remains dry, place a cotton washcloth inside so your child can be awakened by the sensation of wetness. Pinned cloth diapers should be avoided because they can't be taken off and put on by your child. Discontinue disposable diapers when your child stays dry for a whole week or starts to use a bed-wetting alarm. Since odor becomes a problem if urine soaks into the mattress or blankets, protect the mattress with a plastic mattress cover or washable vinyl mattress pad. Protect the blankets (and they should be washable ones) with a sheet of plastic placed between the top sheet and blankets.

A Morning Routine for Wet Pajamas and Wet Bedding • On wet mornings, your child can rinse pajamas and underwear in the sink until the odor is gone. If your child smells of urine, he or she will need to take a quick rinse in the shower to avoid teasing at school. You can cut down on the laundry by placing a dry towel under your child's buttocks each night. This can be rinsed each morning and saved until washday. If a wet bed is left open to the air, the wet sheets will usually be dry by noon. Odor may require the sheets to be washed one extra time per week. You don't need to wash wet bedding for hygienic reasons, since normal urine has no germs in it.

Respond Positively for Dry Nights • Dry mornings should always receive some positive recognition. At least your child should receive words of praise and a hug from everyone in the family. A calendar with gold stars or "happy faces" for dry nights may also help. If you visit your child's physician, bring this calendar with you.

Respond Gently to Wet Nights • Your child does not like being wet. Most bed-wetters feel quite guilty about this problem. They need sympathy, not blame, criticism, or punishment. In addition, siblings should not be allowed to tease bed-wetters. If they do, send them to their room for 15 minutes. Punishment or pressure will only delay a cure and it could cause secondary emotional problems. Be supportive of your child.

ADDITIONAL INTERVENTION WHEN YOUR CHILD REACHES AGE 6 Keep the previous recommendations in effect and add the following:

Bladder Stretching Exercises • Bladder stretching exercises may be helpful for any child with enuresis. However, they should only be initiated if your child wants to try them. During the daytime, encourage your child to hold his or her urine as long as possible. Whenever your child feels the urge to go, he can try to distract himself for the 10 seconds or so it takes for the bladder spasms to stop. Learning to resist and postpone the first urge to urinate is especially important. This will gradually enlarge the size of the bladder so that it can hold more urine at night. Have your child drink adequate fluids during the day so he will have lots of practice holding back his urine.

At least once a day, have your child urinate into a measuring cup to see if he has maintained—or even beaten—his previous record (in ounces). Mark the highest volume achieved with a piece of masking tape on the bottle. The normal bladder capacity is 1 or more ounces per year of age. In a 6-year-old, a capacity of 5 ounces or less is small. A capacity of 6 to 8 is normal and can hold the night's urine production without the need for awakening. Normal adult bladder size is 14 to 16 ounces.

Self-Awakening Program for Children with Small Bladders • These children will not be dry unless they get up to urinate 1 or more times during the night. Children with normal bladder size don't need to do this. The best way to have this happen is for your child to learn to awaken herself at night. It is not helpful for you to awaken her. Have your child practice the following at bedtime:

1. Go to bed before emptying your bladder.
2. Practice the following 3 times:

   • Lie on your bed with your eyes closed.

   • Pretend it's the middle of the night.

   • Pretend your bladder is full.

   • Pretend it's starting to ache.

   • Pretend it's trying to wake you up.

   • Pretend it's saying: "Get up before it's too late."

   • Then run to the bathroom.

   • Urinate a small amount.

   • Return to bed.

3. Empty your bladder on the third (last) practice run.
4. Remind yourself to get up like this if you need to urinate during the night. If you need a flashlight or night light, ask for it.

Note: Some preschoolers can learn to get up at night if a potty chair is kept next to the bed and the parent whispers "Try to get up to pee" into the child's ear at bedtime.

Self-Awakening When Wet • If your child is wet at night, he should try to get up and change himself. First, if he feels any urine leaking out, he should clamp down and try to stop the flow of urine. Second, he should hurry to the toilet to see if he has any urine left in his bladder. Third, he should change himself and put a dry towel over the wet part of the bed. This step can be made easier if dry pajamas and towels are always kept on a chair near the bed. The child who shows the motivation to carry out these steps is close to being able to awaken to the sensation of a full bladder.

Responsibility • Your child should feel that he or she is responsible for solving this problem. The bladder exercises, awakening program, fluid restriction, and record keeping need your child's involvement and commitment. By all means, don't try to awaken your child at night. As long as you're doing it, your child won't do it for himself. Your child should look upon his parents and physician as people who can provide suggestions and support.

Call Your Child's Physician Later If

• Your child is over 6 years of age and is not better after 3 months using this treatment program.

ADDITIONAL INTERVENTION WHEN YOUR CHILD REACHES AGE 8
Keep the previous recommendations in effect. Talk with your physician about possibly adding the following:

Bed-Wetting Alarms • Several new transistorized alarm devices that are lightweight, sensitive to a few drops of urine, not too expensive (about $40), and easy to set up can be used to condition a child to awaken when he or she needs to urinate during the night. They have the highest success rate (about 70 percent) of any available approach. They are the treatment of choice for any bed-wetter with a small bladder who can't otherwise train himself to awaken at night. The brand names are Wet-Stop (from Palco Laboratories, 5026 Scotts Valley Drive, Scotts Valley, CA 95066) and Nytone (from Nytone, Medical Products Inc., Salt Lake City, UT 84119).

Directions for the Youngster on Using a Bed-Wetting Alarm

- This is your alarm. It can help you cure your bed-wetting only if you use it correctly. Remember, the main purpose of the alarm is to help you get up during the night and use the toilet. The alarm won't work unless you listen for it carefully and respond to it quickly. It's the backup system for your self-awakening program.

- Hook up the alarm system by yourself. Trigger the buzzer a few times by touching the sensors with a moist finger and practice what you will do if it goes off during the night (namely, go to the bathroom).

- Have a night light or flashlight near your bed so it will be easy to see what you are doing when the alarm sounds.

- Give yourself a pep talk at bedtime. Try to "beat the buzzer" by waking up when your bladder feels full but before any urine leaks out. If the buzzer does go off, try to wake up and stop urinating at the first moment that you think you hear the alarm—even if you think you are hearing it in a dream.

- Once you've awakened, turn off the buzzer's sound by removing the metal strip from the little pocket in your underwear (if you have a Wet-Stop) or disconnect the electrodes (if you have a Nytone) and dry them off.

- Hurry to the bathroom and see if you were able to keep some urine in your bladder. Empty your bladder.

- Put on dry underwear and pajamas, and reconnect the alarm. Put a dry towel over the wet spot on your bed.

- In the morning write on your calendar DRY, WET SPOT (if you got up after the alarm went off), or WET (if you didn't get up).

- Use the alarm every night until you go 3 or 4 weeks without bed-wetting. This usually takes 2 to 3 months, so don't expect a quick result.

The Parent's Role with Alarms • During the first week, your child may need some help waking up to the sound of the buzzer. The goal is for your child to awaken immediately. Give your child 10 seconds. If he or she hasn't responded by then, turn on the lights. If that doesn't work, run a cold washcloth over your child's face to bring him out of a deep sleep. By all means, don't turn off the buzzer. Your child has to learn to do that for himself. Help your child become completely independent in following the directions listed above. Stay in the background and phase out of your child's alarm program as soon as possible.

Alarm Clock • If your child is unable to awaken herself at night and you can't afford a bed-wetting alarm, teach her to use an alarm clock or clock radio. Set it for 3 to 4 hours after your child goes to bed. Put it beyond arm's reach. Have your child practice responding to the alarm during the day while lying on the bed with eyes closed. Have your child set up the alarm clock each night. Praise your child for getting up at night, even if she isn't dry in the morning.

Drugs • Unfortunately, the available drugs are not helpful to children with small bladders. In addition, none of them is completely safe. The new alarm systems and self-awakening programs have practically eliminated the need to use powerful drugs for bed-wetting. My preference is to prescribe a drug only if a child needs extra help at camp or on a vacation. If you do use a drug, be careful about the amount used, where the drug is stored, and keeping the safety cap on the bottle.

TELEVISION: REDUCING THE NEGATIVE IMPACT

TV has a tremendous influence on how children view our world. Youngsters spend more hours watching TV from birth to age 18 than they spend in the classroom. The positive aspects include seeing different life-styles and cultures and entering school more knowledgeable than children did before the era of TV. Television also presents some positive, even heroic, role models. In addition, TV has great entertainment value, providing humor, excitement, and other types of diversion. Unfortunately, many children watch TV excessively and therefore experience some of its negative consequences.

HARMFUL ASPECTS OF TV

• *TV fosters passive types of recreation.* It decreases time spent with peers, when games and other creative activities are experienced. It decreases daydreaming and thinking time. It takes away the practice time required to become competent at any sport or art form. Television is especially dangerous for children who already tend to be shy or withdrawn.

- *TV interferes with conversation and discussion time,* especially if kept on during meals. It reduces social interactions with family and friends.

- *TV discourages reading.* Reading requires much more brain activity and thinking than television. Reading improves a youngster's vocabulary. A falloff in reading scores may be related to excessive TV time.

- *Heavy TV viewing (more than 4 hours a day) definitely reduces school performance.* This much TV interferes with study, reading, and thinking time. If watching television prevents adequate sleep, the children will not be alert enough to learn well on the following day.

- *TV discourages exercise.* An inactive life-style leads to poor physical fitness. If accompanied by frequent snacking, watching TV may contribute to weight problems. A recent study found that for each additional hour of television watched per week, the tendency toward obesity was increased by 1 percent.

- *TV advertising encourages a demand for material possessions.* Particular toys are highlighted in such a way that young children pressure their parents to buy them. TV portrays materialism as the "American way."

- *TV advertising teaches poor eating habits.* Sweets (such as sugared cereals) tend to be emphasized for young children.

- *TV advertising teaches a magical trust in health products, drugs, and vitamins.* TV suggests that there is a pill for every symptom.

- *TV fosters a poor reality base.* Young children through age 10 have some difficulty separating fact from fantasy. Television frequently presents a distorted view of the world in which most problems have easy solutions. Game shows may give children the sense that they can suddenly become rich and that hard work and delayed gratification are unnecessary.

- *TV depicts unrealistic stereotypes of human beings.* Men outnumber women 3 to 1 on television shows. Minority groups, elderly people, common occupations, and middle-class life-styles are underrepresented.

- *TV is sexually seductive.* Television programs and commercials depict relationships that rapidly progress to sexual activity. The risks and ethics of promiscuity are seldom addressed. Many of the lead characters also smoke and drink heavily.

- *TV violence creates its own set of problems.* Crime and violence occurs on television ten times as often as in real life. Viewing violence may cause pessimism regarding personal safety and the future. Several studies have shown that TV violence can lead to apathy toward violence. TV violence may numb the normal sympathy toward victims. Young children may be more aggressive in their play after seeing violent television shows. While TV violence does not increase aggressive behavior toward people in most children, it may do so in disturbed or impulsive children.

THE PREVENTION OF TV ADDICTION

- *Encourage active recreational outlets.* Help your child become interested in sports, games, hobbies, and music. Occasionally turn off the television and take a walk or play a game with your child.

- *Read more to your children* and encourage their own reading as they become older. Help them improve their conversational skills.

- *Limit TV time to 2 hours per day or less.* Allowing children to view excessive amounts of television is probably an even greater problem in our country than watching violence on TV. Another alternative is to limit TV to 1 hour on school nights and 2 or 3 hours per day on weekends. Special educational programs may receive exemption. Don't allow your child to have a TV set in his or her bedroom, because this limits your control of TV hours. Also, don't use television as a babysitter for preschool children. Preschoolers should be limited to 1 hour of television viewing a day, since they are most confused by what is really happening on TV shows. If you cut back your child's TV watching, don't be surprised if he initially complains. Excessive TV watching is a habit that, once established, is hard to break. Suggest other activities to fill the free time.

- *Turn off the TV set during meals.* Family time is too precious to be squandered on TV shows. After your children are grown up and have left home, you will probably regret it if your mealtimes were not protected and your children were allowed to disappear into their private TV worlds while they ate. In addition, don't use television as a background sound in your house. If you don't like silence, leave a radio or record player on. Television is too engrossing a medium. It demands to be seen as well as heard.

• *Set a bedtime deadline* that is not altered by TV shows that interest your child. Children who are allowed to stay up late and watch television may be tired the following day and perform poorly in school.

• *Teach critical viewing.* Turn the TV on only when a specific program is going to be watched. Don't turn it on at random and scan for something interesting. Teach your child to look first in the program guide. On some nights, nothing worthwhile or entertaining is on television.

• *Teach your child to turn off the TV set* at the end of a show. If it is allowed to stay on, your child will probably become interested in the following show and then it will be difficult to turn it off.

• *If your child is doing poorly in school, limit TV time* to ½ hour per day. Make a rule that homework must be finished before television is watched. If you have a VCR, your child can record a favorite show and watch it later.

• *Encourage the watching of shows that are educational* or teach human values. Point out characters who care about others. Encourage watching documentaries, debates, or programs about great artists. Look at what public television has to offer (including the absence of advertising). Use programs about love, sex, family disputes, drinking, and drugs to open family discussions on these difficult topics.

• *Try to be present with your child* the first time he or she watches a new program. Help decide whether or not this is a program you wish to allow your child to watch on a weekly basis.

• *Forbid violent TV shows.* This means you have to keep track of what your child is watching and turn off the TV set when you don't approve of the program. With children of different ages, don't let your younger children watch the shows that you have approved for your older children (including the evening news). The availability of cable television and videocassette recorders means that any child of any age has access to the uncut versions of R-rated films. Children cannot see R-rated movies in theaters without parents until the age of 17. These films may depict maiming, torture, brutal murder, rape, sadism, profound terror, or slaughtering of masses. The scenes may be presented in slow, agonizing closeup. Some children develop daytime fears and nightmares because they have been allowed to watch such frightening movies. I would strongly suggest that you decide which R-rated films (if any) your child watches on cable TV from age 14 to 17 depending on maturity.

• *Discuss the consequences of violence* if you elect to watch shows that contain it. Point out how violence hurts both the victim and his family. Be sure to discuss any program that has content which upsets your child.

• *Discuss commercials with your children.* Help them identify high-pressure selling and exaggerated claims. If your child wants a toy that is a look-alike version of a TV character, ask him how he will use it at home. Point out foods that cause cavities.

• *Discuss the differences between reality and make-believe.* This type of clarification can help your child enjoy a show and yet realize that what is happening doesn't happen in real life.

• *Set a good example.* If you are a TV addict, you can be sure your child will become one. Start yourself on a TV diet.

THE WORKING MOTHER: JUGGLING CHILDREN, HOME, AND CAREER

THE DECISION TO WORK

Reasons for Working • At this time only 10 percent of American households include a mother whose role is strictly that of homemaker-wife. More than 50 percent of mothers with infants are working outside the home. The frequency is even higher for mothers of preschoolers.

The reasons for working outside the home are many. In some families, it is financial need, as in a single-parent family.

Other mothers work because two incomes are needed for financial stability or are desired to sustain a middle-class life-style. For some mothers it is the personal preference of work over "housekeeping and mothering." For others it is essential for staying up-to-date in a fast-changing career, as well as for the fulfillment work brings. It has often been said that a satisfied parent makes a better parent.

The question of returning to work versus staying at home has no easy or correct answer. The decision is one that each parent must make based on her particular circumstances.

Pros and Cons of Being a Working Mother • If you can provide your child with a consistent nurturing caretaker, there is no evidence that your return to work will cause your child any harm. Children of working mothers develop as well emotionally as do other children. Working does not weaken the mother-child bond. In fact, there are several benefits for your child in having a working mother. These include increased independence, self-esteem, responsibility, and maturity. Young children of working mothers learn to trust other adults and to negotiate better with peers—increased social skills. Other advantages include, for girls, having higher career aspirations and, for boys, learning that fathers share in housework. Each parent must decide how important it is for her to be present during her child's early years. Research does not document any dire consequences to the children of working mothers.

Timing the Return to Work • A mother should try to remain at home for 6 to 8 weeks after the birth of her baby in order to recover physically from normal childbirth. A preferred maternity leave might extend to 4 months after the birth, at which time the mother would have developed greater confidence regarding her mothering skills and have a baby who sleeps through the night. Unfortunately, few mothers can return to work at the time of their preference. Many mothers need to return to work because of financial realities and the limits of subsidized leave. At this time only 40 percent of jobs provide any paid maternity leave, and a smaller percent guarantee job security through unpaid leave until the baby is 4 months of age. In fact, the United States is the only advanced nation without federal legislation guaranteeing maternity leave. (Over 100 nations do have such leave.)

The optimal length of maternity leave is unknown and should probably be based upon individual preference. Although some authorities suggest that mothers should attempt to spend the first 2 or 3 years of their babies' life fully involved with child rearing, the advantages of this commitment remain unproven. Mothers should not feel guilty about returning to work when their babies are 2 to 4 months of age.

CHILD CARE RESOURCES

Types of Child Care • Several types of child care are available in most communities. During the first 2 years of life, children often do better with individual care or family daycare because they need more cuddling and personal attention. The childcare arrangements are listed in descending order of preference for younger infants.

- *Individual Care in Your Own Home.* This is the preferred arrangement for infants. The care is usually provided by a grandmother or professional sitter. Often the parents will need to advertise in the local newspaper. The applicant's references need to be carefully checked, especially for characteristics that are important to you. While most professional sitters provide part-time services, some are available as live-ins (a nanny).

- *Individual Care in Someone Else's Home.* This arrangement is very similar to the previous one except that your child will not have the extra stability of being cared for in his or her own home. In addition, you will need to pack diapers, bottles, and toys, as well as to transport your child to the sitter's home.

- *Family Daycare Homes.* In these settings a mother may care for 2 to 5 children in her home. This is the most common type of daycare used for young children and it's usually less expensive than center-based care. Disadvantages are that the children do not usually receive as much individual attention, and many of these homes are not licensed or monitored by the state.

- *Center-Based Daycare.* In these settings 30 or more children may be cared for. Because of the numbers, many children do not adapt well to these large centers until they are over age 2 or 2½ years. Optimal daycare centers are workplace-based, but they remain uncommon in our country. Daycare centers are state-licensed and must comply with certain standards. If you are looking for a daycare center, assemble a list from friends or by looking in the Yellow Pages under "Child Care" or "Day Nurseries and Child Care."

The Substitute Caregiver: Choosing the Right Person • The most important factor in your decision about choosing a child-care resource is finding a caretaker who understands and meets children's emotional needs. Choose someone who is warm, affectionate, sympathetic, plays with the children, and has a sense of humor. Avoid someone who is harsh, fussy, nagging, regimented, or overly concerned with neatness, cleanliness, and order. Try to find someone who understands children's normal emotional development. Look for someone who listens to and complies with your expectations (e.g., no spanking, and similar toilet training methods). Form a close partnership with your child's caregiver. Choose a center that has a staff with a positive attitude toward parents, and then support that staff for what they provide for your child. Competition and rivalry are unnecessary if you've chosen well. Be sure that no more than two consistent caregivers are assigned to your child. More than three or four parent-equivalents (including the parents) can cause confusion and lack of security for a young child.

Choosing the Right Child-Care Environment • Don't make your final decision about a child-care center until you have visited it for at least half a day. Children deserve high standards of care. During your visit review the following checklist.

• The ratio of staff to children should be 1:3 for infants (especially for those who don't feed themselves) and 1:4 to 1:6 for preschool children, depending upon their age. By and large these ratios are regulated by each state.

• Each child has a regular primary caregiver assigned.

• The staff turnover is low.

• The playground is safe.

• Sinks and toilets are adequate.

• Diapers are changed promptly, not on some schedule.

• Space and time are adequate for rest and naps.

• Staff members wash their hands after changing diapers and before handling food.

• The staff doesn't smoke on the premises.

• A TV or VCR with tapes is absent or viewed minimally.

• The center's atmosphere is positive when one enters it.

- The children appear happy and busy.

- The children receive individualized attention.

- The children receive plenty of verbal stimulation. (Be concerned if the setting is too quiet.)

- The staff works through praise and suggestion rather than criticism and punishment.

- Staff members are warm, affectionate, and not afraid to hug the children.

- The staff welcomes you as a visitor at any time.

- The staff welcomes your suggestions and questions.

- The staff provides feedback about each child at the time of pickup, especially if anything significant has happened.

Helping Your Child Adjust to Daycare • All parents occasionally need to leave their child with another caretaker while they go to an appointment, go shopping, or go out for an evening. Daycare is simply an extension of this concept. However, your child will not be ready to adjust to a daycare setting unless the child has had previous successful experiences with a babysitter within your home. Also, before beginning daycare, your child should have had ample opportunity to visit with other children in friends' homes. Because of the separation fears that children normally experience between 6 months and 2½ years of age, being left at daycare can initially be somewhat stressful during this time. Talk about the daycare center before you actually go there. Then visit it briefly, pointing out the positive aspects.

When you take your child to daycare for the first day, plan on spending that day there. Let your child gradually reach out and become involved with the other children and staff. When the day arrives for you to leave your child at daycare, stay 5 or 10 minutes while your child makes a transition to interacting with a member of the daycare staff. Leave a familiar toy or security object with your child. If the daycare center is near your workplace, visit your child during the day. When you leave, do so with a cheerful attitude and let your child know you are leaving—don't sneak away. Don't be surprised if your child gets teary on the first days that you depart from the daycare center. When you pick your child up, there may also be tears. For the first week your child may talk about not wanting to return. Remain firm in your decision and your child will gradually adapt to the change. Some children take as long as 1 or 2 months to look forward to attending daycare. Usually, this process cannot be hurried.

Dealing with a Sick Child • The onset of illness can be a major disruption for the working mother. Many daycare centers will not accept sick children. Your options are: staying home with your child, using your sick leave; having your spouse take time off from work and stay home with your child; or having your child stay with a friend or relative who has agreed in advance to be a backup for illness care. Rarely, a parent may have the type of job in which an employer will allow an employee to work at home for a day under these conditions. Sick-care programs for children are springing up across the country to help working parents deal with this situation. Many of these services are based in a special sick wing of a large daycare center. Some agencies offer sick-care babysitters who come into the home and look after children for the working mother. Care for sick children is more expensive than regular child care.

When a child becomes sick, the parents first have to decide whether or not their child needs to see a physician. Refer to the guidelines in this book that pertain to your child's symptoms to help answer this question. If your child becomes sick during the working day and your review of his illness indicates that he needs to see a physician, try to arrange for a late-afternoon appointment by calling before 3:00 P.M. More and more physicians are scheduling evening clinic hours to accommodate the high numbers of working parents.

A second decision that a working parent must make is when is the child well enough to return to daycare. Children with a sore throat, moderate cough, runny nose, or cold symptoms (but without a fever or breathing difficulties) can usually return to daycare. In the first place, daycare is where they acquired the infection. In the second place, the spread of colds cannot be prevented. The return should be based mainly on how well your child feels. Children with fevers (over 100° F), chickenpox, vomiting, or diarrhea cannot return to a regular daycare setting. Children with a strep throat or an eye infection can usually return after 24 hours on an antibiotic. Many child-care centers have their own rules about which children will be excluded, and you should become familiar with these rules (see CONTAGIOUS DISEASES AND INCUBATION PERIODS, page 314).

Latchkey Children (Self-Care) • A latchkey child is a school-age child who is left alone either before or after school while his parent is at work. The name comes from the wearing of a house key around the neck. This practice of self-care has been estimated to occur for 3 million children between 6 and 12 years of age, and 7 million children between 12 and 18 years of age. Elementary-school-age children often develop fears from being left alone. They feel unsafe, lonely, and neglected.

The following recommendations may make the practice more acceptable.

• Children shouldn't be left alone unless they are over 10 years of age.

• They should not spend more than 2 hours per day alone—which means they should not be left alone during school holidays or when they are sick.

• They should be taught how to handle household emergencies and what telephone numbers to call for assistance.

• A safe play area should be designated.

• They should not be left with too many chores, because they need time for schoolwork and entertainment.

• Sometimes the availability of pets will provide a sense of protection and companionship.

• The parents should be available by telephone and periodically call the children during this time. Children should also have a backup adult who lives close by and whom they can call or visit if they have any questions.

• The parents should be punctual about the time at which they promise they will come home.

Since the latchkey-child practice is clearly a compromise, the availability of after-school services for these children in schools or churches is a welcome development.

SURVIVING EACH DAY AS A WORKING MOTHER

Look for a Supportive Employer and Workplace • The most difficult part of being a working mother is trying to carry out three jobs. There is not enough time in the day to permit this. If it's financially and emotionally acceptable, try to find part-time work. Some employers offer flexible schedules, with a set number of hours per week fulfilled during different times of the day. Other jobs allow the employee to work in her home. Job sharing by two women, each working 20 hours per week, is another alternative. Clearly the options are changing rapidly in our country. However, many women with financial needs or career obligations continue to work 40 or more hours per week. The following recommendations may help to lessen their burden.

Avoid Fatigue • If you can't get enough sleep, nothing else will seem to turn out right. You won't have the initiative to nurture your children at the end of the day. You won't have the energy necessary to maintain a marriage or friendships. Pick a reasonable bedtime and stay with it. Cut corners in other areas but protect your sleep time.

Provide Contact Time with Your Child • Research has shown that quality time with children is more important than the quantity of time. Try to make breakfast a pleasant, unhurried occasion. Try to talk with your child during the drive to and from the child-care center. Use the 30 minutes before bedtime to discuss the day's events at your child's pace. Set aside special half-days on weekends to do things with your child. If you have a young infant, breast-feeding may be your special time. While many authorities suggest that parents reserve the first 30 minutes upon arrival at home for uninterrupted individualized time, this is usually impractical. Also, don't be surprised when you pick up your child if he or she "falls apart." Your child is only releasing tensions that have built up over the day, and is releasing them to the person he or she feels safest with.

Reduce Your Housework Time • If you can afford it, hire a housekeeper. In any case, try to simplify your home life. A spotless house must become a low priority. Do less cooking. Make triple recipes and freeze leftovers. Ask other family members to help you. It is imperative that the spouse share with the housework and child care. The father must actively participate in what was formerly considered the mother's responsibilities. He must be more than "available" or a "backup." He must look after more than outside work and the car. Child care and housework tasks must be redistributed to prevent the mother from becoming overworked. The father can help buy a son's clothing, do car-pooling, cook, and do housecleaning chores. School-age children can also be assigned some chores.

Watch Out for Guilt • Be proud of your achievements. If you have chosen a good child-care resource, you should be comfortable during the day with your child's well-being. If your child and husband are happy, you are doing an excellent job. Don't compare yourself to your mother or necessarily expect support from her or other relatives for your pursuit of a career. Try to understand that the "Supermom" is a myth. You can't do everything singlehandedly or perfectly. You need help and deserve help. You don't need to apologize to anyone for not doing well enough. And despite your best efforts, your child will sometimes cry when dropped off at daycare and will sometimes become sick. Try not to rethink your career decision every time this happens.

Nurture Your Marriage • The main loss for a working mother is recreational time with her husband. Try to compartmentalize your life. You deserve a break from your endless list of unfinished work. Relaxation time is essential, not frivolous or wasteful. Plan it and savor it. Make a date for a night out with your husband at least once a week. A strong marriage is an important underpinning for a working mother.

Single-Parent Families: Extra Help • Try to find a friend with a child close in age to yours. Share shopping, overnight and weekend visits, babysitting, car-pooling, and other responsibilities with your friend. Trading services will, in this way, save you money. Sometimes, living with another single mother is mutually beneficial. It's crucial that you spend time with other adults and do something for yourself once in a while. Consider joining an organization for single parents.

RECOMMENDED READING

T. Berry Brazelton, *Working and Caring* (Reading, Mass.: Addison-Wesley, 1985).

Earl A. Grollman and Gerri L. Sweder, *The Working Parent Dilemma* (Boston: Beacon Press, 1986).

Lynette Long and Thomas Long, *The Handbook for Latchkey Children and Their Parents* (New York: Arbor House, 1983).

Helen L. Swan and Victoria Houston, *Alone After School: A Self-Care Guide for Latchkey Children and Their Parents* (Englewood Cliffs, N.J.: Prentice-Hall, 1985).

DIVORCE'S IMPACT ON CHILDREN

More than 1 million children are affected by divorce each year. Over a third of U.S. marriages end in divorce. Our primary goal should be to minimize the emotional harm to these children. The main way to achieve this is to help them maintain a close and secure relationship with both parents. The following recommendations may be helpful.

- *Reassure your children that both parents love them.* Clarify that although you are unhappy with each other and disagree about many things, the one subject you both completely agree on is "We love you." Demonstrating this love by time together is even more important. Preschoolers need lots of cuddling from both parents, but don't start bad habits like letting your child sleep with you.

- *Keep constant as many parts of your child's world as you can.* Try to keep your child in the same home or neighborhood. If this is impossible, at least try to keep your child in the same school with the same teachers, friends, and teams (even if it's on a temporary basis). Reassure your child that although your standard of living will decrease some, that you will continue to have the basic necessities of living (i.e., food, clothing, and shelter).

- *Reassure your child that the noncustodial parent will visit.* Young children are confused by divorce and fear that one parent may abandon them. Children need to know that they will have ongoing contact with their father (or mother, if the father has custody). The custodial parent should strongly support the visiting schedule. Your child needs both parents. Have a scheduled predictable time for visiting. One full day every 1 or 2 weeks is usually preferable to more frequent, rushed, brief visits. Your child will eagerly look forward to visiting, so the visiting parent must keep promises, be punctual, and remember birthdays and other special events. If there is more than one child, all should spend equal time or the same time with the noncustodial parent to prevent favoritism. Try not to do too much in one day. Even more important, both parents should work to make these visits pleasant. Allow your child to tell you he had a good time during the visit with your ex-spouse. Children should also be provided with the telephone number of the noncustodial parent and encouraged to call at regular intervals. If the noncustodial parent has moved to a distant city, telephone calls and letters become essential to the ongoing relationship.

- *If the noncustodial parent becomes uninvolved, find substitutes.* Turn to relatives and Big Brother or Big Sister volunteers to spend more time with your son or daughter. Explain to your child that "Your dad [or mom] is not capable right now of being available for you. He's sorting out his own problems. There's not much we can do to change that." Help your child verbalize his or her sense of disappointment and loss. If your child is a teenager, writing and calling may eventually reengage the absent parent.

- *Help your child talk about painful feelings.* At the time of separation and divorce, many children experience symptoms of anxiety, depression, and anger, as would be seen with any crisis. They are frequently on the brink of tears, sleep poorly, have stomachaches, experience a decline in school performance, and so forth. To help these symptoms pass, your child should be encouraged to talk about the unhappy feelings and should receive understanding and support. A divorce talk group at school can help children counter the isolation and shame they often feel. When anger turns into disruptive behavior, limits must be imposed while you help your child express the anger. Your child needs reassurance that he or she didn't in any way cause the divorce.

- *Clarify that the divorce is final.* Some children hold on to a wish to reunite the parents and pretend that the separation is temporary. Clarifying that the divorce is final can help children mourn their loss and move on to more adaptive functioning.

- *Try to protect your child's positive feelings about both parents.* If possible, mention the good points about the other parent. Don't be overly honest about your negative feelings toward your ex-spouse. (You need to unload these feelings on another adult, not your children.) Devaluing or discrediting the other parent in your child's presence can reduce your child's personal self-esteem and create greater stress.

  Don't ask your child to take sides. A child does not need to have a single loyalty to one parent. Your child should not have to choose between parents. Your child should be able to love both of you, even though you don't love each other.

- *Maintain normal discipline in both households.* Children need consistent child rearing practices. Overindulgence or leniency by one parent makes it more difficult for the other parent to get the child to behave. Constant competition for the child's love through gifts or special privileges leads to a spoiled child. The general ground rules regarding discipline should be set by the custodial parent.

- *Don't argue about your child in the child's presence.* Children are quite upset by seeing their parents fight. Most important, avoid any arguments regarding visiting, custody, or child support in your child's presence. Try to resolve your remaining differences in a civilized way.

- *Try to avoid custody disputes.* Your child badly needs a sense of stability. Challenge custody only if the custodial parent is causing obvious harm or repeated distress to your child. False accusations of physical abuse or sexual abuse cause great emotional anguish for the child. If possible, don't split siblings unless they are adolescents and state a clear preference for living in different settings.

CALL YOUR CHILD'S PHYSICIAN DURING OFFICE HOURS IF

- Your child has symptoms that interfere with schoolwork, eating, or sleeping for more than 2 weeks.

- You feel your child is depressed.

- Your child has any physical symptoms, due to the divorce, lasting for more than 6 months.

- Your child continues to want the parents to come back together again for more than 1 year after the divorce.

- You feel the other parent is harming your child.

- Your child refuses visits with the noncustodial parent.

RECOMMENDED READING

Linda B. Francke, *Growing Up Divorced* (New York: Fawcett Crest, 1983).

Richard A. Gardner, *The Boys and Girls Book About Divorce* (New York: Bantam Books, 1970).

Richard A. Gardner, *The Parents Book About Divorce* (New York: Bantam Books, 1976).

SCHOOLWORK RESPONSIBILITY

All parents want their children to grow up to be responsible adults who keep their promises, meet deadlines, and succeed at their jobs. This type of behavior begins with taking responsibility for schoolwork. Responsible children finish schoolwork, homework, and long-term projects on time. They remember their assignments and turn in papers. They occasionally ask for help (e.g., with a spelling list) but usually like to think through their work by themselves.

HOW TO RAISE A CHILD WHO IS RESPONSIBLE FOR SCHOOLWORK

The following suggestions should help you instill the trait of responsibility in your child:

* *Encourage learning and responsibility in the preschool years.* Listen attentively to your child's conversation. Encourage him to think for himself. Take your child to the library and read to him regularly. Watch educational programs together and talk about them. Provide in yourself an adult model who reads, finds learning exciting, enjoys problem-solving, and likes to try new things.

   For responsibility, actively encourage your preschool child to help you with chores: Say "Hand me the screw driver," "Let's water the garden," or "Let's bake some cookies." Provide work experiences that end in success, be it generous praise or a job well done. Don't make life too easy for your child.

* *Clarify that schoolwork is between your child and the teacher.* When your child begins school she should understand that homework, schoolwork, and marks are strictly between her and her teacher. Parents have their jobs, and children have their schoolwork. Both are private matters. The only person who should set goals for better school performance is the teacher, not the parents. For example, don't find fault with, or ask your child to rework, corrected papers she brings home.

* *Clarify that your child alone is responsible for school performance.* Your child must feel solely responsible for successes and failures in school. People take pride in things more if they feel fully responsible for them. Parents who feel responsible for their child's school performance open the door

for the child to turn this responsibility over to them. But forced responsibility is a myth, and shared responsibility is a trap. Occasionally, elementary-school teachers may ask you to review basic facts or see that your child completes work that was put off at school. Since this request comes from the school, it's fine for you to help out temporarily.

• *Praise your child's school accomplishments.* Recognize and comment positively on the graded papers your child brings home. Praise each report card. Listen to your child's comments about school. Show interest in the books your child selects to read. Your child should feel that you are interested in and pleased with his or her school performance.

• *Support the school staff's recommendations.* Convey that you respect both the school system and the teacher, at least in your child's presence. Verbal attacks on the school will pit your child against it. Even when you disagree with the school's policies, you should encourage your child to conform to school rules. In some cases explain to your child that there are many rules in life which all of us have to obey, even though they may not always make sense.

• *Avoid Nagging.* Nagging about schoolwork promotes rebellion. So do moralizing, criticizing, lecturing, and threatening your child. Pressure is different from parental interest and encouragement. Pressure and punishment are negative approaches. They are destructive to self-esteem; and if they work at all, they work only temporarily. Your child's ability to see studying as a pathway to a future career, his desire to please the teacher and be admired by peers, his enjoyment in knowing things, and his own self-reproach when he falls short of his goals are more effective as long-term motivators. Try to expect the best of your child without dwelling on it or demanding it. Many parents fall into the trap of nagging about long assignments. If you rescue your child from missing the deadline once, he will need you again the next time. Help your child learn to schedule his time by staying out of it. His teacher will give periodic reminders.

• *Avoid Bribing.* Bribes (such as money, special trips, movies, or special presents) in exchange for school performance are shortcuts that rarely work. Your child easily recognizes them for what they really are—last-ditch attempts to control the learning process. This does not imply that you cannot give your child a gift because of a significant breakthrough in schoolwork, but it should come unexpectedly and have no strings attached. At the other extreme, canceling something important (like membership in the Scouts) or taking away something (like a pet) because of poor marks is unfair and ineffective.

• *Avoid "Helping" with Homework.* Stay out of your child's homework. Asking if your child has homework, helping nightly, checking the finished homework, or drilling your child in areas of concern all convey to your child that you don't trust her. Doing your child's homework will reduce her confidence that she can do it herself next time. If your child asks for help with homework, help with the particular problem only. The help should concentrate on explaining the question, not on giving the answer. A good example of useful help is reading your child's spelling list to her while she writes the words. But let her check her own answers. The main purpose of homework is to teach your child to work on his or her own.

• *Avoid Dictating a Study Time.* Assigning a definite time for your child to do homework is destined for failure. No one can teach a child how to organize his time except himself. The main thing you can do is provide a conducive setting with a desk and good lighting. If any, the only rule should be "No television until homework is done." Your child's word that the work is done should be accepted without checking.

SPECIAL HELP FOR CHILDREN WITH LEARNING PROBLEMS

Some children have a mild learning problem that interferes with their learning part of the basic-skills subject matter (e.g., reading). Up until this point, my comments have assumed that your child has no learning limitations. If a child with a reading disability slips further behind in class, the normal parent becomes concerned. (Note: The concern under discussion is "Why is my child not reading on grade level?"; it is not "Why is my child not in the highest reading group?") During the early years of school, children develop a concept of themselves as either competent or dumb. With extra help, the children with learning disabilities can preserve their self-esteem and sense of competency.

Ask for a parent-teacher conference. Hopefully your child can be provided with the needed extra tutoring within the school setting. If this is not possible, you can request that the teacher give extra assignments to be carried out with home tutoring. The teacher can send home notes about what he or she wants you to help your child with (for instance, multiplication for two weeks). This approach continues to respect your child's responsibility for schoolwork because it originates with an order from the teacher. Provide this home instruction in a positive, helping way. As soon as you have achieved the original goal, remove yourself from the role of surrogate teacher. In this way you have provided temporary tutoring to help your child over an obstacle that the school does not have time or resources to deal with fully.

HOW TO HELP A CHILD OVERCOME SCHOOLWORK IRRESPONSIBILITY

Symptoms and Characteristics of Schoolwork Irresponsibility

- Performs below his or her potential at school.
- Parents tutor the child one or more hours every night.
- Parents check the child's answers to see if they are correct.
- Doesn't finish or turn in work at school.
- Changes grades on papers brought home.
- "Forgets" to bring homework home.
- Lies about homework being done.
- "Forgets," loses, or doesn't turn in finished homework.
- "Doesn't remember" what parents have taught.
- Has average or better intelligence, with no learning disabilities.

Causes • Some parents and teachers hold the false impression that children are basically lazy. They believe that they must force children to grow up and to learn. This is untrue. Babies are born with motivation, energy, and curiosity. These characteristics lead the normal child to explore and name everything in his or her environment. The normal child therefore finds school achievement rewarding in itself.

When parents exert pressure for better school performance, they can eventually destroy a child's natural motivation and learning drive. School pressure is looked upon as a threat to a child's independence. More pressure brings more resistance. Failing grades become the child's main way of proving that he is independent of his parents. Unlike discipline, responsibility cannot be externally imposed upon a child. It must develop within the child, growing from enjoyable, self-rewarding experiences.

If a family pattern of parental pressure and interference with the child's school performance is maintained for several years, the child learns to respond with resistance to most outside suggestions. The child becomes a school "under-achiever." This can happen in the best of homes. It can occur to the children of parents who know only too well the value of an education and want very much to help their children acquire this education.

How to Help Your Child Regain Responsibility for Schoolwork • The main approach is to withdraw completely from this power struggle you are in with your child. Stop any nagging, reminders, or criticism about your child's schoolwork. Restrictions are not an ultimate solution to any responsibility problem. Your child can learn the lesson of schoolwork accountability only through personal experience. If possible, apologize to your youngster. You can state: "After thinking about it, we have decided you are old enough to manage your own affairs. Schoolwork is your business and we will try to stay out it. We are confident you will do what is best for yourself."

The result of this "sink or swim" approach is that arguments will stop, but schoolwork may temporarily become worse. Your child may throw caution to the winds to see if you really mean what you have said. If your child is beyond sixth grade and very active outside the home, you may also need to ground the child for 1 or 2 weeks "to give you time to catch up in school." This period of standing and waiting for your child to find his or her own reason for doing well in school may be very agonizing. However, if you can avoid "rescuing" your child, his or her grades will show a dramatic upsurge in anywhere from 2 to 9 months. This planned withdrawal of parental pressure is best done in the early grades. At that time, marks are of minimal importance but the acquisition of a personal reason for learning is critical.

We can never force children to learn or be productive. Learning is a process of self-fulfillment. In some ways it is a sacred area that belongs to the child and one that we as parents should try to stay out of, despite our yearnings for our children's success in this dimension.

SHORT ATTENTION SPAN

SYMPTOMS AND CHARACTERISTICS

- Short attention span. Normal attention span is approximately 5 minutes per year of age. Therefore a 2-year-old should be able to concentrate for 10 minutes, and a child entering school for 25 minutes. (Note: The attention span while watching TV doesn't count.)

- Symptoms of short attention span include the following: The child hasn't learned to listen when someone talks, wait his or her turn, complete a task, or return to a task if interrupted. (These symptoms can be normal until 3 or 4 years of age.)

- The short attention span has been verified by two or more adults (e.g., parent and teacher)

- Some children also have associated hyperactivity (increased motor activity) with symptoms of being restless, impulsive, and in a hurry

- Some children also have an associated learning disability. The most common one is an auditory processing deficit (i.e., they can't understand complex instructions)

- Intelligence is usually normal

- Occurs mostly in males

- Also called Attention Deficit Disorder (A.D.D.) or Hyperactive Child

Similar Conditions • Disruptive children, children who don't mind, and aggressive children are sometimes included under the broad definition of hyperactivity. Many problem 2-year-olds are referred to as being "hyperactive." These children should be looked upon as children with behavior problems and approached with appropriate discipline techniques (see THE TERRIBLE TWOS AND TEMPER TANTRUMS, page 208).

Causes • Attention deficit disorder (A.D.D.) is the most common developmental disability. It occurs in 3 percent to 5 percent of children. *Developmental* means that the cause is immaturity of brain development. This delay results in poor self-control, requiring external controls by the parents for a longer period of time. Often this type of temperament and short attention span is hereditary. Your style of child rearing did not cause your child to have this limitation. Remind your friends and relatives that there is no simple way to "straighten out" your child. A small percent of children with A.D.D. are reacting to chaotic home environments. Despite controversy, minor brain damage has not been proven to be a cause of A.D.D.

Expected Course • The children with A.D.D. on a developmental basis can expect an excellent outcome if the parents and teachers provide understanding and direction, and preserve the child's self-esteem. Many of these children as adults have good attention spans but remain restless, have to keep busy, and, in a sense, have not entirely outgrown the problem. However, not only does society learn to tolerate such traits in adults but in some settings the person with endless energy is prized. Children with severe A.D.D. may need vocational counseling as adults.

CALL YOUR CHILD'S PHYSICIAN FOR REFERRAL TO A CHILD PSYCHIATRIST OR PSYCHOLOGIST IF

• Your child shows unprovoked aggression and destructiveness.

• Your child has repeated accidents.

• Your child has been suspended or expelled from school.

• Your child can't make or keep any friends.

• You have "given up" hope of improving your child.

• You can't stop using physical punishment on your child.

• You are at your wit's end.

Premise: All children with A.D.D. should already have been evaluated by their physician and, if of school age, by the school's special education teacher or psychologist.

GUIDELINES FOR LIVING WITH A CHILD HAVING A SHORT ATTENTION SPAN (HYPERACTIVE CHILD)

A.D.D. is a chronic condition that needs special parenting and school intervention. If your child seems to have a poor attention span and is over 3 years of age, these recommendations may assist you in helping your child. Your main obligations will involve organizing your child's home life and improving discipline. Only after your child's behavior has improved will you know for certain if your child also has a short attention span. If he does, specific interventions to help him learn to listen and complete tasks ("stretch" his attention span) can be initiated. Even though you can't be sure about poor attention span until your child is 3 or 4 years of age, you can detect and improve behavior problems at any time after 8 months of age.

• *Accept your child's limitations.* Accept the fact that your child is intrinsically active and energetic and possibly always will be. The hyperactivity is not intentional. Don't expect to eliminate the hyperactivity but merely bring it under reasonable control. Any criticism or other attempt to change an energetic child into a quiet or model child will cause more harm than good. Nothing is more helpful for the hyperactive child than having a tolerant, patient, low-keyed parent.

• *Provide an outlet for the release of excess energy.* This energy can't be bottled up and stored. Daily outdoor activities such as running, sports, and long walks are good outlets. A fenced yard helps. In bad weather your child needs a recreational room where he can play as he pleases with minimal restrictions and supervision. If no large room is available, a garage will sometimes suffice. Your child's toys should not be excessive in number, for this can accentuate his distractibility. They should also be ones that are safe and relatively unbreakable. Encourage your child to play with one toy at a time.

   Although the expression of hyperactivity is allowed in these ways, it should not be needlessly encouraged. Don't initiate roughhousing with your child. Siblings should be forbidden to say "Chase me, chase me," or to instigate other noisy play. Rewarding hyperactive behavior can lead to its becoming your child's main style of interacting with people.

• *Keep your home well organized.* Household routines help the hyperactive child to accept order. Make wake-up, mealtimes, snacks, chores, naps, and bedtime as consistent as possible. Try to keep your environment on the quiet side, since this encourages thinking and listening. In general, leave the radio and TV off. Predictable daily events help your child become more predictable in his or her responses.

• *Avoid fatigue in your child.* When a hyperactive child becomes exhausted, his self-control often breaks down and the hyperactivity becomes worse. Try to have your child sleep or rest when he is fatigued. If he can't seem to "turn off his motor," hold and rock him in a rocking chair.

- *Avoid taking your child to formal gatherings.* Settings where hyperactivity would be extremely inappropriate and embarrassing (such as churches or restaurants) can be completely avoided except for special occasions. To avoid some friction you also may wish to reduce the number of times you allow your child to accompany you to stores and supermarkets. Not only will you be able to shop more efficiently, but the store manager will also be grateful. After your child develops adequate self-control at home, he can gradually be introduced to these situations. Be sure to praise your child when he plays independently rather than interrupting you when you are talking to guests or on the telephone.

- *Maintain firm discipline.* These children are unquestionably difficult to manage. They need more carefully planned discipline than the average child. Rules should be formulated mainly to prevent harm to your child and to others. Aggressive behavior should be no more accepted in the hyperactive child than in the normal child. Unlike the expression of hyperactivity, you can try to eliminate aggressive behaviors, such as biting, hitting, and pushing. Unnecessary or unattainable rules should be avoided—don't expect your child to keep his hands and feet still. Hyperactive children tolerate fewer rules than the normal child. Set down a few clear, consistent, important rules and add other rules at your child's pace. Avoid constant negative comment like "Don't do this," and "Stop that."

- *Enforce rules with nonphysical punishment.* Physical punishment should be avoided in these children, since we want to teach them to be less aggressive rather than to make aggression acceptable. You will need an isolation or timeout room to back up your attempts to enforce rules if a show of disapproval doesn't work. This room can be your child's bedroom or a timeout chair. Your child should be sent there for about 1 minute per year of age. Without a timeout room, overall success is unlikely. Because of your child's short attention span, apply punishment for misbehavior immediately. Your child also needs adult models of control and calmness. Try to correct your child in a friendly, matter-of-fact voice. If you yell, your child will be quick to imitate you (see THE TIMEOUT TECHNIQUE, page 204).

- *Stretch your child's attention span.* Praising attentive (non-hyperactive) behavior is the key to preparing your child for school. Increased attention span and persistence with tasks can be taught at home. Don't wait until your child is of school age and expect the teacher to change him. By age 5 he needs at least a 25-minute attention span to perform adequately in school.

  Set aside several brief periods each day to teach your child listening skills through reading. Start with picture books, and gradually progress to reading stories. Coloring of pictures can be encouraged and praised. Games of increasing difficulty can be taught to your child, starting with building blocks and progressing to puzzles, dominoes, card games, and dice games. Matching pictures is an excellent way to build your child's memory and concentration span. Later, consequence games such as checkers or tic-tac-toe can be introduced. When your child becomes restless, stop, and return for another session later. This process is slow but invaluable in preparing your child for school.

- *Buffer your child against any overreaction by neighbors.* Neighbors with whom your child has contact should be enlisted as helpers. If your child is labeled by some adults as a "bad" kid, it is important that this doesn't carry over into his or her home life. At home the attitude that must prevail is that your child is a "good child with excess energy." It is extremely important that you don't give up on him. Your child must always feel loved and accepted within the family. As long as a child has this, self-esteem and self-confidence will survive. If school is not rewarding, help your child gain a sense of success through a hobby in an area of strength.

- *From time to time, get away from it all.* Exposure to some of these children for 24 hours a day would make anyone a wreck. Periodic breaks help parents to tolerate hyperactive behavior. In a family in which only the father goes out to work, when he comes home he should try to look after the child, not only to give his wife a deserved break but also to understand better what she must contend with during the day. A babysitter an afternoon a week and an occasional evening out with her husband can salvage an exhausted mother. Pre-school is another helpful option. Parents need a chance to rejuvenate themselves so that they can continue to meet their child's extra needs.

- *Utilize special programs at school.* Try to start your child in preschool by age 3 to help him organize his thoughts and ability to focus. On the other hand consider enrolling your child in regular school a year later (i.e., at age 6 rather than 5) to allow the added maturity to help him fit in better with his classmates. Once your child enters school, the school is responsible for providing appropriate programs for your child's attention deficit disorder and any learning disability he might have. Some standard things that teachers use to help children with A.D.D. are smaller class size, isolated study space, spaced learning techniques, and inclusion of the child in tasks like erasing the blackboard or passing out books as outlets for excessive energy. Many of these children spend part of their day with a learning disability teacher who helps improve their skills and confidence.

  If you feel your child has A.D.D. and he has not been tested by the school's special education team, you can request an evaluation. Usually you can obtain the help your child needs by working closely with the school through parent-teacher conferences and special meetings. Your main job is to continue to help your child improve his attention span, self-discipline, and friendships at home.

- *Medications are sometimes helpful.* Some stimulant drugs can improve the powers of concentration. The use of drugs is a matter for you and your child's physician to discuss. In general, medications should not be prescribed before school age. They should also not be prescribed until after your child has received a medical and school evaluation, an individualized educational plan (I.E.P.) is in effect at school, and the preceding guidelines are in effect at home. Medications without special education and home management programs have no long-term benefit. They need to be part of a broader treatment program.

SCHOOL REFUSAL OR PHOBIA

SYMPTOMS AND CHARACTERISTICS

- Your child experiences vague physical symptoms, such as stomachaches, headaches, or sore throats
- Your child has missed 5 or more days of school for these symptoms

- The symptoms start before school or on arrival at school— that is, leaving home is difficult

- There are usually no symptoms on weekends and holidays

- Your child misses you while at school and wants to go home

- The symptoms began during kindergarten or first grade

- Your child otherwise seems healthy and vigorous

  If your child's symptoms are different, call your physician for help.

Causes • The main cause of school refusal is a worry about leaving home and growing up. This common problem occurs in more than 5 percent of families. The parents are usually very conscientious and loving, but sometimes overly protective. The child may find it difficult to separate from them (separation anxiety). The child may not have the self-confidence and independence that comes from handling life's normal stresses without parental help. Obviously, the first required test of a child's independence is daily school attendance. Some children at special risk for school phobia are the first or last child, the only child, and the child with a chronic disease. Sometimes a strict teacher, hard tests, a learning problem, or a bully add to the problem. When such factors are present, your child should still go to school while they are being settled.

Expected Course • Without intervention, the physical symptoms and the desire to stay home become more frequent. The longer your child stays home, the harder it will be for him or her to return. Your child's future social life and education may be at stake. If full school attendance is enforced, the problem will improve dramatically in 1 to 2 weeks.

CALL YOUR CHILD'S PHYSICIAN DURING OFFICE HOURS IF

- You think the cause may be physical rather than emotional.

- Your child is over 12 years old.

- Your child is withdrawn in general or seems depressed.

- Your child is on homebound teaching.

- You have other questions.

OVERCOMING SCHOOL REFUSAL

Insist On an Immediate Return to School • The best therapy for school refusal is to be in school every day. Fears are overcome by facing them as soon as possible. Daily school attendance will cause most of your child's physical symptoms to improve magically. At least they will become less severe and occur less often. Your child will eventually enjoy school again. But in the beginning, your child will test your determination to send her every day. You must make school attendance an ironclad rule. It won't be effective if handled in a hesitant way. Your child can be reminded that it's against the law for children to stay home from school.

Be Extra Firm on School Mornings • In the beginning, mornings may be a difficult time. Never ask your child how she feels, because it may just encourage her to complain. If your child is well enough to be up and around the house, she is well enough to go to school. If your child spontaneously complains of physical symptoms but they are the usual ones, she should be promptly sent to school with minimal discussion. When there is doubt about your child's health, try to err on the side of sending her to school. If things change during the day, the school nurse can reevaluate your child. If your child is late, she should go to school anyway. In case your child misses the school bus, you should have a prearranged alternative plan of transportation. If your child wanders home during lunch or recess, she should be sent back promptly. Sometimes a child may cry and scream and absolutely refuse to go to school. The child then has to be taken there. One parent may be better at enforcing this than the other. Sometimes a relative can take charge of this for a few days.

Have Your Child See His Physician on Any Morning He Has to Stay Home • If your child has a new physical symptom or seems quite sick, you will probably want him to stay home. However, keep in mind that anxiety can cause a wide variety of symptoms. If you are puzzled, your child's physician will usually be able to determine the exact cause. Call the physician as soon as the office opens. The physician will try to see your child that morning. If the symptom is from a disease, treatment can be given. If the symptom is from anxiety, your child should be back in school before noon. Working closely with your child's physician in this way can solve even the most difficult problems.

Some symptoms that might keep your child at home are: fevers (over 100°F), vomiting, frequent diarrhea, a hacky cough, a widespread rash, earaches, or toothaches. The physician should be called about all of these problems, and many need to be seen. On the other hand, children with a sore throat, moderate cough, runny nose, or other cold symptoms (but without fever) can be sent to class. Children with mild stomachaches, headaches, or leg pains can also usually go to school. Children should not be kept home for "looking sick," "poor color," or "tiredness."

Ask the School Staff for Assistance • Schools are usually very understanding about school phobia once they are informed of the diagnosis, because this problem is such a common one. Usually the school nurse will let your child lie down for 5 to 15 minutes in her office if the child's symptoms act up at school, rather than sending him or her home. It is often helpful if you talk to your child's teacher about the situation. If your child has special fears like reciting in class, the teacher will usually make special allowance for these.

Help Your Child Spend More Time with Other Children • Outside of school hours, school-phobic children have a tendency to prefer to be with their parents, play indoors, be alone in their rooms, watch a lot of TV, and so on. Many of them cannot stay overnight at a friend's home without developing overwhelming homesickness. They need encouragement to have more peer contact and less parent contact. This is a difficult task for parents who enjoy their child's company, but it is the best course of action in the long run. Your child can be encouraged to join clubs and athletic teams. Noncontact sports like baseball may be preferred initially. Your child can be sent outside more, or to other children's homes. Your child's friends can be asked to join the family for outings or for overnight stays. Help your child learn to stay overnight with relatives and friends. If he or she can handle weekend camping, a summer camp experience can be a turning point.

Call Your Child's Physician Later If

• The school phobia is not resolved by 2 weeks on this approach.

• The school phobia recurs.

• Your child continues to have other fears or separation problems.

PREVENTION OF SCHOOL REFUSAL

- School refusal tendencies can be reduced or prevented by helping your child develop a sense of independence. Acquiring independence must occur in gradually increasing amounts; your child can't avoid it and then suddenly catch up.

- Start babysitter contact by 6 months of age at the latest. Being apart from you and then having you return builds security and confidence in your child. Babysitter contact is also important for helping your child develop a sense of trust in other adults.

- Begin peer contact by at least 1 year of age, even though the children don't play cooperatively. From 3 years of age onward, your child should be able to interact with peers without your being present. This is a good age for starting shared play groups for children.

- Enroll your child in a preschool by 3 or 4 years of age. This is especially helpful for children who show tendencies to be overly dependent on their parents. Always refer to the school as a "fun place" and the teachers as "nice people."

- Help your child adjust to kindergarten. Over half of children entering kindergarten have transient discomfort and crying for 2 to 5 days. Their symptoms resolve as long as the child returns to school each day and the teacher is supportive. You can sometimes help with the transition by temporarily staying at school (but in the background) for the first hour. By all means, don't take your child out of school, even if he or she is among the 5 percent that urgently want to leave and never return. These children (sometimes labeled "immature" by the teaching staff) need preschool and kindergarten the most.

ADOLESCENTS: DEALING WITH NORMAL REBELLION

The main task of adolescence in our culture is to become psychologically emancipated from the parents. The teenager must cast aside the dependent relationship of childhood. Before he can develop an adult relationship with his parents, the adolescent must first distance himself from the parents of his past. This process is characterized by a certain amount of normal rebellion, defiance, alienation, discontent, turmoil, restlessness, and ambivalence. Emotions usually run high. Wide mood swings are common. Even teenagers who have a mild transition into adolescence hurt their parents' feelings repeatedly with clear messages of "Leave me alone" and "I don't need you."

Under the best of circumstances, this adolescent rebellion continues for approximately 2 years. Not uncommonly it continues for 4 to 6 years. Rebellion can be accentuated or prolonged for the teenager who is doing poorly in school and is unsure of his or her adult role. The teen with a difficult temperament (who had a terrible phase of negativism in the preschool period) is also likely to have a difficult adolescence. Parental high standards or expectations also cause teens to overreact. Defiance will become very intense if the parent tries to eliminate any signs of normal rebellion and regain control over the teenager.

PRACTICAL APPROACHES TO LIVING WITH AN ADOLESCENT

Treat Your Teenager as an Adult Friend • Whatever relationship you would like to have with your child as an adult, start working on it by age 12. Treat your child the way you would like him or her to treat you as an adult. Your goal is mutual respect, support, and having fun together. Strive for relaxed, casual conversations during bicycling, hiking, playing catch, fishing, cooking, mealtime, working, or hobby time. Use praise and trust to help build self-esteem. Recognize and validate your child's feelings by sympathetic listening and nonjudgmental comments. Listening doesn't mean you have to solve your teen's problems. The friendship model is the best basis for family functioning. In this model people do things for each other out of caring and loyalty.

Avoid Criticism About "No-Win" Topics • Most negative parent-adolescent relationships are caused by too much criticism. Much of the objectionable behavior merely reflects conformity with the current preferences of the youngster's peer group. Peer-group immersion is one of the essential stages of adolescent development. Dressing, talking, and acting differently than adults help your child feel independent from you. But take heart, this stage is not a final personality. Try to avoid any criticism of clothing, hair style, makeup, music, dance steps, friends, recreational interests (such as movies, television, or hobbies), how his or her room is kept, courses in school, career choices, how money or free time is spent, speech, posture, religion and philosophy, diet, and sleeping habits. Allowing your teen to rebel in these minor areas often prevents testing in major areas—such as experimentation with drugs. Intervene and try to make a change only if the behavior is harmful or infringes on your rights (see HOUSE RULES, below). Another common error is to criticize your teen's mood, attitude, or facial expression. A negative or lazy attitude can only be changed through good example and praise.

Let Logical Consequences Teach Responsibility • Outside the home your teenager must learn from trial and error. As she experiments, she will learn to take responsibility for her decisions and actions. The parent should speak up only if the adolescent is going to do something dangerous or illegal. Otherwise, the parent must rely on self-discipline, positive peer pressure, and logical consequences.

Curfew laws will help to control late hours. The requirement for punctual school attendance will influence when your teen goes to bed at night. School grades will hold your teenager accountable for homework and other aspects of school performance. If your teen shows a bad attitude on a job, she will be fired. If she selects an excessively violent movie, she may have nightmares. If your teenager makes a poor choice of friends, she may find her confidences broken or that she gets into trouble. If she doesn't practice hard for a sport, she will get pressure from the team and coach to do better. If she misspends her allowance or earnings, she will run out of money before the end of the month. If she abuses her freedom to choose clothes, her fixed clothing allowance will be spent before she buys something she needs, such as a bathing suit. (By age 16, your teenager should have a summer job. These earnings should cover most of the year's expenses, and any allowance can be discontinued.) If your teenager's mood is negative, she will lose friends.

If by chance your teenager asks you for advice about outside activities, try to cover the pros and cons in a brief, impartial way. Then conclude your remarks with a comment such as "Do what you think is best." Teenagers need plenty of opportunity to learn from their own mistakes before they leave home and have to solve problems without a support system.

Clarify the House Rules • You have the right and the responsibility to make rules regarding your house and other possessions. A teenager's preferences can be tolerated within his own room but they need not be imposed on the rest of the house. You can forbid loud music that interferes with other people's activities, or incoming telephone calls after 10:00 P.M. While you should make your teen's friends feel welcome in your home, clarify the ground rules about parties or where snacks can be eaten. Your teen can be placed in charge of cleaning his own room, washing his clothes, and ironing his clothes. You can insist upon clean clothes and enough showers to prevent or overcome body odor. You must decide whether to loan out your car, bicycle, camera, radio, clothes, and so forth.

Your main means of rule enforcement is loss of privileges. (Timeout is rarely useful in this age group, and physical punishment can escalate to a serious breakdown in your relationship.) If your teenager breaks something, he should repair it or pay for its repair or replacement. If he makes a mess, he should clean it up. If your teen is doing poorly in school, you can restrict TV time. You can also put a limit on telephone privileges and weeknights out. If your teen stays out too late or doesn't call you when he's delayed, you can ground him for a day or a weekend. In general, grounding for more than a few days is looked upon as unfair and is hard to enforce.

Use Family Conferences for Negotiating House Rules • Some families find it helpful to have a brief meeting after dinner once a week. At this time your teenager can ask for changes in the house rules or bring up family issues that are causing problems. You can also bring up issues (such as the demand to drive your teen to many places and your need for his or her help in arranging car pools). The family unit often functions better if the decision-making is democratic. The objective of negotiation should be that both parties win. The atmosphere can be one of: "Nobody is at fault; we have a problem. How can we solve it?"

Avoid a Teenager Who Is in a Bad Mood • Generally when your teenager is in a bad mood, he or she won't want to talk about it with you. If teenagers want to discuss a problem with anybody, it will probably be with a close friend. In general, it is advisable at this time to give your teen lots of space and privacy. This is a poor time to talk to your teenager about anything, pleasant or otherwise.

Use "I" Messages for Rudeness • Teenagers commonly say rude or disrespectful things to their parents. Unlike a negative attitude, these nasty remarks should be addressed. You can respond with a comment like "I really hurt inside when you put me down or don't answer my question." Make your statement in as nonangry a way as possible. If your adolescent continues to make angry, unpleasant remarks, leave. Don't get into a shouting match or game of uproar with your teenager because this behavior is not adaptable to outside relationships. Set a good example of the ability to express disapproval without insult or attack. If angry or rude remarks come up in the context of a complaint about something, try to overlook the rudeness and directly engage your teen in a discussion of the issue. If you can focus on objective problem-solving and keep a courteous tone of voice, often your teenager will be able to regain control over his or her emotions and remarks.

What you are trying to teach is that one has the right to disagree and even to express anger. However, screaming and rude conversation are not allowed in your house. When your teen is angry about something, he or she can explain what it is, but in a calm voice. Family friends and other visitors are also to be treated with respect. You can prevent some rude behavior by role-modeling politeness, constructive disagreement, and the ability to apologize.

CALL YOUR TEENAGER'S PHYSICIAN DURING OFFICE HOURS IF

- You think your teenager is depressed, drinking or using drugs, or going to run away.

- Your teenager is taking undue risks (e.g., driving too fast).

- Your teenager has no close friends.

- Your teenager's school performance is declining markedly.

- Your teenager is skipping school frequently.

- Your teenager's outbursts are destructive.

- You feel your teenager's rebellion is excessive.

- You find yourself escalating the criticism and punishment.

- Your relationship with your teenager does not improve within 3 months using this approach.

- You have other questions or concerns.

RECOMMENDED READING

Peter H. Buntman, and E. M. Saris, *How to Live with Your Teenager* (New York: Ballantine Books, 1982).

Lois Davitz and Joel Davitz, *How to Live (Almost) Happily with a Teenager* (New York: Signet, 1983).

Don Dinkmeyer and Gary D. McKay, *The Parent's Guide: The STEP Approach to Parenting Your Teenager* (Circle Pines, Minn.: American Guidance Service, 1983).

V

COMMON
ILLNESSES

GENERAL SYMPTOMS OF ILLNESS

FEVER

SYMPTOMS AND CHARACTERISTICS

- Rectal temperature over 100.4°F (38.0°C)
- Oral temperature over 100°F (37.8°C)
- Axillary (armpit) temperature over 99°F (37.2°C)
- While the body's average temperature is 98.6°F (37°C), it normally fluctuates during the day from a low of 97.6°F in the morning to a high of 100°F in the late afternoon (called normal diurnal variation)
- Mild elevations of 100.4 to 101.2°F (38 to 38.5°C) can be caused by exercise, excessive clothing, hot weather, or warm food or drink. If you suspect one of these causes, retake the temperature in a half hour, after eliminating the possible cause

Similar Conditions • For CONVULSIONS or DELIRIUM (acting very confused), go directly to those guidelines (see pages 31 and 35). Both symptoms should stop if you reduce the fever below 102°F with medicine and cool sponging. Then return to this guideline.

TAKING THE TEMPERATURE
First, shake the thermometer until the mercury line is below 98.6°F (37°C).

Where to Take the Temperature

- Under 5 years old: axillary (armpit) or rectal

- Over 5 years old: oral (mouth)

Taking Axillary Temperatures

- Place the tip of the thermometer in a dry armpit.

- Close the armpit by holding the elbow against the chest for 4 minutes (5 or 6 minutes after 2 years of age).

- If you're uncertain about the result, recheck it with a rectal temperature.

Taking Rectal Temperatures

- Have your child lie stomach-down on your lap.

- Lubricate the end of the thermometer and the opening of the anus with petroleum jelly.

- Carefully insert the thermometer about 1 inch, but never force it.

- Hold your child still while the thermometer is in, and press the buttocks together to stabilize it.

- Leave the thermometer inside the rectum for 2 minutes.

- Practice doing this a few times on days your child is happy rather than sick.

Taking Oral Temperatures

- Be sure your child has not recently taken a cold or hot drink.

- Place the tip of the thermometer beside the back of the tongue.

- Have your child hold it in place with the lips and fingers (not the teeth).

- Have your child breathe through the nose and keep the mouth closed.

- Leave the thermometer in the mouth for 3 minutes.

- If your child can't keep the mouth closed because the nose is blocked, take an axillary temperature.

Reading the Thermometer • Find where the mercury line ends by rotating the thermometer slightly until the line appears.

Substituting Rectal and Oral Thermometers • If necessary, a rectal thermometer can be used in the mouth and an oral thermometer can be used in the rectum, as long as the thermometer is cleaned with rubbing alcohol and you are extra careful with rectal insertion.

Broken Thermometer in the Rectum or Mouth • Call your child's physician if you can't find all the pieces of glass. Usually the only harm caused by a broken thermometer is a superficial scratch of the lining of the mouth or rectum. The type of mercury found in thermometers is not poisonous.

Temperature Strips • Liquid crystal strips applied to the forehead have been studied and found to be inaccurate. They miss fevers in many children. Touching the forehead also tends to miss mild fevers, but it can accurately detect higher fevers. Disposable chemical-dot oral strips are accurate, but must be kept beside the tongue for 60 seconds.

CONVERSION OF DEGREES FAHRENHEIT TO CENTIGRADE
Remember that 1°C equals 1.8°F and that 1°F equals 0.55°C. Despite attempts to learn metric, most Americans conceptualize fever in degrees Fahrenheit.

98.6°F	= 37°C	103°F	= 39.5°C
100°F	= 37.8°C	104°F	= 40°C
100.4°F	= 38°C	105°F	= 40.6°C
101°F	= 38.4°C	106°F	= 41.1°C
102°F	= 38.9°C	107°F	= 41.7°C

CAUSES OF FEVER
Fever is the body's normal response to infections and it may be helpful in fighting them. The usual fevers (100 to 104°F) that all children get are not harmful. Most are due to viral illnesses; some are due to bacterial ones. Teething does not cause fever.

EXPECTED COURSE OF FEVER
Most fevers associated with viral illnesses range between 101 and 104°F and last for 1 to 3 days. In general, the height of the fever doesn't relate to the seriousness of the illness. How

sick your child acts is what counts. Fever causes no symptoms until it reaches 102° or 103°F. Fever causes no permanent harm (such as brain damage) until it reaches 107° or 108°F. Fortunately, the brain's thermostat keeps untreated fevers below this level. While all children get fevers, only 4 percent develop a brief febrile convulsion. Since this type of seizure is generally harmless, it is not worth worrying about, especially if your child has experienced high fevers without one.

CALL YOUR CHILD'S PHYSICIAN

Immediately If

• Your child is under 2 months old.

• The fever is over 105°F.

• Your child is crying inconsolably or whimpering.

• Your child cries if you touch him or move him.

• Your child is difficult to awaken.

• The neck is stiff. (Note: The inability to touch the chin to the chest is an early symptom in meningitis.)

• Any purple spots are present on the skin.

• Breathing is difficult *and* no better after you clear the nose.

• A convulsion has occurred.

• Your child is acting very sick.

During Office Hours If

• Your child is 2 to 4 months old (unless fever is due to a DPT shot).

• The fever is between 104 and 105°F (especially if your child is under 2 years old).

• Burning or pain occurs with urination.

• The fever has been present more than 72 hours.

• The fever has been present more than 24 hours without an obvious cause or location of infection.

• The fever went away for more than 24 hours and then returned.

• Your child has a history of febrile seizures.

• You have other questions.

HOME CARE FOR FEVER

Fever-Reducing Medicines: Acetaminophen • Children older than 2 months of age can be given one of the acetaminophen products listed on page 310. Use drugs if the fever is over 102°F (39°C), but preferably only if your child is also uncomfortable. Give the correct dosage for your child's weight or age every 4 to 6 hours, but no more often. Acetaminophen will reduce the fever but usually not bring it down to normal. The drug often needs repeating, since the fever will go up and down as it pleases until the disease runs it course. Once acetaminophen is started, my custom is to continue it for 24 hours because the fever usually stays at an uncomfortable level for the first day and the continuous medicine prevents the fever from making big swings. Thereafter, give it only for symptoms. If your child is sleeping, don't awaken him or her for medicines. If the fever is high enough to need an antipyretic, your child will awaken. In general, these medicines are overused in our country.

CAUTIONS:

• Do not use these drugs for more than 3 days *or* in children less than 4 months old without consulting your physician.

• Since all these drugs are poisonous if taken in overdosage, keep them out of the sight and reach of children.

Cautions About Aspirin • The American Academy of Pediatrics and other national health organizations have recommended that children (through age 21 years) not receive aspirin if they have chicken pox or influenza (any cold, cough, or sore throat symptoms). This recommendation stems from several studies that have linked aspirin to Reyes syndrome, a severe encephalitis-like illness. As evidence mounts, many pediatricians have stopped using aspirin for fevers associated with any illness. For the present, I agree with that position. On the other hand, aspirin may be a better drug than acetaminophen for pain relief with muscle and bone pains, menstrual cramps, and sunburn. (See page 51 for dosage.) If you have teenagers, be sure they are aware of this warning about aspirin, since they tend to self-medicate.

Sponging for Fever • If the fever is over 104°F (40°C) half an hour after medicines have been given, sponge for at least 30 minutes in lukewarm water (85 to 90°F). Sponge immedi-

ACETAMINOPHEN DOSAGES

TYPE AND BRAND	STRENGTH	CHILD'S WEIGHT (POUNDS)			AGE (YEARS)				
		6–11	12–17	18–23	2–3	4–5	6–8	9–11	12+
Total amount (mg.)		40 mg.	80	120	160	240	325	485	650
Acetaminophen drops (Tylenol, Tempra, Panadol, or Liquiprin drops)	80 mg/dropper*	½ dropper	1	1½	2	3	—	—	—
Acetaminophen syrup (Tylenol, Tempra, Panadol syrup or elixir)	160/5 ml.(1 tsp.)	—	½ tsp.	¾	1	1½	2	2½	4
Chewable acetaminophen	80 mg. tablets	—	—	1½	2	3	4	5–6	8
Adult acetaminophen	325 mg. tablets	—	—	—	—	—	1	1–1½	2

*The dropper that comes with one product should not be used with other brands.
Note: Acetaminophen comes in 120, 325, and 650 mg suppositories. They are useful in febrile children with vomiting or in children with febrile seizures. The rectal dose is the same as the oral dose. Since the drug is dispersed uniformly throughout the newer suppositories, they can be cut.

ately with cooler water for delirium, a seizure from fever, or any fever over 106°F. Sponging works much faster than immersion, so sit your child in 2 inches of water and keep wetting the skin surface. If your child shivers, raise the water temperature. Don't expect to get the temperature down below 101°F. Don't add rubbing alcohol to the water; it can cause a coma or seizure if breathed in. Never leave your child alone in the tub; accidents can happen quickly. If your child is seizing or thrashing about, sponge him in a safer place than the bathtub.

Retaking the Temperature • In general, take the temperature once a day in the morning until the fever is gone. Take it more often if your child feels very hot or is acting miserable; he may need sponging. With most infections, the level of fever bounces around for 2 or 3 days. Shivering (or feeling cold) means the fever is going up, a flushed (pink) appearance means the fever has peaked, and sweating means it is coming down. The main purpose of temperature taking is to determine if a fever is present or absent, not to chart its every move.

Extra Fluids • Extra fluids should be encouraged but not forced. Popsicles and iced drinks are helpful. Body fluids are lost during fevers because of sweating.

Less Clothing • Clothing should be kept to a minimum, because most heat is lost through the skin. Do not bundle up your child; it will cause a higher fever. Be especially careful with infants who are unable to undress themselves if they become overheated. During the time your child feels cold or has shivering (the chills), give him a light blanket.

Reduced Activity • Discourage any vigorous activities, because they produce additional heat that the body must release. Normal play, however, is fine.

Call Your Child's Physician Later If

• The fever goes over 104°F (40°C) (especially if it stays over 104°F or your child is under 2 years old).

• The fever lasts more than 24 hours without an obvious cause or location of infection.

• The fever lasts more than 72 hours.

• You feel your child is getting worse.

Remember: The response, or lack of response, of the fever to medicines tells us little about the severity of the infection. If your febrile child smiles, plays, and drinks adequate fluids, you need not worry about the fever.

DECREASED APPETITE WITH ILLNESS

SYMPTOMS AND CHARACTERISTICS

• Reduced food intake of recent onset

• Associated acute illness

If your child's symptoms are different, call your physician for help.

Cause • A falloff in appetite is normal with most minor illnesses. This is not harmful. It is not very helpful in assessing the seriousness or cause of the illness.

HOME CARE

Temporarily, serve your child his favorite foods. Let him decide how much he eats. Avoid the tendency to pressure him to eat more when he is sick. Usually, his fluid intake will remain normal and that is the only important aspect of diet during an illness. Look at other guidelines for information on the treatment of associated symptoms.

CALL YOUR CHILD'S PHYSICIAN IF

• Your child is under 2 months old (call immediately).

• Your child is not drinking adequate fluids.

• Your child has not urinated in more than 8 hours.

• Poor appetite lasts for more than 1 week.

• You feel your child is getting worse.

INCREASED SLEEP WITH ILLNESS

Most children are less active, and sleep several extra hours a day when they are sick with any infectious illness. It helps them fight the illness and speeds recovery. Increased sleep is not very useful in judging the seriousness of the illness.

CALL YOUR CHILD'S PHYSICIAN

Immediately If

• Your child is drowsy or confused when awake (rather than alert and thinking clearly).

• Your child could have taken any sleeping pills or other drugs.

• Your child is acting very sick.

During Office Hours If

• Your child is on any medicines that could cause drowsiness.

• Your child is otherwise not sick.

• Your child could be upset or depressed.

• You have other questions.

HOME CARE

Treatment • No special treatment is needed. Refer to the guidelines regarding the basic illness your child is suffering from.

Call Your Child's Physician Later If

• Your child becomes difficult to arouse or confused when awake.

• New symptoms develop that worry you.

• The increased sleeping and tiredness last for more than 1 week.

RELATED TOPIC

DELIRIUM (see page 35)

CONTAGIOUS DISEASES AND INCUBATION PERIODS

Young children are afflicted with infectious diseases 10 to 15 times per year. The attack rate decreases with age because with each new infection we build up antibodies against future ones. Most of these infections are due to viruses or bacteria, but occasionally fungi or parasites are involved. Your child's symptoms are probably due to an infection if fever is present or the illness spreads to others. The following information is intended to improve your understanding of contagious diseases.

THE INCUBATION PERIOD

The incubation period is defined as the time interval between exposure to a contagious disease and the onset of symptoms. This information should help answer the questions (1) "When will my child come down with it?" and (2) "Should we cancel our weekend plans?"

If the outer time limit of the incubation period passes and your child is still well, he or she has probably escaped that infection for now (or has previous antibodies against it).

THE CONTAGIOUS PERIOD

The contagious period is defined as that time interval during which a sick child's disease is contagious to others. Knowing the period of contagion helps answer the question "How long does my child have to stay home from school or daycare?"

For major illnesses (such as hepatitis), a child will need to remain in isolation at home or in the hospital until all chance of spread has passed. For minor illnesses (like the common cold) we are less strict. Most physicians would agree that a child should stay home at least until he feels well enough to return to school, and the fever has been gone for 12 hours.

INFECTIONS THAT ARE NOT CONTAGIOUS

Try not to become preoccupied with infections. Some of the more serious ones are not even contagious. Some infections are due to blockage of a passageway followed by an overgrowth of bacteria. Examples of these are ear infections, sinus infections, and urinary tract infections. Lymph node and bloodstream infections are also rarely contagious. Pneumonia is a complication of a viral respiratory infection in most cases and is usually not contagious. While exposure to meningitis requires consultation with your child's physician, most children exposed to this disease just develop cold symptoms. Venereal diseases are usually noncontagious unless there is sexual contact or shared bathing arrangements.

GUIDELINES FOR COMMON CONTAGIOUS DISEASES

DISEASE	INCUBATION PERIOD (DAYS)	CONTAGIOUS PERIOD (DAYS)
Skin Infections:		
Chicken pox	14–16	Until all sores have crusts (7)
Fifth disease (*Erythema infectiosum*)	10–14	*
Hand, foot, and mouth disease	3–6	Until fever gone
Impetigo (strep)	2–5	Until 24 hours on antibiotic
Lice	7	Until 1 treatment
Measles	10–12	Until rash gone (7)
Roseola	10–15	Until rash gone (2)
Rubella	14–21	Until rash gone (4)
Scabies	30	Until 1 treatment
Scarlet fever	3–6	Until 24 hours on antibiotic
Shingles (contagious for chicken pox)	14–16	Until all sores have crusts (7) (Note: No need to isolate if sores can be kept covered.)
Staph skin infections	2–3	Until 24 hours on antibiotic ointment (Note: Keep draining boils covered until healed.)
Warts	30–120	*
Respiratory Infections:		
Colds	2–5	Until fever gone
Cold sores (herpes)	2–12	†
Coughs (viral)	2–5	Until fever gone
Croup (viral)	2–6	Until fever gone
Influenza	1–2	Until fever gone
Sore throat, strep	2–5	Until 24 hours on antibiotic
Sore throat, viral	2–5	Until fever gone

DISEASE	INCUBATION PERIOD (DAYS)	CONTAGIOUS PERIOD (DAYS)
Tuberculosis	14–70	Until 2 weeks on drugs
Whooping cough	7–10	Until 7 days on antibiotic
Intestinal Infections:		
Diarrhea, bacterial	1–5	‡
Diarrhea, giardia	7–21	‡
Diarrhea, traveler's	1–6	‡
Diarrhea, viral	2–5	‡
Hepatitis	14–42	Until jaundice resolved
Pinworms	21–28	*
Vomiting, viral	2–5	Until vomiting stops
Other Infections:		
Infectious mononucleosis	20–30	Until fever gone
Meningitis, bacterial	2–10	Hospital isolation until 24 hours on IV antibiotics
Mumps	16–18	Until swelling gone (7)
Pinkeye without pus (viral)	1–5	*
Pinkeye with pus (bacterial)	2–7	Until 1 day on antibiotic eyedrops

*Staying home is unnecessary because the infection is very mild or minimally contagious.

†Cold sores: Less than 6 years old, home until sores are dry, 4–5 days. (No isolation if sores are on part of body that can be covered.) More than 6 years old, no isolation if beyond touching, picking stage.

‡Diarrhea: Less than 6 years old, home until stools are formed. More than 6 years old, home until fever is gone, diarrhea is mild, and child has control over loose BMs.

References:
(1) Incubation periods are from American Academy of Pediatrics, Committee on Infectious Diseases, 1982 Red Book, 19th edition, Evanston, Illinois.
(2) Isolation recommendations are from Garner, J.S., and Simmons, B.P. "Guideline for Isolation Precautions in Hospitals, Infection Control 4" (Suppl.), 1983, pp. 245–325.

FREQUENT INFECTIONS

Some children seem to have the constant sniffles. They get one cold after another. Many a parent wonders: "Isn't my child having too many colds?" Children start to get colds after about 6 months of age. During infancy and the preschool years, they average 7 or 8 colds a year. During the school-age years, they average 5 or 6 colds a year. During adolescence they finally reach an adult level of approximately 4 colds a year. Colds account for more than 50 percent of all acute illnesses with fever.

In addition, children can have diarrhea illnesses (with or without vomiting) 2 or 3 times per year. Some children are especially worrisome to their parents because they have a tendency to get high fevers with most of their colds or they have a sensitive gastrointestinal (GI) tract and develop diarrhea with the majority of their colds. These repeatedly ill children cause their parents a great deal of consternation.

Similar Condition • If your child is over age 3, has lots of sneezing, has a clear nasal discharge that lasts over a month, doesn't have a fever, and especially if these symptoms occur during pollen season, your child probably has a nasal allergy and you should refer to the guideline on HAY FEVER, page 442.

Causes • The main cause of all these infections is that your child is being exposed to new viruses. There are at least 150 different cold viruses. The younger the child, the less the previous exposure and subsequent protection. Your child is exposed more if he or she attends daycare, play group, a church nursery, or a preschool. Your child has more indirect exposures if he has older siblings in school. Therefore, colds are more common in large families. The rate of colds triples in the wintertime when people spend more time crowded together indoors. In addition, smoking in the home increases your child's susceptibility to colds.

WHAT DOESN'T CAUSE FREQUENT INFECTIONS
Most parents are worried that their repeatedly ill child has some serious underlying disease. Children with immune system diseases (inadequate antibody or white blood cell production) don't experience any more colds than the average child.

Instead, they have two or more bouts per year of pneumonia, sinus infection, draining lymph nodes, or boils. They also heal slowly from these infections. In addition, most children with serious disease do not gain weight adequately. Tell your physician if your family is worried about a particular diagnosis so your physician can discuss this concern with you. Also, recurrent ear infections don't mean that your child has a serious health problem, only that his eustachian tubes don't drain properly.

Other parents worry that they have in some way neglected their child or done something wrong to cause frequent colds. On the contrary, having all these colds is an unavoidable part of growing up. Colds are the one infection we can't prevent yet. From a medical standpoint, colds are an educational experience for your child's immune system.

DEALING WITH FREQUENT INFECTIONS

Look at the Brighter Side of Things • If your child is vigorous and gaining weight, you don't have to worry about his or her health. Your child is no sicker than the average child. Children get over colds by themselves. While you can do something to reduce the symptoms, you can't shorten the course for each cold (see COLDS, page 435). Your child will just have to muddle through like every other child. The long-term outlook is good. The number of colds will decrease over the years as your child's body builds up a good antibody supply to the various viruses. To help put infections in perspective, a recent survey found that on any given day, 10 percent of children have a cold, 8 percent have a fever, 5 percent have diarrhea, and 3 percent have an ear infection.

Send Your Child Back to School as Soon as Possible • The main requirement for returning your child to school is that the fever is gone and the symptoms are not excessively noisy or distracting to classmates. It doesn't make sense to keep a child home until we can offer some guarantee that he or she is no longer shedding any viruses (as this could take 2 or 3 weeks). If isolation for respiratory infections were taken seriously, insufficient days would remain to educate children. Also the "germ warfare" that normally occurs in schools is fairly uncontrollable. Most children shed germs during the first days of their illness before they even look sick or have symptoms. In other words, contact with respiratory infections is unavoidable in group settings, such as schools or daycare. Also, as long as your child's fever has cleared, there is no reason not to attend parties, play with friends after school, and go on scheduled trips. The overexertion of gym and team sports may need to wait a few extra days.

Try Not to Miss Work • When both parents work, these repeated colds are extremely inconvenient and costly. Since the complication rate is low and the improvement rate is slow, don't hesitate to leave your child with someone else at these times. If your babysitter is willing to accept the care of a child with a fever, take advantage of the offer. If your child is in daycare or a preschool, send him or her back once the fever is gone. No need to prolong the recovery at home if you need to return to work. Early return of a child with a respiratory illness won't increase the complication rate of your child or the exposure rate for other children.

Likewise, you don't need to cancel an important social engagement because your child has a minor acute illness. There will be many more of these. You also don't need to take your child out of preschool or daycare permanently because of the nuisance aspect of all these repeated illnesses. Because there are so many more working mothers, "sick child" daycare programs are starting to spring up around the country.

WHAT DOESN'T HELP

There are no instant cures for recurrent colds and other viral illnesses. Antibiotics are not helpful unless your child develops complications such as an ear infection, sinus infection, or pneumonia. Since the colds are not caused by bad tonsils, having your child's tonsils removed is not helpful (see TONSIL AND ADENOID SURGERY, page 461). Colds are not caused by poor diet or lack of vitamins. They are not caused by bad weather, air conditioners, or wet feet. Again, the best time to have these infections and develop immunity is during childhood.

RELATED TOPICS

PREVENTION OF COLDS (see page 440)

THE PREVENTION OF INFECTIONS

Public health measures have had the greatest impact in preventing the spread of infectious diseases. Proper sewage disposal and safe water supplies have largely eliminated epidemics such as typhoid fever and cholera. Immunizations and vaccinations constitute the other aspect of modern medicine that has controlled infectious diseases like smallpox and polio. Precautions within the home can limit the spread of gastrointestinal illnesses. Unfortunately, the spread of colds, coughs, and sore throats within a family unit is uncontrollable for practical purposes.

HOW DIFFERENT INFECTIOUS DISEASES ARE SPREAD

- Nose, mouth, and eye secretions are the most common sources of respiratory infections. These secretions are usually spread by contaminated hands or occasionally by kissing. Toddlers are especially prone to spreading these infections because of their habits of touching or mouthing everything.

- Droplet spread from coughing or sneezing is a less common means of transmission of respiratory infections. Droplets can travel up to 6 feet.

- Fecal contamination of hands or other objects accounts for the spread of most diarrhea, as well as infectious hepatitis. Unlike urine, which is usually sterile, bowel movements are composed of up to 50 percent bacteria.

- The discharge from sores such as chicken pox and fever blisters can be contagious. However, most red rashes without a discharge are not contagious by skin contact.

- Contaminated food or water accounted for many epidemics in earlier times. Even today, some foods frequently contain bacteria that cause diarrhea. (For example, raw turkey or chicken often contains Campylobacter or salmonella.)

- Contaminated utensils such as bottles and dishes can occasionally be a source of respiratory or intestinal infections.

- Contaminated objects such as combs, brushes, and hats can lead to the spread of lice, ringworm, or impetigo.

HOW TO PREVENT OR REDUCE THE SPREAD OF INFECTIOUS DISEASES

The following preventive actions can help reduce the spread of disease within your household.

• *Hand washing has greater value in preventing the spread of gastrointestinal infections than all other approaches combined.* Rinsing the hands vigorously with plain water is probably as effective as using soap and water. Hand washing is especially important after using the toilet, changing diapers, and blowing the nose. Choose a daycare center where the staff practices good hand washing after changing diapers. Young children must be supervised in their use of toilets and sinks. A surprising finding of recent studies was that hand washing is also the mainstay in preventing the spread of respiratory disease.

• *Discourage habits of touching the mouth and nose.* Again this is helpful in preventing the spread of respiratory infections.

• *Don't smoke around your children.* Passive smoking increases the frequency and severity of your child's respiratory infections.

• *Discourage the kissing of pets.* Pets (especially puppies) can transmit bloody diarrhea, worms, and more. Pets are for petting.

• *Cook all poultry thoroughly.* If it is frozen, thaw it in the refrigerator rather than at room temperature to prevent multiplication of the bacteria. After preparation, carefully wash your hands and any object that comes in contact with raw poultry (such as the knife and cutting board) before using them with other foods.

• *Choose a small daycare center over a large one.* Daycare provided in private homes has a lower rate of infectious disease. If you can afford it, children who are cared for in their own homes by babysitters have the lowest rate of infection.

• *Clean contaminated areas with disinfectants.* These products kill most bacteria, including staph. Disinfecting the diaper-changing area, cribs and strollers, play equipment, and food service items is effective in limiting intestinal diseases at home and in daycare centers.

• *Contact your child's physician if your child is exposed to meningitis or hepatitis.* Antibiotics are useful in preventing some types of bacterial meningitis in exposed children under 4 years of age. An injection of gamma globulin is helpful in preventing hepatitis in those who have had intimate contact (i.e., greater than 4 hours) with someone having this disease.

- *Don't attempt to isolate your child.* Isolation is mentioned last because it is of doubtful value within a family unit. By the time a child shows symptoms, he or she has already shared the germs with the family. Also, from a practical standpoint, isolation at home is impossible to enforce.

BRAIN

ALTITUDE SICKNESS

SYMPTOMS AND CHARACTERISTICS

- Headache, fatigue, dizziness, nausea
- Shortness of breath and rapid heartbeat on exertion
- Insomnia or restless sleep
- Onset at 8,000 feet elevation or higher
- Onset within 6 to 8 hours of arrival at higher altitude

If your child's symptoms are different, call your physician for help.

Cause • Altitude sickness is caused by the reduced level of oxygen at higher altitudes. Many people travel to mountainous areas to hike or ski. Symptoms occur in 50 percent of nonacclimated people who abruptly go from sea level to 10,000 feet. The likelihood of symptoms increases with the altitude.

Expected Course • Most people with acute mountain sickness (the most common type of altitude sickness) feel normal in 2 or 3 days. With overexertion and ascent above 10,000 feet, 4 percent of people can develop life-threatening complications of pulmonary edema (lung failure) or cerebral edema (swelling of the brain).

CALL A PHYSICIAN IMMEDIATELY IF

- Your child is confused.
- Your child can't talk normally.
- Your child can't walk normally.
- The lips are bluish.
- Breathing is labored or fast.
- The headache is severe.
- Vomiting has occurred 3 or more times.
- Your child is acting very sick.

HOME CARE

First Aid for Symptoms of Severe Altitude Sickness • Rapidly transport your child to a lower altitude. Descend at least 2,000 feet, and always go below 10,000 feet elevation. If your child cannot walk, carry him or her in a sitting position. Administer oxygen as soon as it becomes available.

Rest for Mild Symptoms • The symptoms usually respond to 2 or 3 days of rest, fluids, and a light diet. Acetaminophen can be given for the headache (aspirin may make it worse). The dizziness and headache can usually be improved by deliberately breathing *slower*. Skiing, hiking, or any other type of exercise should be postponed. Once your child feels healthy again, activity should be increased gradually. Breathing from an oxygen tank can improve symptoms temporarily, but generally this is unnecessary.

Call Your Physician Later If

- The symptoms become worse.
- The symptoms last more than 3 days.

PREVENTION

- Try to stage your mountain visit. Spend a few days at 5000 to 7000 feet before journeying to the high country.
- Take it easy on the day of arrival. Some exercise (like short walks) is important, but take rest breaks. Gradually increase the amount of exertion during days 2 and 3.

- Avoid dehydration by drinking ample fluids.

- While mountain climbing, gain only 1,000 feet per day.

- If your child has experienced severe altitude sickness before, talk to your physician about taking Diamox tablets (a prescription medicine) preventively in the future.

DIZZINESS

Dizziness is a sensation of lightheadedness, faintness, or apparent movement of stationary objects in one's environment. All people occasionally get temporary dizziness if they skip a meal, become a little dehydrated, get too much sun, get exhausted, stand up suddenly, stand for too long in one place, or have a viral illness. If the dizziness relates to riding in a car, going to an amusement park, or playing twirling games (turning somersaults, for instance), see the guideline on MOTION SICKNESS, page 329.

CALL YOUR CHILD'S PHYSICIAN

Immediately If

- Your child is unable to stand and walk.

- Your child is acting very sick.

During Office Hours If

- Ear pain or congestion is also present.

- Your child is taking any medicines that could be causing the dizziness.

- Dizziness is a recurrent problem for your child.

- You have other questions.

HOME CARE

Treatment • Have your child lie down with the feet elevated for the next hour and offer something to drink. Always prevent dizziness from progressing to fainting (passing out) by reminding your child early on to lie down or sit with the head between the knees.

Call Your Child's Physician Later If

• Your child passes out.

• The dizziness is still present after 2 hours of rest.

RELATED TOPIC

FAINTING (see below)

FAINTING

SYMPTOMS AND CHARACTERISTICS

Fainting is defined as falling down and being unconscious briefly (usually less than 1 minute). The four most common causes are sudden stress (such as seeing a bad accident), severe pain, prolonged standing in one position with the knees locked, or standing up suddenly (especially after bed rest). These conditions quickly respond to lying horizontally for 10 minutes with the feet elevated.

Similar Conditions • If appropriate, turn directly to the following guidelines:

BREATH-HOLDING SPELLS (see page 190)
COMA (remaining unconscious in an *emergency*) (see page 31)
HEAT REACTIONS (see page 41)

CALL YOUR CHILD'S PHYSICIAN

Immediately If

• The fainting followed a head injury.

• Any shaking or jerking occurred while your child was unconscious.

• The unconsciousness lasted more than 2 minutes.

• The cause of the fainting isn't obvious.

• Your child is also acting sick.

During Office Hours If

• Fainting is a recurrent problem for your child.

• You have other questions.

HOME CARE

First Aid • Have your child lie down for 10 to 20 minutes with the feet elevated. Do not place a pillow under the head. Also, offer a glass of fruit juice. In hot weather, your child may also need several glasses of water and a cool compress to the forehead. If fainting was due to stress or fear, help your child talk about it.

Call Your Child's Physician Later If

• Your child isn't feeling better by 1 hour.

• Your child passes out again on the same day.

PREVENTION

For fainting that occurs following prolonged standing, remind your child that keeping the knees locked interferes with recirculation of the blood. Under these circumstances, your child should pump the blood by repeatedly relaxing and retightening the leg muscles.

For fainting that occurs with standing up suddenly, have your child sit up first and take some deep breaths.

Also, feeling faint at any time or place is a warning to sit or lie down quickly.

RELATED TOPIC

DIZZINESS (see page 325)

HEADACHE

SYMPTOM

• Your child complains that his or her head hurts

Similar Condition • If a blow to the head is suspected, save time by turning directly to the guideline for HEAD TRAUMA, page 58.

Causes • A mild headache commonly occurs as part of a cold or other viral illness. A high fever almost always causes a headache. Many children get a headache in the late afternoon when they are hungry.

In children and adults, the most common cause of recurrent headaches is tension. These headaches can be caused by unusual excitement or concentration, as well as by stress or worries. A tension headache gives a constant dull pain that covers the entire forehead and often the neck muscles. Recurrent headaches can have numerous causes and deserve a medical evaluation.

Expected Course • Many headaches clear when a fever comes down. Others come and go during an illness. Tension headaches usually last 2 to 8 hours, and tend to recur.

CALL YOUR CHILD'S PHYSICIAN

Immediately If

- The pain is very severe.
- Your child is confused.
- Your child is difficult to awaken from sleep.
- Speech is slurred.
- Vision is blurred or double.
- Walking is unsteady.
- Vomiting has occurred 3 or more times.
- The neck is stiff.
- The pupils are unequal in size.
- Your child is acting very sick.

During Office Hours If

- Headaches are a recurrent problem for your child.
- The pain is just on one side of the head.
- The headache has lasted more than 12 hours despite using a pain-relieving medicine.
- You have other questions.

HOME CARE

Treatment • Have your child lie down and rest until he or she is feeling better. If your child is hungry, offer some food. Give a pain-relieving medicine and repeat it in 4 hours if needed. If your child also has a fever, use acetaminophen. If your child doesn't have a fever, give aspirin. (See FEVER, page 305, for dosage.) Apply a cool washcloth to the forehead. If something is bothering your child, help him talk about it and get it off his mind.

Call Your Child's Physician Later If

• The headache lasts for more than 12 hours despite the medicine.

• It worsens after 2 hours on pain-relieving medicine.

• New symptoms develop that concern you.

RELATED TOPIC

SINUS CONGESTION (see page 447)

Consider this diagnosis if the pain is on one side and near the eye, the nose is runny or blocked, and your child has previously experienced sinus problems.

MOTION SICKNESS

Motion sickness is a common condition, especially in young children. The same children who get dizzy and nauseated in the car are also prone to becoming seasick, trainsick, airsick, and sick on amusement park rides. The problem is due to an inherited sensitivity of the equilibrium center found in the semicircular canals (inner ear). It is not related to emotional problems, nor can your child control it. The sensitivity to motion is usually a lifelong problem.

HOME CARE

Treatment for the Nausea • Have your child lie down, and keep a vomiting pan handy. Give only sips of clear fluids until the stomach settles down. If your child goes to sleep, all the better. Usually, children don't vomit more than once, and all symptoms disappear in about 4 hours.

PREVENTION

Anti-Nausea Medicine • Buy some nonprescription Dramamine tablets at your drugstore. They come in 50 mg tablets or 15 mg-per-teaspoon liquid. The dosage is 1 teaspoon for children 2 to 6 years old, 1 tablet for children 6 to 12 years old, and 2 tablets for children over 12. Give the Dramamine 1 hour before traveling or going to an amusement park. The tablets give 6 hours of protection and are very helpful.

Car trips • Have your child sit in the front seat and at window level. Have your child look out the front window, not the side one. Ask your child not to look at books or play games during car travel. Keep a window cracked to provide fresh air.

Sea travel • Avoid it. Boating on small lakes is usually tolerated.

Air travel • Airsickness can be helped by selecting a seat near the wings or center of the aircraft, since turbulence is felt least there.

Amusement parks • Have your child avoid rides that spin (like the Tilt-a-Whirl). Some children can't even look at whirling rides without becoming sick.

Meals • Have your child eat light meals on these days.

SOFT SPOT, BULGING

The soft spot (called the anterior fontanel) is open during the first 12 to 18 months of life. Normally it is flat or slightly sunken. Normally it moves up and down (pulsates) with each beat of the heart, if the child is sitting up and quiet. It can be slightly elevated while your child is crying. If the soft spot is tense and bulging, the brain is under pressure. Many of the causes are serious.

CALL YOUR CHILD'S PHYSICIAN IMMEDIATELY IF

• Your child has a bulging soft spot.

SKIN: WIDESPREAD PINK OR RED RASHES

RASHES, UNKNOWN CAUSE (WIDESPREAD)

SYMPTOMS AND CHARACTERISTICS

- Red or pink rash (erythema)
- Smooth or slightly bumpy
- Spots or solid red
- Over most of body (widespread or generalized)
- Not itchy

Similar Condition • Fever over 103 or 104°F can cause a pinkness of the skin. Sometimes it's blotchy. If it clears with fever reduction, it's normal "fever erythema." If the rash is itchy, turn directly to the guideline on ITCHING, UNKNOWN CAUSE (WIDESPREAD), page 332.

Causes of Widespread Rashes • The possible causes of a nonitchy, pink or red rash are many. If one of the following is suspected, save time by turning directly to that guideline.

AMPICILLIN RASH (see page 334)
CHICKEN POX (see page 335)
HEAT RASH (see page 343)
MEASLES (see page 346)
MEASLES VACCINE RASH (see page 348)
NEWBORN RASHES (less than 2 weeks old) (see page 88)
ROSEOLA (see page 349)

SCARLET FEVER (see page 351)
SUNBURN (see page 398)

Expected Course • Depends on the diagnosis

CALL YOUR CHILD'S PHYSICIAN

Immediately If

• The rash is purple or blood-colored.

• It is bright red *and* tender to the touch.

• It looks like a burn.

• Your youngster is a female adolescent *and* she currently is having her menstrual period.

• Your child is acting very sick.

During Office Hours If

• Your child has a fever (over 100°F).

• The rash has been present longer than 48 hours.

• Your child is taking a medicine.

• You have other questions.

HOME CARE FOR WIDESPREAD RASHES

Treament • Widespread rashes can occur with viral illnesses. No treatment is necessary. These rashes are unimportant and usually disappear within 48 hours.

Call Your Child's Physician Later If

• The rash becomes itchy.

• It becomes purple.

• It lasts more than 48 hours.

ITCHING, UNKNOWN CAUSE (WIDESPREAD)

CAUSES OF WIDESPREAD ITCHING

The possible causes are many. If one of the following is suspected, turn directly to that guideline.

BITES, INSECT (see page 361)
CHICKEN POX (see page 335)
DRY SKIN (see page 338)
ECZEMA (see page 339)
HEAT RASH (see page 343)
HIVES (see page 344)

CALL YOUR CHILD'S PHYSICIAN

Immediately If

- Breathing or swallowing is difficult.

- The itching started immediately after your child took medicine or was stung by an insect.

- The itching keeps your child from sleeping.

During Office Hours

All other children with a widespread itchy rash need medical consultation. (Exception: If you know the cause and can eliminate it, proceed to HOME CARE, below.)

HOME CARE FOR ITCHY, WIDESPREAD RASHES

The following measures may help to relieve itching regardless of the cause:

- Wash the skin once with soap to remove any irritants.

- Give your child cool baths without soap every 3 to 4 hours. (Exception: If the cause is dry skin, see the guideline on page 338.)

- Follow with calamine lotion (no prescription needed) or a baking soda solution (1 teaspoon in 4 ounces water). For very itchy spots, apply ½ percent hydrocortisone cream (no prescription needed). (Exception: If the cause is chicken pox, see the guideline on page 336.)

- Encourage your child not to scratch. Cut the fingernails short.

- Since sweating aggravates itching, temporarily avoid excessive heat, sunbathing, exercise, or sleeping with several blankets.

- Since they cause dry skin, also avoid soaps and swimming pools.

- Your child should not wear itchy or tight clothes.

AMPICILLIN RASH

SYMPTOMS AND CHARACTERISTICS

- Pink or red spots
- The spots are small, flat, and non-itchy
- Always on the trunk
- Spreads to the face in 50 percent of cases
- Occurs while on ampicillin or amoxacillin
- Usual day of onset is day 5 from start of medicine (with a range of 1 to 16 days)

  If your child's symptoms are different, call your physician for help.

Cause • From 5 to 10 percent of children taking ampicillin get a skin rash. This is a harmless "toxic rash" and does not indicate any allergy to ampicillin or penicillin.

Expected Course • The rash usually lasts 3 days, with a range of 1 to 6 days.

CALL YOUR CHILD'S PHYSICIAN DURING OFFICE HOURS IF

- The rash looks like hives.
- The rash is itchy.
- The rash has been present more than 6 days.
- Your child has any joint pains or swelling.
- You have other questions.

HOME CARE
No treatment is necessary.

Ampicillin • Keep your child on the ampicillin until it is gone. The rash will disappear just as quickly whether or not your child continues on ampicillin. Your child can receive ampicillin in the future when necessary and probably won't get a rash next time.

Call Your Child's Physician Later If

• The rash becomes itchy.

• The rash lasts more than 6 days.

• You feel it is a drug allergy.

CHICKEN POX (VARICELLA)

SYMPTOMS AND CHARACTERISTICS

• Multiple small red bumps that progress to thin-walled water blisters, then cloudy blisters or open sores, and finally dry brown crusts (all within 24 hours)

• Repeated crops of these sores for 4 to 5 days

• The sores or crusts are usually less than ¼ inch across

• Rash is on all body surfaces, but usually starts on the head and back

• Fever (The more the rash, the higher the fever. However, your child may not have a fever on the first day of chicken pox or if the rash remains mild.)

• Some sores in the mouth

• Exposure to a child with chicken pox 14 to 16 days previously

If your child's symptoms are different, call your physician for help. Usually the diagnosis of chicken pox is easy.

Cause • A highly contagious virus. A chicken pox vaccine has been tested extensively and should be available for general use by 1989.

Expected Course • New eruptions continue to crop up daily for 4 to 5 days. The fever is usually the highest on the third or fourth day. Children start to feel better and their fevers clear once they stop getting new bumps. Since chicken pox often looks terrible, reassure your child that the bumps are not serious and will go away. Chicken pox rarely leaves any permanent scars unless the eruptions become badly infected with impetigo or your child repeatedly picks off the scabs.

Normal chicken pox, however, can leave temporary marks on the skin that take 6 to 12 months to fade. One attack gives lifelong immunity. Very rarely, a child may develop a mild second attack.

CALL YOUR CHILD'S PHYSICIAN

Immediately If

• Your child is difficult to awaken or confused.

• Your child has trouble walking.

• The neck is stiff.

• The breathing is difficult.

• Vomiting occurs 3 or more times.

• Your child is acting very sick.

During Office Hours If

• The scabs drain yellow pus.

• The scabs are soft and golden.

• One lymph node becomes larger and more tender than the others.

• You have other questions.

HOME CARE FOR CHICKEN POX

Itching and Cool Baths • The best treatment for skin discomfort and itching is a cool bath every 3 to 4 hours for the first few days. Adding 2 ounces of bleach to a tub of water once a day may reduce the bacterial superinfection rate. Rinse well. Baths don't spread the chicken pox. To protect the scabs, pat rather than rub your child dry. Calamine lotion can be placed on itchy spots after the bath.

Fever • Acetaminophen may be given for a few days if your child develops a fever over 102°F (39°C). (For dosage, see FEVER, page 305.) For the present, aspirin should be avoided in children with chicken pox because of the possible link with Reyes syndrome.

Sore Mouth • Since chicken pox sores also occur in the mouth and throat, your child may be picky about eating for a few days. Encourage cold fluids. Offer a soft diet (e.g., ice cream, eggs, pudding, Jell-O, mashed potatoes). Avoid salty foods and citrus fruits.

Sores also normally occur on the eyelids; this carries no danger to vision.

Sore Genital Area • Sores normally occur in the genital area. These can be very painful. If your child (especially a girl) complains of a lot of pain or holds back her urine, buy a local anesthetic like 2.5 percent Xylocaine ointment (no prescription needed). Apply it to the genital ulcers as often as necessary to relieve the pain (every 2 to 3 hours). The cool baths should also help.

Prevention of Impetigo (Infected Sores) • To prevent the sores from becoming infected with bacteria, trim your child's fingernails short. Also, wash the hands with an antibacterial soap (such as Dial or Safeguard) frequently during the day. Discourage picking and scratching, especially of the face. For young babies who are scratching badly, you may want to cover their hands with cotton socks.

Contagiousness and Isolation • Children with chicken pox are contagious until all the sores have crusted over, usually about 7 days after the rash begins. Therefore, they should be kept out of school for about 1 week. Your child does not have to stay home until all the scabs fall off, since this may take 2 weeks.

Avoid sunlight, since extra chicken pox will occur on sun-exposed parts of the skin.

To avoid exposing other children, try not to take your child to the physician's office. If you must, leave your child in the car with a sitter while you check in.

If a child with a serious disease is exposed to chicken pox, he should see his physician promptly because he may need protection with a special kind of gamma globulin.

Call Your Child's Physician Later If

• The scabs turn from brown to gold, get any pus under them, or become larger in size.

• Itching interferes with sleep.

• Breathing becomes difficult or fast.

• Your child becomes confused or difficult to awaken.

• Your child has severe pain when passing urine.

• You feel your child is getting worse.

DRY SKIN

Dry, rough skin is mainly caused by removing the skin's natural oils through too much bathing and soap ("soapy dermatitis"). Once the oils are gone, the skin can't hold moisture. Dry climates make it worse, as does winter weather ("winter itch"). The problem is less common in teenagers, because the oil glands are more active. Dry, rough skin on the back of the upper arms is called keratosis pilaris. Dry, pale spots on the face are called pityriasis alba. Both are complications of scrubbing dry skin with soap. The dry areas are often itchy, and this is the main symptom.

HOME CARE

Soap and Bathing • For children with dry skin, avoid all soaps. Have your child bathe or shower less often than usual—perhaps twice a week. Keep bathing time to less than 10 minutes. Avoid soaps, detergents, and bubble baths. Don't let a bar of soap just float around in the tub. For teenagers, buy a special soap for dry skin (Dove received high ratings in a recent study). Teenagers can get by with applying soap only to the armpits, genitals, and feet. Use no soap on itchy areas. Don't lather up—the outer arms are often affected for this reason. Rinse well.

Lubricating Creams • Buy a large bottle of a lubricating cream (see ECZEMA, below, for details). Apply the cream to any dry or itchy areas several times a day, especially immediately after bathing. You will probably have to continue this throughout the winter. If the itch persists after 4 days, use ½ percent hydrocortisone cream (no prescription needed) temporarily.

Humidifier • If your winters are dry, you can protect your child's skin from the constant drying effect by running a room humidifier full time. The presence of static electricity means your home is much too dry.

Bath Oils • It does not make sense to pour bath oils into the bathwater; most of the oil goes down the drain. It also makes the bathtub slippery and dangerous. If you prefer a bath oil over hand lotion, it should be applied (usually in a diluted form) immediately after the bath. Baby oil (mineral oil) is inexpensive and keeps the skin moisture from evaporating.

Call Your Child's Physician Later If

• No improvement occurs within 2 weeks.

ECZEMA (ATOPIC DERMATITIS)

SYMPTOMS AND CHARACTERISTICS

• Red, extremely itchy rash

• Most common on flexor surfaces (creases) of the elbows, wrists, and knees

• Occasionally the neck, ankles, and feet are involved

• If scratched, the rash becomes raw and weeping

• Constant dry skin

• Previous confirmation of this diagnosis by a physician is helpful

If your child's symptoms are different, call your physician for help.

Cause • Eczema results from an inherited type of sensitive skin and lowered itch threshold. A personal history of asthma or hay fever or a family history of eczema adds weight to the diagnosis. Flare-ups occur when there is contact with irritating substances (especially soaps and chlorine). While food allergies are not the underlying cause of eczema, in a few infants a particular food may cause the eczema to flare up. If you suspect some food (e.g., cow's milk, eggs, or peanut butter), feed it to your child as a single challenge. If it plays any role, the eczema should become itchy or develop hives within 2 hours of ingestion. If this occurs, avoid this food in the future and talk to your child's physician about food substitutes.

Expected Course • This is a chronic condition and will usually not go away before adolescence. Eczema of the face usually clears by age 2 or 3 years. Early treatment of any itching or change in the skin is the key to preventing a severe rash.

CALL YOUR CHILD'S PHYSICIAN

Immediately If

• The rash appears to be infected and your child has a fever.

• Your child is acting very sick.

During Office Hours If

• Your child is under 2 years of age.

• The rash is raw and bleeding in several places.

• The itching interferes with sleep.

• The rash appears to be infected, as evidenced by pus or soft yellow scabs.

• You have other questions.

HOME CARE

Steroid Cream • Steroid cream is the main treatment for eczema. Use the one your physician prescribes or nonprescription ½ percent hydrocortisone cream. Apply it up to 6 times a day when the eczema flares up. When the rash quiets down, use it at least once a day for an additional 2 weeks. After that, break the itch cycle by using it immediately on any spot that itches. This cream should be applied in small amounts and rubbed in until it can't be seen. When you travel with your child, always take the steroid cream with you, and always leave it available for babysitters. If your supply starts to run out, get it renewed.

Bathing • Your child should have 1 bath a day (less often in the wintertime) for 10 minutes or less. Don't use any soap on the areas of rash. Eczema is very sensitive to soaps. Young children can usually be cleaned without any soap. Teenagers need a soap to wash under the arms, the genital area, and the feet. They can use a nondrying soap such as Dove for these areas. Try to keep shampoo off the eczema.

Lubricating Cream • Children with eczema always have dry skin. After a 5- to 10-minute bath, the skin is hydrated and feels good. Help trap the moisture in the skin by applying an outer layer of cream to the entire skin surface while it is damp. Apply it after steroid cream has been applied to any itchy areas. Apply the lubricating cream once daily (twice a day during the winter). Some lubricating creams are Eucerin, Keri, Lubriderm, Nivea, and Nutraderm. Avoid applying any ointments, petroleum jelly, or vegetable shortening, because they can block the sweat glands and worsen the rash. They cause the most trouble during hot weather. Also, soap is needed to wash them off.

Itching • At the first sign of any itching, apply the steroid cream to the area that itches. Keep your child's fingernails cut short so they are less damaging to the skin. Also, wash your child's hands with water frequently to avoid infecting the eczema. When itching is present, it is always worse at bedtime compared to the rest of the day, because your child has little else by way of distraction. Therefore, steroid cream at bedtime is important.

Call Your Child's Physician Later If

• Itching interferes with sleep.

• The rash becomes infected.

• The rash hasn't greatly improved within 7 days on this treatment.

PREVENTION

• Clothes made of cotton, or of cotton in combination with other fibers, should be worn as much as possible.

• Avoid wool fibers and clothes made of other scratchy, rough materials. They make eczema worse.

• Avoid materials that hold in heat, such as most synthetic fibers, which can worsen the rash.

• Avoid triggers that cause eczema to flare up, such as excessive heat, sweating, excessive cold, dry air, chlorine, harsh chemicals, and soaps.

• In dry climates, place a humidifier in your child's bedroom.

• Never use bubble bath, because it can have a disastrous effect on eczema.

- Keep your child off the grass during grass pollen season (May and June).

- Keep your child away from anyone with fever blisters. The herpes virus can cause a serious skin infection in children with eczema.

FIFTH DISEASE (ERYTHEMA INFECTIOSUM)

SYMPTOMS AND CHARACTERISTICS

- Bright red rash of both cheeks for 1 to 3 days ("slapped cheek" appearance)
- Followed by pink "lacelike" rash of extremities
- "Lacy" rash mainly on thighs and upper arms
- "Lacy" rash that comes and goes several times over 1 to 3 weeks
- No fever or minimal one

  If your child's symptoms are different, call your physician for help. Fifth Disease was so named because it was the fifth pink-red infectious rash to be described. Despite some controversy about roseola being fourth disease, the other 4 are:

  SCARLET FEVER (see page 351)
  MEASLES (see page 346)
  RUBELLA (see page 350)
  ROSEOLA (see page 349)

  See those guidelines for details.

Cause • Fifth disease is caused by the parvovirus. The attack rate in schools is usually 50 percent of the students.

Expected Course • This is a very mild disease with either no symptoms or a slight runny nose and sore throat. Complications are very rare. The lacelike rash can come and go for 5 weeks. Heat seems to be the main precipitant; therefore it returns following warm baths, exercise, and sun exposure.

CALL YOUR CHILD'S PHYSICIAN DURING OFFICE HOURS IF

- Your child was on any medicine when the rash began.

- A fever over 101°F is present.

- The rash is itchy.

- You have other questions.

HOME CARE

Treatment • No treatment is necessary. This distinctive rash is harmless and causes no symptoms. Although exposed children may come down with it in 10 to 14 days, isolation or exclusion from school is inappropriate, since the condition is so mild.

Call Your Child's Physician Later If

- It becomes itchy.

- A fever over 101°F occurs.

- You feel your child is getting worse.

HEAT RASH (MILIARIA)

A heat rash consists of tiny pink bumps, mainly of the neck and upper back. It is caused by blocked-off sweat glands. Lots of children get it during hot, humid weather when sweat glands are overworked. Infants can also get it in the wintertime with fever, overdressing, or ointments applied to the chest for coughs. It is also called prickly heat.

HOME CARE

Treatment • Heat rash will clear up completely in 2 to 3 days with techniques that cool off the skin. Give cool baths every 2 to 3 hours, without soap. Let your child's skin air-dry. Leave as many clothes off as possible. Use a fan if your child is asleep or in a playpen. Have your child lie on a towel so the face isn't constantly wet.

Calamine lotion (no prescription needed) can be applied to the worst spots. Cornstarch applied to body creases can prevent some heat rashes. Avoid all ointments or oils, because they can block off sweat glands.

Call Your Child's Physician Later If

• The rash lasts more than 72 hours on this treatment.

HIVES (URTICARIA)

SYMPTOMS AND CHARACTERISTICS

• Very itchy rash

• Raised pink spots with pale centers

• Sizes of spots range from ½ inch to several inches across.

• Shapes are quite variable

• Location, size, and shape change rapidly and repeatedly

If your child's symptoms are different, call your physician for help.

Causes • Hives are an allergic reaction to a food (especially shrimp, fruits, and nuts), drug, viral infection, insect bite, or a host of other substances. Usually a child has been exposed to the substance many times in the past before developing an allergy to it. Often the cause is not found.

Expected Course • More than 10 percent of children get hives. Most children who develop hives have it only once. The hives come and go for 3 or 4 days and then mysteriously disappear. Large swellings are common about the eyes, lips, and genitals if hives occur there.

CALL YOUR CHILD'S PHYSICIAN

Immediately If

• Breathing or swallowing is difficult.

• The tongue is swollen.

• Any abdominal pain is present.

- The hives started immediately after your child took medicine or was stung by an insect.

- Your child is acting very sick.

During Office Hours If

- A fever (over 100°F) is present.

- Joint swelling or pain is present.

- Your child had hives before *and* the cause wasn't found.

- Your child is on any medicine.

- You have other questions.

HOME CARE

Treatment • The best drug for hives is an antihistamine. If you have one at home (e.g., for hay fever) use it. Otherwise ask your pharmacist to recommend a good nonprescription product. While an antihistamine won't cure the hives, it will reduce their numbers and relieve itching. A cool bath will also make your child feel better. In the meantime, avoid anything you think might have brought on the hives. If the cause was definitely a food or drug your child swallowed in the last 4 hours, give one large dose of a laxative to speed its passage out of the body. (Such as 1 or 2 tablespoons of Milk of Magnesia.) Since hives are not contagious, your child can be with other children.

Common Mistakes • Many parents wait to give the antihistamine until new hives have re-appeared. This means your child will become itchy again. The purpose of the medicine is to keep your child comfortable until the hives go away. Therefore, give the medicine regularly until you are sure the hives are completely gone.

Call Your Child's Physician Later If

- Most of the itch is not relieved within 24 hours on the medicine.

- The hives last for more than a week.

- You feel your child is getting worse.

MEASLES (RUBEOLA)

SYMPTOMS AND CHARACTERISTICS

- 3 or 4 days of red eyes, cough, runny nose, and fever before the rash begins
- Pronounced blotchy red rash starting on the face and spreading downward over the entire body in 3 days
- White specks on the lining of the mouth, especially by the molars (Koplik's spots)
- Exposure to a child with measles 10 to 12 days earlier

(Note: Because of the measles vaccine, this disease has become rare in our country.)

If your child's symptoms are different, call your physician for help.

Cause • A highly contagious virus.

Expected Course • Measles can be a miserable illness, and there's not much we can do to shorten it. The Koplik's spots (which cause no symptoms) appear 1 day before the rash and are gone by day 2 of the rash. The rash usually lasts 7 days (this is why it's called 7-day measles). Your child will usually begin to feel a lot better by the fourth day of the rash. Ear infections, eye infections, and pneumonia are common complications.

CALL YOUR CHILD'S PHYSICIAN

Immediately If

- Breathing is difficult *and* no better after you clear the nose.
- Your child is confused or delirious.
- Your child is hard to awaken completely.
- Your child has a severe headache.
- Your child is acting very sick.

During Office Hours

All other children with suspected measles need medical consultation. This disease must be reported to the public health department to prevent spread.

HOME CARE

Fever • Use acetaminophen (for dosage, see FEVER, page 305).

Cough • Use corn syrup or honey (1 to 4 years old) or cough drops (over 4 years old). If the cough interferes with sleep, give a cough suppressant such as dextromethorphan (DM). Also, use a humidifier. (See COUGH, page 469, for further information.)

Red Eyes • Wipe your child's eyes frequently with a clean wet cotton ball. The eyes are usually sensitive to bright light, so your child may prefer the curtains drawn in his room and probably won't want to go outside for several days unless he wears sunglasses. Light exposure, however, can't damage the eyes.

Rash • The rash requires no treatment.

Diet • Offer a diet of your child's own choosing. The appetite will be poor for several days.

Contagiousness • The disease is no longer contagious after the rash is gone and your child can then see friends and go to school. This usually takes 7 days.

Measles Exposure • Any child or adult who has been exposed to your child and who has not had natural measles or the measles vaccine should call his or her physician. If given early, a measles vaccine is often protective.

Call Your Child's Physician Later If

• An earache develops.

• The eyes develop a yellow discharge.

• The nasal discharge becomes yellow for more than 24 hours.

• The breathing becomes labored *and* not due to a stuffy nose.

• Fever is still present on the fourth day of the rash.

• Fever returns after the temperature has been normal for more than 24 hours.

• You feel your child is getting worse.

MEASLES VACCINE RASH

The live measles vaccine has prevented many deaths and serious complications of the natural disease. The vaccine is given to children over 15 months of age. About 20 percent of children develop some mild symptoms 7 to 10 days after the vaccine. A slight, pink rash of the trunk usually lasts 2 or 3 days. A fever is usually 101 to 103°F and lasts less than 72 hours.

HOME CARE
Treatment is not usually needed. The measles vaccine rash is harmless and not contagious.

Call Your Child's Physician During Office Hours If

• The rash becomes itchy.

• The rash changes to purple spots.

• The rash lasts more than 3 days.

PURPLE SPOTS

If your child develops purple to blood-red spots of the skin or unexplained bruises, call your child's physician *immediately*. The size of the bleeding into the skin can vary from small dots (petechiae) to large spots (purpura). These spots can be caused by a serious bloodstream infection (especially if your child also has a fever) or by a bleeding tendency.

(Note: Bruises due to injuries or blue birthmarks don't count.)

RELATED TOPIC

SKIN TRAUMA, BRUISES (see page 64)

ROSEOLA (ROSEOLA INFANTUM)

SYMPTOMS AND CHARACTERISTICS

- Age 6 months to 3 years
- Presence of a fine pink rash, mainly on the trunk
- High fever during the preceding 2 to 4 days which cleared within 24 hours before the rash appeared
- Your child was only mildly ill during the time with fever
- Your child acts fine now

  If your child's symptoms are different, call your physician for help.

Cause • Roseola is caused by a virus.

Expected Course • The rash lasts 1 or 2 days, followed by complete recovery.

HOME CARE

Treatment • No particular treatment is necessary, since the fever is usually gone when the rash appears. Roseola is contagious, and other children under age 3 who have been with your child may come down with roseola in about 12 days. Once the rash is gone, the disease is no longer contagious.

Call Your Child's Physician Later If

- The spots become purple or blood-colored.
- The rash lasts more than 3 days.
- The rash becomes itchy.
- Any new symptoms develop that concern you.

RELATED TOPIC

RASHES, UNKNOWN CAUSE (WIDESPREAD) (see page 331)

RUBELLA (GERMAN MEASLES)

SYMPTOMS AND CHARACTERISTICS

• Widespread pink-red spots

• Starts on the face

• Moves rapidly downward, covering the body in 24 hours

• Lasts 3 to 4 days ("3-day measles")

• Associated enlarged lymph nodes at back of neck

• Mild fever

• Your child never had the rubella vaccine

> The rash is not distinctive. Many other viral rashes look like it. Physicians have difficulty being certain of this diagnosis even after examining the child. Don't try to make this diagnosis at home unless there is an epidemic of it in your community.

Cause • Rubella is a viral illness. The incubation period is 14 to 21 days.

Expected Course • The disease is mild with complete recovery in 3 or 4 days. Complications are very rare except for about 10 percent of teenagers (especially girls) who develop associated joint pains. However, complications to the unborn child are disastrous and include deafness, cataracts, heart defects, growth retardation, and encephalitis. Pregnant women should avoid anyone with suspected rubella.

CALL YOUR CHILD'S PHYSICIAN DURING OFFICE HOURS IF

• Your child has a widespread, pink rash with fever.

• You think your child might have rubella.

HOME CARE

If your physician has confirmed that your child probably has rubella, the following may be helpful:

Treatment • None is probably necessary. Give acetaminophen for fever over 102°F, sore throat, or other pains. (For dosage, see FEVER, page 305.)

Avoid Pregnant Women • If your child might have rubella, keep him away from any pregnant women. He is contagious for 5 days after the start of the rash.

EXPOSURE OF ADULT WOMEN TO RUBELLA
The nonpregnant woman exposed to rubella should avoid pregnancy during the following 3 months, and the pregnant woman should see her obstetrician. If she has already received the rubella vaccine, she (and her unborn child) should be protected. If she thinks she had German measles as a child, this history is too unreliable. Even if the present exposure was minor or brief, she should have a blood test to determine her immunity against rubella.

RUBELLA VACCINE
Get your children protected against rubella at 15 months of age so we won't have to worry about pregnant women when kids get a pink or red rash. It's quite safe to immunize the child of a pregnant woman.

SCARLET FEVER

SYMPTOMS AND CHARACTERISTICS
- Reddened, sunburned-looking skin (especially of the chest and abdomen)
- On close inspection, the redness is speckled (i.e., tiny pink dots)
- Increased redness in skin folds (especially the groin, armpits, and elbow creases)
- The rash is everywhere within 24 hours
- Rough, sandpapery feeling to the reddened skin
- Flushed face with paleness around the mouth
- Sore throat and fever (usually preceding the rash by 18 to 24 hours)

  If your child's symptoms are different, call your physician for help.

Cause • Scarlet fever is a strep throat infection with a rash. The complication rate is no different from that for strep throat alone. The rash is caused by a special rash-producing toxin that is present in some strep bacteria.

Expected Course • The red rash usually clears in 4 or 5 days. Sometimes the skin peels in 1 or 2 weeks where the rash was most prominent. The skin may peel and flake for several weeks. The sore throat and fever clear after 1 or 2 days on penicillin. Your child can return to school then. The penicillin will need to be continued for 10 days to completely eliminate the strep.

CALL YOUR CHILD'S PHYSICIAN

Immediately If

• Your child is drooling or having great difficulty swallowing.

• The urine is red or cola-colored.

• Your child is a female adolescent *and* she is also having her menstrual period.

• Your child is acting very sick.

During Office Hours

All other children with suspected scarlet fever need medical consultation. Your child's physician will advise you about a throat culture and antibiotics.

RELATED TOPIC

Sore Throat (see page 457)

SKIN: LOCALIZED PINK OR RED RASHES

RASHES, UNKNOWN CAUSE (LOCALIZED)

SYMPTOMS AND CHARACTERISTICS

- Red or pink rash (erythema)
- Smooth or slightly bumpy
- Spots or solid red
- On one part of body (localized or clustered)
- Not itchy

Similar Condition • If the rash is itchy, turn directly to the guideline for ITCHING, UNKNOWN CAUSE (LOCALIZED), page 355.

Causes of Localized Rashes • The possible causes are many. If one of the following is suspected, turn directly to that guideline:

- Scalp location
  CRADLE CAP (see page 151)

- Face location
  ACNE (see page 356)

- Genital location
  DIAPER RASH (see page 152)

- Hand and foot location
  HAND, FOOT, AND MOUTH DISEASE (see page 368)

- Shoulder location
  TINEA VERSICOLOR (see page 380)

- Variable location
  BOILS (see page 365)
  IMPETIGO (see page 369)
  NEWBORN RASHES (less than 2 weeks old) (see page 88)
  RINGWORM (see page 377)
  SHINGLES (see page 378)

Expected Course • Depends on the diagnosis

CALL YOUR CHILD'S PHYSICIAN

Immediately If

- The rash is purple or blood-colored.

- It is bright red *and* tender to the touch.

- It looks like a burn.

- Red streaks that look like a spreading infection are present.

- Your child is acting very sick.

During Office Hours If

- You have other questions.

HOME CARE FOR LOCALIZED RASHES

Treatment • Localized red rashes can be due to a chemical or plant irritant that got on your child's skin. No treatment is necessary. Wash the rash once with soap to remove any irritating substances. Thereafter cleanse it only with water. Don't apply any medicine or petroleum jelly. If the rash seems dry, apply hand lotion twice a day.

Call Your Child's Physician Later If

- The rash spreads.

- It becomes tender to the touch.

- It lasts more than 1 week.

ITCHING, UNKNOWN CAUSE (LOCALIZED)

CAUSES
The possible causes are many. If one of the following is suspected, turn directly to that guideline:

- Itching of anus
  PINWORMS (see page 497)

- Itching of eyes
  EYES, ALLERGIES (see page 409)
  EYE, ITCHY (see page 411)

- Itching of foot
  ATHLETE'S FOOT (see page 359)

- Itching of genitals
  JOCK ITCH (see page 372)

- Itching of head
  LICE (HEAD) (see page 373)
  DANDRUFF (see page 386)

- Itching of lip
  LIP, SWOLLEN (see page 456)

- Itching of variable locations
  BITES, INSECT (see page 361)
  POISON IVY (see page 374)
  RINGWORM (see page 377)

CALL YOUR CHILD'S PHYSICIAN DURING OFFICE HOURS IF

- The itching is severe.

- The rash is larger than 2 inches in size.

- You have other questions.

HOME CARE

Clarification • The itchy spot is probably due to contact with an irritant like a plant, chemicals, Fiberglas, detergents, a new cosmetic, or new jewelry (called contact dermatitis). Try to figure out what caused it and avoid this substance in the future.

Treatment • Wash the area once thoroughly with soap to remove any remaining irritants. Thereafter avoid soaps to this area. Apply cold-water compresses or ice for 20 minutes every 3 to 4 hours to reduce itching. Follow this with calamine lotion. If the itch is more than mild, apply ½ percent hydrocortisone cream (no prescription needed) every 2 hours until it feels better. Encourage your child not to scratch; cut the fingernails short.

Call Your Child's Physician Later If

• The rash spreads.

• The itching becomes worse.

• It lasts more than 1 week.

ACNE

SYMPTOMS AND CHARACTERISTICS

• Blackheads, whiteheads (pimples), or red bumps

• Face, neck, and shoulders involved

• The larger red lumps are quite painful

• Occurs during adolescent and young adult years

Cause • Acne is due to an overactivity and plugging of the oil glands. More than 90 percent of teenagers have some acne. The main cause of the changes in the oil glands is increased levels of hormones during adolescence. Heredity is also a factor. It is not caused by diet, and it is unnecessary to restrict fried foods, chocolate, or any other food. Acne is not caused by sexual activity of any kind, or by dirt or not washing the face often enough. The tops of blackheads are black because of the chemical reaction of the oil plug with the air.

Expected Course • Acne usually lasts until age 20 or even 25. It is rare for acne to leave any scars, and people worry needlessly about this.

CALL YOUR CHILD'S PHYSICIAN DURING OFFICE HOURS IF

- There are any boils.
- There are any red streaks.
- There are more than five tender, red lumps.
- You have other questions.

HOME CARE

There is no magic medicine at this time that will cure acne. However, good skin care can keep acne under control and at a very mild level.

Basic Treatment for All Acne

- Soap. The skin should be washed twice a day, the most important time being at bedtime. A mild soap such as Dove should be used, because overly dry skin makes acne harder to treat. Lack of washing does not cause acne.

- Hair. The hair should be shampooed daily. Acne can be made worse by friction if the hair is too long.

- Avoid picking. Many young people pick at their acne when they are not thinking about it. This keeps it from healing. They should try not to touch the face at all during the day.

- Avoid looking in mirrors more than 1 or 2 minutes a day. Your youngster will just find something to pick and make the acne worse.

- Get out and meet people. Acne is not contagious.

Additional Treatment for Pimples • Pimples are infected oil glands. They should be treated with the following:

- Benzoyl peroxide cream or gel. This cream helps to open pimples and blackheads, and it also kills bacteria. It is available without a prescription. Ask your pharmacist to recommend a brand. The cream should be applied in a thin film once a day at bedtime. In redheads and blonds, it should be applied every other day initially. Apply the cream to the entire face (except for next to the eyes and mouth), not just the areas that have currently flared up. If the skin peels or becomes red, you are using the medicine too often, so slow down. After a desirable effect has been achieved, the benzoyl peroxide cream may be needed only every other night.

• Pimple opening. Pimples can be opened after they have come to a head. This should be done only after the face and hands have been washed thoroughly. Opening and draining the pimples will help them to clear up in 2 days instead of 7. However, this must be done correctly. Use a sterile needle (sterilized by alcohol or a flame). The opening must be sufficiently large, and any squeezing should be done gently. Scarring will not result from opening small pimples, but it can result from squeezing boils or other red, tender lumps. This should never be done, because it damages the skin.

Additional Treatment for Blackheads (Comedones) • Blackheads are the plugs found in blocked-off oil glands. Blackheads are not infected and should be treated with the following:

• Benzoyl peroxide. This agent is the best nonprescription medicine for removing thickened skin inside the openings to oil glands. It should be used as previously described. (Note: A stronger agent for stopping blackhead formation is retinoic acid A, but a prescription is required.)

• Blackhead extractor. Blackheads that are a cosmetic problem can usually be removed easily with a blackhead or comedone extractor. This instrument costs about a dollar and is available at any drugstore. By placing the hole in the end of the small metal spoon directly over the blackhead, uniform pressure can be applied that does not hurt the normal skin. If the blackhead does not come out the first time, it should be opened carefully with a sterile pin before pressing again. Obviously, the face should be washed before using a blackhead extractor.

Results of Treatment • Even the best of medicines takes 4 to 6 weeks to improve acne. Success depends on your patience. There are no shortcuts. The proper treatment program will need to remain in effect for several years.

Common Mistakes in Treating Acne

• Alcohol wipes, medicated soaps, or abrasive soaps have no benefits.

• Avoid rubbing the skin. Hard scrubbing of the skin is harmful because it breaks the walls of the oil glands, which leads to pimples and large lumps.

- Avoid applying any oily or greasy substances to the face. They make acne worse by blocking off oil glands. If you must use cover-up cosmetics, use water-based ones and wash them off at bedtime.

- Avoid hair tonics or hair creams (especially greasy ones). With sweating, these will spread to the face and aggravate the acne.

- Avoid any friction. Friction or pressure on the face, such as from headbands, scarves, turtlenecks, or resting the cheek or chin on the palm of the hand will worsen the acne in these areas.

- Avoid close shaves. Attempts to look extra good for a date usually nick the openings of the oil glands and cause the acne to flare up.

- Avoid self-medication with high dosages of zinc or Vitamin A. The former can increase the risk for strokes and the latter can cause brain swelling and bone pain.

Call Your Child's Physician Later If

- A boil develops on the face.

- Several large, tender, red lumps appear.

- Acne is not improved after treating it with benzoyl peroxide for 6 weeks.

- Benzoyl peroxide makes the face itchy or swollen.

ATHLETE'S FOOT (TINEA PEDIS)

SYMPTOMS AND CHARACTERISTICS

- A red, scaly, cracked rash between the toes
- The rash itches and burns
- With itching the rash becomes raw and weepy
- Scaly rash often involves the insteps of the feet
- Unpleasant foot odor
- Mainly occurs in adolescents

Similar Condition

CRACKED SKIN (see page 386)

Cause • A fungus infection that grows best on warm, damp skin. The condition is worse in summer, in people who sweat a lot (e.g., athletes), and in people who rarely take off their shoes.

Expected Course • With proper treatment, athlete's foot usually clears in 2 to 3 weeks.

CALL YOUR CHILD'S PHYSICIAN DURING OFFICE HOURS IF

• The rash is not confined to the instep and between the toes.

• Pus is draining from the rash.

• The feet are very painful.

• You have other questions.

HOME CARE

Antifungal Cream • Buy Tinactin or Micatin lotion at your drugstore (no prescription needed). Before applying, rinse the feet in plain water and dry them carefully, especially between the toes. Apply the lotion twice a day to the rash and well beyond its borders. Continue Tinactin or Micatin for several weeks, or for at least 7 days after the rash seems to have cleared.

Dryness • Athlete's foot improves dramatically if the feet are kept dry. It helps to go barefoot or wear sandals or thongs as much as possible. Canvas tennis shoes are good. Plastic or tight shoes are bad because they don't allow the feet to breathe. Cotton socks should be worn because they absorb sweat and keep the feet dry. Change the socks twice daily. Dry the feet thoroughly after baths and showers. Sun exposure also helps.

Foot Odor • Foot odor will often clear as the athlete's foot improves. Rinsing the feet and changing the socks twice daily are essential. If you can still smell your child coming, take off his tennis shoes and throw them in your washing machine with some soap and bleach.

Discourage Scratching • Scratching infected feet will delay a cure.

Contagiousness • The condition is not very contagious. The fungus won't grow on dry, normal skin. Your child may take gym and continue with sports. The socks don't need to be boiled, nor do shoes need to be discarded. Taking special precautions in community showers or swimming pools is pointless. If a preadolescent child has athlete's foot, usually a parent or older sibling also has it and requires treatment.

Call Your Child's Physician Later If

• The athlete's foot is not improved in 1 week.

• It is not completely cured after 4 weeks of this treatment.

BITES, INSECT

The following 4 types of insect bites are covered. Go directly to the one that applies to your child.

BEE-STINGS (below)
ITCHY INSECT BITES (see page 362)
PAINFUL INSECT BITES (see page 364)
TICK BITES (see page 364)

If your child has difficulty breathing, difficulty swallowing, hives, or other worrisome symptoms within 30 minutes following an insect bite (especially bees) or had a previous severe allergic reaction to bee-stings, turn directly to ALLERGIC REACTION, SEVERE, page 12.

BEE-STINGS

Your child was stung by a honeybee, bumblebee, hornet, wasp, or yellow jacket. These bites cause immediate painful red bumps. While the pain is usually better in 2 hours, the swelling may increase for up to 24 hours. Multiple stings (more than 10) can cause vomiting, diarrhea, a headache, and fever. This is a toxic reaction related to the amount of venom received (i.e., not an allergic reaction). A bite on the tongue can cause swelling that interferes with breathing.

CALL YOUR CHILD'S PHYSICIAN IMMEDIATELY IF

• Breathing or swallowing is difficult.

• Hives are present.

• There are 10 or more stings.

• A bite is inside the mouth.

HOME CARE

Treatment • If you see a little black dot in the bite, the stinger is still present. Remove it by scraping it off with a knife or a credit card. If only a small fragment remains, use a tweezers or sterile needle just as you would to remove a sliver. Then rub each bite for 15 minutes with a cotton ball soaked in a meat-tenderizer-and-water solution. This will neutralize the venom and relieve the pain. If meat tenderizer is not available, apply an ice cube while you obtain some.

Call Your Child's Physician During Office Hours If

• You can't remove the stinger.

• The swelling continues to spread after 24 hours.

• Swelling of the hand (or foot) spreads past the wrist (or ankle).

• You want the bite looked at.

PREVENTION OF BEE-STINGS

Some bee-stings can be prevented by avoiding gardens, clover fields, orchards in bloom, perfumes, and going barefoot. Insect repellents are not effective against these stinging insects.

ITCHY INSECT BITES

Bites of mosquitoes, chiggers (harvest mites), fleas, and bedbugs usually cause itchy red bumps. The size of the swelling following a mosquito bite means very little. Mosquito bites near the eye always cause massive swelling for 2 days. Clues to a bite's being due to a mosquito are itchiness, a central raised dot in the swelling, bites on surfaces not covered by clothing, summertime, and the child's being an infant. Some mosquito bites in sensitive children form hard lumps that last for months. In contrast to mosquitoes, fleas and bedbugs don't fly; therefore, they crawl under clothing to nibble. Flea bites often turn into little blisters in young children. Some children appeal to these insects more than other children and repeatedly acquire numerous bites.

HOME CARE

Treatment • Apply calamine lotion or a baking soda solution. If the itch is severe (as with chiggers), apply nonprescription ½ percent hydrocortisone cream. Encourage your child not to pick at the bites or they will leave marks and could become infected.

Call Your Child's Physician Later If

• Itching interferes with sleep.

• The bites become infected due to scratching.

PREVENTION OF ITCHY INSECT BITES

Mosquitoes and Chiggers • Many of these bites can be prevented by applying an insect repellent to the ankles, wrists, and other exposed areas before going outdoors or into the woods. Repellents are essential for infants (especially those less than 1 year of age), because their inability to bat away the pesky critters leaves them helpless targets. Excessive application of repellents can cause seizures or coma through skin absorption or ingestion. Therefore, avoid repellent on the hands of young children and teach older children that 3 drops are enough to protect the face and backs of the hands.

Bedbugs • Beds and baseboards can be sprayed with 1 percent malathion, which can be obtained from any garden supply store. Keep young children away from the area until it dries, because this substance is somewhat poisonous. You may need to call in an exterminator.

Fleas • Usually you will find the fleas on your dog or cat. If the bites started after you moved into a different house or apartment, fleas from the previous owner's pet are the most common cause. Fleas can live in carpeting for several months without a meal. Fleas can often be removed by bringing a dog or cat inside the house for 2 hours to collect the fleas—they prefer the dog or cat to living in the carpet. In either case, apply flea powder or soap to your animal outdoors. Careful vacuuming will usually capture any remaining fleas. Malathion bug spray (see BEDBUGS, above) can be used for persistent cases.

PAINFUL INSECT BITES

Bites of horseflies, deerflies, sandflies, gnats, fire ants, harvester ants, cone-nosed bugs, blister beetles, and centipedes usually cause a painful (sometimes burning) red bump. Within a few hours, fire ant bites change to blisters or pimples.

HOME CARE

Treatment • Rub the bite area with a cotton ball soaked in meat-tenderizer-and-water solution. This will relieve the pain. Ammonia rubbed on the area is helpful if you have no meat tenderizer. If these substances are not available, an ice cube applied to the area may help.

Call Your Child's Physician Later If

• The bites are from fire ants.

• Pain interferes with sleep.

• The bites become infected.

PREVENTION

Apply insect repellent sparingly to exposed parts.

TICK BITES

A tick is a half-inch brown insect that stays attached to the skin. The bite is usually painless and also doesn't itch. Therefore, your child will usually be unaware of its presence.

HOME CARE

Tick Removal • The simplest and quickest way to remove a tick is to pull it off. Use a tweezers to grasp the tick as close to the skin as possible (try to get a grip on its head). Apply a steady upward traction until it releases its grip. Do not twist the tick or jerk it suddenly because these maneuvers can break off the tick's head or mouth parts. Do not squeeze the tweezers to the point of crushing the tick, because the secretions released may be contagious. If you have no tweezers, pull the tick off in the same way, using your fingers or a needle for traction.

If the body is removed but the head is left in the skin, it must be removed. Use a sterile needle (as with a sliver). Dispose of the tick by returning it to nature or flushing it down the toilet. Don't crush ticks with your hands; some of them carry disease. Wash the wound and your hands with soap and water after removal.

A recent study showed that embedded ticks do not back out when covered with petroleum jelly, fingernail polish, or rubbing alcohol. We used to think that this would block the tick's breathing pores and take its mind off eating. Unfortunately, ticks breathe only a few times per hour. The application of a hot match to the tick failed to cause it to detach, and also carried the risk of inducing the tick to vomit infected secretions into the wound. (Yuck! Let's change the subject.)

Call Your Child's Physician Later If

- You can't remove the tick.
- The tick's head remains embedded.
- A fever or rash occurs in the week following the bite.
- An enlarging red spot develops at the site of a tick bite.

PREVENTION
Use an insect repellent on exposed parts and wear long clothing. Children and adults who are hiking in tick-infested areas should be checked every 3 hours and immediately after the hike, because the bites are usually painless and ticks are easier to remove before they become firmly attached. Ticks most commonly are found on the scalp, neck, armpit, waist, groin, or feet. Removing ticks promptly may also prevent Rocky Mountain spotted fever, because transmission requires several hours of feeding.

BOILS (ABSCESSES)

SYMPTOMS AND CHARACTERISTICS

- Tender, red lump in the skin
- Causes pain even when not being touched
- Usually ½ inch to 1 inch across

If your child's symptoms are different, call your physician for help.

Cause • A bacterial infection of a hair root or skin pore caused by staph (*Staphylococcus aureus*). Rubbing can cause additional boils. The back of the neck is especially vulnerable because of friction from collars.

Expected Course • Without treatment, the body will wall off the infection. After about a week, the center of the boil becomes soft and mushy (filled with pus). The overlying skin then develops a pimple or becomes thin and pale ("comes to a head"). The boil is now ready for draining. Without lancing, it will drain by itself in 3 or 4 days. Until it drains, a boil is extremely painful.

CALL YOUR CHILD'S PHYSICIAN

Immediately If

• An unexplained fever (over 100° F) is present.

• A spreading red streak runs from the boil.

• Your child is acting very sick.

During Office Hours

All children with boils need medical consultation to decide if antibiotics and/or lancing are needed. Boils on the face are especially dangerous and should always be treated by a physician.

HOME CARE

Lancing • In general, it's better not to open a boil on your own child because it's a very painful procedure. However, if your physician has agreed that you can open the boil, the following information may help: Until the abscess comes to a head or becomes soft, apply warm compresses 3 times a day for 20 minutes. When the boil is ready, use a sterile needle (sterilized with alcohol or a flame), make a large opening, and squeeze very gently or not at all. Once opened, it will drain pus for 2 or 3 days and then heal up. Since this pus is contagious, the boil must be covered by a large 4-by-4-inch gauze and microporous tape. This bandage should be changed and the area washed with Dial or Safeguard soap 3 times a day.

Contagiousness • Boils are very contagious. Be certain that other people in your family do not use your child's towel or washcloth. Any clothes, towels, or sheets that are contaminated with drainage from the boils should be washed with Lysol. Any bandages with pus on them should be carefully thrown away.

Common Mistakes in the Treatment of Boils • Sometimes friends or relatives may advise you to squeeze a boil until you get the core out. The pus in a boil will come out easily if the opening is large enough. Vigorous squeezing is not only very painful, but also entails the risk of forcing bacteria into the bloodstream or causing other boils in the same area. Again, squeezing should be done very gently or not at all. A boil on the face should be treated by a physician.

Call Your Child's Physician Later If

• You want him to open the boil.

• Your child develops more boils.

• A fever (over 100°F) occurs.

PREVENTION OF MORE BOILS
Boils can easily become a recurrent problem. The staph bacteria on the skin can be decreased by showering and washing the hair daily with an antibacterial soap (e.g., Dial or Safeguard). Showers are preferred to a bath because, during a bath, bacteria are just relocated to other parts of the skin. Often the staph bacteria are carried inside the nose. Eliminate them by applying Bacitracin ointment (no prescription needed) with a cotton swab twice a day for 2 weeks. Also discourage your child from picking the nose.

RELATED TOPICS

FINGERNAIL INFECTION (PARONYCHIA) (see page 387)
PIMPLES (see page 397)
STYE (see page 414)

HAND, FOOT, AND MOUTH DISEASE

SYMPTOMS AND CHARACTERISTICS

- Small ulcers in the mouth
- A mildly painful mouth
- Small water blisters or red spots located on the palms and soles, and between the fingers and toes
- 5 or fewer blisters per extremity
- Sometimes, small blisters or red spots on the buttocks
- Low-grade fever (over 100°F)
- Mainly occurs in children age 6 months to 4 years

  If your child's symptoms are different, call your physician for help.

Similar Conditions • If one of the following is suspected, save time by turning directly to that guideline:

CANKER SORES (see page 452)
COLD SORES (see page 454)
THRUSH (see page 159)

Cause • Hand, foot, and mouth disease is always caused by a Coxackie A virus. It has no relationship to hoof and mouth disease of cattle.

Expected Course • The fever and discomfort are usually gone by day 3 or 4. The mouth ulcers resolve by 7 days, but the rash on the hands and feet can last 10 days. The only complication seen with any frequency is dehydration from refusing fluids.

CALL YOUR CHILD'S PHYSICIAN

Immediately If

- Your child has not urinated for more than 8 hours.
- The neck is stiff.
- Your child is confused or delirious.
- Your child is hard to awaken completely.
- Your child is acting very sick.

During Office Hours If

• Fluid intake is poor.

• The mouth pain is severe.

• The gums are red, swollen, or tender.

• You have other questions.

HOME CARE

Diet • Avoid giving your child citrus, salty, or spicy foods. Also avoid foods that need much chewing. Change to a soft diet for a few days and encourage plenty of clear fluids. Cold drinks, Popsicles, and sherbet are often well received. Have your child rinse the mouth with warm water after meals.

Fever • Acetaminophen may be given for a few days if the fever is above 102°F (39°C). (For dosage, see FEVER, page 305.)

Contagiousness • Hand, foot, and mouth disease is quite contagious and usually some of your child's playmates will develop it at about the same time. The incubation period after contact is 3 to 6 days. Because the spread of infection is extremely difficult to prevent and the condition is harmless, these children do not need to be isolated. They can return to school when the fever returns to normal range.

Call Your Child's Physician Later If

• Signs of dehydration develop.

• The fever lasts more than 3 days.

• You feel your child is getting worse.

IMPETIGO (INFECTED SORES)

SYMPTOMS AND CHARACTERISTICS

• Sores smaller than 1 inch in diameter
• Begin as small red bumps which rapidly change to cloudy blisters, then pimples, and finally sores
• Sores increase in size (any wound that doesn't heal)

- Sores often covered by a soft, yellow-brown (honey-colored) scab
- Scabs may be draining pus
- Sores increase in number
- Often starts near the nose or mouth

If your child's symptoms are different, call your physician for help.

Cause • Impetigo is a superficial infection of the skin, caused by streptococcus bacteria (90 percent) and occasionally by staphylococcus bacteria (10 percent). It is more common in the summertime when the skin, which normally is a barrier to infection, is often broken by cuts, scrapes, and insect bites.

Expected Course • With proper treatment the skin will be completely healed in 1 week. Some blemishes will remain for 6 to 12 months, but scars are unusual unless your child picks his sores.

CALL YOUR CHILD'S PHYSICIAN

Immediately If

- A red streak runs from the impetigo.
- The urine is red or cola-colored.
- The face is bright red *and* tender to the touch.
- Any big blisters (larger than 1 inch across) are present.

During Office Hours

All children with impetigo need medical consultation. Impetigo is an active strep infection, and the physician will decide if your child needs an antibiotic.

HOME CARE

Antibiotic (Oral or Injectable) • If your physician prescribes an antibiotic, be certain to take it as directed until the drug is completely gone. The following measures will also help clear up the infection.

Removing the Scabs • The bacteria live underneath the soft scabs, and until the scabs are removed, the antibiotic ointment cannot get through to the bacteria to kill them. Scabs can be soaked off initially using a warm 1:60 bleach solution (1 tablespoon of bleach to 1 quart of water), with a little dishwashing detergent added to help with penetration. The area may need to be gently rubbed, but it should not be scrubbed. A little bleeding is common if you remove all the crust.

Antibiotic Ointment • After the crust has been removed, antibiotic ointment should be applied to the raw surface 6 times a day. Buy Betadine or Bacitracin ointment at your drugstore (no prescription needed). Apply for 7 days, or longer if necessary. The area should be washed off with an antibacterial soap (Dial or Safeguard) 2 times a day. Any *new* thin crust that forms should not be removed, since that would delay healing. If your child has received oral or injectable antibiotics, the antibiotic ointment is needed for only 48 hours.

Preventing the Spread of Impetigo to Other Areas on Your Child's Body • Every time your child touches the impetigo and then scratches another part of the skin with that finger, a new site of impetigo can form. To prevent this, discourage your child from touching or picking at the sores. Keep the fingernails cut short, and wash the hands often with one of the antibacterial soaps.

Contagiousness • Impetigo is quite contagious. Be certain that other people in the family do not use your child's towel or washcloth. Any clothes, towels, or sheets that are contaminated with drainage from the impetigo should be washed with Lysol or bleach. Your child should be kept out of school until he or she has been on treatment for 24 hours with oral (or injectable) antibiotics, or 48 hours with antibiotic ointment alone.

Call Your Child's Physician Later If

• Other people in the family develop impetigo.

• The impetigo increases in size and number of sores after 48 hours on treatment.

• A fever or a sore throat occurs.

• Cola-colored urine or swollen eyelids occur.

JOCK ITCH

Jock itch is also called ringworm of the crotch, or *Tinea cruris.*

SYMPTOMS AND CHARACTERISTICS

• Pink, scaly, itchy rash

• Inner thighs, groin, and scrotum are involved

• Occurs almost exclusively in males

If your child's symptoms are different, call your physician for help.

HOME CARE

Antifungal Medicine • Buy Tinactin or Micatin powder or spray at your drugstore. You won't need a prescription. It needs to be applied twice a day. Make sure you get it in all the skin creases. Continue it for several weeks, or for at least 7 days after the rash seems to have cleared.

Dryness • Jock itch will improve dramatically if the groin area is kept dry. Loose-fitting cotton shorts should be worn (avoid nylon or synthetic-fiber underwear because these fabrics don't absorb moisture). Shorts and athletic supporters should be washed frequently. After showers and baths, all creases should be carefully dried. The rash areas should be carefully cleansed once a day with plain water. Avoid using soap on the rash.

Scratching • Scratching will delay the cure, so have your child avoid scratching the area. Also keep the fingernails cut short.

Call Your Child's Physician During Office Hours If

• Any pimples, pus, or yellow crusts develop.

• There is no improvement in 1 week.

• The rash is not completely cured in 1 month.

LICE (PEDICULOSIS)

SYMPTOMS AND CHARACTERISTICS

- Nits (white eggs) firmly attached to hair shafts near the skin
- Unlike dandruff, nits can't be shaken off
- Gray bugs (lice) are 1/16-inch long, move quickly, and are difficult to see
- Itching and rash of the scalp
- The back of the neck is the favorite area
- The nits are easier to see than the lice because they are white and very numerous

    If your child's symptoms are different, call your physician for help.

Cause • Head lice live only on human beings and can spread quickly despite good health habits. They are spread by close contact or using the hat, comb, or headphones of an infected person. The nits (eggs) normally hatch in about 1 week. Pubic lice ("crabs") are slightly different but are treated the same way. They can be transmitted from bedding or clothing and do not signify sexual contact. Pets can get a different type of lice, but they will not spread to humans.

Expected Course • With treatment, all lice and nits will be killed. A recurrence usually means another contact with an infected person. There are no lasting problems from having lice and they do not carry other diseases.

HOME CARE

Anti-Lice Shampoos • Buy some nonprescription pyrethrin shampoo (A-200, R & C, or Rid). Pour about 2 ounces of the shampoo into dry hair. Add a little warm water to work up a lather. Scrub the hair and scalp for 15 to 20 minutes, by the clock. Rinse the hair thoroughly and dry it with a towel. These shampoos kill both the lice and the nits. Reapplication of the anti-lice shampoo is necessary in 7 days.

Removing Nits • Remove the dead nits by backcombing with a fine-tooth comb or pull them out individually. The nits can be loosened using a mixture of half vinegar and half rubbing alcohol. Fortunately, the hair does not need to be shaved to cure lice.

Lice in the Eyelashes • If you see any lice or nits in the eyelashes, apply plain petrolatum to the eyelashes twice a day for 8 days. The lice won't survive.

Cleaning the House • Lice can't live for over 72 hours off the human body. Your child's room should be vacuumed. Combs and brushes should be soaked for 1 hour in a solution containing some anti-lice shampoo. Wash your child's sheets, blankets, pillow cases, and any clothes worn in the past 72 hours in hot water (140°F kills lice and nits). Items which can't be washed (e.g., hats, coats, or scarves) should be set aside in airtight plastic bags for 3 weeks (the longest period that nits can survive). Anti-lice sprays are unnecessary.

Contagiousness of Lice • Check the heads of everyone else living in your home. If any have scalp rashes, sores, or itching, they should be treated with the anti-lice shampoo even if lice and nits are not seen. Your child can return to school after 1 treatment with the shampoo. Reemphasize not sharing combs and hats. Also notify the school nurse so she can check other students in your child's class.

Call Your Child's Physician Later If

• Itching interferes with sleep.

• The rash is not cleared by 1 week after treatment.

• The rash clears and then returns.

• New eggs appear in the hair.

• The sores start to spread or look infected.

POISON IVY

SYMPTOMS AND CHARACTERISTICS

- Redness, swelling and weeping blisters
- Eruption on exposed body surfaces (such as the hands)
- Shaped like streaks or patches
- Extreme itchiness
- Onset 1 or 2 days after the patient was in a forest or field

    If your child's symptoms are different, call your physician for help.

Cause • Poison ivy, poison oak, and poison sumac cause the same type of rash and are found throughout the United States (except Nevada, Alaska, and Hawaii). Over 50 percent of people are sensitive to the oil of these plants. When the plants are burned, the toxic substance becomes airborne in the smoke and soot.

Expected Course • Usually lasts 2 weeks. Treatment reduces the symptoms but doesn't cure. The best approach is prevention. Swelling or rash near the eye will not harm the eye in any way.

CALL YOUR CHILD'S PHYSICIAN

Immediately If

- The face is red or coughing begins following exposure to smoke.
- The rash involves more than one fourth of the body.
- Your child had a severe poison ivy reaction in the past.

During Office Hours If

- The face, eyes, lips, or genitals are involved.
- The itching interferes with sleep.
- Any big blisters are present.
- The rash is open and oozing.

- Signs of infection occur, such as pus or soft yellow scabs.
- You have other questions.

HOME CARE

Cool Soaks • Soak the involved area in cool water or massage it with an ice cube for 20 minutes as many times a day as necessary. Then let it air-dry. This will reduce itching and oozing.

Hydrocortisone Cream • Buy some ½ percent hydrocortisone cream (no prescription needed). If you already have a stronger steroid (the gels are the most effective), use it. Apply the cream 4 times a day or as often as the rash begins to itch. The sores should be dried up and no longer itchy in 10 to 14 days. In the meantime, cut your child's fingernails short and discourage scratching. Keep your child busy with other activities.

Contagiousness • Anything that has poison ivy oil or sap on it is contagious for several weeks. This includes the shoes and clothes you last wore into the woods, as well as any pets that may have oil on their fur. Routine laundering will remove oil from clothing and a bath with soap will cleanup "Old Yeller." The rash begins 1 to 2 days after skin contact. The fluid from the blisters, however, is not contagious. Therefore, scratching the poison ivy sores will not cause it to spread.

Call Your Child's Physician Later If

- The itching becomes severe.
- Your child can't sleep.
- The poison ivy becomes infected as suggested by pus, soft yellow scabs, or increasing tenderness.

PREVENTION

- Learn to recognize poison ivy plants. They tend to grow near river banks. At least, avoid all plants with 3 large shiny leaves. Another clue is the presence of shiny black spots on damaged leaves. On the West Coast you will need to identify poison oak.
- Wear long pants or socks when walking through woods that may contain poison ivy.

- If you think your child has had contact with poison ivy, wash the exposed areas of skin with any available soap several times. Do this as soon as possible, because after one hour, it is of little value in preventing absorption of the oil.

- Currently, allergy shots or pills are not of value for poison ivy.

RINGWORM (TINEA CORPORIS)

SYMPTOMS AND CHARACTERISTICS

- Ring-shaped pink patch
- Scaly raised border (always has scales)
- Clear center
- Usually ½ to 1 inch in size
- Ring slowly increases in size
- Mildly itchy

  If your child's symptoms are different, call your physician for help.

Cause • A fungus infection of the skin, often transferred from puppies or kittens who have it. It is not caused by a worm.

Expected Course • Ringworm responds well to appropriate treatment. Without treatment, natural immunity will develop in about 4 months.

CALL YOUR CHILD'S PHYSICIAN DURING OFFICE HOURS IF

- The scalp is involved. (Reason: pills are needed for treatment.)
- More than 3 spots are present.
- You have other questions.

HOME CARE

Antifungal Cream • Buy Micatin or Tinactin cream at your drugstore (no prescription needed). Apply the cream twice a day. Continue this treatment for 1 week after the ringworm patch is smooth and seems to be gone. Encourage your child to avoid scratching the area, because scratching will delay a cure.

Contagiousness • Ringworm of the skin is not contagious to humans. Your child doesn't have to miss any school (or daycare) and can play with other children.

Treatment of Pets • Kittens and puppies with ringworm usually have no symptoms. If ringworm patches are seen, apply Micatin or Tinactin cream as described for humans. If no patches are present, treat the animal only if ringworm recurs in your child. Use Micatin or Tinactin powder and apply it to the entire fur twice a week for 3 weeks. Also have your child avoid close contact with the animal. Natural immunity also develops in animals after 4 months. Call your veterinarian for other questions.

Call Your Child's Physician Later If

• The ringworm continues to spread after 1 week on treatment.

• The rash is not cleared in 4 weeks.

RELATED TOPICS

IMPETIGO (see page 369)
POISON IVY (see page 375)
DRY SKIN (see page 338)

SHINGLES (ZOSTER)

SYMPTOMS AND CHARACTERISTICS

• A linear rash that follows the path of a nerve

• The rash occurs on only 1 side of the body

• The rash starts with clusters of red bumps, changes to water blisters, and finally becomes dry crusts

• The back, chest, or abdomen are the most common sites

• The rash usually doesn't burn or itch in children (in contrast to the adult form)

- Your child does not have a fever or feel sick
- Your child had chicken pox in the past

  If your child's symptoms are different, call your physician for help.

Cause • Zoster is caused by the chicken pox virus. The disease is not caught from other people with active shingles or chicken pox. The chicken pox virus lies dormant in the body of some people and is reactivated for unknown reasons in this form. Children with zoster are usually over 3 years old.

Expected Course • New shingles continue to appear for several days. All the rash dries up by 7 to 10 days. Complications do not occur unless the eye is involved. Most people have shingles just once; repeated attacks are rare.

CALL YOUR CHILD'S PHYSICIAN DURING OFFICE HOURS IF

- The rash is very painful or very itchy.
- The rash is near the eye.
- You have other questions.

HOME CARE

Relief of Symptoms • Most children have no symptoms. For pain, give acetaminophen as necessary. (For dosage, see FEVER, page 305.) Avoid aspirin for zoster because of the possible link with Reyes syndrome. Discourage itching or picking the rash. The rash does not need any cream.

Contagiousness • Children with zoster can transmit chicken pox (but not zoster) to others. Although they are far less contagious than children with chicken pox, children with zoster should stay home from school for 7 days unless they can keep the rash covered until it crusts over. Children or adults who have not had chicken pox should avoid visiting the child with zoster (unless the rash is covered).

Call Your Physician Later If

- The rash lasts more than 14 days.
- The rash becomes infected with pus or soft yellow scabs.
- You feel your child is getting worse.

SORES

Sores are coin-sized ulcerated, weeping, or scabbed areas on the skin. Many begin as blisters which quickly break open. The possible causes are many. If one of the following is suspected, save time by turning directly to that guideline:

BURNS, THERMAL (see page 28)
CHICKEN POX (see page 335)
COLD SORES (see page 454)
IMPETIGO (see page 369)
BITES, INSECT (see page 361)
POISON IVY (see page 375)
RINGWORM (see page 377)

If the cause of the sores is unknown, call your child's physician during office hours for an appointment.

TINEA VERSICOLOR

SYMPTOMS AND CHARACTERISTICS

• The name means "multicolored ringworm"

• The condition occurs in adolescents and adults

• Numerous spots and patches on the neck, upper back, and shoulders

• The spots are covered by a fine scale

• The spots vary in size

• In summer, the spots are light and don't tan

• In winter, the spots are darker (often pink or brown) compared to normal Caucasian skin

If your child's symptoms are different, call your physician for help.

Cause • This superficial infection is caused by a yeastlike fungus called *Malassezia furfur*. It occurs more commonly in warm, humid climates.

Expected Course • The problem tends to wax and wane for many years. Since complications do not occur, tinea versicolor is solely a cosmetic problem. Itching is uncommon.

HOME CARE

Selsun Blue Shampoo • Selsun Blue (selenium sulfide) is a non-prescription medicated shampoo that can cure this condition. Apply this shampoo once a day for 14 days. Apply it to the affected skin areas as well as 2 or 3 inches onto the adjacent normal skin. Rub it in and let it dry. Be careful to keep it off the eyes or genitals, since it is irritating to these tissues. After 20 minutes, take a shower. By 2 weeks, the scaling should be stopped, and the rash is temporarily cured. The normal skin color will not return for 6 to 12 months.

Prevention of Recurrences • Tinea versicolor tends to recur. Prevent this by applying Selsun Blue shampoo to the formerly involved areas once a month for several years. Leave it on for 1 to 2 hours. This precaution is especially important in the summer months, because this fungus thrives in warm weather.

Contagiousness • Tinea versicolor is not contagious. This fungus is a normal inhabitant of the hair follicles in many people. Only a few develop the overgrowth of the fungus and a rash.

Call Your Child's Physician Later If

• The rash is not improved with this treatment by 2 weeks.

• You feel your child is getting worse.

RELATED TOPIC

RINGWORM (see page 377)

SKIN: CONDITIONS WITHOUT A RASH

BLISTERS, FOOT OR HAND

SYMPTOMS AND CHARACTERISTICS

- Water blister on the sole or palm
- The toes or heel are most commonly involved
- Caused by friction
- Foot blisters are due to sports, hiking, or new shoes
- Hand blisters are due to prolonged use of a tool (such as a shovel) or playground equipment

HOME CARE

Treatment • Do not open the blisters, since this increases the possibility of infection. The blisters will dry up and peel off in 1 to 2 weeks. In the meantime, take the pressure off the area by placing a foam "donut" or a Band-Aid with a hole cut in the center over the blister. Also, temporarily wear a more comfortable shoe. If the blister accidentally breaks open, trim off the loose skin. Keep the surface clean by washing it twice a day with an antibacterial soap (such as Dial or Safeguard) and changing to clean socks (for foot blisters). The open blister can be covered with an antibiotic ointment (like Bacitracin), surrounded by a "donut" of foam rubber, and then the whole area patched over with tape for a few days.

Call Your Child's Physician Later If

• The blister becomes infected.

PREVENTION OF FOOT BLISTERS

Avoid shoes that are too tight or too loose. If your child frequently gets blisters on certain pressure areas, cover that spot with petroleum jelly or tape before athletic activities to decrease the friction on the spot. Friction can also be reduced by wearing 2 pairs of socks if the shoes are not too tight. If blisters occur under a callus, file the callus down and lubricate it so it won't contribute to the friction.

SIMILAR CONDITIONS THAT ALSO HAVE BLISTERS

BURNS, THERMAL (see page 28)
IMPETIGO (see page 369)
POISON IVY (see page 375)

BLUISH LIPS (CYANOSIS)

If your child's lips, mouth, ears, or nail beds have become bluish or dusky, call your child's physician *immediately*. Bluish skin (cyanosis) can indicate reduced oxygen in the blood, and serious disease. If your child is bluish and very cold, check first if the normal color returns with warming. Also, normal newborns can have bluish hands and feet (acrocyanosis) from sluggish circulation until 3 or 4 days of age.

RELATED TOPIC

BREATH-HOLDING SPELLS (see page 190)

CALLUSES, CORNS, AND BUNIONS

Calluses and corns are areas of thickened, hard skin. Calluses are located on the palms or soles and are painless. They occur over areas of prolonged friction or pressure, as with walking barefoot or using a hand tool. Corns can be located anywhere on the foot except the sole, are caused by pressure from tight shoes, and are painful. Bunions occur on the side of the foot over the protruding bone at the base of the first or fifth toe. Occasionally a bunion will occur where the back of a shoe rubs against the back of the heel. A bunion is painful and often causes a swollen area due to damage to both the skin and underlying bone. Bunions can also result from tight shoes, especially narrow or pointed ones.

CALL YOUR CHILD'S PHYSICIAN DURING OFFICE HOURS IF

- A callus is quite painful.
- A callus has black dots in it.
- A bunion is extremely painful or swollen.
- An unexplained fever (over 100°F) is present.
- You have other questions.

HOME CARE

Calluses • No treatment is necessary. The callus is protective. If it cracks, see CRACKED SKIN, page 386. If a blister develops, see BLISTERS, FOOT OR HAND, page 383.

Corns • Change to properly fitting shoes. Temporarily protect the corn with donut-shaped foam pads or a Band-Aid with a hole cut from the center. The pain should resolve in 1 week.

Bunions • The key to recovery is changing to properly fitting (i.e., wider or longer) shoes. Your youngster may need to wear soft slippers for a week. While most tight shoes must be discarded, a prized shoe (if it is long enough) may be salvaged by having the constricting area stretched out by a shoemaker with a shoe punch. (Note: The leather-stretching chemicals give disappointing results.) Soak the feet in warm water for 15 minutes twice a day. Take aspirin or acetaminophen for pain. (For dosage, see FEVER, page 305.) Protect the area with donut-shaped bunion pads. The pain and swelling will take 2 to 3 months to resolve. Call your child's physician if it gets worse instead of better.

CRACKED SKIN

Cracked skin most commonly occurs on the soles of the feet, especially the heels and big toes (called juvenile plantar dermatosis). Deep cracks are painful and periodically bleed. The main cause is wearing wet shoes and socks, or swimming a lot. Cracks can also develop on the hands in children who frequently wash dishes or suck their thumbs. The lips can become cracked (chapped) in children with a habit of licking their lips or from excessive exposure to sun or wind.

HOME CARE

Even deep cracks of many years duration can be healed in about 2 weeks if they are constantly covered with an ointment (like petroleum jelly). If the crack seems mildly infected, use Bacitracin ointment (no prescription needed). Covering the ointment with a Band-Aid, socks, or gloves speeds recovery even more. For chapped lips, a lip balm can be applied frequently. Call your child's physician during office hours if any of the cracks develop pimples or yellow drainage.

DANDRUFF

Dandruff is normal shedding and regeneration of skin. On most of the body surface, the flakes of dead skin fall to the ground without fanfare, but they can accumulate in the hair. Some children shed skin faster than others, making the dandruff more noticeable. Keep in mind that the shedding of skin cells is a normal process that occurs throughout life on the entire body surface. It is not contagious.

HOME CARE FOR DANDRUFF

Daily Shampooing • The key to fighting dandruff is removing the flakes as fast as they form by washing the hair daily. A regular shampoo usually works very well. Brush the hair before each washing. Eventually, you may be able to wash the hair every other day without seeing dandruff, but you probably won't ever be able to wash it less often than that.

Anti-Dandruff Shampoos • If the scalp is red and irritated or the scales are quite greasy, use a medicated shampoo (one that contains selenium sulfide) for 3 days in a row and then once a week. Your pharmacist can help you select one that does not require a prescription (e.g., Selsun Blue). These shampoos not only remove the dandruff but also cut down on the rate of shedding. They are used in a special way: Lather the hair, wait 3 minutes, then rinse thoroughly. Continue to use a regular shampoo on other days.

Avoid Hair Tonics • Hair tonics and creams just cover up the problem, and the dandruff eventually comes off in bigger flakes.

Call Your Child's Physician Later If

• The dandruff is not improved after 2 weeks of treatment.

FINGERNAIL INFECTION (PARONYCHIA)

SYMPTOMS AND CHARACTERISTICS

• A large pimple at the junction of the cuticle and the fingernail
• Redness and tenderness of this area
• Occasionally, pus draining from this area

If your child's symptoms are different, call your physician for help.

Cause • Paronychia are usually infected with the staphylococcus bacteria, but are occasionally due to strep bacteria. The primary event, however, is usually a break in the skin secondary to pulling or chewing on the cuticle. Thumbsucking may also contribute.

Expected Course • With proper treatment, this infection should clear up in 7 days. If not, your physician will probably prescribe an oral antibiotic.

CALL YOUR CHILD'S PHYSICIAN

Immediately If

- Fever or chills are present.
- A red streak spreads beyond the cuticle.
- The finger pad is swollen or tender.

During Office Hours If

- You want your physician to open the pus pockets.
- You can see pus under the base of the nail.
- The infection encircles the nail.
- This is a recurrent problem.
- You have other questions.

HOME CARE

Lancing • Open and drain any visible pus pockets with a sterile needle (sterilized with rubbing alcohol or a flame). Make a large opening where the pus pocket joins with the nail. Squeeze the pus out gently.

Antiseptic Soaks • Soak the infected finger 3 times a day for 20 minutes in a warm 1:60 bleach solution (1 tablespoon of bleach to 1 quart of water) with a little dishwashing detergent added. Do this for 4 days or longer if the wound has not healed.

Antibiotic Ointments • Apply an antibiotic ointment (Bacitracin or Betadine) 6 times a day.

Call Your Child's Physician Later If

- The infection is not improved by 48 hours on home treatment.
- The infection is not totally resolved by 7 days.

PREVENTION

Discourage any picking or chewing of hangnails (loose pieces of cuticle). Instead, cut these off with nail clippers.

RELATED TOPIC

TOENAIL, INGROWN (see page 403)

FOREIGN BODY IN SKIN (SLIVERS)

A sliver is a foreign object embedded in the skin. Most of these are wood slivers (splinters) that go in very superficially. Others are thorns or glass or metal fragments. Most slivers are painful to pressure unless they are very superficial. While organic slivers (e.g., wood) usually become infected if they are not removed, nonorganic slivers (e.g., metal) generally do not. If appropriate, turn to the guideline on SKIN TRAUMA (SCRAPES), page 67.

CALL YOUR CHILD'S PHYSICIAN

Immediately If

• The sliver is deeply embedded (for instance, a needle or toothpick in the foot).

• It is a fish hook.

• You think you won't be able to get it out.

During Office Hours If

• It was removed but went deeply (a puncture wound) *and* more than 5 years have passed since the last tetanus booster.

• You have other questions.

HOME CARE

Removing Slivers • Most slivers can be removed with a needle and tweezers. Check the tweezers beforehand to be certain the pickups meet exactly. (If they do not, bend them.) These items can be sterilized with rubbing alcohol or a flame. The skin surrounding the sliver should also be washed with soap before you try to remove the sliver. Use the needle to expose the end of the sliver fully. Then grasp the sliver firmly with the tweezers and pull it out at the same angle that it went in. Getting a good grip the first time is especially important with slivers that go in perpendicular to the skin or those trapped under a fingernail. Sometimes a wedge of the fingernail must be cut away with a fine scissors to expose the end of the sliver.

Superficial horizontal slivers (where you can see all of it) can be removed by opening the skin along the length of the sliver and flicking it out. If superficial slivers are numerous and pain-free, they can be left in. Eventually they will work their way out with normal shedding of the skin.

Cactus Spines • The following method can also be used for small Fiberglas spicules or plant stickers (e.g., stinging nettle). Usually these break when pressure is applied with a tweezers. Apply a layer of facial gel or wax depilatory (hair remover). Let it air-dry for 5 minutes, or accelerate the process with a hair dryer. Then peel it off with the spicules. White glue can also be tried, but it is less effective.

Call Your Child's Physician Later If

• You can't get it all out *and* the sliver is glass, metal, or colored pencil lead.

• You can't get it all out *and* it's painful.

• The site of penetration becomes infected.

FRECKLES

Freckles are pigmented spots brought out by sunlight. Thus, they usually are confined to the face, neck, chest, and shoulders. They occur mainly in fair-skinned people and are due to an inherited tendency to have tanning pigment (melanin) scattered irregularly, rather than evenly, throughout the skin. They start around age 5, and although they fade somewhat each winter, they become prominent each summer.

HOME CARE

Sunscreens cannot prevent them, and lemon juice cannot bleach them. Therefore, the child who has freckles must learn to live with them. Family and friends can help by referring to the freckles as special and attractive. They never turn into skin cancer. People with freckles sunburn easily and need to be extra careful about sun overexposure (see SUNBURN, page 398).

FROSTBITE

Frostbitten skin is cold, white, tingly, or numb. The most common sites are toes, fingers, tip of the nose, earlobes, or cheeks. The nerves, blood vessels, and other cells are temporarily frozen. The frostbite is much worse if the skin is also wet at the time of cold exposure. Touching bare hands to cold metal or volatile products (like gasoline) stored outside during freezing weather can cause immediate frostbite. Cold injuries are painful and sometimes dangerous. Severe cold exposure (hypothermia) with shivering and sleepiness is an emergency.

CALL YOUR CHILD'S PHYSICIAN IMMEDIATELY IF

• Three or more areas are involved.

• A large area is involved.

• The frostbite resulted from severe cold exposure.

• Your child's temperature is less than 95°F.

• Severe shivering is present.

• Speech is slurred or confused.

• You have other urgent questions.

HOME CARE

Treatment • The main treatment for frostbite is to rewarm the area rapidly. Place the frostbitten part in very warm water or cover it with warm wet compresses. A bath is often the quickest approach. The water should be very warm (104° to 108°F, or 40° to 42°C) but not hot enough to burn. Immersion in this warm water should continue until a flush returns to the frostbitten part (usually 30 minutes). If your child has lots of frostbite, the last 10 minutes of rewarming is usually quite painful. The rest of your child's body should also be kept warm by plenty of blankets. If there is any pain, your child can take aspirin or acetaminophen. Offer warm fluids to drink.

Common Mistakes • A common error is to apply snow to the frostbitten area or to massage it; both can cause damage to thawing tissues. Do not rewarm with a heat lamp or electric heater, because frostbitten skin is easily burned.

Call Your Child's Physician Later If

- The color and sensation doesn't return to normal after 60 minutes of rewarming.

- The frostbitten part develops blisters.

HAIR LOSS

Hair loss can occur in patches or throughout the scalp. The causes are many, including ringworm, which requires medical diagnosis and treatment.

CALL YOUR CHILD'S PHYSICIAN DURING OFFICE HOURS

All children who have hair loss should be seen by a physician with the following exceptions:

- The hair of many newborns falls out during the first few months of life. This baby hair is replaced by permanent hair.

- Babies from 3 to 6 months of age commonly rub off a patch of hair on the back of the head due to friction during head-turning against the mattresses of cribs, playpens, and infant seats. This grows back nicely once they start sitting up.

- Hair can be lost because of vigorous hairbrushing, hot combs, tight pony tails or braids, or exercising while wearing head-phones.

JAUNDICE

A jaundiced child has yellowish skin and sclera (the white part of the eyes). The yellow color is due to the accumulation of bilirubin pigment in the blood and skin. The most common cause of jaundice is hepatitis (a liver infection). Usually these infections are not serious, but they need to be evaluated by a physician.

While jaundice occurs in over 30 percent of newborns and is usually harmless, the follow-up of jaundiced newborns should be carried out under the direction of your baby's physician.

Be certain to notify your physician if the jaundice worsens after discharge from the hospital. (See JAUNDICE OF THE NEW-BORN, page 154.)

CALL YOUR CHILD'S PHYSICIAN

Immediately If

• Your child has vomited any blood.

• Your child is confused or difficult to awaken.

• Your child is acting very sick.

During Office Hours

• All other children with jaundice need medical consultation.

CAROTENEMIA: THE JAUNDICE IMITATOR

Your child has carotenemia if the following are present:

• Lemon-yellow coloration of the skin

• No yellow coloration of the sclera (white part of the eye)

• High intake of yellow and green vegetables

• Age under 2 years

Carotenemia is harmless and temporary. The yellow color is due to a pigment (carotene) found in yellow and green vegetables, as well as fruits such as oranges, apricots, and peaches. The intake of these vegetables and fruits needs to be reduced only if you want to change your child's skin tone. After a return to a more normal diet, the carotenemia color will disappear in 3 or 4 weeks. Even without dietary change, the skin color will gradually return to normal by 2 or 3 years of age.

LYMPH NODES (OR GLANDS), SWOLLEN

SYMPTOMS AND CHARACTERISTICS

• Normal nodes are smaller than ½ inch across (often the size of a pea or baked bean). The body contains more than 500 lymph nodes. They can always be felt in the neck and groin.

Normal nodes are largest at age 10 to 12. At this age they can be twice the normal adult size.

• Active nodes with viral infections are usually ½ to 1 inch across. Slight enlargement and mild tenderness means the lymph node is fighting infection and succeeding.

• Active nodes with bacterial infections are larger than 1 inch across and exquisitely tender. If they are over 2 inches across or the overlying skin is pink, the nodes are not controlling the infection, and may contain pus.

Causes • Lymph glands stop the spread of infection and protect the bloodstream from invasion (blood poisoning). They enlarge with cuts, scrapes, scratches, splinters, burns, insect bites, rashes, impetigo, or any break in the skin. Cancer is an extremely rare cause in children. Try to locate and identify the cause of the swollen gland by remembering that the groin nodes drain lymph from the legs and lower abdomen, the armpit nodes drain the arms and upper chest, the back of the neck nodes drain the scalp, and the front of the neck nodes drain the lower face, nose, and throat. Most enlarged neck nodes are due to colds and throat infections. A disease like chicken pox can cause all the nodes to swell.

Expected Course • With the usual viral infections or skin injuries, nodes quickly swell up to a peak size in 2 or 3 days and then slowly return to normal size over 2 to 4 weeks. However, you can still see and feel nodes in most normal children, especially in the neck and groin. Don't look for lymph nodes, because you can always find some.

CALL YOUR CHILD'S PHYSICIAN

Immediately If

• The node is 2 or more inches in size.

• The node is quite tender to the touch.

• Red streaks go to the node.

• The node is in the neck *and* there is any difficulty with breathing or swallowing.

• Your child is acting very sick.

During Office Hours If

• The node is 1 to 2 inches in size.

• The cause of the swollen node is unknown.

• Your baby is under 1 month old.

• An unexplained fever (over 100°F) is present.

• An explained fever lasts more than 3 days.

• You have other questions.

HOME CARE

Clarification • Minor skin infections and irritations can cause lymph nodes to double in size. It may take a month for them to slowly return to normal size. However, they won't completely disappear.

Treatment • No treatment is necessary for the nodes, just for the underlying disease—for instance, remove the sliver.

Call Your Child's Physician Later If

• The node becomes quite tender.

• The node enlarges to greater than 1 inch in size.

• The node remains larger than ½ inch for more than 1 month.

• You feel your child is getting worse.

MOLES (NEVI)

Moles, or nevi, are tan, brown, or black spots on the skin. Most adults have 20 to 30 moles. They first appear around 1 year of age, and we are constantly getting new ones. They do not fade and they last throughout our lives. In general, they are harmless. Even the moles removed for the changes listed below are usually not cancerous.

CALL YOUR CHILD'S PHYSICIAN DURING OFFICE HOURS IF

• You want a mole removed for cosmetic purposes.

• The mole is pitch-black *and* your child was born with it.

• The mole is growing rapidly in size.

• The mole has bled or become an open sore.

• The mole has changed colors (especially to red or blue).

• The surface has become lumpy.

(Note: Moles are no longer routinely removed just because they are in areas of friction or pressure.)

PALE SKIN

SYMPTOMS AND CHARACTERISTICS

The skin color is white or very pale. This concern is rarely voiced about non-Caucasian children.

Causes • Most of these children simply have a fair complexion. They have always been fair, have light hair, and usually have a parent with similar skin coloring. Another factor is lack of sun exposure; hence pallor (pale color) is noted more during winter months. Temporary paleness also occurs when someone is very cold; the normal color returns after warming up.

Pale skin (pallor) rarely is due to anemia (low red blood cell count). In anemia, the lips, gums, and nailbeds are also pale. In a child with fair complexion who is not anemic, these areas should be nice and pink.

CALL YOUR CHILD'S PHYSICIAN

Immediately If

• Your child has fainted.

• Your child becomes dizzy when standing up.

• Nosebleeds have been heavy.

• Menstrual periods have been heavy.

• Blood has been passed in stools or vomited material.

• The whites of the eyes are yellow.

• Your child is acting very sick.

During Office Hours If

- The paleness is of recent onset.
- The paleness is longstanding, but the cause is unclear.
- You have other questions.

PIMPLES

SYMPTOMS AND CHARACTERISTICS

Pimples (pustules or whiteheads) are small blisters filled with pus. They are caused by the staph bacteria (unlike acne). While they can occur on any part of the body, they commonly occur in areas of friction (as where a diaper rubs). Tight braids combined with pomades (perfumed ointments) are a common cause of pimples in the scalp. The tight braid injures the hair follicles and the pomade seals them off, thus predisposing them to infection. Pimples are a superficial skin infection and never leave scars.

Similar Conditions • If appropriate, turn directly to the following guidelines:

ACNE (see page 356)
BOILS (see page 365)
FINGERNAIL INFECTION (see page 387)
IMPETIGO (see page 369)

CALL YOUR CHILD'S PHYSICIAN

Immediately If

- Your child is under 2 weeks old (Exception: erythema toxicum, see under NEWBORN RASHES, page 88).
- An unexplained fever (over 100°F) is present.
- Your child is acting very sick.

During Office Hours If

- Your child is under 1 year old.
- There are 6 or more pimples.

- The pimples are larger than ⅛ inch across.

- You have other questions.

HOME CARE

Treatment • The best inexpensive agent for killing the staphylo-cocci that are causing the pimples is a 1:60 bleach solution, made by mixing 1 tablespoon of bleach in 1 quart of water. Open any pimples that have come to a head, using a needle sterilized with rubbing alcohol or flame, and then throw the needle away. Gently squeeze out any pus and wipe it away. Clean the pimples with the weak bleach solution before and after you do this. Do this at least twice a day; then rinse the skin with plain water.

Common Mistakes • A common mistake is to cover pimples with a Band-Aid. This can cause them to spread. The application of petroleum jelly or any ointment can also make them much worse.

Call Your Child's Physician Later If

- The pimples are not completely gone in 3 days.

- New pimples develop after 24 hours on treatment.

PREVENTION

To prevent spread, ask your child not to touch the pimples or rub the skin. Cut the fingernails short and wash the hands frequently. Give your child a shower once a day with an antibacterial soap (Dial or Safeguard). Be sure to use a separate washcloth and towel for this child. Wash your child's clothes and sheets with Lysol or bleach to remove the staph bacteria from them. For pimples of the scalp, pomades should be discontinued and braiding done loosely.

SUNBURN

Sunburn is due to overexposure of the skin to the ultraviolet rays of the sun or a sun lamp. Most people have been sun-burned many times. Vacations can quickly turn into painful experiences when the power of the sun is overlooked. Unfortunately, the symptoms of sunburn do not begin until 2 to 4 hours after the sun's damage has been done. The peak reaction of redness, pain, and swelling is not seen for 24 hours.

Minor sunburn is a first-degree burn which turns the skin pink or red. Prolonged sun exposure can cause blistering and a second-degree burn. Sunburn never causes a third-degree burn or scarring because it is limited to the superficial layer of skin (epidermis). Repeated sunburn does cause premature aging of the skin (wrinkling, sagging, and brown sunspots) and eventually increases risk of skin cancer in the damaged areas.

CALL YOUR CHILD'S PHYSICIAN

Immediately If

• The sunburn is extremely painful *and* widespread.

• Your child is unable to look at lights because of eye pain.

• Your child has an unexplained fever over 102°F.

• Your child has fainted with the sunburn.

• Your child is acting very sick.

During Office Hours If

• More than 2 blisters are present.

• Any of the blisters are broken.

• You have other questions.

HOME CARE

Pain Relief • The sensation of pain and heat will probably last for 48 hours.

• Aspirin started early and continued for 2 days can reduce the discomfort. (For dosage, see chart on page 51.)

• Nonprescription ½ percent hydrocortisone cream may cut down on swelling and pain, but only if used early. Apply 3 times a day.

• The symptoms can also be helped by cool baths or compresses several times a day. Add 2 or 3 tablespoons of baking soda to the tub.

• Showers are usually painful because of the force of the spray.

- Don't use any soap on the burned skin.

- Offer extra water on the first day to replace the fluids lost into the sunburn.

- Peeling will usually occur on the fifth to seventh day. Peeling and itching can be reduced by applying the ½ percent hydrocortisone cream or a lubricating cream (see ECZEMA, page 339) to the involved skin once or twice a day. (Avoid petrolatum or other ointments because they keep heat and sweat from escaping.)

Common Mistakes in Sunburn Treatment

- Avoid applying ointments or butter to sunburn; they just make the symptoms worse and are painful to remove.

- Don't buy any of the common first aid creams or sprays for burns. They often contain benzocaine, which can cause an allergic rash, and they don't relieve the pain of first-degree burns.

- Don't confuse sunscreens, which block the sun's burning rays, with suntan lotions or oils, which mainly lubricate the skin. Despite advertisements to the contrary, suntan oils cannot help your child tan faster or more deeply. Also, they offer no protection against sunburn.

Call Your Child's Physician Later If

- Blisters start to break open.

- The sunburn looks infected.

- You feel your child is getting worse.

PREVENTION

- Try to keep sun exposure to small amounts early in the season until a tan builds up. Start with 15 or 20 minutes per day and increase by 5 minutes per day. Decrease daily exposure time if the skin becomes reddened. Because of the 2-to-4-hour delay before sunburn starts, don't expect symptoms to tell you when it's time to get out of the sun.

- About 15 percent of white people have skin that never tans but only burns. These fair-skinned children (especially redheads) need to be extremely careful throughout the summer. The skin of infants is also thinner and more sensitive to the sun.

Sunscreens, longer clothing, and a hat with a brim are essential for these children.

- Avoid the hours of 10:00 A.M. to 3:00 P.M., when the sun's rays are most intense.

- Don't let overcast days give you a false sense of security. Over 70 percent of the sun's rays still get through the clouds. Over 30 percent of the sun's rays can also penetrate loosely woven fabrics (for instance, a T-shirt).

- Water or snow increases the sun exposure. A hat or umbrella won't protect you from reflected rays.

Sunscreens • There are good sunscreens on the market that prevent sunburn but still permit gradual tanning to occur. The sun protection factor (SPF) or filtering power of the product determines what percent of the ultraviolet rays get through to the skin. The SPF of various products ranges from 2 to 15. An SPF of 4 allows ¼ of the rays to get through and thereby permits the child to stay in the sun 4 times longer than usual without sunburning. An SPF of 15 allows only ⅟₁₅ (7 percent) of the sun's rays to get through and thereby extends safe sun exposure from 20 minutes to 5 hours. Redheads need a sunscreen with an SPF of 15, fair-skinned whites need a 12, darker whites need an 8 to 10, and Mediterranean whites need a 6 to 8. If you're working on a suntan, apply your sun screen to all uncovered skin after 15 to 20 minutes of sun exposure.

Apply the sunscreen before any sun exposure to areas that are most likely to become sunburned, such as your child's nose, ears, cheeks, and shoulders. Most products need to be reapplied every 3 to 4 hours, as well as immediately after swimming or profuse sweating. A "waterproof" sunscreen stays on for about 30 minutes in water. To prevent sunburned lips, apply a lip coating that also contains PABA. This is especially important in children who develop fever blisters after sun exposure. If your child's nose or some other area has been repeatedly burned during the summer, protect it completely from all the sun's rays with zinc oxide ointment.

SWEATING, EXCESSIVE

SYMPTOMS AND CHARACTERISTICS

The parent may be concerned because a child has a wet pillow after naps. Sometimes the entire bed is wet, since sweat glands are found throughout the body's surface. Neither of these examples is necessarily abnormal.

Your adolescent may be unduly worried about underarm perspiration. Teenagers may be reassured that sweating normally increases with exercise and tension, and this is never abnormal.

Similar Conditions • Sweating occurs with fever (so take your child's temperature). If fever is present, save time by turning directly to that guideline. (See FEVER, page 305.)

Causes • The purpose of sweating is to cool off the body by evaporation. The most common cause of sweating is overheating due to hot weather, a hot room, overdressing, or too many blankets. When a child is covered up in bed, the *only* way to release heat is through the head. Night sweats in a child who is otherwise well mean nothing. Some parents worry unduly about diseases from another era (such as tuberculosis or malaria).

CALL YOUR CHILD'S PHYSICIAN DURING OFFICE HOURS IF

• Your child is under 2 months old.

• Your child has unexplained fevers (over 100°F).

• Your child has unexplained weight loss.

• You have other questions.

HOME CARE

Turn down the heat in your home. Dress your child in lighter clothing for naps. Offer your child extra fluids in hot weather to prevent dehydration. Adolescents, of course, need to be introduced to underarm antiperspirants/deodorants to prevent body odor.

TOENAIL, INGROWN

SYMPTOMS AND CHARACTERISTICS

- Tenderness, redness, and swelling of the skin surrounding the corner of the toenail on one of the big toes

Causes • Ingrown toenails are usually due to tight shoes (such as cowboy boots) and/or improper cutting of the toenails. Children with wide feet are predisposed, since many shoes come in only one width. Ingrown toenails take several weeks to clear up.

CALL YOUR CHILD'S PHYSICIAN DURING OFFICE HOURS IF

- Any pus or yellow drainage is present.
- The corner of the nail is impossible to locate.
- The problem is a recurrent one.
- You have other questions.

HOME CARE

Soaking • Soak the foot twice a day in a 1:60 bleach solution (1 tablespoon of bleach to 1 quart of water) for 20 minutes. This solution kills most germs. Add a little dishwashing detergent to help penetration. While soaking, massage outward the part of the cuticle (skin next to the nail) that is swollen. A "cuticle pusher" (available in most drugstores) may be helpful.

Cut Off the Corner of the Toenail • The pain is always caused by the corner of the toenail rubbing against the raw cuticle. Only this once, cut the corner off so the irritated tissue can quiet down and heal. If the corner is buried in the swollen cuticle, have your physician remove it. The main purpose of treatment is to help the nail grow *over* the nail cuticle rather than get stuck in it. Therefore, during soaks, try to bend the nail corners upward. You can try to wedge some cotton under the edge of the nail, but for practical purposes, this is impossible during the infected phase. Filing or cutting a wedge out of the center of the upper edge of the nail may help the corners bend upward.

Antibiotic Ointment • If your child's cuticle is just red and irritated, an antibiotic ointment is probably not needed. But if the cuticle is swollen or oozing, apply Neosporin ointment (no prescription needed) 5 or 6 times a day.

Shoes • Have your child wear sandals or go barefoot as much as possible to prevent pressure on the toenail. When your child must wear closed shoes, protect the ingrown toenail as follows: If the inner edge is involved, tape cotton between the first and second toes to keep them from touching. If the outer edge is involved, tape cotton to the outside of the ball of the toe to keep the toenail from touching the side of the shoe.

Call Your Child's Physician Later If

• The ingrown toenail becomes infected.

• The problem is not much better in 1 week.

• The problem is not totally resolved in 2 weeks.

PREVENTION
Prevent recurrences by making sure that your child's shoes are not too narrow. Give away those pointed or tight shoes. After the cuticle is healed, cut the toenails straight across, leaving the corners. Don't cut them too short. After baths, while the nails are pliable, bend the corners of the nails upward.

WARTS

SYMPTOMS AND CHARACTERISTICS

• Raised, round, rough-surfaced growth on the skin

• Skin-colored or pink

• Most commonly occur on the hands

• Not painful unless located on the sole of the foot (plantar wart)

• Unlike a callus, the wart has brown dots within it and clearly has a boundary with the normal skin

If your child's symptoms are different, call your physician for help.

Cause • Warts are caused by viruses (not by playing with toads).

Expected Course • Most warts disappear without treatment in 2 or 3 years. With treatment, they resolve in 2 to 3 months. There are no shortcuts in treating warts. Itching and redness mean the wart is responding to treatment. If the treatment of warts becomes painful or expensive, it may be better to step back and wait for them to go away naturally.

CALL YOUR CHILD'S PHYSICIAN DURING OFFICE HOURS IF

• Some warts are on the bottom of the feet.

• Some are on the face.

• Some are on the genital area.

• A wart is open and infected-looking.

• You have other questions.

HOME CARE

Adhesive Tape • Apply adhesive tape to cover the wart completely. Leave it on for 6½ days; then remove it for 12 hours. Repeat the procedure weekly. The total treatment usually takes 6 weeks. Don't apply the tape so tightly that it interferes with circulation. This method is surprisingly effective at turning on the body's immune system to the wart virus. Try it.

Wart-Removing Acids • If no progress is being made in 4 weeks with adhesive tape, switch to a nonprescription acid. Ask your pharmacist to recommend one. Apply it once a day to the top of the wart after soaking the wart in water for 5 minutes. Since you are using an acid, avoid getting any near the eyes or mouth. Keep the lid closed tightly so it won't evaporate. The acid will turn the wart into dead skin. The acid will work faster if it is covered with adhesive tape.

Once or twice a week, remove the dead wart material by paring it down with a razor blade. The dead wart will be softer and easier to slice if you soak the area first in warm water for 10 minutes. If the cutting causes any pain or minor bleeding, you have cut into living wart tissue. If your child won't let you cut off the dead wart material or you are afraid you might hurt the child, file it down with an emery board or have your child's physician pare down the wart.

Contagiousness • Encourage your child not to pick at the warts, because this may cause them to spread. If your child chews or sucks the wart, cover the area with a Band-Aid. Encourage your child to give up the habit of chewing on the wart, because doing so can lead to warts on the lips or face. Warts are not very contagious to other people. The incubation period is 1 to 4 months.

Call Your Child's Physician Later If

• A wart becomes open *and* looks infected.

• New warts develop after 2 weeks of treatment.

• The warts are still present after 8 weeks of treatment.

WOUND INFECTIONS

Most contaminated wounds that are going to become infected do so 24 to 72 hours after the initial injury. An infected wound develops redness, tenderness, and pus. Keep in mind that a 2 mm to 3 mm rim of pinkness or redness, confined to the edge of a wound, can be normal, especially if the wound is sutured. However, the area of redness should not be spreading. Pain and tenderness also occur normally, but the pain and swelling are at a peak during the second day and thereafter diminish. If the infection spreads beyond the wound, it will follow the lymph channels and cause a red streak. If the infection reaches the bloodstream ("blood poisoning"), a fever will be present. The healing process can normally cause mild swelling and tenderness of the lymph nodes that drain the injured area.

CALL YOUR CHILD'S PHYSICIAN

Immediately If

• The wound is extremely tender.

• An unexplained fever (over 100°F) occurs.

• A red streak runs from the wound.

• The wound is located on the face.

During Office Hours If

- You can see pus in the wound, or there is pus draining from it.

- A pimple starts to form where a stitch comes through the skin.

- The wound is becoming more tender than it was on the second day.

- You have other questions.

HOME CARE

Treatment of Mild Redness • Use warm salt water soaks or compresses (1 tablespoon of table salt per quart of water) on the wound for 15 minutes, 3 times a day. Dry the area thoroughly afterward.

Call Your Child's Physician Later If

- The wound becomes more tender.

- Pus or drainage develops.

- The redness starts to spread.

- You feel your child is getting worse.

EYES

ALLERGIES OF THE EYES

SYMPTOMS AND CHARACTERISTICS

- Itchy eyes (without pain)
- Increased tearing (without pus)
- Red or pink eyes
- Mild swelling of the eyelids
- Similar symptoms during the same month of the previous year
- Previous confirmation of this diagnosis by a physician is helpful

  If your child's symptoms are different, call your physician for help.

Similar Condition • If the nose is also involved, save time by turning directly to the guideline on HAY FEVER, page 000.

Causes • For cases that occur during the same season each year, the cause is pollens. For cases that are not seasonal, the allergic factor can be pets (cats, for instance), feathers, perfumes, and so forth.

Expected Course • Most eye allergies due to a pollen last for 4 to 6 weeks, which is the length of most pollen seasons. If the allergic substance can be identified *and* avoided (a cat, perhaps), the symptoms will not recur.

CALL YOUR CHILD'S PHYSICIAN DURING OFFICE HOURS IF

- The eye allergy keeps your child from playing or sleeping.
- The eyelids are swollen tight.
- Sacs of clear yellow fluid are seen inside the eyelids.
- The eyelids become matted together with pus.
- You have other questions.

HOME CARE

Removing Pollen • First wash the pollen off the face. Then use a clean washcloth and cool water to clean off the eyelids. Tears will wash the pollen out of the eyes. This rinse of the eyelids may need to be repeated every time your child comes in on a windy day. Pollen also collects in the hair and on exposed body surfaces. This pollen can easily be reintroduced into the eyes. Therefore, give your child a shower and shampoo every night before bedtime. Encourage your child not to touch the eyes unless the hands have been washed recently.

Vasoconstrictor Eyedrops • Usually, the eyes will feel much better after the pollen is washed out and cold compresses are applied. If they are still itchy or bloodshot (i.e., the blood vessels are swollen), instill some long-acting vasoconstrictive eyedrops (no prescription needed). Ask your pharmacist for help in choosing a reliable product. Use 2 drops every 6 to 8 hours as necessary.

Antihistamines • If these measures aren't effective, your child probably also has hay fever (i.e., allergic symptoms of the nose). Give your child an oral antihistamine. (For dosage, see HAY FEVER, page 442.)

Call Your Child's Physician Later If

- This treatment and an antihistamine do not relieve most of the symptoms in 2 or 3 days.

  Keep in mind that the pollen season lasts for 1 to 2 months. You need to continue the treatment for that length of time and start it again next year.

ITCHY EYE

For itchy, watery, red eyes, the possible causes are many. Turn directly to the guideline that pertains to your child.

ALLERGIES (see page 409)
CHEMICAL IN EYE (see page 38)
RED OR PINKEYE (includes minor irritants) (see below)

RED OR PINKEYE (CONJUNCTIVITIS)

SYMPTOMS AND CHARACTERISTICS

• Redness of the sclera (white part of the eye)

• Redness of the inner eyelids

• A watery discharge ("watery eyes")

• No yellow discharge or matting of eyelids

• Not from crying

• Also called pinkeye or bloodshot eyes

If your child's symptoms are different, call your physician for help.

Similar Conditions • If one of the following is suspected, save time by turning directly to that guideline:

ALLERGIES (see page 409)
CHEMICAL IN EYE (see page 38)
FOREIGN BODY IN EYE, (e.g., blowing dust or eyelash) (see page 39)
EYE TRAUMA (see page 63)
YELLOW DISCHARGE (see page 416)
HAY FEVER (see page 442)

Causes • Red eyes are usually caused by a viral infection, and commonly accompany colds. If a bacterial superinfection occurs, the discharge becomes yellow and the eyelids are commonly matted together after sleeping. The second most common cause is getting an irritant into the eyes. The irritant can be smog, smoke, or chlorine from a swimming pool. More commonly in young kids, it comes from touching the eyes with hands carrying dirt, soap, or food (such as cinnamon, chili powder, or other spice). Contact with mother's perfume or father's after-shave can also be irritating, as can rubbing faces with the family pet. The main symptom in children with irritants in the eye is constant rubbing and tearing of the eyes.

Expected Course • Viral conjunctivitis usually lasts as long as a cold does (4 to 7 days). Red eyes from irritants usually are cured within 4 hours of washing out the irritating substance, unless reexposure occurs.

CALL YOUR CHILD'S PHYSICIAN

Immediately If

• The eyelids are red or swollen.

• The eyes are constantly tearing or blinking.

• Your child is complaining of pain in the eyes.

• Vision is blurred.

• Your child is acting very sick.

During Office Hours If

• Your child is under 1 month old.

• The eye has been red for more than 7 days.

• You have other questions.

HOME CARE

Washing with Soap • Wash the face, then the eyelids, with a mild soap and water. This will remove any irritants.

Irrigating with Water • Rinse the eyes out with warm water as often as possible, at least every 1 to 2 hours while your child is awake. Use warm (not hot) water, and use a fresh cotton ball each time. Wipe toward the inside of the eye. This usually will keep a bacterial infection from occurring.

Vasoconstrictor Eyedrops • Viral conjunctivitis usually is not helped by eyedrops. Red eyes from irritants usually feel much better after the irritant has been washed out. If they remain uncomfortable and bloodshot, instill some long-acting vasoconstrictor eyedrops (no prescription needed). Ask your pharmacist for help in choosing a reliable product. Use 2 drops every 6 to 8 hours as necessary. Products called "artificial tears" are not helpful, since they do not contain any vasoconstrictors.

Contagiousness • If your child has pinkeye from a viral infection, the secretions can cause eye infections in other people if they get some of it on their eyes. Therefore, it is important for the sick child to have his or her own washcloth and towel. However, the infection is so mild that staying home is unnecessary. If the pinkeye is due to irritants or chemicals, obviously your child is not contagious.

Call Your Child's Physician Later If

• A yellow discharge develops.

• The eyelids become matted together with pus.

• The eyelids become red or swollen.

• The redness lasts more than a week.

• The vision becomes blurred.

SWELLING OF EYELID

SYMPTOMS AND CHARACTERISTICS

This guideline deals with eyelid swelling due to an insect bite near it. This is especially common with mosquito bites of the upper face. The eyelid is not red, but it can be pink.

Similar Conditions • If one of the following is suspected, save time by turning directly to that guideline:

EYE TRAUMA (see page 53)
ALLERGIES (see page 409)
RED OR PINKEYE (see page 411)

CALL YOUR CHILD'S PHYSICIAN

Immediately If

• Both eyelids are swollen. (Exception: eye allergies.)

• The swollen eyelid is tender to the touch.

• The eyelid is red.

• A fever (over 100°F) is present.

• There is pain on movement of the eye.

• Your child is acting very sick.

During Office Hours If

• You are unsure of the cause of the swelling.

• You have other questions.

HOME CARE FOR EYELID SWELLING FROM AN INSECT BITE

Treatment • Cool compresses or ice in a washcloth help. Give your child an antihistamine to decrease the swelling and help any itching. (See HAY FEVER, page 000, for dosages.) Many common cold medicines contain antihistamines. In 2 or 3 days, the swelling from insect bites is usually gone.

Call Your Child's Physician Later If

• The swelling hasn't cleared in 3 days.

• The eyelid becomes red or tender.

• Other symptoms develop that concern you.

RELATED TOPIC

BITES, INSECT (see page 361)

STYE

SYMPTOMS AND CHARACTERISTICS

• A tender, red bump at the base of an eyelash

• A small pimple at the base of an eyelash

If your child's symptoms are different, call your physician for help.

Cause • A stye is an infection of the hair follicle of an eyelash, usually caused by staphylococcus bacteria.

Expected Course • It usually comes to a head and forms a pimple in 3 to 5 days. In a few more days, it usually drains and heals. Recurrences are common, especially in children who rub their eyes.

CALL YOUR CHILD'S PHYSICIAN

Immediately If

• The infection is spreading.

• The eyelid is red or swollen.

During Office Hours If

• Styes are a recurrent problem for your child.

• There are 2 or more styes.

• You have other questions.

HOME CARE

Warm Compresses • Wash the outer eyelids daily with an antibacterial soap (like Dial or Safeguard). Apply a warm washcloth to the eye for 10 minutes 4 times a day to help the stye come to a head. Continue to cleanse the eye several times a day even after the stye drains.

Opening the Pimple • When the stye does display a center of pus, you can open it by pulling out the eyelash that goes into the pimple with a tweezers. This will initiate drainage and healing. Your other option is just to continue warm compresses. Most styes will drain spontaneously in a few days after they have come to a head.

Antibiotic Eye Ointment • The ointments do not cure styes, but they may keep them from spreading and recurring. If your child has recurrent styes or more than 2 styes, call your child's physician, since this ointment requires a prescription. Most single styes respond to the treatment outlined.

Prevention of Recurrences • Ask your child not to touch the eyes, because rubbing can cause spread to other eyelashes.

Call Your Child's Physician Later If

• Infection seems to be spreading.

• The stye is not draining or improved by 3 days.

• The stye is not completely healed by 10 days.

• Styes recur.

YELLOW DISCHARGE

SYMPTOMS AND CHARACTERISTICS

• Yellow discharge in the eye

• Eyelids stuck together with pus, especially after sleep

• Dried eye discharge on the upper cheek

• The eyes are also red or pink

• Also called runny eyes or mattery eyes (Note: Everyone can normally have a small amount of cream-colored mucus, called "sleep," in the inner corner of the eyes after sleeping.)

Causes • Caused by various bacteria. After ear infections, bacterial eye infections are the next leading complication of a cold. Red eyes without a yellow discharge, however, are more common and are due to a virus (see RED OR PINKEYE, page 411).

Expected Course • With proper treatment, the yellow discharge should clear up in 72 hours. The red eyes (which are part of the underlying cold) may persist for several more days.

CALL YOUR CHILD'S PHYSICIAN

Immediately If

• The outer eyelids are red or swollen.

• Any ulcer or sore is seen on the eyeball.

• Your child is acting very sick.

During Office Hours If

- Your child is under 3 years of age. (Simultaneous ear infections are very common.)

- There is any suggestion of an earache.

- Your child has frequent eye infections.

- You have other questions.

HOME CARE

Cleaning the Eye • Before putting in any medicines, remove all the dried and liquid pus from the eye with warm wet cotton balls. This should be done as often as you see pus in the eye, sometimes every hour. Unless this is done, the medicine will not have a chance to work. Remove the dried crusts carefully so they don't scratch the eyeball.

Antibiotic Eyedrops or Ointments • A bacterial conjunctivitis must be treated with an antibiotic eye medicine. Acceptable ones are sulfacetamide (Sulamyd), Gantrisin, Garamycin, Polysporin, or Neosporin. If you have one of these products in your home, use it. If not, you must call your physician during office hours for a prescription. Some physicians will want to examine your child before prescribing.

Holding Your Child • Putting eyedrops or ointment in the eyes of younger children can be a real battle. Ideally, it's done with two people. One person can hold the child still while the other person opens the eyelids with one hand and puts in the medicine with the other. One person *can* do it alone, sitting on the floor, holding the child's head (face up) between the knees to free both hands to put in the medicine.

Using Antibiotic Eyedrops • Put 2 drops in each eye every 2 hours while your child is awake. Do this by gently pulling down on the lower lid and placing the drops inside the lower lid. As soon as the eyedrops have been put in, have your child close the eyes for 2 minutes so the eyedrops will stay inside. If it is difficult to separate your child's eyelids, put the eyedrop over the inner corner of the eye. As your child opens the eye, the eyedrop will flow in. Continue the eyedrops until your child has awakened 2 mornings in a row without any pus in the eyes. If the eyedrops are stopped sooner, the infection will probably come back.

Using Antibiotic Eye Ointment (instead of eyedrops) • Eye ointment needs to be used only 4 times a day because it can remain in the eyes longer than eyedrops. Separate the eyelids and put in a ribbon of ointment from one corner to the other. If it is very difficult to separate your child's eyelids, put the ointment on the lid margins. As it melts, it will flow onto the eyeball and give equal results. Again, continue until 2 mornings have passed without any pus in the eye.

Contagiousness • The pus from the eyes can cause eye infections in other people if they get some of it on their eyes. Therefore, it is very important for the sick child to have his or her own washcloth and towel. Your child should be discouraged from touching or rubbing the eyes, because it can make the infection last longer, and it puts a lot of germs on the fingers. Therefore, your child's hands should also be washed often to prevent spreading the infection. Your child can return to school after using the eyedrops for 24 hours if the pus is minimal.

Call Your Child's Physician Later If

• The infection isn't cleared up in 72 hours.

• The eyelids become red or swollen.

• The vision becomes blurred.

• Your child develops an earache.

• The eyes become itchy or redder after eyedrops are begun.

EARS

EARACHE

SYMPTOMS AND CHARACTERISTICS

Your child complains of ear pain. Children too young to talk may cry several times during the night and be cranky during the day. Most of these children also have a fever and symptoms of a cold. The peak age range for earaches is 6 months to 2 years, but they continue to be a common complaint until age 8 or 10.

Similar Conditions • If your child is doing lots of swimming and it hurts when you move the outer ear up and down, save time by going directly to the guideline on SWIMMER'S EAR (page 432).

Cause • Most earaches are due to a middle-ear infection (acute otitis media). A middle-ear infection is a bacterial infection of the space behind the eardrum. The earache is due to the bulging of the eardrum. Most children (70 percent) have one or more ear infections, and 25 percent of these will have repeated ear infections. Ear infections are the most common complication of a cold. While colds are contagious, ear infections are not.

A temporary earache can occur for 10 to 15 minutes after being outside in cold weather. When your child comes inside, the cold air inside the middle ear warms up, expands, and causes some pain. Chewing gum or drinking fluids should relieve it. However, cold wind or weather cannot cause an ear infection.

Another cause of temporary pain in front of the ear is muscle pain from excessive chewing.

Expected Course of Ear Infection • In 5 to 15 percent of children with otitis media, the pressure in the middle ear causes the eardrum to rupture and drain. The ear drainage does not mean that the ear infection is any more serious. This small tear usually heals in a few days. Most ear infections respond nicely to a course of antibiotics. At the 2-week visit for ear recheck, about 10 percent will still be infected and need a second course of antibiotics. Another 40 percent or more will have fluid in the middle ear (serous otitis) and reduced hearing. Over the following 1 to 3 months, hearing will return to normal without treatment in most of these children. A few children will need "ventilation tubes" placed in their eardrums.

CALL YOUR CHILD'S PHYSICIAN

Immediately If

• The pain is extreme.

• The neck is stiff.

• Your child can't walk normally.

• The earache followed injury to the ear.

• Your child is acting very sick.

During Office Hours

• All other children with earaches that last more than 2 hours need medical consultation.

HOME CARE

Relieving Pain

• An earache is not an emergency. Until you see the physician, give acetaminophen for pain. (For dosage, see FEVER, page 305.) If your child is still uncomfortable, use a cough medicine containing dextromethorphan or codeine. These agents are strong anti-pain medicines. (For dosage, see COUGH, page 469.) You may also put an ice bag or ice in a wet washcloth over the painful ear. Many physicians recommend a hot water bottle, but cold seems to provide greater relief.

• Do not use any ear drops unless your physician recommends them.

- If the ear is draining, wipe the material away as it appears.

- Don't plug the canal with cotton.

RELATED TOPICS

COLDS (see page 435)
EAR CONGESTION (below)
EAR DISCHARGE (see page 422)
PULLING AT EAR (see page 431)

EAR CONGESTION

SYMPTOMS AND CHARACTERISTICS

- Sudden onset of muffled hearing

- Crackling or popping noises in the ear

- A stuffy, full sensation in the ear

- No ear pain except in cases related to airplane travel

Similar Conditions • If one of the following is suspected, save time by turning directly to that guideline:

EARACHE (see page 419)
EAR DISCHARGE (see page 422)
EARWAX, PACKED (see page 423)
HAY FEVER (see page 442)

Cause • The most common cause of ear congestion is fluid in the middle ear due to intermittent blockage of the Eustachian tube (the channel connecting the middle ear to the back of the nose) by a cold, hay fever, or overvigorous nose-blowing. Sudden increases in barometric pressure, such as occur in descent from mountain driving or airplane travel, also cause ear congestion (but usually with pain, as the eardrum is pulled inward).

CALL YOUR CHILD'S PHYSICIAN DURING OFFICE HOURS IF

- Your child could have put something in the ear canal.

- You have other questions.

HOME CARE

Treatment • Have your child chew gum, yawn frequently, and swallow (or puff out the cheeks) while the nose is pinched closed. If this isn't effective, use a long-acting decongestant nasal spray 1 hour before air travel. Ask your pharmacist to recommend a good product (no prescription needed). If your child could have water in the ear canal from a recent shower or swim, help drain it by gravity while gently pulling the ear in different directions. If your child has hay fever, an antihistamine medication should also be taken. If your child is in pain, give aspirin or acetaminophen (see FEVER, page 305, for dosage). Swimming is permitted.

Call Your Child's Physician Later If

• The ear congestion lasts more than 48 hours.

• Ear pain or fever develops.

PREVENTION OF EAR CONGESTION DUE TO ALTITUDE CHANGE • Have your child repeatedly "pop" the ears by yawning or swallowing during the typical 30 to 60 minutes of descent. If this fails, attempt to blow the nose (and puff out the cheeks) against closed nostrils and a closed mouth. A baby can be given water to drink or a pacifier to suck on during descent, and the nose can be pinched closed periodically during swallowing. Obviously, the child should not sleep during descent.

People with recurrent problems should take an oral antihistamine and long-acting decongestant nasal spray (see HAY FEVER, page 442, and COLDS, page 435, respectively, for drug names and dosage) 1 hour before travel. If severe pain occurs despite these precautions, ask the stewardess for a hot towel to place over the ear canal. (The heat will expand the air in the middle ear and relieve the negative pressure on the eardrum.)

EAR DISCHARGE

YELLOW OR CLOUDY DISCHARGE

Call your child's physician during office hours.

BLOODY DISCHARGE
See the guideline on EAR TRAUMA, page 52.

EARWAX DISCHARGE
For a brown or orange discharge, see the guideline on EAR-WAX, PACKED, below.

CLEAR DISCHARGE

• If it followed head or ear trauma, call your child's physician immediately.

• If it followed an earache, call your child's physician during office hours.

• If it could be tears, bath water, or eardrops someone put in, your worries are over.

HOME CARE
Pending the office visit for a suspected ear infection, give acetaminophen for pain. (For dosage, see FEVER, page 305.) Wipe away the drainage as it appears. Don't pack the ear canal closed with cotton, because this will block the natural drainage. Don't put any cotton swabs in the ear canal.

EARWAX, PACKED

Earwax is present in everyone. The color can vary from light yellow to dark brown. It has chemicals in it which can kill germs, it keeps dust off the eardrum, and it protects the lining of the ear canal. Earwax is not abnormal or dirty. Earwax also moves outward naturally during chewing and the normal growth of the ear canal's lining. Every day or two, you may notice a little earwax at the opening of the ear canal. The amount varies from person to person, and as long as it comes out, your child can't have too much of it. Proceed with this guideline if earwax is completely blocking one of the ear canals (i.e., impacted wax). If the hearing seems normal on that side, the blockage is only partial and you can leave it alone.

CALL YOUR CHILD'S PHYSICIAN DURING OFFICE HOURS IF

• Any discharge comes from the ear canal other than earwax.

• The eardrum has been ruptured in the past.

• Blockage from earwax is a recurrent problem for your child.

• You have other questions.

HOME CARE

Flushing Out Packed Earwax • Keep in mind that complete blockage is rare. Regular removal of earwax is not necessary to prevent wax buildup.

• If the wax is hard, soften it first. Mineral or baby oil is a good earwax softener. Put in 3 drops twice a day for 3 days. Lying with the ear against a heating pad for 20 minutes may help remove the wax by melting it.

• When the wax is soft, irrigate it out with a rubber ear syringe or Water Pik at the lowest setting. The water must be at body temperature to prevent dizziness. Irrigate several times, until the return is clear and the ear canal seems open when you look in with a light. Never put water in your child's ear if there is any chance the eardrum has a hole in it.

Call Your Child's Physician Later If

• Your irrigation doesn't clear out the ear canal and return the hearing to normal.

• Any other questions come up.

PREVENTION

Earwax can usually be removed from the opening of the ear canal with a wet cloth or your fingernail. Nothing should be put into the ear canal to try to hurry this process along, because it usually ends up packing the wax deeper. The most common cause of earwax retention is putting cotton swabs or hairpins into the ear canal.

FOREIGN BODY IN EAR

Young children often put foreign objects in their ear canals. Some common ones are erasers, beads, food, and cotton.

FIRST AID
If a live insect is within your child's ear canal, take your child into a dark room and shine a light by the ear. The insect will often come out on its own. If this fails, kill the intruder by pouring in some alcohol. You can use 80 proof gin if you have no rubbing alcohol. Then remove the insect by irrigating the canal with water and an ear syringe (or a nasal suction bulb). For other objects, make one simple attempt at removing it. Turn the involved side down. Wiggle the ear at the same time you gently shake the head, and try to get the object to fall out with the help of gravity.

CALL YOUR CHILD'S PHYSICIAN IMMEDIATELY IF THESE MEASURES FAIL
It is critical that you do not try to remove the object by putting tweezers, fingers, or any other device into the ear canal. This almost always pushes the object in farther and makes the physician's job very difficult, even with special instruments. Watch closely that your child doesn't push it in.

ITCHY EAR

SYMPTOMS
Your child repeatedly scratches his ear or complains that it itches.

Causes • Most older children who complain of itchy ear canals have a mild otitis externa from:

• Water accumulation during swimming or showers

• Soap or shampoo retention

• Irritation from hair sprays

• Canal irritation from cotton swabs. These swabs remove the earwax that normally protects the lining of the ear canal, and this leads to itching and irritation.

Similar Conditions • If one of the following is suspected, save time by turning directly to that guideline:

SWIMMER'S EAR (see page 432)
EARACHE (see page 419)
EAR DISCHARGE (see page 422)

HOME CARE

Treatment • White vinegar has acetic acid in it and can usually restore the ear canal to its normal chemistry. Fill one ear canal at a time with white vinegar. Do this by running the vinegar down the side of the opening of the ear canal so that air doesn't get trapped under it. Leave it in for 5 minutes; then remove it by putting that side of the head down and pulling the ear in different directions to help the vinegar run out. Do this twice a day for 3 or 4 days.

Call Your Child's Physician Later If

• The canals itch for more than a week.

• The ear becomes painful.

• A discharge from the ear occurs.

• A fever (over 100°F) occurs.

PREVENTION

• Keep soap and shampoo out of the ear canal.

• Don't use cotton swabs in the ear canal.

• Do plug the openings with cotton prior to using hair spray.

• After swimming, get all water out of the ear canals by turning the head to the side and pulling the ear in different directions to help the water run out. Dry the opening to the ear canal carefully.

MUMPS

SYMPTOMS AND CHARACTERISTICS

- Swollen parotid gland, in front of the ear and crossing the corner of the jaw. (Both parotid glands are swollen in 70 percent of children with mumps.)
- Tenderness of the swollen gland
- Pain increased by jaw movement (chewing or even talking)
- Fever (over 100°F) is present
- No prior mumps vaccine
- Exposure to another child with mumps 16 to 18 days earlier adds weight to the diagnosis.

  If your child's symptoms are different, call your physician for help.

Cause • Mumps is an acute viral infection of the parotid, a gland which produces saliva and is located in front of and below each ear.

Expected Course • The fever is usually gone in 3 to 4 days. The swelling and pain are cleared by 7 days.

CALL YOUR CHILD'S PHYSICIAN

Immediately If

- Your child has a stiff neck or severe headache.
- Your child is vomiting repeatedly.
- Your child has definite abdominal pain.
- Your child is acting very sick.

During Office Hours If

- It could be an enlarged lymph node rather than mumps.
- The skin over the mumps gland is reddened.
- The gland has been swollen more than 7 days.
- In adolescent males, the testicles become tender.

- Your child received the mumps vaccine.

- Your child had mumps before.

- You have other questions.

HOME CARE

Pain and Fever Relief • Give acetaminophen. (For dosage, see
FEVER, page 305.) Cold compresses (e.g., ice in a wet washcloth) applied to the swollen area may also relieve pain.

Diet

- Avoid sour foods or citrus fruits that increase saliva production and parotid swelling.

- Avoid foods that require lots of chewing.

- Consider a liquid diet if chewing is very painful.

Contagiousness • The disease is contagious until the swelling is
gone (usually 6 or 7 days). Your child should be kept out of
school and away from other children who have not had mumps
or mumps vaccine.

Mumps Exposure • Mumps exposure can be a problem if a person has never received the mumps vaccine or had past swelling of the parotid gland (mumps). Only 10 percent of adults
are really susceptible, however. Adults who as children lived
in the same household with siblings who had mumps can be
considered protected. People who are not protected should
call their physician during office hours, if they are exposed to
mumps, to see if the mumps vaccine would be helpful, based
on the following guidelines:

- Children: Call for all.

- Adolescent or adult males: Calling is optional. There is a 2.5
percent chance of mumps infection of the testicles (orchitis).

- Adult females: Calling is unnecessary. No serious complications occur.

Call Your Child's Physician Later If

- The swelling lasts for 8 days or more.

- The fever lasts for 5 days or more.

- The skin over the swelling becomes red.

- Your child develops a stiff neck, severe headache, or prolonged vomiting.

- You feel your child is getting worse.

RELATED TOPIC

LYMPH NODES, SWOLLEN (see page 393)

PIERCED EAR INFECTIONS

SYMPTOMS AND CHARACTERISTICS

Earrings for pierced ears have become very popular in our country. Ear piercing no longer awaits the teenage years; even infants are seen with pierced ears. For safety reasons, pierced earrings should not be worn until a child is old enough (usually past age 4) to know not to take the earrings out and swallow them. Ideally, the ears should not be pierced until the girl can play an active part in the decision (usually past age 8).

The most common complication of pierced ears is a bacterial infection of the channel. Signs of an infection are tenderness, a yellow discharge, redness, and some swelling.

Causes • The most common causes of infection are piercing the ears with unsterile equipment, inserting unsterile posts, or frequently touching the earlobes with dirty hands. Another frequent cause is wearing tight earrings because the post is too short (earlobes come in various thicknesses) or the clasp is applied too tightly. Tight earrings don't allow air to enter the channel. Also, the pressure from tight earrings reduces blood flow to the earlobe and sets it up for infection. Some inexpensive earrings have rough areas on the posts that scratch the channel and allow infection to enter. Inserting the post at the wrong angle also can scratch the channel, so a mirror should be used until insertion becomes second nature. Posts containing nickel can also cause an itchy, allergic reaction.

Expected Course • If the proper precautions are taken, most mild earlobe infections will clear up in 1 to 2 weeks. Recurrences are common if the youngster does not become conscientious in earring care.

CALL YOUR CHILD'S PHYSICIAN DURING OFFICE HOURS IF

- An unexplained fever (over 100°F) occurs.

- The lymph node in front of or behind the earlobe becomes swollen.

- Swelling or redness spreads beyond the pierced area of the earlobe.

- The earring clasp becomes embedded in the earlobe and can't be removed.

- You have other questions.

HOME CARE

Treating Mild Pierced Ear Infections • Remove the earring and post three times a day. Cleanse them with rubbing alcohol. Clean both sides of the earlobe with rubbing alcohol. Apply Bacitracin ointment (a nonprescription item) to the post and reinsert it. Continue the antibiotic ointment for 2 days beyond the time the infection seems cleared. Carefully review all the recommendations on preventing infections and be certain they are in effect.

Call Your Physician Later If

- Fever (over 100°F) occurs.

- The infection worsens.

- The infection is not improving after 48 hours of treatment.

PREVENTION OF INITIAL INFECTIONS

Have your child's earlobes pierced by someone who understands sterile technique and does them frequently. Using someone inexperienced can result in infections or a cosmetically poor result.

- The initial post should be 14 carat gold or stainless steel.

- Do not remove the post for 6 weeks.

- Apply the clasp loosely to allow for swelling.

- After washing the hands and cleaning both sides of the earlobe with rubbing alcohol, turn the posts approximately 3 rotations. Do this twice a day.

- By the end of 6 weeks, the lining of the channel should be healed and earrings may be changed as often as desired.

Prevention of Later Infections

- Remind your youngster not to touch the earrings except when inserting or removing them. The fingers are often dirty and can contaminate the area.

- Clean the earring, post, and earlobe with rubbing alcohol before each insertion.

- Apply the clasp loosely to prevent any pressure on the earlobe and to provide an air space on both sides.

- Polish or discard any posts with rough spots.

- At bedtime, remove the earrings to permit air exposure and drying of the channel during the night.

Prevention of Injury to the Earlobe • Remind your daughter that dangling earrings can lead to a torn earlobe requiring plastic surgery. Avoid them during sports. Also, take precautions while dancing, hair washing, or handling young children who might yank them.

PULLING AT EAR

Most young children who are pulling at or rubbing their ears, but have no other symptoms, do not have an ear infection. Many of them have an itchy ear canal from getting soap or shampoo in it. Some have just discovered their ears and are playing with them (6 months to 2 years old). If it occurs only when your child is sleepy, it may be a reassuring habit like clutching a security blanket.

CALL YOUR CHILD'S PHYSICIAN DURING OFFICE HOURS IF

- You think your child is in any pain.

- Your child has been crying without an obvious cause.

- Your child had any trouble sleeping last night.

- Your child has a fever (over 100°F) or any signs of a cold.

- You have other questions.

HOME CARE

Treatment • Mix a solution of one-half rubbing alcohol and one-half white vinegar. Place 1 to 2 drops in each ear daily for 3 days.

Call Your Child's Physician Later If

• Pulling at the ear continues beyond 3 days.

• Ear pain occurs.

• A discharge from the ear occurs.

• Any other symptoms develop that concern you.

PREVENTION

• Keep soap and shampoo out of the ear canal.

• Don't use cotton swabs in the ear canal, since they remove the earwax that protects the lining of the canal, and this can cause irritation or itching.

• After swimming, get all water out of the ear canals by turning the head to the side and pulling the ear in different directions to help the water run out. Dry the opening to the ear canal carefully.

SWIMMER'S EAR (OTITIS EXTERNA)

SYMPTOMS AND CHARACTERISTICS

• Itchy and painful ear canals

• Currently engaged in swimming

• Pain when the ear is moved up and down

• Pain when the tab of outer ear overlying the ear canal is pushed in

• Discharge is slight in amount and clear

If your child's symptoms are different, call your physician for help.

Cause • Swimmer's ear is an infection of the skin lining the ear canal. When water gets trapped in the ear canal, the lining becomes swollen and prone to infection. Ear canals were meant to be dry. Swimming pools are worse than lakes, because the chlorine kills all the good bacteria in the ear canal, and harmful bacteria tend to take over. However, this doesn't mean anything is wrong with the water.

Expected Course • With treatment, symptoms should be better in 3 days.

CALL YOUR CHILD'S PHYSICIAN DURING OFFICE HOURS IF

- A fever (over 100°F) is present.
- A yellow discharge issues from the ear canal.
- The canal appears full of gunk.
- The ear is very painful.
- The outer ear becomes red or swollen.
- A swollen lymph node is present behind the earlobe.
- You have other questions.

HOME CARE

Treatment • White vinegar has acetic acid in it and can usually restore the ear canal to its normal chemistry. Fill one ear canal at a time by running the vinegar down the side of the opening so that air isn't trapped under it. Leave it in for 5 minutes; then remove it by putting that side of the head down and pulling the ear in different directions to help the vinegar run out. Do this twice a day. Use aspirin or acetaminophen for pain relief (for dosage, see FEVER, page 305). Generally, your child should not swim until the symptoms are gone. If your child is on a swim team, he or she may continue but should use a white vinegar rinse after each session.

Common Mistakes • Don't use earplugs of any kind for prevention or treatment. They tend to jam earwax back into the ear canal. Also, they don't keep all water out of the ear canals.
Cotton swabs also should not be inserted in ear canals.

Call Your Child's Physician Later If

- The symptoms are not cleared up in 3 days.
- The pain becomes worse after 24 hours on treatment.

- A yellow discharge from the ear canal occurs.

- A fever (over 100°F) occurs.

PREVENTION
After swimming, get all water out of the ear canals by turning the head to the side and pulling the ear in different directions to help the water run out. Dry the opening to the ear canal carefully. If recurrences are a big problem, rinse your child's ear canals with rubbing alcohol for 1 minute each time he or she finishes swimming.

NOSE

COLDS

SYMPTOMS AND CHARACTERISTICS

- Also called an upper respiratory infection (URI)
- Runny or stuffy nose
- Usually associated with fever and sore throat
- Sometimes associated with a cough, hoarseness, red eyes, and swollen lymph nodes in the neck

If your child's symptoms are different, call your physician for help.

Cause of Colds • A cold or upper respiratory infection (URI) is a viral infection of the nose and throat. The cold viruses are spread from one person to another by the mouth (kissing) or hands. Cold germs can get on your child's hands from a cold sufferer's hands or contaminated objects. Cold viruses can live on toys, phones, doorknobs, desks, tables, and other objects for up to 3 days. The virus is then transmitted to the nose or eyes, by normal face-touching habits. Airborne droplets of germs from sneezing or coughing are a rare means of cold transmission.

Once the cold germs get a foothold in the nasal passages, they start to multiply and spread downward into the throat and windpipe, causing a sore throat and cough. Since there are up to 150 cold viruses, most healthy children get at least 6 colds a year. By adolescence, the number per year starts to taper off. Cold weather, cold winds, drafts, air conditioners, and wet feet do not increase the chances of coming down with a cold.

Expected Course • Usually the fever lasts less than 3 days, and all nose and throat symptoms are gone by a week. A cough may last 2 to 3 weeks. The main things to watch for are secondary bacterial complications such as ear infections, yellow drainage from the eyes, thick pus from the nose (often indicating a sinus infection), or pneumonia. These complications may occur in 5 percent of colds because the viral infection temporarily lowers your child's resistance. In young infants, a blocked nose can interfere so much with the ability to suck, that dehydration can occur.

SIMILAR CONDITIONS

Vasomotor Rhinitis • Many children and adults have a profusely runny nose in the wintertime when they are breathing cold air. This usually clears within 15 minutes of coming indoors. It requires no treatment beyond a handkerchief and has nothing to do with infection. If you or your child must spend all day in a cold environment (for instance, on a skiing trip), you can prevent the endless nasal drip by using a long-acting vasoconstrictor spray beforehand (see under in *Home Care*, below).

Chemical Rhinitis • Chemical rhinitis is a dry stuffy nose from excessive and prolonged use of vasoconstrictor nose drops (more than 5 days). It will be better within a day or two of stopping the nose drops.

Hay Fever • For a runny nose that sounds like an allergy, save time by turning directly to the guideline on HAY FEVER, page 442.

CALL YOUR CHILD'S PHYSICIAN

Immediately If

• Breathing is difficult *and* no better after you clear the nose.

• Your child is acting very sick.

During Office Hours If

- There is any suggestion of an earache.
- The skin under the openings of the nose is raw or scabbed over (looks like impetigo).
- The nasal discharge has been yellow (pus) for more than 24 hours.
- The discharge has been present for more than 7 days.
- The nasal discharge contains blood that is not from a simple nosebleed.
- The eyes have a yellow discharge (not just red and watery).
- A fever (over 100°F) has been present for more than 72 hours.
- You have other questions.

HOME CARE FOR COLDS

Remember: If you treat a cold it will be gone in a week. If you don't treat it, it will last 7 days. However, we can relieve many of the symptoms. Keep in mind that the treatment for a runny nose is quite different from that for a stuffy nose (see below).

Treatment for a Runny Nose with Profuse Clear Discharge • The only treatment needed is to blow the nose periodically. Sniffing and swallowing the secretions is even better, because blowing the nose may force the infection into the ears or sinuses. Since most children developmentally are unable to blow the nose or sniff until age 4, use a soft rubber suction bulb to remove the secretions if they are bothering your child. Nasal discharge is the nose's way of eliminating viruses. Medicine for this stage is not recommended unless your child has a nasal allergy. However, if nasal secretions are profuse and socially inconvenient (and your child is over 1 year old), try an oral antihistamine. (See HAY FEVER, page 442, for drugs and dosages.)

Treatment for a Stuffy (Dry) Nose with Only a Little Discharge

Warm Water Nose Drops and Suctioning • Most stuffy noses are blocked by dry mucus. Suction alone cannot remove dry secretions. Warm tap-water nose drops are better than any medicine you can buy when it comes to loosening up mucus. If you prefer normal saline nose drops, mix ¼ level teaspoon of table salt in 4 ounces of water. Make up a fresh solution every few days and keep it in a clean bottle. Use a clean eyedropper or wet cotton ball to drip in drops of water.

• For the younger child who cannot blow the nose: Place 3 drops of warm water in each nostril. After 1 minute, use a soft rubber suction bulb to suck out, or a cotton swab to wipe out, the loosened mucus. Clean the bulb tip by squirting the secretions into a tissue. To remove secretions from the back of the nose, you will need to seal off both nasal openings completely with the tip of the suction bulb on one side and your finger closing the other side. You can get a suction bulb at your drugstore for about two dollars. Buy the short, stubby one with a clear-plastic mucus trap. If you cause a nosebleed, you are putting the tip of the suction bulb in too far. If your child is breast- or bottle-feeding, you must clear his nose out so he can breathe while he's sucking. Clearing the nasal passages is also important before putting your child down to sleep. Some babies can't breathe through the mouth during the first 6 months of life (obligate nasal breathers), so the nose must be kept open.

• For the older child who can blow the nose: Use 3 drops as necessary in each nostril while your child is lying on her back on a bed with her head hanging over the side. Wait 1 minute for the water to soften and loosen the dried mucus. Then have your child blow her nose. This can be repeated several times in a row for complete clearing of the nasal passages.

• Errors in using warm water nose drops: The main errors are not putting in enough water, not waiting long enough for secretions to loosen up, and not repeating the procedure until the breathing is easy. The front of the nose can look open while the back of the nose is all gummed up with dried mucus. Obviously, putting in warm water nose drops without suctioning afterward is of little value.

Decongestant Nose Drops or Spray for a Stuffy Nose • If nasal congestion interferes with breathing despite warm water nose drops, buy some nonprescription vasoconstrictor nose drops.

• For 6 months to 2 years of age: ⅛ percent Neosynephrine nose drops every 2 to 3 hours as needed (especially before feeding).

• For 2 to 6 years of age: Pediatric strength, long-acting nose drops or spray every 8 to 12 hours as needed.

- Over 6 years of age: adult-strength, long-acting nose drops or spray every 8 to 12 hours as needed. (These products usually contain oxymetazoline or xylometazoline.)

Cautions

- Use 1 drop or spray on each side.

- Do not use for children under 6 months of age.

- Use only after the nose has been cleaned out with saline or nose drops.

- Don't repeat unless nasal congestion recurs.

- Don't use for more than 5 days because they can irritate the nose and make it more congested.

- Don't use for noisy breathing unless it makes your child uncomfortable or interferes with feeding.

Treatment for Associated Symptoms of Colds

Fever • Use acetaminophen for aches or moderate fever (over 102°F). (For dosage, see FEVER, page 305.) For the present, avoid aspirin because of the possible link with Reyes syndrome.

Sore Throat • Use hard candies and saltwater gargles for children over 4 years old.

Cough • Use cough drops for children over 4 years old, and corn syrup for younger children.

Red Eyes • Rinse frequently with wet cotton balls.

Poor Appetite • Encourage fluids of the child's choice. A recent study showed that eating chicken noodle soup loosened nasal mucus.

Common Mistakes • Most cold remedies or tablets are worthless. Also, oral medicines have no ability to remove dried nasal secretions. If the nose is really running, consider a pure antihistamine such as chlorpheniramine products. (See HAY FEVER, page 442, for dosages.) Prescription cold medicines offer no advantages over nonprescription products. Avoid drugs that have several ingredients; they increase the risk of side effects. Avoid oral decongestants if they make your child jittery or keep the child from sleeping at night. Also, these medicines give much shorter relief than antihistamines.

Use acetaminophen for a cold only if your child also has fever, sore throat, or muscle aches.

Leftover antibiotics should not be given because they have no effect on viruses and may be harmful.

Call Your Child's Physician Later If

• Your child is under 3 months of age *and* develops a fever.

• The fever lasts more than 3 days.

• The nasal discharge lasts more than 7 days.

• The discharge becomes consistently thick and yellow for more than 24 hours.

• The skin under the openings of the nose becomes raw or scabbed over.

• The eyes become mattery.

• You can't unblock the nose enough for your infant to take adequate fluids.

• Breathing becomes difficult *and* not due to the stuffy nose.

• There is any suggestion of an earache or sinus pain.

• You feel your child is getting worse.

PREVENTION OF COLDS

Over the years, we all become exposed to many cold viruses and develop some immunity to them.

• Since complications are more common in children during the first year of life, try to avoid undue exposure of young babies to other children or adults with colds, to daycare nurseries, church nurseries, and crowded shopping centers. A parent can't control the majority of contact, however.

• Since the cold viruses are commonly transmitted by hand contamination, frequent hand washing and keeping the hands away from the nose and mouth are the most helpful steps in prevention.

• A humidifier prevents dry mucus membranes, which may be more susceptible to infections. Clean the humidifier once per week with a bleach solution.

• Vitamin C, unfortunately, has not been shown to prevent or shorten colds. Large doses (like 2 grams) can cause diarrhea.

RELATED TOPICS

FEVER (see page 305)
SORE THROAT (see page 457)
COUGH (see page 469)
EYES, RED OR PINKEYE (see page 441)
EYES, YELLOW DISCHARGE (see page 416)
EARACHE (see page 419)
SINUS CONGESTION (see page 447)

FOREIGN BODY, NOSE

Young children often put foreign objects in their nostrils and then forget about them. Favorites are food, seeds, nuts, paper, cotton, foam, stones, and beads. The body tries to reject these intruders by producing a foul-smelling yellow nasal discharge.

FIRST AID

Have your child blow his nose vigorously several times while closing the other nostril. Sometimes this action will expel the object. If you successfully remove the object, call your child's physician later if a yellow nasal discharge occurs.

CALL YOUR CHILD'S PHYSICIAN IMMEDIATELY IF THESE MEASURES FAIL

It is critical that you do not try to remove the object by putting anything into the nose, including tweezers and fingers. This almost always pushes the object in farther and makes the physician's job very difficult, even with special instruments. Watch closely to see that your child doesn't push it in.

HAY FEVER (ALLERGIC RHINITIS)

SYMPTOMS AND CHARACTERISTICS

- Clear nasal discharge with sneezing, sniffing, and nasal itching
- Symptoms occur during pollen season
- Similar symptoms during the same month of the previous year
- Previous confirmation of this diagnosis by a physician is helpful
- Eye allergies are commonly associated
- A tickling sensation in the back of the throat can be associated
- Sinus or ear congestion are sometimes associated
- No fever

  If your child's symptoms are different, call your physician for help.

Cause • These children are not allergic to hay (nor do they have a fever). Hay fever is an allergic reaction of the nose (and sinuses) to an inhaled substance. The sensitivity is often inherited, so other family members may also have hay fever. During late April and May the most common offending pollen is from trees. From late May to mid-July, the offending pollen is usually grass. From late August to the first frost, the leading cause of hay fever is ragweed pollen. Although the inhaled substance is usually a pollen, it can also be animal dander, feathers, or other agents your child is allergic to. Hay fever is the most common allergy; over 15 percent of people have it.

Expected Course • This is a chronic condition that will probably recur every year, perhaps for a lifetime. Therefore, it is important to learn how to control it.

CALL YOUR CHILD'S PHYSICIAN DURING OFFICE HOURS IF

- Your child is also coughing a lot.
- The symptoms are constant rather than seasonal.
- You have other questions.

HOME CARE FOR HAY FEVER

Antihistamine Medicine • The best drug for hay fever is an antihistamine. Some effective nonprescription ones are Chlortrimeton, Dimetane, and Teldrin. Symptoms clear up faster if antihistamines are given at the first sign of sneezing or sniffing. For children with occasional symptoms, the antihistamines can be taken on days when symptoms are present or expected. For children with daily symptoms, the best control is attained if antihistamines are taken continuously throughout the pollen season. The bedtime dosage is especially important for helping the nose repair itself during the night.

Dosages for chlorpheniramine: the short-acting liquid or tablet preparations must be given every 6 to 8 hours. For children over 20 pounds, give 1 mg. For children 3 to 6 years, give 1½ mg. For children 7 to 11 years, give 2 mg. Adolescents and adults can take 4 mg.

For convenience, children age 6 to 12 can take 8 mg long-acting pills every 12 hours for prevention of symptoms. Those over age 12 (more than 90 pounds) can take 12 mg long-acting pills of chlorpheniramine every 12 hours.

The main side effect of antihistamines is drowsiness. If your child gets drowsy, continue the drug, but temporarily decrease the dosage. In 1 to 2 weeks the regular dosage will be tolerated without much drowsiness.

Pollen Removal • Pollen tends to collect on the exposed body surface and especially in the hair. Shower your child and wash the hair any time lots of symptoms (especially itchy or burning skin) are present, following heavy exposure to pollen. At a minimum, shower your child every night before going to bed. Avoid handling pets that have been outside and are probably covered with pollen.

Eye Allergies Associated with Hay Fever • If your child also has itchy, watery eyes, some additional treatment measures are in order. Wash the face and eyelids to remove the pollen. Then apply a cold compress to the eyelids. Also, instill 2 drops of long-acting vasoconstrictor eyedrops every 8 to 12 hours as necessary (no prescription needed). Ask your pharmacist for help in choosing a reliable product.

Common Mistakes • Nose drops or nasal sprays usually do not help hay fever, because they are washed out of the nose by nasal secretions as soon as they have been instilled. Also, when used for more than 5 days, they can irritate the nose and make it more congested.

Call Your Child's Physician Later If

• The treatment does not relieve most of the symptoms.

• Your child is missing any school, work, social activities, or sleep because of hay fever.

• Any other changes concern you.

Good News • *Severe* hay fever can now usually be controlled by cromolyn or steroid nasal sprays (called Nasalcrom or Beclomethasone respectively) rather than requiring hyposensitization (allergy shots). These sprays must be used when the nose is not dripping. Antihistamines can be used first to turn it off.

PREVENTION OF HAY FEVER SYMPTOMS

• Reduce pollen exposure by not taking your child on drives in the country, by closing car windows (if possible) during necessary drives, staying indoors when it is windy, closing the windows that face the prevailing winds, turning off attic fans, and not having your child near when someone is cutting the grass during pollen season (especially when the pollen count is high).

• Avoid feather pillows, pets, farms, stables, and tobacco smoke if any of them seem to bring on or accentuate symptoms of nasal allergy.

• If the hay fever is especially bad, you may wish to take your child to an air-conditioned store or theater for a few hours.

• For exposure you can't avoid, give an antihistamine 1 hour before and a shower immediately afterward.

Pollen-Free Vacations • If your child is allergic to ragweed, you may wish to plan an August vacation to an area that has little or no ragweed. In essence, the pollen count is highest in the Midwest, and only the coastal areas of Washington, Oregon, and California are free of ragweed pollen. You may wish to write to Abbott Laboratories, Public Affairs Section, North Chicago, Illinois 60064, for a free map of the country with details on ragweed distribution. This booklet is called "Hayfever Holiday." Moving to another part of the country to avoid pollens is usually not worth the sacrifice, because within 3 years your child will usually develop allergies to plants in the new location.

RELATED TOPICS

EAR CONGESTION (see page 421)
EYE, ALLERGIES (see page 409)
SINUS CONGESTION (see page 447)

NOSEBLEED

Nosebleeds (epistaxsis) are very common throughout childhood. They are usually caused by dryness of the nasal lining, plus the normal rubbing and picking that all children do. Vigorous nose-blowing can also cause them. Many times they begin unexpectedly, even during sleep. If the nosebleed was caused by an injury, turn directly to the guideline on NOSE TRAUMA, page 63.

CALL YOUR CHILD'S PHYSICIAN

Immediately If

• There are any skin bruises not caused by an injury.

• Your child has fainted or feels dizzy when he or she stands up.

• A huge amount of blood has been lost.

• Your child is acting very sick.

During Office Hours If

• A concerning amount of blood has been lost.

• Your child is under 1 year old.

• Difficult-to-stop nosebleeds are a recurrent problem for your child.

• You have other questions.

HOME CARE

Treatment • Have your child sit up and lean forward so he or she does not have to swallow the blood. Have a basin so your child can spit out any blood that drains into the throat. Your child's nose should be blown free of any large clots that interfere with pressure. Then tightly pinch the soft parts of the nose against the center wall for 10 minutes. Don't release the pressure until 10 minutes are up. If the bleeding continues, you may not be pressing on the right spot. During this time, tell your child to breathe through the mouth. Reassure your child that you can stop the bleeding. If the nosebleed hasn't stopped, insert a gauze covered with vasoconstrictor nose drops (e.g., Neosynephrine) or petroleum jelly into the nostril. Squeeze again for 10 minutes. Leave the gauze in for another 10 minutes before removing it. If bleeding persists, call your physician, but continue the pressure in the meantime.

Common Mistakes

• A cold washcloth applied to the forehead, back of the neck, or under the upper lip does not help stop nosebleeds.

• Avoid packing the nose with anything, because when it is removed, bleeding usually recurs.

• Swallowed blood is irritating to the stomach. Don't be surprised or worried if it is vomited up.

Call Your Child's Physician Later If

• The bleeding has not stopped after two 10-minute attempts at pinching the nostrils closed.

• Nosebleeds occur daily even after petroleum jelly and humidification are used.

• Any other symptoms concern you.

PREVENTION

• A small amount of petroleum jelly applied twice a day to the center wall (septum) inside the nose is often helpful for relieving dryness and irritation.

• Increasing the humidity in the home by using a humidifier may also be helpful.

• Get your child into the habit of putting 2 or 3 drops of warm water in each nostril before blowing a stuffy nose.

• In addition, avoid aspirin temporarily. Aspirin can increase the tendency of the body to bleed and can make nosebleeds last longer.

SINUS CONGESTION

SYMPTOMS AND CHARACTERISTICS

- Sensation of fullness, pressure, or pain on the face overlying a sinus

- Pain can be above the eyebrow, behind the eye, or over the cheekbone

- Pain is usually just on one side of the face

- Runny or blocked nose

- A sensation of continuous postnasal drip

- Sinus congestion documented by a physician one or more times in the past is helpful

  If your child's symptoms are different, call your physician for help.

Cause • The nose has seven bony, air-filled chambers (sinuses) that help to warm and humidify the air passing through it. Sinus congestion occurs when the sinus openings are blocked and normal sinus secretions accumulate and cause a sensation of pressure and fullness. Sinusitis occurs mainly with colds and hay fever.

Expected Course • Without treatment, the sinuses usually open after about a week. The main complication is when bacteria multiply within the blocked sinus. This leads to a yellow nasal discharge and increased pain. Sometimes the overlying skin becomes red or swollen. This type of sinusitis needs antibiotics. Frequent throat-clearing of postnasal secretions usually leads to sore throat, and swallowing secretions commonly leads to nausea and mild stomach discomfort.

CALL YOUR CHILD'S PHYSICIAN

Immediately If

- Redness or swelling occurs on the skin overlying the sinus.

- Your child is acting very sick.

During Office Hours If

• Your child is under 5 years old.

• A fever (over 100°F) is present.

• The nasal secretions are yellow.

• Your child is also coughing a lot.

• The pain keeps your child from getting enough sleep.

• You have other questions.

HOME CARE

Inhalation of Warm Mist • The main purpose of treatment is to open the sinuses so they can drain. Inhalation of warm moisture for 10 to 20 minutes, 4 times a day, is helpful. The easiest method is to cover the nose and mouth with a warm wet washcloth and have your child breathe through it. Your child also could lean over a basin of hot water with a towel placed over the head and breathe in the vapors coming from the basin. Another way to do this is to put warm water into a humidifier (not a vaporizer) and lean over the mist it gives off.

Decongestant Nose Drops or Spray • If the sinus still seems blocked after the inhalation of warm mist, long-acting vasoconstrictor nose drops or sprays should be used. These are nonprescription items; ask your pharmacist to recommend a brand. The usual dose is 2 drops or sprays per side twice a day. Don't repeat them unless the sinus congestion or pain recurs. The nose should first be cleared by sniffing or nasal suction.

The openings to the sinuses are on the outer side of the nasal passages. Point the nasal spray in this direction. To deliver nose drops to this location, they must be put in while your child is lying on a bed with the head tipped back and turned to one side.

The drops or spray must be stopped for 2 days out of every 7 to prevent rebound swelling.

Pain Relief Medicines • Your child will usually need to take acetaminophen temporarily to relieve pain until the obstructed sinus is opened. The application of ice over the sinus may also help to relieve pain.

Oral Antihistamines • If your child also has hay fever, give him his allergy medicine.

Call Your Child's Physician Later If

• Your child develops a fever.

• A yellow nasal discharge occurs *and* lasts for more than 24 hours.

• Redness or swelling of the overlying skin occurs.

• The sinus discomfort persists for more than 1 week.

• The sinus pain becomes so bad that it interferes with sleep.

• You feel your child is getting worse.

PREVENTION

Jumping into the water feet first can cause sinusitis of the frontal sinuses and should be avoided unless the nose is pinched. Swimming does not worsen sinusitis, but deep diving should be forbidden unless your child wears nose plugs.

RELATED TOPICS

COLDS (see page 435)
HAY FEVER (see page 442)

MOUTH AND THROAT

BAD BREATH (HALITOSIS)

SYMPTOMS AND CHARACTERISTICS

- An unpleasant odor to the exhaled breath
- The problem can be a recent or longstanding one
- Bad breath only on awakening is normal and due to poor saliva flow at night

Causes • Causes are numerous. If your child has one of the following, turn directly to that guideline:

CANKER SORES (see page 452)
COLDS (see page 435)
SINUS CONGESTION (see page 447)
SORE THROAT (see page 457)

- If your child has dental cavities, make a dental appointment.
- If your child is forgetful about brushing her teeth, help her brush more frequently.
- If your child sucks the thumb, a blanket, or other object, the bad breath will resolve when this habit is given up. Over age 4, ask your child's physician about some ways to discourage it before the permanent teeth come in. (See THUMBSUCKING, page 132).

CALL YOUR CHILD'S PHYSICIAN DURING OFFICE HOURS IF

- Your child has bad breath of unknown cause.

HOME CARE
More frequent toothbrushing improves most cases of mild bad breath. Also brush the surface of the tongue. Mouthwashes and chewable breath fresheners are heavily promoted in our society but provide temporary improvement at best. Since some products contain 20 to 30 percent alcohol, they also carry a risk of poisoning in children who swallow them. The complaint of foul breath is unusual in children, and the cause should be uncovered and dealt with directly.

CANKER SORES (MOUTH ULCERS)

SYMPTOMS AND CHARACTERISTICS

- Painful, shallow ulcers of the lining of the mouth

- The gums or inner sides of the lips or cheeks are the usual sites

- No fever

  If your child's symptoms are different, call your physician for help.

Similar Condition • If thrush is suspected, save time by turning directly to the guideline for Thrush, page 159.

Cause • The cause of canker sores is unknown, but some may be due to prolonged contact with food that gets stuck in the teeth. Others may be due to forgotten injuries from toothbrushes, hot foods or self-biting. Herpes simplex causes recurrent fever blisters (on the outside of the lip) but does not cause recurrent canker sores.

Expected Course • The white color of canker sores is the normal color of healing tissue in the mouth. This is not pus. They heal up in 1 to 2 weeks. For many people they are a recurrent problem.

CALL YOUR CHILD'S PHYSICIAN
Immediately If

- Your child could have swallowed an acid or alkali.

During Office Hours If

• Four or more mouth ulcers are present.

• The gums are red, swollen, and tender.

• A raised yellow (or red) bump is present on the gums.

• A fever (over 100°F) is present.

• Fluid intake is poor.

• The eyelids or genitals have any ulcers.

• The canker sores began after taking a medicine.

• You have other questions.

HOME CARE

Pain Relief • To reduce the pain, swish milk of magnesia (MOM) solution in the mouth for several minutes. For a single ulcer, apply a MOM tablet and let it dissolve. This can be repeated 3 or 4 times a day. Give acetaminophen as necessary for pain (especially at bedtime).

Diet • The diet can be changed to reduce the pain. Use a glass instead of a bottle if your child is a baby. Avoid giving your child salty or citrus foods and foods that need much chewing. Change to a soft diet for a few days. Cold drinks and milk-shakes are especially good. If toothbrushing is painful, have your child rinse the mouth with water after meals.

Call Your Child's Physician Later If

• The pain is severe.

• Your child can't take adequate fluids.

• The mouth ulcers increase to 4 or more in number.

• They last for more than 2 weeks.

• Your child develops a fever or other symptoms.

• You feel your child is getting worse.

PREVENTION

Canker sores tend to recur throughout life. Good attention to toothbrushing after meals may prevent some. Try to identify any offending foods. Were tomato, citrus fruit, peppermint, cinnamon, nuts, or shellfish taken within the last day? If you find a food that you think may be causing the problem, eliminate it from the diet for 2 weeks and then offer some to see whether it causes a recurrence of the canker sores. If it does, the food should be eliminated from the diet permanently.

COLD SORES (FEVER BLISTERS)

SYMPTOMS AND CHARACTERISTICS

- A cluster of painful 1 mm to 2 mm bumps or blisters on the outer lip
- On one side of the mouth only
- Pain or burning on the outer lip where cold sores previously occurred (i.e., an early diagnosis of recurrent cold sores)

If your child's symptoms are different, call your physician for help.

Cause • Cold sores are caused by the herpes simplex virus (usually Type I). The first bout follows contact with someone else with herpes. Thereafter, recurrences occur when the virus (which lives in the sensory nerve) is reactivated by sunburn, fever, friction, menstrual periods, or physical exhaustion.

Expected Course • The blisters go on to rupture, scab over, and dry up. The whole process takes 10 to 14 days. They do not cause scars. Treatment can shorten the course by many days.

HOME CARE

Treatment

- If blisters are not yet present, apply an ice cube or ice pack continuously for 90 minutes. This will often abort the infection.
- If blisters are present, apply rubbing alcohol for 2 minutes 4 times per day until the cold sores begin to dry up. While this approach stings, it is most effective at reducing the swelling.
- Avoid ointments, because air exposure speeds drying and healing. If the lips later crack, apply petroleum jelly.

Call Your Child's Physician Later If

• The sores are spreading.

• Any sores occur near the eye.

• The sores last more than 2 weeks.

PREVENTION

Since fever blisters are often triggered by exposure to intense sunlight, prevent them in the future by using a lip balm containing sunscreen. Avoid spreading this germ to the eye, because an infection there can be serious. Therefore, discourage picking or rubbing and wash the hands frequently.

Since the condition is contagious, avoid kissing other people during this time. If your child is young and puts everything in his or her mouth, avoid sharing toys with other children for a week. In general, most children under age 6 need to stay away from other children until the sores are dry (4 or 5 days). Although one should be careful about contagion, the child with herpes should not be made to feel like a leper. Fever blisters are not a sexually transmitted disease. By age 6, more than 50 percent of children already have antibodies to the cold sore virus.

GEOGRAPHIC TONGUE

SYMPTOMS AND CHARACTERISTICS

• The tongue develops smooth red patches of various shapes and sizes

• The pattern resembles a map, and can change from week to week

• The bare spots are painless, and the sense of taste is preserved

• The condition usually occurs in children under 6 years of age and the cause is unknown, but it is not due to a vitamin deficiency

• The tongue returns to normal appearance after a period of months to years

HOME CARE

The condition is harmless and no treatment is helpful or necessary. No disease looks like geographic tongue, but if you are uncertain of the diagnosis, call your child's physician during office hours.

LIP, SWOLLEN

The sudden onset of a swollen lip without an injury is usually due to a local allergic reaction. Symptoms of itching or tingling are also present. The allergic substance can be a food, toothpaste, lipstick, lip balm, or other irritant (such as an evergreen resin) that inadvertently is transferred from the hands.

If one of the following is suspected, save time by turning directly to that guideline:

BITES, INSECT (see page 361)
COLD SORES (see page 454)
MOUTH TRAUMA (see page 61)
POISONING (see page 42)

CALL YOUR CHILD'S PHYSICIAN IMMEDIATELY IF

• Breathing or swallowing is difficult.

• The area looks like a burn.

• The swelling is tender to the touch.

• A fever (over 100°F) is present.

• Your child is acting very sick.

HOME CARE

Wash the lips and face with soap and water to remove any irritating substances. Apply ice to the swelling for 20 minutes out of every hour. If you have an antihistamine in your home (see HIVES, page 344, for details), give your child the correct dosage 1 or 2 times. In the future, avoid any substance you are suspicious of.

Call your child's physician if the swelling becomes worse or it lasts more than 2 days.

SORE THROAT (PHARYNGITIS)

SYMPTOMS AND CHARACTERISTICS

- Complaint of a sore throat

- In children too young to talk, a sore throat may be suspected if they refuse to eat or begin to cry during feedings

- When examined with a light, the throat is bright red

If your child's symptoms are different, call your physician for help.

Causes • Most sore throats are caused by viruses and are part of a cold. About 10 percent of sore throats are due to strep bacteria. A throat culture is the only way to tell strep pharyngitis from viral pharyngitis. This identification of strep throat is important because without treatment some rare but serious complications (rheumatic fever or glomerulonephritis) can occur.

Tonsillitis (temporary swelling and redness of the tonsils) is usually present with any throat infection, viral or bacterial. The presence of tonsillitis does not have any special meaning.

Children who sleep with their mouths open often wake in the morning with a dry mouth and sore throat. It clears within an hour of having something to drink. Use a humidifier to help prevent this problem. Children with a postnasal drip from draining sinuses often have a sore throat from frequent throat-clearing.

Expected Course • Sore throats with viral illnesses usually last 3 or 4 days. Strep throat responds nicely to penicillin. After 24 hours on medication, strep is no longer contagious, and your child can return to daycare or school if the fever is gone and the child is feeling better.

CALL YOUR CHILD'S PHYSICIAN

Immediately If

- Your child is drooling or having great difficulty swallowing.

- Your child can't fully open his mouth.

- Breathing is difficult *and* not due to a stuffy nose.

- Your child is acting very sick.

During Office Hours to Make an Appointment for a Throat Culture If

• The temperature is over 101°F.

• The pain is severe.

• The sore throat has been present more than 48 hours.

• There are any swollen or tender lymph glands in the neck.

• There is any associated abdominal pain.

• There was any recent contact with a person with a strep throat or impetigo.

• Your child has a sunburned-looking rash.

• You see any yellow or white spots on the tonsils while looking at them with a light.

• You have other questions.

HOME CARE

Local Pain Relief • Older children can gargle with warm salt water (1 teaspoon salt per glass) or suck on hard candy (butterscotch seems to be a soothing flavor) as often as needed. Younger children can be given a teaspoon of corn syrup or honey periodically to soothe the throat. (Avoid giving honey under 1 year of age because of the small risk of botulism in this age group.)

Swollen tonsils can make some foods hard to swallow. Provide your child with a soft diet for a few days if it is preferred.

Fever • Acetaminophen may be given for a few days if your child has a fever over 102°F (39°C) or a great deal of throat discomfort. (For dosage, see FEVER, page 305.)

Common Mistakes

• Avoid expensive throat sprays or throat lozenges. Not only are they no more effective than hard candy, many also contain an ingredient (benzocaine) that may cause a drug reaction.

• Avoid using leftover antibiotics from siblings or friends. These should be thrown out because they deteriorate faster than other drugs. Unfortunately, antibiotics only help strep throats. They have no effect on viruses, and they can cause harm. They also make it difficult to find out what is wrong if your child becomes sicker.

- Avoid rapid strep tests performed in shopping malls or at home. These tests are accurate only if positive. If they are negative, a throat culture should be performed to pick up the 20% of strep infections that the rapid tests miss. Discuss this new concern with your child's physician.

Call Your Child's Physician Later If

- A sunburned-looking rash appears.

- Breathing or swallowing becomes difficult.

- The sore throat lasts more than 48 hours (without major improvement).

- A fever (over 101°F) occurs.

RELATED TOPIC

CANKER SORES (see page 452)

SWALLOWING DIFFICULTY (DYSPHAGIA)

Difficulty in swallowing is usually due to a sore throat or mouth ulcers in a child too young to tell us what's happening. However, it can be caused by some serious conditions.

CALL YOUR CHILD'S PHYSICIAN

Immediately If

- Your child is having any difficulty breathing.

- Your child has croup.

- Your child is drooling saliva and unable to swallow anything.

- This could be a reaction to a food, drug, or insect sting.

- A foreign object or bone could possibly be caught in the throat.

- Your child could have swallowed some acid, alkali, or other poison.

- Your child can't fully open his mouth.

- Your child has not urinated in more than 8 hours.

- Your child is acting very sick.

During Office Hours If

• You do not know the cause of your child's swallowing difficulty.

RELATED TOPICS

CANKER SORES (see page 452)
SORE THROAT (see page 457)

TEETHING

Teething is the normal process of new teeth working their way through the gums. The first teeth normally erupt between 6 and 10 months of age in the lower jaw. Most children have completely painless teething. The only symptoms are increased saliva, drooling, and a desire to chew on things. Teething occasionally causes some mild gum pain, but not enough to interfere with sleep. Your child won't be miserable from teething. When the back teeth (molars) come through (6 to 12 years old), the overlying gum may become bruised and swollen (an eruption hematoma). This is harmless and temporary.

Usually the primary (baby) tooth falls out before the corresponding permanent tooth erupts. Occasionally both teeth are temporarily present. As long as the baby tooth is a little loose, everything should go well. Have your child wiggle the baby tooth each day. The permanent tooth will find its way to the correct position once the baby tooth is out. If the primary tooth is still in place after 1 month of rocking, go to your child's dentist.

HOME CARE

Gum Massage • Find the irritated or swollen gum. Vigorously massage it with your finger for 2 minutes. Do this as often as necessary. If you wish, you may use a piece of ice to massage the gum.

Teething Rings • Your baby's way of massaging the gums is to chew on a smooth, hard object. Solid teething rings and ones with liquid in the center (as long as it's purified water) are fine. Most children like them cold. A wet washcloth placed in the freezer for 30 minutes will please many infants.

Your child may also like some ice, a Popsicle, or a frozen

banana (cut it into pieces first). Avoid hard foods that your baby might choke on (like raw carrots), but teething biscuits are fine.

Diet • Avoid salty or acid foods. Your baby probably will enjoy sucking on a nipple, but if that seems to cause pain, use a cup for fluids temporarily. A few babies may need acetaminophen for pain relief for a few days.

Common Mistakes

• Teething does not cause fever, sleep problems, diarrhea, diaper rash, or lowered resistance to any infection. It probably doesn't cause crying. If your baby develops fever while teething, the fever is due to something else, so refer to the guideline on FEVER, page 305.

• Special teething gels and lotions are unnecessary. Since many contain benzocaine, there is a risk that they may cause choking due to numbing the throat or a drug reaction.

• Don't tie the teething ring around the neck. It could catch on something and strangle your child.

TONSIL AND ADENOID SURGERY

Surgical removal of the tonsils and adenoids (known as a T&A) is the most common operation performed on children in our country (400,000 per year). It has been described as "an American ritual." While as many as 30 percent of children in some communities undergo a T&A, only 2 or 3 percent of children have adequate medical indications for this procedure. Although the decision to proceed is a medical one, the frequency of questionable surgery means that parents need to be armed with more facts.

The tonsils are not just some worthless pieces of tissue that block our view of the throat. They have a purpose. They produce antibodies that fight nose and throat infections. They confine the infection to the throat, rather than allowing it to spread to the neck or bloodstream. Other beneficial functions of the tonsils and adenoids are under study.

RISKS OF A T&A

T&A procedures are not without risk. Under ideal conditions, the death rate is still 1 child per 15,000 operations. Approximately 5 percent of children bleed on the fifth to eighth postoperative day and require a transfusion or additional surgery. All the children experience throat discomfort for several days. Some children with previously normal speech develop hypernasal speech because the soft palate no longer closes completely. In addition, the operation is expensive (costing $1,500 per patient).

ERRONEOUS REASONS FOR A T&A

Many T&A's are performed for the following unwarranted reasons. By all means, don't pressure a physician to remove your child's tonsils. A few physicians have difficulty saying no. You can always find someone to perform surgery on your child; in fact, this is the main risk of "doctor shopping."

"Large Tonsils" • Large tonsils do not mean "bad" tonsils or "infected" tonsils. The tonsils are normally large during childhood (called "physiological hypertrophy"). They can't be "too large" unless they touch each other. The peak size is reached between 8 and 12 years of age. Thereafter, they spontaneously shrink in size each year, as do all of the body's lymph tissues.

Recurrent Colds and Viral Sore Throats • Several studies have shown that T&A's do not decrease the frequency of viral upper respiratory infections. These URIs are unavoidable. Eventually your child develops immunity to these viruses and experiences fewer colds per year.

Recurrent Strep Throats • Newer studies have shown that the frequency of streptococcal infections of the throat do not decrease after the tonsils are removed unless your child experiences 7 or more per year (a rare occurrence). In children with 7 or more severe throat infections per year, some physicians would recommend daily penicillin for 6 months instead of a T&A, since penicillin can almost always eradicate the strep bacteria from the tonsils. The strep carrier state (which causes no symptoms, is harmless, and is not contagious) is not an indication for a T&A.

Recurrent Ear Infections • While formerly controversial, newer studies have shown that removal of the adenoids will not open the Eustachian tube and decrease the frequency of ear infections or fluid in the middle ear. The exceptions are children who also have persistent nasal obstruction and mouth breathing due to large adenoids. Recurrent ear infections usually respond to a 3-month course of antibiotics. Persistent middle-ear fluid may need ventilation tubes inserted in the eardrums.

School Absence • If your child misses school for vague reasons (including sore throats), removing the tonsils will not improve attendance. (See SCHOOL REFUSAL OR PHOBIA, page 293.)

Miscellaneous Conditions • A T&A will not help a poor appetite, hay fever, asthma, febrile convulsions, or bad breath. There is little in medicine that has not at one time or another been blamed on the tonsils.

MEDICAL INDICATIONS FOR A T&A

Yes, sometimes the tonsils should come out. But the benefits must outweigh the risks. All of the following valid reasons are rare, with the exception of the first two. The ear, nose, and throat doctor will decide if the tonsils, adenoids, or both need removal.

Persistent Mouth-Breathing • Mouth-breathing during colds or hay fever is common. Continued mouth breathing is less common and deserves an evaluation to see if it is due to large adenoids. The open-mouth appearance results in teasing, and the mouth breathing itself leads to changes in the facial bone structure (including an overbite which could need orthodontia).

Abnormal Speech • The speech can be muffled by large tonsils or made hyponasal (no nasal resonance) by large adenoids. Although other causes are possible, an evaluation is in order.

Severe Snoring • Snoring can have many causes. If the adenoids are the cause, they should be removed. In severe cases, the loud snoring is associated with retractions (pulling in of the spaces between the ribs) and is interrupted by 30- to 60-second bouts of stopped breathing (sleep apnea).

Heart Failure • Rarely, large tonsils and adenoids interfere so much with breathing that blood oxygen is reduced, and the right side of the heart goes into failure. Children with this condition are short of breath, have limited exercise tolerance, and have a rapid pulse.

Persistent Swallowing Difficulties • During a throat infection, the tonsils may temporarily swell enough to cause swallowing problems. If the problem is persistent and the tonsils are seen to be touching, an evaluation is in order. This problem usually occurs in children with a small mouth to begin with.

Recurrent Abscess (Deep Infection) of the Tonsil • Your child's physician will make this decision.

Recurrent Abscess of a Lymph Node Draining the Tonsil • Your child's physician will make this decision.

Suspected Tumor of the Tonsil • These rare tumors cause one tonsil to be much larger than the other. The tonsil is also quite firm to the touch, and usually enlarged lymph nodes are found on the same side of the neck.

CALL YOUR CHILD'S PHYSICIAN DURING OFFICE HOURS IF

• You think your child has a valid indication for a T&A.

• You have other questions.

(*Remember:* Do not give permission for a T&A unless your child has one of the preceding indicators or until you have received a second opinion from another physician.)

TOOTHACHE

If your child complains of a painful tooth, it may just be a temporarily sensitive tooth, but usually it means decay or a cavity is present. One complication of a decaying tooth is a gumboil just below the gumline. The infection in the tooth may also spread to the face (giving a swollen cheek) or the lymph node just under the jawbone. Dental decay must be treated in both the baby and permanent teeth. Unchecked cavities in primary teeth not only cause pain, they also can damage the underlying permanent teeth.

CALL YOUR CHILD'S DENTIST

Immediately If

• The pain is very severe.

• Fever (over 100°F) is present.

• The face is swollen.

During Office Hours If

• The pain has been present for more than 24 hours.

• You can see a brown cavity in the painful tooth.

• There is a red (occasionally yellow) bump at the gumline of the painful tooth.

• You have other questions.

HOME CARE

Flossing • First use dental floss on either side of the painful tooth. The removal of a jammed piece of food may bring quick relief.

Pain Relief Medicines • For now, treat the toothache with aspirin or acetaminophen. If the pain lasts for more than 24 hours or becomes severe, call your dentist. For severe toothaches, use dextromethorphan or codeine, if you have a cough syrup containing them. (For dosage, see COUGH, page 469.) An ice pack on the jaw may also help.

Oil of Cloves for Severe Toothache • If you cannot see a dentist for several days and an open cavity is visible: Clean all food out of the cavity with a toothpick, Water Pik, or water in a syringe. Buy some oil of cloves (80 percent eugenol) at a pharmacy; no prescription is needed. Place a few drops of the oil of cloves into the open pit, keeping in mind that it has no effect if applied to the tooth's surface. If the cavity is large, pack it with a small piece of cotton soaked with oil of cloves. Try to keep the oil of cloves off the tongue, because it stings. The cavity can also be temporarily sealed with melted candle wax. Just rub it in with your fingertip.

Call Your Child's Physician Later If

• You can't reach your dentist and it's an emergency.

RELATED TOPIC

TOOTH DECAY PREVENTION (page 117)

LUNGS (RESPIRATORY)

BREATHING, NOISY

CALL YOUR CHILD'S PHYSICIAN IMMEDIATELY IF

- Your child has serious and sudden difficulty in breathing. (See also BREATHING DIFFICULTY, SEVERE, page 26.)

- Wheezing is present. (See also WHEEZING, page 480.) Wheezing is a high-pitched meowing or whistling sound produced during breathing-out (expiration).

TYPES OF NONEMERGENCY NOISY BREATHING
Keep in mind that noisy breathing is due to vibrations set up somewhere in the airway (nose, throat, vocal cords, or chest).

Croup • Croup, or stridor, gives a harsh, vibrating sound on breathing-in (inspiration) and is associated with a brassy, tight, hoarse cough. (See the guideline on CROUP, page 474.)

Rattling Sounds • Rattling sounds are due to mucus pooling in the lower throat. These gurgling sounds can be eliminated by coughing or swallowing. Many parents are needlessly concerned about a rattly chest. (See the guideline on COUGH, page 469.)

Snorting Sounds • Intermittent snorting sounds are due to mucus partially blocking the nasal passages. If the snorting makes your child uncomfortable, the problem can be eliminated by warm water nosedrops and nasal suction. (See the guideline on COLDS, page 435.) Increased humidity in the home will also help prevent dried secretions. During the first year of life, many babies normally make nasal sounds off and on during sleep simply because the nasal passages are so narrow. Since the sounds do not interfere with sleep, no treatment is necessary.

Snoring • Nightly snorting sounds (snoring) can be caused by partial obstruction of the nose or throat during sleep. The most common cause in children is large tonsils and adenoids. Call your child's physician during office hours. Observe your child during sleep so you can report whether or not cyanosis (bluish lips), retractions (pulling in of the spaces between the ribs), and temporary interruptions (arrests) of breathing occur during snoring.

CHEST PAIN

Your child may complain of pain in the chest. Most chest pain is associated with a hacking cough. Coughing can cause sore muscles in the chest wall, upper abdomen, or diaphragm. Occasionally, chest pain follows strenuous exercise or work, and these harmless muscle cramps last 5 to 10 minutes. Heart disease is hardly ever the cause of chest pain in children.

CALL YOUR CHILD'S PHYSICIAN
Immediately If

• The pain is very severe.

• The breathing is difficult or fast.

• The pain prevents taking a deep breath.

• Your child is acting very sick.

During Office Hours If

• Coughing is also present.

• Fever (over 100°F) is present.

• The pain followed a direct blow to the chest.

• The pain is unexplained *and* has lasted more than 12 hours.

- Chest pains are a recurrent problem for your child.

- You have other questions.

HOME CARE

Treatment • Treat the chest pains with local heat. They will probably clear. Avoid aspirin for now, so we can see what happens without painkillers. If the pain is due to coughing, begin a cough suppressant medicine while waiting to talk with your physician. (See the guideline on COUGH, page 000.)

Call Your Child's Physician Later If

- The pains last more than 24 hours on treatment.

- You feel your child is getting worse.

RELATED TOPIC

COUGH (below)

CONGESTION, RESPIRATORY

Congestion means many things to different people. One of the following guidelines will probably meet your needs:

BREATHING, NOISY (see page 467)
COLDS (see page 435)
COUGH (see below)
EAR CONGESTION (see page 421)
SINUS CONGESTION (see page 447)

COUGH

SYMPTOMS AND CHARACTERISTICS

- The cough reflex expels air from the lungs with a sudden explosive noise

- Cough can be dry and hacky or wet and productive

- A coughing spasm is more than 5 minutes of continuous coughing

Similar Conditions • If one of the following is suspected, save time by turning directly to that guideline:

CROUP (see page 474)
WHEEZING (see page 480)

Causes • Keep in mind that coughing has a purpose: It clears the lungs and protects them from pneumonia.

Most coughs are due to a viral infection of the trachea (windpipe) and bronchi (larger air passages). This is called acute bronchitis and can be part of a cold. Most children get this a couple of times a year.

While coughs may be associated with sinus infections, they are not due to postnasal drip. People swallow while they are asleep, so secretions don't pool in the throat.

The role of milk in thickening the secretions is also doubtful, except for the 1 to 2 percent of infants with proven milk allergy.

Expected Course • Usually bronchitis gives a dry tickly cough that lasts for 2 to 3 weeks. Sometimes it becomes loose (wet) for a few days, and your child coughs up a lot of phlegm (mucus). This is usually a sign that the end of the illness is near.

CALL YOUR CHILD'S PHYSICIAN

Immediately If

• Your child is less than 1 month old.

• Breathing is difficult *and* not better after you clear the nose.

• The respirations are fast or labored (when your child is not coughing).

• Your child has passed out with coughing spasms.

• The lips have turned bluish with coughing spasms.

• Any blood-tinged sputum has been coughed up.

• A toy, food, or other foreign object could possibly be caught in the windpipe (especially likely if the cough came on suddenly after a choking episode *and* your child is under 3 years old).

• Your child is acting very sick.

During Office Hours If

- A fever (over 100°F) has lasted more than 72 hours.

- The cough has been present for more than 3 weeks.

- Your child is 1 to 3 months old *and* the cough has been present for more than 72 hours.

- The cause could be an allergy (like pollen).

- Your child also has sinus congestion.

- Coughing spasms cause lots of lost sleep.

- The coughing has caused vomiting 3 or more times.

- The coughing has caused bad chest pains.

- The cough has caused your child to miss 3 or more days of school.

- You have other questions.

HOME CARE FOR COUGH

Cough-Loosening Medicines

Cough Drops • Most coughs in children over age 4 can be controlled by sucking on cough drops freely.

Homemade Cough Syrup • Children under age 4 can be given a teaspoon of honey or corn syrup instead. (Avoid giving honey to babies under 1 year of age, because of the small risk of botulism for this age group.)

Warm Liquids • Warm liquids usually relax the airway. Start with warm lemonade, warm apple cider, or warm tea. Avoid adding any alcohol, because of the aggravation of the cough as the fumes of alcohol are inhaled into the lungs, and also the risk of intoxication from unintentional overdosage.

Cough-Suppressant Medicines • Since the cough reflex protects the lungs, cough-suppressant drugs are given in a dosage to reduce (but not eliminate) coughing. They are indicated only for dry coughs (nonproductive of mucus) that interfere with sleep, school attendance, or work. They also help children who have chest pain from coughing spasms. They should not be given to infants under 12 months of age or for wet productive coughs.

A nonprescription cough suppressant is dextromethorphan (DM). Ask your pharmacist for help in choosing a brand that contains DM without any other active ingredients. Dosage is 0.2 mg per pound of body weight, every 4 to 6 hours as needed. It usually comes as a liquid in a strength of 15 mg per teaspoon. DM is also available as a cough lozenge for easy carrying and as a long-acting (12 hour) liquid.

20-pound child	can take	4 mg of DM
30-pound child	can take	6 mg of DM
4–6 years	can take	7.5 mg of DM
7–11 years	can take	15 mg of DM
Adults	can take	30 mg of DM

Often corn syrup or honey can be given during the day, and DM given at bedtime and during the night.

Cold Mist Humidifiers • Dry air tends to make coughs worse. Dry coughs can be loosened up by encouraging a good fluid intake and using a humidifier in your child's bedroom. Don't add medicine to the water in the humidifier, because it irritates the cough in some children. The new ultrasonic humidifers not only have the advantage of quietness, they also kill molds and most bacteria that might be in the water.

Postural Drainage for Coughing Spasms • Some coughing spasms are due to choking on lung mucus that comes up and sticks to the vocal cords. If your child is under 3 years old and coughing up lots of mucus at night, try to improve matters by giving postural drainage at bedtime. Start by having your child breathe in warm mist from a wet washcloth over the face or a humidifier. Have your child lie stomach down on your outstretched legs, with the head lower than the rest of the body. Then gently pat your child on the back of the rib cage, working from the lower back to the shoulders. Do this for 10 minutes, and expect some productive coughing.

Vomiting with Coughing Spasms • Refeed your child after this type of vomiting. Offer smaller amounts with each feeding to reduce the chances of repeated vomiting.

Smoking and Exercise • Since tobacco smoke agitates coughing, don't let anyone smoke around your coughing child. Better yet, try to protect your child from all passive smoking. If one parent smokes in the house, that's equivalent to your child actively smoking 30 to 40 cigarettes per year. Remind the teenager who smokes that his or her cough may last weeks longer than it normally would without smoking.

Teenagers will find that required gym and exercise trigger coughing spasms when they have bronchitis. If so, these activities should be avoided temporarily.

Common Mistakes • Antihistamines, decongestants, and antipyretics are found in many cough syrups. These ingredients have no impact on coughs, but they can have side effects. Antihistamines are illogical for productive coughs, because they dry secretions and make them harder to cough up. While the expectorants are safe, they have recently been shown to be ineffective. Stay with the simple remedies mentioned previously, or give DM for severe coughs. Keep in mind that prescription cough medicines (unless they contain codeine) offer no advantage over nonprescription ones.

Milk does not need to be eliminated from the diet, since most sick babies want their formula, and restricting it rarely improves the cough.

Raising the head of the bed is of questionable value, since more coughing is caused by lung mucus than nasal mucus.

Lastly, physicians can usually evaluate coughs and exclude pneumonia without a chest X-ray (so don't expect one).

Call Your Child's Physician Later If

• Breathing becomes labored or difficult.

• Coughing spasms cause passing out or bluish lips.

• Coughing spasms cause exhaustion or lost sleep.

• Coughing spasms occur continuously for more than 1 hour.

• Any fever lasts more than 72 hours.

• The cough lasts more than 3 weeks.

• The cough causes your child to miss 3 or more days of school.

• You feel your child is getting worse.

CROUP (CROUPY COUGH AND STRIDOR)

SYMPTOMS AND CHARACTERISTICS OF CROUPY COUGH

- A special cough that occurs with infections of the voice box (larynx)
- The cough is tight, metallic, and like a barking seal
- The voice is usually hoarse

SYMPTOMS AND CHARACTERISTICS OF STRIDOR

- A harsh, vibrating sound during inspiration
- Breathing-in is very difficult
- Usually only present with crying or coughing
- As the disease becomes worse, the stridor occurs continuously

Similar Conditions to Croup • WHEEZING (see page 480)—a high-pitched meowing or whistling sound produced during expiration. If this is what your child has, call your physician immediately.

Cause • Croup is a viral infection of the vocal cords. It is usually part of a cold. The hoarseness is due to swelling of the vocal cords. Stridor occurs as the opening between the vocal cords becomes more narrow.

Expected Course • Croup usually lasts for 5 to 6 days and generally gets worse at night. During that time, it can change from mild to severe many times.

FIRST AID FOR ATTACKS OF STRIDOR WITH CROUP

If your child suddenly develops stridor or tight breathing, do the following:

Inhalation of Warm Mist • Warm, moist air seems to work best to relax the vocal cords and break the stridor. The simplest way to provide this is to have your child breathe through a warm, wet washcloth placed loosely over the nose and mouth. Another good way, if you have a humidifier (not a hot vaporizer), is to fill it with warm water (a little warmer than body temperature) and have your child put his or her face in the stream of humidity and breathe deeply through an open mouth.

The Foggy Bathroom • In the meantime, have the hot shower running with the bathroom door closed. Once the room is all fogged up, take your child in there for at least 10 minutes. Try to allay fears by cuddling your child and reading a story. Fear and crying make croup worse. If the crying can be stopped, the breathing will be easier.

If the house is closed up, an occasional child will do better if taken outside for 5 minutes. Why the fresh air should break the stridor remains a mystery.

Results of First Aid • Most children settle down with the above treatments and then sleep peacefully through the night. If the stridor continues in your child, call your physician immediately.

CALL YOUR PHYSICIAN (AND ALSO BEGIN THE FIRST AID FOR STRIDOR, ABOVE)

Immediately If

- Your child is drooling or having great difficulty swallowing.

- Your child can't bend the neck forward.

- Your child has passed out. (Also call the Rescue Squad.)

- The stridor is present constantly.

- Breathing is difficult.

- There are any retractions (tugging in) between the ribs.

- The lips are bluish or dusky.

- Your child is constantly uncomfortable.

- Your child has been unable to sleep.

- Coughing spasms occur continuously for over 1 hour.

- A toy or other small foreign object could be caught in the windpipe.

- The croup started suddenly after taking a medicine or being stung by an insect.

- Your child is acting very sick.

During Office Hours If

• Your child is under 1 year old.

• The attacks of stridor are occurring more than 3 times a day.

• The fluid intake is poor.

• A fever (over 104°F) is present.

• You have other questions.

HOME CARE FOR A CROUPY COUGH

Mist • Keep the child's room humidified. Use a cool mist humidifier if you have one. Have it run 24 hours a day. Be sure to empty and wash the container with soap and water every day. Don't add any camphor or menthol oils to the water, because they are irritating to the cough in most children. If you don't own a humidifier, hang wet sheets or towels in your child's room.

Increase Fluid Intake • Encourage your child to drink more than usual. Clear fluids (ones you can see through) are the best. Warm fluids help relax the vocal cords and may help clear stridor occuring with coughing spells.

Cough Medicines • Medicines are less helpful than either mist or increased fluid intake. Older children can be given cough drops for the cough, and younger children can be given some corn syrup. Avoid strong cough medicines (like codeine) which could suppress the brain's respiratory center and interfere with keeping the lungs clear. If your child has a fever (over 102°F) you may give him acetaminophen. (See FEVER, page 305, for dosage.)

Close Observation • While your child is croupy, sleep in the same room temporarily. Croup can be a dangerous disease. By all means, don't let anyone smoke around your child; smoke can make croup worse.

CALL YOUR CHILD'S PHYSICIAN IMMEDIATELY IF

• Breathing becomes difficult.

• The lips turn bluish.

• Your child is drooling or having great difficulty swallowing.

- Your child is unable to sleep because of the croup.

- The warm mist fails to clear the stridor in 20 minutes.

- You feel your child is getting worse.

RELATED TOPICS

CHOKING (see page 9)
COUGH (see page 469)

HOARSENESS

SYMPTOMS AND CHARACTERISTICS

- The voice is raspy

- If hoarseness is severe, your child can do little more than whisper

- A cough is often associated

Similar Conditions • If appropriate, turn directly to the following guidelines:

CROUP (see page 474)
HAY FEVER (see page 442)

Causes • Hoarseness is usually caused by a cold or croup virus (laryngitis) or overuse of the vocal cords (e.g., shouting or screaming). Cheerleaders and avid sports fans are prone.

Expected Course • Hoarseness usually lasts 1 to 2 weeks. Repeated vocal cord abuse can cause thickening of the cords and a slow recovery.

CALL YOUR CHILD'S PHYSICIAN

Immediately If

- Breathing is difficult.

- A toy, food, or other foreign object could possibly be caught in the windpipe.

- Your child choked on anything recently.

During Office Hours If

- Your child is under 2 months old.
- The hoarseness has been present more than 2 weeks.
- You have other questions.

HOME CARE FOR HOARSENESS

Treatment • Have your child gargle with warm salt water and suck on hard candy or cough drops several times a day. Younger children can sip warm liquids like apple juice. Encourage your child to rest the voice and avoid the vocal strain that comes from yelling and screaming. Encourage your child to talk as little as possible for a few days. If the hoarseness gets really bad, have your child whisper or write notes. Also run a humidifier in your child's bedroom.

Call Your Child's Physician Later If

- The hoarseness gets worse.
- The hoarseness lasts more than 2 weeks.

INFLUENZA

Influenza is a viral infection of the nose, throat, trachea, and bronchi that occurs in epidemics every 3 or 4 years (e.g., Asian influenza). The main symptoms are a stuffy nose, sore throat, and nagging cough. There may be more muscle pain, headache, and fever than with usual colds. Spread is rapid because the incubation period is only 24 to 36 hours. Influenza is usually just a "bad" cold. The dangers of influenza for normal healthy people (under 65 years of age) are overrated.

WHEN TO CALL YOUR CHILD'S PHYSICIAN

See the guidelines on fever, cough, colds, sore throat, sinus congestion, earache, and so forth. Ear infections and pneumonia are the most common complications.

HOME CARE FOR INFLUENZA

The treatment of influenza depends on your child's main symptoms and is no different from that suggested for other viral respiratory infections.

Fever or Aches • Use acetaminophen every 4 to 6 hours. (See FEVER, page 305, for dosage.) Aspirin should be avoided in children with suspected influenza because of the possible link with Reyes syndrome.

Cough or Hoarseness • Cough drops for children over 4 years of age and corn syrup for younger children should help. (See the guidelines on COUGH, page 469, or HOARSENESS, page 477.)

Sore Throat • Salt water gargles and soft diet should help. (See the guideline on SORE THROAT, page 457.)

Stuffy Nose • Warm water nose drops and suction (or nose blowing) will open most blocked noses. Vasoconstrictor nose drops or spray may be added for resistant ones. (See the guideline on COLDS, page 435.)

INFLUENZA VACCINE AND PREVENTION

Influenza vaccine gives protection for only 1 or 2 years. In addition, the vaccine itself can cause fever and a sore arm. Therefore the vaccine is not recommended for healthy children (unless an especially severe form of influenza comes along).

However, children over 6 months of age with the following conditions have a high complication rate from influenza (especially pneumonia) and need to visit the physician's office during the fall for yearly influenza boosters. During influenza Type A epidemics, these same children may be helped by taking an oral antiviral drug called amantadine for 2 weeks until the vaccine takes effect.

- Lung disease (e.g., asthma, cystic fibrosis, bronchopulmonary dysplasia)

- Heart disease (e.g., congenital heart disease, rheumatic heart disease)

- Muscle disease (e.g., muscular dystrophy)

- Metabolic disease (e.g., diabetes mellitus)

- Renal disease (e.g., nephrotic syndrome)

- Malignant and immunodeficient diseases

- Diseases requiring longterm aspirin therapy.

(*Exception:* Children allergic to eggs should not receive this vaccine.)

WHEEZING

SYMPTOMS AND CHARACTERISTICS
Wheezing is a high-pitched meowing or whistling sound produced during breathing-out (expiration).

Similar Conditions • Some other respiratory sounds can be confused with wheezing. If one of the following is suspected, save time by turning directly to that guideline:

- CROUP (see page 474) or stridor gives a harsh, vibrating sound on breathing-in (inspiration) and is associated with a hoarse, metallic, tight cough.

- Snorting sounds are due to mucus partially blocking the nasal passages. These sounds can be eliminated by warm water nose drops and nasal suction. (See the guideline on COLDS, page 435.)

- Rattling sounds are due to mucus in the lower throat. These sounds can be eliminated by coughing or swallowing.

WHEN TO CALL YOUR CHILD'S PHYSICIAN
If your child definitely has wheezing, call your child's physician immediately. Although there are many causes of wheezing, it can be an emergency situation. Let your physician help you sort out what is going on.

ABDOMEN (GASTROINTESTINAL)

ABDOMINAL PAIN

SYMPTOM

- Your child complains that his stomach (abdomen) hurts

Similar Condition • For babies under 3 months old with fussy crying, see CRYING BABY (COLIC), page 124.

Causes • The causes are numerous. Usually it's something simple like overeating, gas pains from too much soda pop, or other types of indigestion. Sometimes it signals the onset of a viral gastroenteritis, and vomiting or diarrhea soon follow. Recurrent stomachaches deserve a medical evaluation.

Expected Course • With harmless causes, the pain is usually better or resolved in 2 hours. With gastroenteritis, belly cramps may precede each bout of vomiting or stooling. With serious causes (such as appendicitis) the pain worsens and becomes constant.

CALL YOUR CHILD'S PHYSICIAN

Immediately If

- The pain is very severe.
- The pain is constant *and* has lasted more than 2 hours.
- Your child walks bent over or holding the abdomen.

- Your child is lying down and refuses to walk.

- Your child is under 2 years old.

- The pain is in the scrotum or testicle.

- Any blood has appeared in the bowel movements.

- Poisoning with a plant, medicine, or chemical is a possibility.

- The abdomen was recently injured.

- Your child is acting very sick.

- When you press on your child's abdomen with your hand, the abdomen is quite tender to the touch.

During Office Hours If

- The pain comes and goes (cramps) *and* lasts more than 12 hours.

- This is a recurrent problem for your child.

- You have other questions.

HOME CARE

Treatment • Have your child lie down and rest until feeling better. A warm washcloth or heating pad on the abdomen may speed recovery. Avoid giving your child solid foods; permit only sips of clear fluids. Keep a vomiting pan handy. Younger children are especially likely to refer to nausea as "a stomachache."

Common Mistakes • Do not give any medicines for stomach cramps unless you have talked with your physician. Painkillers (like aspirin or codeine) may mask the problem. More importantly, avoid laxatives and enemas. If your child has appendicitis, these medicines could cause the appendix to rupture.

Call Your Child's Physician in 2 Hours If

- The pain is constant *and* no better.

- Call sooner if it rapidly becomes worse.

- Call in 12 hours if it's the kind of pain that comes and goes.

RELATED TOPICS
Pain with:

CONSTIPATION (see page 483)
COUGH (see page 469)
DIARRHEA (see page 488)
MENSTRUAL CRAMPS (see page 514)
URINATION (see page 407)
VOMITING (see page 502)

AMPICILLIN DIARRHEA

Ampicillin causes diarrhea in 20 to 30 percent of children receiving it, depending on the dosage. (Amoxacillin causes diarrhea less commonly.) This is an irritative reaction (i.e., ampicillin acts like a laxative), not an allergic one. The loose stools begin within a day or two of starting the antibiotic. Ampicillin diarrhea is usually mild and occasionally moderate in degree. Dehydration and weight loss do not occur. As soon as you finish the course of ampicillin, the BMs will return to normal.

HOME CARE

The ampicillin does not need to be discontinued. The diet does not need to be changed, unless you wish to cut back on foods like bran products, beans, and fresh fruits and vegetables. Sometimes the diarrhea causes a diaper rash. Wash the irritated area with water and then protect the skin with a thick layer of petroleum jelly or other ointment. Call your child's physician if you feel the ampicillin needs to be changed.

CONSTIPATION

SYMPTOMS AND CHARACTERISTICS

- Painful passage of stools. The best sign of constipation is the occurrence of pain or discomfort with the passage of a bowel movement.

- Inability to pass stools. These children feel a desperate urge to have a BM, have discomfort in the anal area, strain, but are unable to pass anything.

- Infrequent movements. Going more than 3 days without a BM can be considered constipation, even though this may cause no pain in some patients and even be normal for a few. *Exception:* After the second month or so of life, many breast-fed babies have normal, large, soft BMs at infrequent intervals (up to 7 days is normal). These are infrequent normal stools.

Common Misconceptions in Defining Constipation • Large or hard BMs unaccompanied by any of the conditions just described are usually normal variations. Some people normally have hard BMs each day without any pain. Others have large BMs every 3 days without pain. Babies less than 6 months of age commonly grunt, push, strain, draw up the legs, and become flushed in the face during passage of bowel movements. However, they don't cry. These behaviors are normal and should remind us that it takes some time for the bowels and rectum to become coordinated. Also, it is difficult to have a bowel movement while lying down. Help your straining baby by holding the knees against the chest to simulate squatting (the natural position for pushing out a BM).

Causes • Constipation is usually due to a diet deficient in fiber (found in fruits, vegetables, and whole-grain foods). Fiber is not digested and makes stools larger, softer, and easier to pass. Another common cause is repeated postponement of the urge to go because of embarrassment about school toilets, public toilets, or long waiting times for the home bathroom. If constipation begins during toilet training, the parent is usually applying too much pressure. (See the guideline on TOILET TRAINING, page 253.)

Expected Course • Constipation usually is easy to relieve with dietary changes. After your child is better, be sure to keep him or her on a high-fiber diet so that it doesn't happen again. On some occasions, the trauma to the anal canal causes an anal fissure (a small tear). This is confirmed by finding small amounts of bright-red blood on the toilet tissue or the stool surface.

CALL YOUR CHILD'S PHYSICIAN

Immediately for Advice about an Enema or Suppository If

- Your child is in extreme pain.
- Pain is constant *and* has persisted for more than 2 hours.

During Office Hours If

- More than 6 days have passed without a BM.
- You are giving suppositories or enemas.
- The anal area has any tears (fissures) that are deep or won't heal.
- Anal fissures have bled more than twice.
- Toilet training is in progress *and* there is any resistance.
- Your child soils himself.
- Constipation is a recurrent problem for your child.
- You have other questions.

HOME CARE

Diet Treatment for Babies Under 1 Year Old • For babies on only formula or breast milk, add fruit juices (like grape or prune juice) twice a day. Switching to soy formula may also give looser stools. If your baby is over 4 months old, add strained peas, beans, apricots, prunes, peaches, pears, plums, or spinach twice a day. In my experience, corn syrup usually doesn't help. (Note: If necessary, strained peas can be added to the formula of younger babies.) Avoid strained carrots, squash, bananas, and apples (foods which make some kids constipated). Also put your child in a tub with warm water several times a day to help relax the anus.

Diet Treatment for Children Over 1 Year Old

- Increase fruits/vegetables. Have your child eat fruits or vegetables high in fiber content at least 3 times a day (raw ones are best, and peelings are most helpful). Peas, beans, and dates are especially good because they are palatable and high in fiber. Other examples are prunes, figs, raisins, peaches, pears, apricots, cauliflower, broccoli, and cabbage. (Warning: Avoid any foods your child can't easily chew.)

- Increase bran. Bran is an excellent natural laxative, since it has high fiber content. Have your child eat bran daily in one of the new "natural" cereals, bran flakes, bran muffins, shredded wheat, graham crackers, oatmeal, high-fiber cookies, brown rice, or whole wheat bread. Popcorn is a high fiber food that is acceptable to most children.

- Decrease constipating foods. Milk, ice cream, cheese, white rice, applesauce, bananas, and cooked carrots are constipating and should be kept to moderate amounts.

- Increase water. Be sure your child drinks plenty of water.

- Increase carbonated fluids. The gas from soft drinks can pass quickly through the intestines and increase the sense of fullness in the rectum. School-age children can try a can of pop each day and see if it improves their frequency of BMs.

- Exercise. If your child tends to be inactive, encourage him or her to become more outgoing in the neighborhood or join a team.

Sitting on the Toilet • Encourage your child to establish a regular bowel pattern by sitting on the toilet for 10 minutes after meals, especially breakfast. If your child is resisting toilet training by holding back, temporarily discontinue the training.

Natural Laxative Medicine • If diet alone doesn't work, a good natural laxative is Maltsupex (a malt extract from barley). No prescription is needed. It comes in liquid or powder and is best mixed with any beverage. The starting dosage is:

Infants:	½ tablespoon twice daily
Children:	1 tablespoon twice daily
Adolescents:	2 tablespoons twice daily (or 2 tablets)

Another product that can be mixed with foods (such as orange juice or applesauce) is unprocessed (unmilled) bran, available in most health food stores. The starting dosage is ½ to 1 teaspoon twice daily, depending on age. Try this for one week and then only as necessary.

Treatment for Anal Fissure • Streaks or flecks of blood noted on the surface of the stool or toilet tissue indicate that your child probably has an anal fissure. Anal fissures are prevented with the diet changes already discussed and are treated with

20-minute sitz baths in warm salt water 3 times a day, followed by ½ percent hydrocortisone cream (no prescription needed). If the pain is severe, apply 2½ percent Xylocaine ointment (no prescription needed) 4 times a day for a few days to numb the area.

Common Mistakes • Don't use any suppositories or enemas without your physician's advice. These can cause irritation or fissures (tears) of the anus, resulting in pain and stool holding. Do not use strong laxatives by mouth without asking your physician, because they can cause cramps and become somewhat habit-forming. Keep in mind that constipation will probably become a recurrent problem if the dietary changes aren't continued.

Enemas for Acute Constipation • If your child has acute rectal pain needing immediate relief and your physician has given you clearance, proceed with the following: A glycerine suppository, a gentle rectal dilation with a lubricated finger (covered with plastic wrap), or a normal saline enema will usually provide quick relief. Enemas with soapsuds, hydrogen peroxide, or tap water are dangerous. The normal saline enema is made by adding 2 teaspoons of table salt to a quart of water and is given lukewarm. Your child should lie on the stomach with knees pulled under. The enema tube should be lubricated and inserted 1½ to 2 inches. The enema fluid should be delivered gradually by gravity, with the enema bag no more than 2 feet above the level of the anus. Your child should hold the enema until a strong need to defecate is felt (2 to 10 minutes). If you do not have an enema apparatus, you can use a rubber bulb syringe. The amount of normal saline for different ages is:

1 year:	4 ounces
1–3 years:	6 ounces
3–6 years:	8 ounces
6–12 years:	12 ounces
Adolescents and Adults:	16 ounces

Call Your Child's Physician Later If

• Cramps or pains last more than 2 hours.

• 3 days on this dietary approach does not bring a BM.

- BMs continue to cause pain.

- Anal fissures bleed 3 or more times.

- You feel your child is getting worse.

RELATED TOPIC

STOOLS, BLOOD IN (see page 499)

DIARRHEA

SYMPTOMS AND CHARACTERISTICS

Diarrhea is the sudden increase in the frequency and loose-ness of bowel movements. Mild diarrhea is the passage of a few loose or mushy stools. Moderate diarrhea gives many watery stools. The best indicator of the severity of the diarrhea is its frequency. A green stool also points to a very rapid passage and moderate to severe diarrhea. Keeping your child on nothing but clear fluids for more than 2 days can cause green, watery BMs ("starvation stools").

Causes • Diarrhea is usually caused by a viral infection of the intestines (gastroenteritis). Occasionally it is caused by bacteria. If only 1 or 2 loose stools are passed, the cause often turns out to be something unusual your child ate ("indigestion"). Remember that diarrhea is the body's way of purging itself of harmful organisms until it can build up immunity to them.

Expected Course • Diarrhea stools usually last from several days to a week, regardless of the type of treatment. The main goal of therapy is to prevent dehydration (excessive water loss) by giving enough oral fluids to keep up with the fluids lost in the diarrhea. Don't expect a quick return to solid stools. Since 1 loose stool can mean nothing, don't start dietary changes until there have been at least two.

CALL YOUR CHILD'S PHYSICIAN

Immediately If

- Your child has not urinated in more than 8 hours.

- Crying produces no tears.

- The mouth is dry rather than moist.
- Any blood appears in the diarrhea.
- Severe abdominal cramps are present.
- More than 8 diarrhea stools have occurred in the last 8 hours.
- The diarrhea is watery *and* your child has vomited clear fluids 3 or more times.
- Your child is acting very sick.

If your child has vomited more than once, turn directly to the guideline on VOMITING, page 502. The treatment of vomiting takes priority over the treatment of diarrhea, until your child has gone 8 hours without vomiting.

During Office Hours If

- Mucus or pus is present in the stools.
- The diarrhea has caused loss of bowel control in a toilet-trained child.
- Your child was exposed to someone with bacterial diarrhea (especially in foreign travel).
- Abdominal cramps come and go for more than 12 hours.
- A fever (over 100°F) has been present for more than 72 hours.
- Your child is on any medicines that could cause diarrhea.
- The diarrhea has been present for more than 1 week.
- Diarrhea is a recurrent problem for your child.
- You have other questions.

HOME CARE

Dietary changes are the mainstay of home treatment for diarrhea. The optimal diet depends on your child's age and the severity of the diarrhea. There are 5 basic scenarios—go directly to the part that pertains to your child.

Diet Treatment for *Mild* Diarrhea (Mushy Stools) in Children *Under 2 Years Old* • Give extra fluids by mixing your baby's formula or milk with 1 or 2 ounces of extra water per bottle. If your baby is on solids, offer only applesauce, strained bananas, strained carrots (the ABCs) and rice for the next few days. Avoid other foods temporarily.

Diet Treatment for *Moderate* Diarrhea (Watery or Frequent Stools) in Children *Under 1 Year Old*

Clear Fluids for 24 Hours • Have your baby take one of the following special clear fluids (oral rehydration solutions) for the first 24 hours: Lytren, Pedialyte, Resol, or Infalyte. These are available without a prescription in most pharmacies and supermarkets. Until you obtain this special solution, Gatorade or Jell-O water can be used. Jell-O water must be mixed one package per quart of water (twice as much water as usual). Don't use any red-colored Jell-O water, since it can look like blood. Give as much of the liquid as your baby wants. Diarrhea makes children thirsty and your job is to prevent dehydration. Never restrict fluids in diarrhea. (If none of these are available, temporarily use a homemade mixture of ½ level teaspoon of table salt and 5 teaspoons of sugar to 1 quart of water. Be careful not to add too much salt.)

Soy Formulas • After being on clear fluids for 6 to 24 hours, your baby will be hungry, so begin a soy formula. There is much less diarrhea with soy formulas than with cow's milk formulas because they don't contain milk sugar (lactose). Mix the formula with 1 or 2 ounces of extra water per bottle until the stools begin to look normal. Plan on keeping your baby on soy formula for at least 2 weeks. If your baby wants solids, offer only applesauce, strained bananas, strained carrots, and rice cereal with water until the diarrhea improves.

Diet Treatment for *Moderate Diarrhea* (Watery or Frequent Stools) in Children *1 to 2 Years Old* • The infant on table foods doesn't need formula or milk of any kind for the first week of diarrhea. After 24 hours on clear fluids (see the preceding section), gradually phase in the special solids detailed below. During this week, water, Kool-Aid, and soft drinks can be used for fluids. Keep in perspective that adding milk or solids at a faster rate won't harm your child in any way but will cause increased stools.

Day 1:   Clear fluids and Popsicles
             (If your toddler is hungry, add some foods from the Day 2 list.)
Day 2:   Saltine crackers, white toast with corn-oil margarine or honey, rice, applesauce, bland soups

Day 3:   Lean meats, soft-boiled eggs, noodles, and active culture yogurt

Days 4 and 5:   Soft cooked fruits and vegetables (for example: pears, carrots, potatoes)

Days 6 and 7:   Regular diet but no milk products

Day 8:   Milk and milk products can gradually be added

(Note: Avoid cheeses, which still contain 80 percent of the lactose found in milk, until day 8. By contrast, the lactose in active culture yogurt will be digested by the lactobacillus organisms present in the yogurt.)

Diet Treatment for Children *Over 2 Years Old* (With *Mild or Moderate* Diarrhea) • For the child who is toilet trained for BMs, the approach to diarrhea is the same as for any adult: namely, eat a regular diet with a few simple changes. Avoid raw fruits and vegetables, bran products, beans, spices, and any foods that can cause loose BMs. Increase the intake of water or clear fluids (ones you can see through). Reduce or eliminate the intake of milk and milk products (exception: active culture yogurt is fine). A normal diet can be resumed one day after the diarrhea is gone, which is usually in 3 or 4 days.

Diet Treatment for *Breast-feeding Babies* with Any Diarrhea

Special Considerations • No matter how it looks, the stool of the breast-fed infant must be considered normal unless it contains mucus or blood or develops a bad odor. In fact, breast-fed babies can normally pass some green stools. Frequency of movements is also not much help. During the first 2 or 3 months of life, the breast-fed baby may normally have as many stools as one after each feeding. The presence of something in the mother's diet that causes rapid passage should always be considered in these babies (e.g., coffee, cola, or herbal teas). Diarrhea can be diagnosed if your baby's stools abruptly increase in number. Additional clues are if your baby feeds poorly, acts sick, or develops a fever.

Treatment • If your breast-fed baby has diarrhea, treatment is straightforward. Breast-feeding should never be discontinued because of mild to moderate diarrhea. The only treatment necessary is to offer extra water between breast-feedings. Breast-feeding may have to be temporarily discontinued if your baby requires hospitalization for severe diarrhea and dehydration. Pump your breasts to maintain milk flow until nursing can be restarted (usually within 1 day).

Common Mistakes in Treating Diarrhea • Using boiled skim milk or any concentrated solution can cause serious complications for babies with diarrhea, because they contain too much salt. Kool-Aid, soda pop, or rice water should not be used as the only food because they contain little or no salt. Fruit juices (especially apple and grape) should be avoided because they are too concentrated and can pull water out of the baby. Use only the clear fluids mentioned.

By 24 hours, add formula or solids to the diet, because your baby needs more calories than clear fluids alone can provide (that is, avoid starvation).

The most dangerous myth is that the intestine should be "put to rest"; restricting fluids can cause dehydration.

Keep in mind that there is no effective, safe drug for diarrhea and that extra water and diet therapy work best.

Diaper Rash from Diarrhea • The skin near your baby's anus can become "burned" from digestive enzymes and other chemicals found in the diarrhea stools. Wash it off after each BM and then protect it with a thick layer of petroleum jelly or other ointment. This protective shield is especially needed during the night and during naps. Changing the diaper quickly after BMs also helps.

Overflow Diarrhea in a Child Not Toilet Trained • For children in diapers, diarrhea can be a mess. Despite treatment, loose stools usually continue for a week. Place a cotton washcloth or a 6-inch piece of cut-up towel inside the diaper to trap some of the more watery stool. Use disposable diapers temporarily to cut down on cleanup time. Use the ones with snug leg bands or cover the other type with a pair of plastic pants. Wash your child under running water in the bath tub. Someday your child will be toilet trained.

Call Your Child's Physician Later If

• Any signs of dehydration occur.

• Your child vomits the clear fluids 3 or more times.

• The diarrhea becomes severe (such as a BM every hour for more than 8 hours).

• Any blood, pus, or mucus appears in the diarrhea.

• Abdominal pain develops and lasts more than 12 hours.

- The diarrhea does not improve after 48 hours on the special diet.

- Mild diarrhea lasts more than a week.

PREVENTION
Diarrhea is very contagious. Hand-washing after diaper changing or using the toilet is crucial for keeping everyone in the family from getting diarrhea.

FOREIGN BODY, SWALLOWED

Most swallowed nonfood solid items are coins. Fortunately, most children are given only pennies to play with, and these almost always pass with ease. Dangerous objects are pointed ones such as nails, needles, and toothpicks. Swallowed glass usually passes harmlessly.

CALL YOUR CHILD'S PHYSICIAN
Immediately If

- Your child is choking or coughing severely. (Also, turn directly to the guideline on CHOKING, page 9.)

- There is any increased salivation, drooling, gagging, or difficulty swallowing.

- There is any discomfort in the throat or chest.

- There is any abdominal pain or vomiting.

- The object was sharp.

- The object was larger than a penny.

- The object was a small button battery (as found in calculators and watches).

- You're not sure what your child swallowed.

- You have other urgent questions.

During Office Hours

In all other cases when your child has probably swallowed a foreign body. The medical evaluation of this situation is somewhat controversial.

HOME CARE

Diagnostic Trial of Eating • If no symptoms are present, give your child some water to drink. If this causes no symptoms such as gagging or pain, your child should eat some bread or other soft solid food. If this goes smoothly, the object is probably in the stomach. Swallowed foreign bodies almost always make it to the stomach, travel through the intestines, and are passed in a normal bowel movement in 3 or 4 days. There is nothing you can do to hurry it along.

Checking Bowel Movements • Normally, for small, smooth objects, bowel movements do not need to be checked. However, for sharp, long (larger than 1 inch), or valuable objects, the bowel movements should be collected and strained through a piece of screen until the object is retrieved.

Call Your Child's Physician Later If

• The stools are being checked *and* the foreign body hasn't passed in 7 days.

• Abdominal pain, vomiting, or blood stools develop in the next 2 weeks.

PREVENTION

Young children who put everything in their mouths must be protected from small objects they might inadvertently swallow. Check your floors periodically for coins, peanuts, pins, and the like. The new button-size batteries used for watches can cause intestinal damage or death if swallowed. Dispose of them carefully. Avoid pierced earrings in children under 4 years of age.

GAS, EXCESSIVE

A normal but embarrassing part of the human condition is to pass bowel gas on a daily basis. Most people also belch or burp up stomach gas occasionally. In fact, the average adult on a regular diet passes gas 10 to 20 times a day. This amounts to approximately 1 quart of gas per day. Gas should not be considered excessive unless it occurs at more than twice the normal frequency.

Causes • The main causes of normal gas are swallowed air, gas-producing foods, and certain diseases that interfere with sugar absorption. Every baby is somewhat "gassy" because of swallowing air during sucking. This process is increased by sucking on a clogged nipple, a bottle that does not have milk in it, a pacifier, the thumb, or a blanket. Babies also swallow air during crying. Children at a later age swallow air with gum-chewing. Children with nasal allergies swallow air if they are "sniffers." Some children have a nervous habit of frequent swallowing. The carbonation in soft drinks releases gas in the stomach. Stomach gas is more likely to pass into the intestines if a child is lying down. Gas (unlike food) can pass through the gastrointestinal tract in 20 minutes.

Some foods (such as beans) are made up of complex carbohydrates that are not completely digested in the small bowel. These foods are converted into gas by bacteria in the large bowel. Ingestion of beans can increase gas production tenfold.

The most common medical condition that causes increased gas production is milk intolerance. The enzyme (lactase) that normally digests milk sugar (lactose) progressively decreases in amount between ages 4 and 20 years in large segments of our population. Those most affected people are Orientals, Blacks, and Eastern Europeans. The undigested lactose is converted into hydrogen by the bacteria in the large bowel. The amount of gas produced depends upon the amount of milk ingested. Symptoms of bloating, abdominal cramps, and increased passage of gas usually don't occur until a person drinks more than 1 quart a day.

Gas can be temporarily increased with bouts of infectious diarrhea. Gas can also build up behind constipation and be released in large amounts.

CALL YOUR CHILD'S PHYSICIAN DURING OFFICE HOURS IF

• You think your child has excessive gas and you don't know the cause.

• Your child is losing weight.

• You have other questions or concerns.

HOME CARE

In general, the passage of gas causes no symptoms. By age 5 or 6 most children can be taught to release gas in a socially acceptable manner. Gas does not need to be released by inserting anything in the rectum.

Air swallowing can be reduced by eliminating some of the previously mentioned habits.

The reduction in intake of beans and carbonated beverages will decrease gas production in all children.

If you feel your child has a milk intolerance (especially if your family history is positive), reduce the milk intake to 2 or 3 glasses a day. Milk does not need to be completely eliminated in most people with a lactose intolerance. Yogurt is easily digested and can be continued. If you suspect milk intolerance and symptoms persist after minor dietary change, consult your child's physician about current recommendations for this disorder.

RELATED TOPIC

DIARRHEA (see page 488)

HICCUPS

Hiccups are an inspiratory sound made during spasms or sudden contractions of the diaphragm. They usually are quite uncomfortable in older children. They often accompany indigestion or an overfull stomach that presses against the diaphragm. Drinking excessive carbonated beverages is a common cause of recurrent hiccups. In small infants, hiccups are normal.

HOME CARE

Treatment • Give 1 teaspoon of dry granulated sugar and have your child swallow it quickly. If this doesn't work the first time, repeat it 3 times at 2-minute intervals. For younger children, corn syrup can be used. Babies can be given a swallow of water.

Also, lying down usually helps, possibly because this position relaxes the abdominal wall. If this doesn't work, gag your child 3 or 4 times by pushing down the back of the tongue with the handle of a spoon.

Call Your Child's Physician Later If

• The hiccups last more than 3 hours (the usual time needed to empty the stomach).

NAUSEA

Nausea is an urge to vomit or a general uneasiness in the stomach. Nausea is often caused by a stomach virus and accompanied by vomiting. If so, turn directly to the guideline for VOMITING, page 502. Nausea can also be due to indigestion or fear.

HOME CARE

Treatment • Temporarily, serve your child clear fluids and light foods. Avoid medicines such as aspirin which can irritate the stomach.

Call Your Child's Physician Later If

• New symptoms develop that worry you.

• The nausea lasts more than 1 week.

RELATED TOPICS

MOTION SICKNESS (see page 329)
VOMITING (see page 505)

PINWORMS

A pinworm is a white, very thin worm, about ½ inch long, that moves. If it doesn't wiggle it's probably lint or a thread. Pinworms are usually seen in the anal and buttock area, especially at night or early in the morning. Occasionally one is found on the surface of a bowel movement. They infect the anal area and large intestine. More than 10 percent of children have them. They do not cause any serious health problems, but they can cause considerable itching and irritation of the anal area and buttocks. Occasionally in girls, vaginal itching becomes a symptom. If the skin around the anus is red and tender, it is probably a strep infection, so call your child's physician during office hours.

HOME CARE WHEN PINWORM IS SEEN

Anti-Pinworm Medicine • The drugs for killing pinworms all require a prescription. If you have definitely seen a pinworm, call your child's physician during office hours for a prescription. The following information may also help you.

Treatment of Other Family Members • Children are usually infected by children outside the family. If anyone else in your family has symptoms or anyone sleeps with your child, call your physician during office hours for instructions. Physicians do not agree on whether to treat everyone in the family or only those with symptoms. If any of your child's friends have similar symptoms, be sure to tell their parents to get them tested.

Call Your Child's Physician During Office Hours If

• The skin around the anus becomes red or tender.

• The anal itching is not resolved within a week after treatment.

• You have other questions or concerns.

HOME CARE FOR SUSPICIOUS SYMPTOMS WITHOUT PINWORM BEING SEEN

Suspicious Symptoms • If your child has itching or irritation of the anal area, it could mean pinworms. Keep in mind that many children get itching here solely from washing their anal area too frequently or vigorously with soap. The anal area can also become red and sore from diarrhea or local strep infections. The only way to tell for certain is to do a Scotch-tape test for pinworm eggs.

Instructions for Scotch-tape Test • Pick up glass slides at your physician's office (2 for each child) and mark your child's name on the slide. Touch a piece of clear Scotch tape (with the sticky side down) to the skin on both sides of the anus. Do this in the morning soon after your child has awakened, and definitely before any bath or shower. Do it 2 mornings in a row. Apply the piece of tape to the slide. If slides are unavailable, the transparent tape that has touched the skin can be applied to a second piece of tape. Bring the slides in for examination with a microscope. Your physician will call the results to you. If pinworm eggs are seen, a medicine will be prescribed. (See PINWORM IS SEEN, above, for details on home treatment.)

HOME CARE FOR PINWORM EXPOSURE OR CONTACT

If your child had recent contact with a child with pinworms but has no symptoms, your child probably won't get them. Pinworms are harmless and are never present very long without causing some anal itching. If you want to be sure your child doesn't have them, wait for at least a month. The swallowed egg will not mature into an adult pinworm for 3 to 4 weeks. Then contact your physician about doing a Scotch-tape test for pinworm eggs. (See above, instructions on doing the Scotch-tape test.)

PREVENTION

Infection is caused by swallowing pinworm eggs. Your child can get pinworms no matter how carefully you keep the kids and your house clean. The following hygiene measures, however, can help to reduce the chances of reinfection of your child or new infections in other people. Pets don't carry pinworms.

- Have your child scrub hands and fingernails thoroughly before each meal and after each use of the toilet. Keep the fingernails cut short, because eggs can collect here. Thumb-sucking and nail-biting should be discouraged.

- Don't eat food that has fallen on the floor.

- Vacuum or wet-mop your child's entire room once a week, because any eggs scattered on the floor are infectious for 1 to 2 weeks.

- Machine-washing at hot temperature will kill any eggs present in clothing or bedding.

STOOLS, BLOOD IN

SYMPTOMS AND CHARACTERISTICS

Blood in the stools (or bowel movements) is usually bright red. Rarely, blood comes out tar-black if it is from bleeding in the stomach. Swallowed blood also will look this way, so your child may have a tarry stool within 24 hours after a severe nosebleed.

Similar Condition • If your child has eaten anything red in the last 24 hours, turn first to the guideline for STOOLS, UNUSUAL COLOR OF, page 501. Most red stools are not due to blood.

ANAL FISSURE

Although the causes of actual blood in the stools are many, more than 90 percent of these children have an anal fissure. Suspect this diagnosis if:

• The blood is bright red.

• The blood is only a few streaks or flecks.

• It is on the surface of the stool or on the toilet tissue after wiping.

• The bleeding was preceded by passage of a large or hard BM, or insertion of a rectal thermometer or suppository.

• Sometimes you can see the shallow tear of the skin at the opening of the anus (usually at 6 or 12 o'clock).

• Touching the fissure will cause mild pain.

If your child's symptoms are different, call your physician for help.

CALL YOUR CHILD'S PHYSICIAN

Immediately If

• Bright-red blood is mixed throughout the stool.

• There is a large amount of bright-red blood.

• There has been a tar-black stool.

• Diarrhea is also present.

• Any blood has been vomited.

• A stomachache is also present.

• There are any skin bruises not caused by an injury.

• Your child is acting very sick.

During Office Hours If

• The cause of bleeding is unknown (i.e., not an anal fissure).

• You have other questions.

Be sure to bring a sample of the blood in your child's stool with you to the physician's office for testing.

HOME CARE FOR ANAL FISSURE

Warm Saline Baths • Give your child warm baths for 20 minutes, 3 times a day. Have your child sit in a basin or tub of very warm water with 2 tablespoons of table salt or baking soda added. Don't use any soap on the irritated area. Then gently dry the anal area. If it seems irritated, you can apply ½ percent hydrocortisone cream (no prescription needed). If the pain is severe, apply 2½ percent Xylocaine ointment (no prescription needed), 4 times a day for a few days to numb the area.

Diet for Anal Fissure • The most important aspect of treatment is to keep your child on a nonconstipating diet. Increase the intake of fresh fruits and vegetables, salads, beans, and bran products. Reduce the consumption of milk products.

Call Your Child's Physician Later If

• The anal fissure is not completely healed after 3 days of treatment.

• The bleeding increases in amount.

• The bleeding occurs more than 2 times.

RELATED TOPIC

CONSTIPATION (see page 483)

STOOLS, UNUSUAL COLOR OF

Unusual colors of the stool (some color other than brown) are almost always due to food color or food additives. In children with diarrhea, the passage time is very rapid and stools often come out the same color as the Kool-Aid or Jell-O water that went in. Stool color relates more to what is eaten than to any disease.

UNUSUAL STOOL COLORS AND COMMON CAUSES

• Red: Blood, red Jell-O, red cereals, tomato juice or soup, beets, red medicines

• Black: Blood from the stomach, iron, bismuth (e.g., Pepto-Bismol), licorice, cigarette ashes, spinach, grape juice

- Green: Green Jell-O, iron, diarrhea (due to rapid passage of normal bile), breast-feeding (especially during the first 2 months of life)

- Yellow-white: Aluminum hydroxide (antacids), hepatitis

WHEN TO CALL YOUR CHILD'S PHYSICIAN

- If stools are red without an explanation, see the guideline on STOOLS, BLOOD IN, above.

- If tar-black without an explanation, also see the guideline on STOOLS, BLOOD IN, above.

- If other unusual colors continue for more than 72 hours without an explanation, call during office hours. Be prepared to bring a stool sample with you.

VOMITING

SYMPTOMS AND CHARACTERISTICS

Vomiting is the forceful ejection of a large portion of the stomach's contents through the mouth. Nausea and abdominal discomfort usually precede each bout of vomiting. The mechanism is strong stomach contractions against a closed stomach outlet.

By contrast, regurgitation is the effortless spitting up of 1 or 2 mouthfuls of stomach contents, which is commonly seen in babies under 1 year of age.

Similar Conditions • If appropriate, turn directly to the following guidelines:

COUGH (when vomiting is strictly triggered by coughing spells) (see page 469)
MOTION SICKNESS (see page 329)
SPITTING UP (REGURGITATION) (see page 156)

Causes • Most vomiting is caused by a viral infection of the stomach (stomach flu) or by your child's eating something that is hard to digest. Often the viral type is associated with DIARRHEA (see page 488). Vomiting is a protective mechanism to keep harmful substances out of the intestines.

Expected Course • The vomiting usually stops in 6 to 24 hours. Dietary changes usually speed recovery.

CALL YOUR CHILD'S PHYSICIAN

Immediately If

• Your child has not urinated in more than 8 hours.

• Crying produces no tears.

• Any blood appears in the vomited material *and* it's not from a recent nosebleed.

• Any abdominal pain has persisted for more than 4 hours (especially if the abdomen is swollen).

• Your child has vomited clear fluids 3 or more times *and* has passed 3 or more diarrhea stools.

• Your child is difficult to awaken.

• Your child is confused or delirious.

• The neck is stiff.

• The abdomen was recently injured.

• Poisoning with a plant, bad food, medicine, or other chemical is a possibility.

• A foreign object could have been swallowed and caught in the esophagus.

• Your child is acting very sick.

During Office Hours If

• Your child has been vomiting for more than
12 hours (under 6 months old).
24 hours (6 months to 2 years old).
48 hours (over 2 years old).

• Your child is on any medicine that could cause vomiting.

• Vomiting is a recurrent problem for your child.

• You have other questions.

HOME CARE

Special Diet for Vomiting

1. Avoid All Solids for 8 Hours.

2. Clear Fluids for 8 Hours • Offer clear fluids (not milk) in small amounts until 8 hours have passed without vomiting. For infants, use one of the new oral rehydration solutions (such as Lytren or Pedialyte). After this age, soft drinks (cola, lemon-lime soda, or ginger ale) or water work fine. Stir or warm up on the stove until no fizz (carbonation) remains. (The bubbles inflate the stomach and increase the chances of continued vomiting.) Weak tea or Kool-Aid can also be used. Choose a flavor your child likes. Avoid diet pops. Older children may prefer to chew on a Popsicle.

Start with 1 teaspoon to 1 tablespoon, depending on age, every 10 minutes. Double the amount each hour. If your child vomits using this treatment, rest the stomach completely for 1 hour and then start over, but with small amounts. The 1-swallow-at-a-time approach rarely fails.

3. Bland Foods After 8 Hours Without Vomiting • After 8 hours without vomiting, your child can gradually return to a normal diet. For older children, start with foods like saltine crackers, honey on white bread, bland soups like "chicken with stars," rice, mashed potatoes, and so on. For babies, start with foods like applesauce, strained bananas, and rice cereal. If your baby takes only formula, give 1 or 2 ounces less per feeding than usual.

Usually your child can be back on a normal diet within 24 hours after recovery from vomiting. It won't hurt your child not to eat much for a few days.

Medicines • Discontinue all medicines for 8 hours. Oral medicines can irritate the stomach and make vomiting worse. If your child has a fever, treat it with cool compresses to the forehead. If necessary, use acetaminophen suppositories (no prescription necessary). Call your physician if your child needs to take a prescription medicine such as an antibiotic.

Common Mistakes • A common error is to give as much of clear fluids as the child wants, rather than gradually increasing the amounts. This almost always leads to continued vomiting. Another error is to force the child to drink when he or she doesn't want anything.

Keep in mind that there is no effective drug for vomiting. Various suppositories have caused serious reactions; in addition, they alleviate only vomiting related to anesthesia, poisoning, or motion sickness—but not the type caused by an irritated stomach lining. Diet therapy is the answer. Vomiting alone rarely causes dehydration unless you give your child drugs, milk, or too much of clear fluids at one time.

Special Advice for Vomiting with Breast-feeding • If your baby has vomited only once or twice, continue breast-feeding, but nurse on only one side each time. After 24 hours, return to both sides, but limit the time your baby nurses. If vomiting occurs 3 or more times, put your baby on clear fluids. As soon as 4 hours elapse without vomiting, return to nursing, but with small amounts for 8 hours.

Call Your Child's Physician Later If

• Your child develops diarrhea *and* vomits clear fluids.

• The vomiting continues for more than 48 hours (12 hours if your child is under 6 months old, and 24 hours if between 6 and 24 months).

• Any signs of dehydration occur. (See EMERGENCY SYMPTOMS page 5.)

• Your child becomes difficult to awaken or acts confused.

• Any blood appears in the vomited material.

• Abdominal pain develops and lasts more than 4 hours.

• You feel your child is getting worse.

VOMITING OF BLOOD

Blood in the vomited material can be bright red or the dark-brown color of coffee grounds, if it has been acted on by stomach acid.

CALL YOUR CHILD'S PHYSICIAN IMMEDIATELY

- In every case.

- *Exception:* If your child swallowed blood from a cut in the mouth or a nosebleed in the preceding 4 to 6 hours, don't call. One episode of vomited blood under these circumstances can be presumed to be due to swallowed blood and is unimportant.

- If you are asked to come in, bring a sample of the "bloody" material with you, so that it can be tested.

BLADDER (URINARY)

URINATION, PAIN WITH (DYSURIA)

SYMPTOMS AND CHARACTERISTICS

- Discomfort with passing urine
- Burning or stinging with passing urine
- Urgency (can't wait), frequency (passing small amounts), and straining (difficulty starting) are occasionally associated
- In children too young to talk, suspect dysuria if your child begins to cry regularly when passing urine

If your child's symptoms are different, call your physician for help.

Causes • The most common cause of mild pain or burning with urination in young girls is an irritation and redness of the vulva and opening of the urethra. The irritation is usually caused by bubble bath, shampoo, or soap that was left on the genital area. Occasionally it is due to poor hygiene. This chemical urethritis occurs almost exclusively prior to puberty. Circumcised boys are also susceptible to urethral irritation from soap. Since 5 percent of young girls get urinary tract infections (UTI), one must always consider this diagnosis. A UTI is a bacterial infection of the bladder (cystitis) and sometimes the kidneys (pyelonephritis).

Expected Course of Bubble Bath (Chemical) Urethritis • With warm-water soaks, the pain and burning usually clear in 12 hours.

CALL YOUR CHILD'S PHYSICIAN

Immediately If

- The pain with urination is severe.
- Your child has a fever (over 100°F) or chills.
- Any abdominal or back pain is present.
- Your child is able to pass only very small amounts of urine.
- The urine is bloody or cola-colored.
- Your child is acting very sick.

During Office Hours If

- Your child is a male.
- There is any frequency, urgency, or straining with urination.
- There is a recent onset of day or night wetting.
- Your child is female *and* she had previous urinary tract infections.
- She has any vaginal discharge.
- You think she may have pinworms.
- She has started the body changes of puberty.
- You have other questions.

HOME CARE

Warm Vinegar-Water Soaks • Have your daughter soak her bottom in a basin or bathtub of warm water for 20 minutes. Put ½ cup of white vinegar in the water. Be sure she spreads her legs and allows the water to cleanse the genital area. No soap should be used. Help her dry herself completely afterward. Repeat this in 2 hours and again in 12 hours. This will remove any soap, concentrated urine, or other chemicals from the genital area. Thereafter, cleanse the genital area once a day with warm water.

Instructions for Collecting a Midstream, Clean-Catch Urine Specimen at Home • If you are told to bring a urine sample with you, try to collect the first one in the morning. Use a sterile jar. Wash off the genital area several times with cotton balls and warm water. Have your child then sit on the toilet seat with her legs spread widely so that the labia (skin folds of the vagina) don't touch. Have her start to urinate into the toilet, and then place the clean container directly in line with the urine stream. Remove it after you have collected a few ounces but before she stops. Catch urine from the middle of the stream without any stopping or starting. The first or last ounce that comes out of the bladder may be contaminated. Store the urine in the refrigerator until you take it to the physician's office.

Call Your Child's Physician Later If

- The pain and burning are not cleared within 12 hours after having a warm vinegar-water soak. (You will probably need to bring a urine specimen with you.)

PREVENTION OF RECURRENCES

- Don't use bubble bath or put any other soaps into the bath water. Don't let a bar of soap float around in the bathtub. Wash the genital area with water, not soap. (The tissue inside the vaginal lips is very sensitive to soap.) If you are going to shampoo your child's hair, do this at the end of the bath.

- Keep bath time less than 15 minutes. Have your child urinate immediately after baths.

- Teach your daughter to wipe herself correctly from front to back, especially after a bowel movement.

- Try not to let your child get constipated. (If she does, see the guideline for CONSTIPATION, page 483.)

- Encourage her to drink enough fluids each day. This will increase the amount of urine she makes, and the extra urine "washes out" the kidneys and bladder.

- Encourage her to empty the bladder at least every 3 to 4 hours during the day. (If she avoids public restrooms, help her overcome this reluctance.)

- Have her wear loose cotton underpants. Polyester or nylon underpants, tights, or panty hose don't allow the skin to "breathe." Discourage wearing of underpants during the night.

URINE, BLOOD IN

Blood in the urine can make it pink, red, brown, or cola-colored. There are some harmless causes for these colors—beets, for instance. Keep in mind that dark-yellow (amber) urine is usually due to being a little dehydrated from a poor fluid intake, sweating, and/or fever.

If blood in the urine is suspected, your child needs to have the urine checked. Collect a specimen of the "bloody" urine in a clean container and keep it in the refrigerator until you go to your physician's office. If your child is in diapers, bring along the diaper with the pink or red spot on it. Also measure and record (in ounces) all the urine that your child passes if he or she is toilet trained.

CALL YOUR CHILD'S PHYSICIAN

Immediately If

• A headache is present.

• The eyelids are puffy.

• Your child is urinating much less than usual.

• Pain is present in the back or side.

• The back has recently been injured.

• Your child is acting very sick.

During Office Hours

• All other children with suspected blood in the urine need medical consultation. If your child is male and the opening at the tip of the penis appears to have a crack in it that is bleeding, apply petrolatum while waiting.

URINE, STRONG ODOR

SYMPTOMS AND CHARACTERISTICS

The urine has a pungent, often unpleasant odor of recent onset. The color of the urine is usually darker than normal at these times.

Similar Conditions • A dark-yellow urine may contain bilirubin; check the whites of the eyes for a yellow color change (i.e., jaundice). Urinary tract infections cause a foul-smelling urine. Blood in the urine can cause pink, red, or cola-colored urine.

If one of the following is suspected, save time by turning directly to that guideline:

JAUNDICE (see page 392)
URINATION, PAIN WITH (see page 407)
URINE, BLOOD IN (see above)

Causes • Most strong-smelling urine is produced when your child is mildly dehydrated. Exercise, a fever, hot weather, or a hot room can lead to slight dehydration. Children in cloth diapers can acquire a strong odor of ammonia if the bacteria in the stool have time to break down the urine. Certain drugs (e.g., penicillin and ampicillin) are excreted in the urine and cause an unusual odor. Certain foods (e.g., asparagus) or a high-protein diet lead to strong-smelling urine.

CALL YOUR CHILD'S PHYSICIAN DURING OFFICE HOURS IF

• The unusual odor has been present since birth.

• The unusual odor lasts more than 24 hours without explanation.

• You have other questions.

HOME CARE

Increase your child's water intake during warm weather or fevers. Reduce your youngster's protein intake (remember that milk is largely a protein). Refer to the guideline on DIAPER RASH, page 152, if the odor is ammonia. By and large, most of these odors are not caused by anything harmful.

GENITALS

FOREIGN BODY, VAGINA

During normal exploration of the body, young girls may put a foreign object in their vagina. Common ones are toilet tissue, a crayon, or a bead. The objects must be removed to prevent a vaginal infection. Often they are not discovered until after the girl is brought in for a bad-smelling vaginal discharge.

CALL YOUR CHILD'S PHYSICIAN

Immediately If

- The object was sharp.
- There is any bleeding.
- The object is causing any discomfort.

During Office Hours

- All other children need medical consultation. In the meantime, leave the object alone lest it be pushed in farther.

MENSTRUAL CRAMPS (DYSMENORRHEA)

SYMPTOMS AND CHARACTERISTICS

- Cramps during the first 1 or 2 days of a period
- Pain in lower mid-abdomen
- Pain may radiate to the lower back or both thighs

  If your child's symptoms are different, call your physician for help.

Cause • Menstrual cramps (dysmenorrhea) are experienced by more than 50 percent of girls and women during menstrual periods. Therefore, cramps are not abnormal. They are caused by strong contractions (even spasms) of the muscles in the womb (uterus) as it tries to expel menstrual blood. Menstrual periods usually are not painful during their first 1 to 2 years. However, once ovulation (the release of an egg from the ovary) begins, the level of progesterone and other hormones in the bloodstream increases and leads to stronger contractions and some cramps.

Expected Course • Cramps last 2 or 3 days and usually occur with each menstrual period. Current drugs usually can keep the pain to a very mild level. The cramps may be reduced after the first pregnancy and childbirth, probably due to the stretching of the opening of the womb (cervical os). Other women gain some improvement by age 25.

CALL YOUR CHILD'S PHYSICIAN

Immediately If

- The pain is so bad that your daughter is unable to walk normally.
- She also has an unexplained fever (over 100°F).
- She is acting very sick.

During Office Hours If

- More than 1 day of school is missed with each period.
- Vaginal discharge was also present before the period.

- Any pain occurs with urination or bowel movements.

- The pain is located on one side only.

- Any pain persists beyond the last day of flow.

- You have other questions.

HOME CARE

Ibuprofen (Advil, Nuprin, and Medipren Are Some of the Brand Names) • Ibuprofen is a special drug for menstrual cramps. It not only decreases the pain but also decreases contractions of the uterus. Until the fall of 1984, it was available only by prescription (as Motrin). Because of an excellent safety record, it can now be obtained over the counter in 200 mg tablets, of which 1 or 2 can be given 4 or 5 times a day. The drug should be started as soon as there is any menstrual flow, or the day before if possible. Don't wait for the onset of menstrual cramps. Ibuprofen should make your child feel good enough not to miss anything important.

If you don't have ibuprofen, give aspirin until you can obtain some. (For dosage, see the chart on page 51.) Acetaminophen products are not as effective as aspirin for treating dysmenorrhea. Most nonprescription products that are advertised as providing special, fast relief for menstrual cramps are overrated. If you read the label carefully, you will notice that they contain aspirin or acetaminophen (sometimes with a small amount of caffeine).

Local Heat • A heating pad or hot washcloth applied to the area of pain may be helpful. A 20-minute warm bath twice a day usually reduces the pain.

Aggravating Factors • Any type of pain will hurt more in people who are tired or upset. Avoid long hours and inadequate sleep during menstrual periods. If your daughter has undue troubles or worries on her mind, encourage her to share them with someone.

Full Activity • The main goal should be to stay active and take pain medications as necessary. There are absolutely no restrictions; your child can go to school, take gym, swim, take a shower or bath, wash her hair, go outside in bad weather, date, etc., during her menstrual period. A common mistake is to go to bed; people who are busy have a better chance of repressing their pain. If the pains are getting her down despite using ibuprofen, see a physician for stronger medication.

Prevention of Toxic Shock Syndrome • Over 80 percent of cases of this life-threatening disease occur in girls during a menstrual period. Most cases occur in girls who use a tampon overnight. This condition can usually be prevented if tampons are changed every 3 to 4 hours during the day and external pads are used during sleep.

Call Your Teenager's Physician Later If

• Ibuprofen does not provide adequate pain relief.

• The menstrual cramps are causing her to miss school or other important activities.

• An unexplained fever occurs.

• The pain lasts more than 3 days.

• Premenstrual weight gain or swelling occurs.

SWELLING, GROIN OR SCROTUM

SYMPTOMS

This guideline covers a swelling, bulge, or lump in the scrotum or groin in males.

Similar Conditions • If one of the following is present, save time by turning directly to that guideline:

GENITAL TRAUMA (see page 57)
LYMPH NODES, SWOLLEN (see page 393)

Causes • A hydrocele is a painless collection of clear fluid above the testicle, present at birth. (See HOME CARE OF A HYDROCELE, below.) Unlike the other conditions, both sides are commonly involved.

An inguinal hernia may be diagnosed at birth or later.

A lymph node in the groin can swell up following a rash or infection of the leg on that side. While all the other conditions cause swelling of the scrotal sac, the enlarged node is found in the groin crease.

Two emergency conditions that begin with scrotal swelling and severe pain are torsion (rotation) of the testicle, and an infected testicle (orchitis). Don't assume it's just a pulled groin muscle.

CALL YOUR CHILD'S PHYSICIAN

Immediately If

- The area is tender to the touch.
- The area is painful.

During Office Hours

- All other cases of scrotal swelling should be seen by a physician, except a hydrocele diagnosed at birth.

HOME CARE OF A HYDROCELE

Hydroceles are present in about 10 percent of normal newborn males. If your child's physician has made this diagnosis, the following information may be helpful. A hydrocele is usually caused by the pressure on the abdomen during delivery, which pushes clear fluid downward through the channel that surrounds the spermatic cord and blood vessels to the testicle. A hydrocele may take 6 to 12 months to clear completely. It is harmless, but can be rechecked during regular visits. If the swelling frequently changes in size (especially becoming larger with crying), a hernia may also be present, and you should call your physician during office hours for an appointment.

VAGINAL IRRITATION

SYMPTOMS AND CHARACTERISTICS

- Genital area pain, burning, or itching
- No pain or burning with urination

If your child's symptoms are different, call your physician for help.

Similar Conditions • If pain accompanies urination, save time by turning directly to the guideline on URINATION, PAIN WITH, page 407.

If your child also has itching of the anus and buttocks, see the guideline on PINWORMS, page 497.

Causes • Most vaginal itching or discomfort is due to a chemical irritation of the vulva or outer vagina. The usual irritants are bubble bath, shampoo, or soap left on the genital area. Occasionally it is due to poor hygiene. This chemical vulvitis occurs almost exclusively prior to puberty. If the vagina becomes infected, a vaginal discharge will be noted.

Expected Course of Chemical Vulvitis • It responds within 1 to 2 days with proper treatment.

CALL YOUR CHILD'S PHYSICIAN

Immediately If

• An unexplained fever (over 100°F) is present.

• There is any severe abdominal pain.

• Sexual abuse could be the cause.

During Office Hours If

• There is any vaginal discharge.

• Your child has started the body changes of puberty.

• You have other questions.

HOME CARE

Warm Vinegar-Water Soaks • Have your daughter soak her bottom in a basin or bathtub of warm water for 20 minutes. Put ½ cup of white vinegar in the water. Be sure she spreads her legs and allows the water to cleanse the genital area. No soap should be used. Help her dry herself completely afterward. Repeat this in 2 hours and again in 12 hours. This will remove any soap, concentrated urine, or other chemicals from the genital area. Thereafter, cleanse the genital area once a day with warm water on a washcloth.

Hydrocortisone Cream • Apply ½ percent hydrocortisone cream (no prescription needed) 4 times a day to the genital area for 2 or 3 days.

Call Your Child's Physician Later If

• The pain and itching are not cleared within 48 hours on treatment.

• Your child develops a vaginal discharge.

PREVENTION

• Don't use bubble bath or put any other soaps into the bath water. Don't let a bar of soap float around in the bathtub. Wash the genital area with water, not soap. If you are going to shampoo your child's hair, do this at the end of the bath.

• Your child should wear cotton underpants. Polyester or nylon underpants, tights, or panty hose don't allow the skin to "breathe." Discourage wearing underpants during the night.

• Teach your daughter to wipe herself correctly from front to back, especially after a bowel movement.

BONES AND JOINTS

BACKACHE, ACUTE

SYMPTOMS AND CHARACTERISTICS

- Your child complains of back pain
- Usually the mid or lower back is involved
- The pain is worsened by bending
- The muscles on one side of the spine are tender and in spasm
- Mainly occurs in adolescents

Causes • Backaches are usually a symptom of a strain of some of the 200 muscles in the back that allow us to stand upright. Often the triggering event is carrying something too heavy, lifting from an awkward position, bending too far backward or sideways, or prolonged digging in the garden (overexertion of back muscles).

Expected Course • The pain and discomfort usually resolve in 1 to 2 weeks. Recurrences are common.

CALL YOUR CHILD'S PHYSICIAN

Immediately If

- The pain is very severe.
- Your child can't walk.
- The back pain shoots into the buttock or back of the thigh.

- A tingling sensation occurs in the legs.

- The backache followed an accident or injury.

- A fever (over 100°F) is present.

- Passing the urine causes pain or burning.

- Your child is acting very sick.

During Office Hours If

- Your child is under 5 years old.

- Your child doesn't walk normally.

- The pain interferes with sleep.

- The cause of the pain is unknown.

- You have other questions.

HOME CARE

Pain-Relief Medicines • Give aspirin (for dosage, see the chart on page 51) 4 times a day. Aspirin usually gives more relief of muscle and bone pain than acetaminophen. Continue this until 24 hours have passed without any pain. This is the most important part of the therapy, because back pain causes muscle spasm, and the aspirin can greatly reduce both the spasm and the pain.

Local Heat • A heating pad or hot water bottle applied to the most painful area helps to relieve muscle spasm. Do this whenever the pain flares up. Don't allow your child to go to sleep on a heating pad, because it can cause burns.

Sleeping Position • The most comfortable sleeping position is usually on the side with a pillow between the knees. If your child sleeps on the back, it may help to place a pillow under the knees. Avoid sleeping on the adomen. The mattress should be firm or reinforced with a board.

Activity • Complete bedrest is unnecessary. Have your child avoid lifting, jumping, horseback riding, motorcycle riding, and exercise until he or she is completely well.

Call Your Child's Physician Later If

- The pain becomes worse.
- The pain begins to shoot into the leg.
- The pain is no better in 72 hours.
- The pain is still present after 2 weeks.

PREVENTION

The only way to prevent future backaches is to keep the back muscles in excellent physical condition. This will require 5 minutes of back and abdominal exercises per day, possibly for the rest of your child's life. Helpful exercises are sit-ups, 6-inch leg raises, flattening the back against the floor, tucks of the leg to the chest, chest lifts while on the abdomen, and various stretching exercises. These exercises should be started gradually and should be avoided when your child is having active back pain. Remind your child to lift objects with the leg muscles and not by bending or twisting the back.

LIMB PAIN

SYMPTOMS AND CHARACTERISTICS

- Your child complains of pains in the arms or legs
- Your child does not have a limp
- The pain is not due to a known injury

Similar Conditions • If appropriate, turn directly to the following guidelines:

LIMP (see page 525)
BONE AND JOINT TRAUMA (see page 49)

Causes • There are 2 main causes of *mild* limb pain. *Brief* pains (1 to 15 minutes) are usually due to muscle spasms. Foot or calf muscle cramps are especially common at night. *Continuous* acute pains (hours to 3 days) are usually due to overstrenuous activities or forgotten muscle injuries. Both of these normal pains have been erroneously referred to as "growing pains" (although they have nothing to do with growth). Mild muscle aches also occur with many viral illnesses.

CALL YOUR CHILD'S PHYSICIAN

Immediately If

- The limb pain is very severe.
- A joint is swollen.
- A joint can't be moved fully.
- Your child is acting very sick.

During Office Hours If

- The pain interferes with sleep.
- A fever (over 100°F) is present.
- The pain has lasted more than 3 days.
- Limb pain is a recurrent problem for your child.
- You have other questions.

HOME CARE

Treatment for Muscle Cramps • Muscle cramps in the feet or calf muscles occur in a third of children. During attacks, stretch the foot and toes upward as far as they will go to break the spasm. Massage and heat to the painful muscle can also help.

Future attacks may be prevented by daily stretching exercises of the heel cords. (Lean forward at the ankles with the knees straight.) A glass of tonic (quinine) water at bedtime may prevent some of these night cramps, as will adequate fluids during sports.

Treatment for Acute Strained Muscles • Massage the sore muscles with ice for 20 to 30 minutes several times on the first day. Aspirin usually gives more relief of muscle pain than acetaminophen. (For dosage, see the chart on page 51.) For muscle pains with fever, give acetaminophen instead.

If stiffness persists after 48 hours, have your child relax in a hot bath for 20 minutes twice a day, and gently exercise the involved part under water.

Call Your Child's Physician Later If

- Your child develops a limp, a swollen joint, or a fever.
- The pain lasts more than 3 days.
- You feel your child is getting worse.

LIMP

A limp is a painful type of walking (gait), in which the child tries to avoid putting much weight on one leg or hurries off it when walking. Some children flat-out refuse to stand or walk at all. Most of these children have limb pain but may be too young to express this in words. The most common cause of an unexplained limp in young children is a minor injury from jumping off of furniture.

CALL YOUR CHILD'S PHYSICIAN

Immediately If

• A severe limp followed a recent injury.

• Your child won't walk at all.

• A fever (over 100°F) is present.

• A joint is swollen.

• A joint can't be moved fully.

During Office Hours If

• The limp has no obvious cause. (First consider a simple cause such as tight new shoes, a sliver in the foot, a plantar wart, or an intramuscular injection within the previous 24 hours.)

• A slight limp (due to an injury) lasts more than 72 hours (as with a pulled muscle, bruised bone, stubbed toe, or scraped knee).

NECK PAIN, ACUTE

SYMPTOMS AND CHARACTERISTICS

• Your child complains of pain in the back of the neck or upper back

• Pain in the front of the neck usually is due to a sore throat or swollen lymph node

• The head is often cocked to one side

Similar Condition • LYMPH NODES, SWOLLEN (see page 393)

Causes • Acute neck pain (wryneck) is usually caused by sleeping in an awkward posture, painting a ceiling, reading in bed, or prolonged typing.

Serious spinal cord injury can follow diving injuries, trampoline injuries, or other accidents involving the neck. Children who have suffered such an accident should not be moved until a neck brace or spine board has been applied.

A stiff neck (in which your child can't bend forward and touch the chin to the chest) is an early finding in meningitis. (Fever should also be present.)

Expected Course • A strained neck isn't serious and usually lasts 5 to 7 days.

CALL YOUR CHILD'S PHYSICIAN

Immediately If

• The pain was caused by contact sports or an accident.

• Numbness or tingling is present in the arms or upper back.

• The pain is severe.

• Your child cannot touch the chin to the center of the chest.

• A fever (over 100°F) is present.

During Office Hours If

• Your child is under 5 years old.

• The pain interferes with sleep.

• You have other questions.

HOME CARE

Pain-Relief Medicines • Give aspirin 4 times a day until your child has gone 24 hours without any pain. (For dosage, see the chart on page 51.) Aspirin usually gives more relief of muscle and bone pain than acetaminophen. This is the most important part of therapy, because neck pain causes muscle spasm, and the aspirin can interrupt this cycle.

Local Heat • A heating pad, hot water bottle, or hot shower spray applied to the most painful area helps to relieve muscle spasm. Do this whenever the pain flares up.

Sleeping Position • Instead of a pillow at night, your child may prefer a folded towel wrapped around the neck. This collar will keep the head from moving too much during sleep. (A foam cervical collar with Velcro closure can be obtained at a pharmacy.) Avoid sleeping on the abdomen.

Exercises • Your child should avoid any neck exercises until completely well.

Call Your Child's Physician Later If

• The pain becomes worse.

• The pain begins to shoot into the arms or upper back.

• The pain is no better in 72 hours.

• The pain is still present after 1 week.

• Other questions come up.

PREVENTION

If your child has had more than one neck ache, usually the child has an activity or habit that overstresses the neck muscles or bones (cervical spine). Such activities are working with the neck turned or bent backward, carrying heavy objects on the head, carrying heavy objects with one arm (instead of both arms), standing on the head, contact sports, or even friendly wrestling. Avoid these triggers. Also improve the tone of the neck muscles with 2 or 3 minutes of gentle neck exercises per day. Helpful exercises are touching the chin to each shoulder, touching the ear to the shoulder, and moving the head forward and backward against mild resistance.

VI

GLOSSARY

A GLOSSARY OF CHILDREN'S DISEASES REQUIRING PHYSICIAN CONSULTATION

All of these conditions require a physician's input for diagnosis or treatment. Therefore, they are purposely not covered in this book. Your education on how to manage them should come from your child's physician and his or her associates.

If your child is born with or develops a chronic (long-term or lifetime) disease, to best serve your child you will need to learn almost as much about symptoms and treatment as your physician. To gain such a knowledge base, you can turn to local parent support groups or a national organization, as well as medical specialists. In many cases, a parents' handbook on your child's disease is available. If your child is hospitalized, you have the right to ask the staff your questions, and they will usually be able to schedule a meeting with you once or twice a day for this purpose.

This chapter is divided into three parts: chronic diseases or conditions; severe acute illnesses usually requiring admission to the hospital; and acute illnesses usually treatable at home but requiring diagnosis by a physician or lab test.

CHRONIC DISEASES OR CONDITIONS

Acquired Immune Deficiency Syndrome (AIDS): A life-threatening disease due to markedly reduced lymphocytes and immunity. Pediatric cases are rare except for the offspring of affected adults, or children who have required multiple transfusions (hemophiliacs, for instance).

Adrenogenital syndrome: An inherited disease present at birth in which the infant has accelerated sexual development and an inability to produce steroids. Females with this disease may resemble male newborns (ambiguous genitals).

Amblyopia: Decreased vision or blindness.

Anorexia nervosa: In adolescents, excessive weight loss (more than 20 percent below ideal weight) and denial of being underweight. Over 90 percent are female. Psychotherapy is essential.

Asthma: An allergic condition of the lungs. The smaller airways (bronchioles) go into spasm and become swollen with colds and when allergens or irritants are inhaled, leading to attacks of wheezing. Occurs in 5 percent of children.

Astigmatism: Distorted vision due to variations in refractive power on different parts of the cornea.

Attention deficit disorder: The new medical term for the hyperactive child's condition. These children cannot concentrate or complete tasks. The causes are many.

Bifid uvula: A splitting of the tag of tissue hanging down from the center of the soft palate in the mouth. Looks like 2 uvulas. No symptoms except increased ear infections in some children.

Biliary atresia: Blockage of the bile ducts at birth leading to severe liver damage. Sometimes treatable with surgery.

Bronchopulmonary dysplasia (BPD): Lung damage that occurs in some prematures who needed mechanical ventilation for survival. Portable oxygen administration may be needed over the first 1 or 2 years until lung improvement occurs.

Bulimia: In adolescents, periodic food binging followed by self-induced vomiting or laxative-induced diarrhea to prevent weight gain. The weight, however, is usually kept in the normal range. Psychotherapy is essential.

Cerebral palsy: A motor handicap due to brain injury either before or during birth. The most common type is spastic diplegia (weakness and tightness of both legs).

Chorea: Abnormal and unexpected muscle jerks. The location of the chorea changes. Sydenham's chorea is a type seen following rheumatic fever.

Cleft lip and/or palate: The incomplete closure of the lip and/or roof of the mouth. Can occur in various combinations. A birth defect of unknown cause. Requires surgical repair and speech therapy.

Clubfoot: A fixed (inflexible) deformity of the foot (usually downward and inward) present at birth. Requires repeated casts or surgical correction.

Congenital heart disease: A birth defect of the heart which is usually not inherited. The defects are of many types. Surgery is frequently required.

Cow's milk allergy: An allergy to cow's milk protein resulting in the onset of diarrhea (often bloody) during the first 8 weeks of life. Responds to a non-cow's milk formula. Occurs in 1 to 2 percent of newborns and resolves spontaneously by 1 year of age in most children.

Craniosynostosis: An early closure of the sutures (growth lines) of the skull. Surgery is required if multiple sutures are involved, and should be done before 6 months of age.

Cryptorchidism: An undescended testicle that remains in the abdomen. Needs to be surgically brought down into the scrotal sac by 2 years of age.

Cystic fibrosis: An inherited disease causing very thick mucus that blocks the lungs and pancreas. The main symptoms are recurrent pneumonia, diarrhea, and poor weight gain.

Diabetes insipidus: The inability to concentrate the urine, making the child predisposed to dehydration. Symptoms of increased drinking (polydipsia) and urination (polyuria). The causes are several.

Diabetes mellitus: The inability of the pancreas to produce insulin, leading to high blood sugar and sugar in the urine. The main symptoms are increased drinking and eating, excessive urination, and weight loss. The child needs daily insulin injections.

Down's syndrome: Newborns with Down's syndrome are mentally retarded, floppy, and have a characteristic facial appearance (mongolism). They are commonly the offspring of older mothers. Caused by an extra chromosome (Trisomy 21). Can be diagnosed during pregnancy by amniocentesis.

Epilepsy: A recurrent seizure disorder. The types and causes are many. In grand mal epilepsy the child falls and the entire body jerks for several minutes. In petit mal epilepsy (staring spells) a child loses consciousness and stops what he or she is doing for 5 to 15 seconds, but doesn't fall down.

Exercise-induced bronchospasm: Attacks, lasting 20 to 30 minutes, of coughing and wheezing after (but sometimes during) exercise. Running in cold air is the main offender. Occurs in 10 to 20 percent of people (90 percent of those with asthma). Prevented by taking an asthma medicine before sports.

Fetal alcohol syndrome: Birth defects due to maternal alcohol intake in excess of 1 drink per day during pregnancy. The most common abnormalities are small eyes, a small head, low birth weight, and delayed development.

Fragile X syndrome: In males, an abnormal X chromosome. Accounts for 25 percent of mental retardation in males. Features include a long face, large jaw, large testes, and scars from hand-biting.

Galactosemia: An inherited enzyme defect that causes vomiting, diarrhea, liver damage, and mental retardation. Detection by newborn screening permits treatment with a galactose-free diet. Galactose is one of the sugars in milk.

Gastroesophageal reflux: The regurgitation or vomiting of food because the junction of the esophagus (food tube) and stomach doesn't close completely. The mild form is common in newborns and resolves by 1 year of age. The severe form can cause poor weight gain or vomited blood due to acid irritation of the end of the esophagus. This form may require surgery.

Hemophilia: An inherited bleeding tendency due to the inability to produce certain clotting factors. Mainly occurs in males.

Hip, congenital dislocation: Being born with the hip out of the socket. A brace is needed for 3 months to correct the problem. Early diagnosis is important to prevent permanent damage.

Hydrocephalus: Blockage of spinal fluid flow out of the brain; resulting in a large head if not treated early. Treatment is a surgical shunt to drain the fluid to the abdomen.

Hydronephrosis: An enlarged kidney due to obstruction of its drainage system. Usually requires surgical correction.

Hyperopia: Farsightedness. Close objects are difficult to see.

Hypertension: High blood pressure. The causes are many in children. In adolescents, the cause is usually genetic (i.e., essential hypertension).

Hypospadias: A birth defect in which the urethra opens onto the shaft of the penis rather than the end. Surgical correction is usually required.

Hypothyroidism: An underactive thyroid gland. When this condition occurs in newborns, it can cause very slow growth and development. Treated with thyroid medicine. Diagnosis before 6 weeks of age is important.

Inborn errors of metabolism: Genetic diseases that involve the absence of a particular enzyme the body requires. Examples are phenylketonuria and galactosemia.

Irritable colon of childhood: The most common cause of chronic diarrhea in infants. The loose, mushy stools do not interfere with normal weight gain. The cause is unknown but the condition miraculously clears at 2½ to 3 years of age.

Klinefelter's syndrome: In males, an extra X chromosome (i.e., XXY). Features include tall stature, borderline intelligence, breast development, small testes, and sterility.

Lactose intolerance: An inherited reduction in lactase, the enzyme needed to break down lactose in milk. Milk intake causes loose stools and gas. The condition is most common in dark-skinned races, and usually has an onset at 5 to 10 years of age.

Learning disabilities: Specific learning limitations (e.g., in mathematics or reading) in children of normal intelligence and motivation. Usually inherited. Illiteracy (the inability to read and write adequately to function in our society) is often due to untreated severe reading disability. Most schools have special programs to help these children.

Leukemia: A cancer of the white blood cells. With modern treatment, over half of children can be cured.

Malabsorption: An intestinal condition that interferes with the absorption of fat, protein, or sugar. Symptoms are severe diarrhea and weight loss. The causes are legion.

Mental retardation: An intelligence quotient (I.Q.) less than 70. Children with I.Q.'s over 50 can often learn to function independently. The causes are many.

Microcephaly: Small head size. Due to below-average brain growth. Extremely small heads are associated with mental retardation.

Migraine headaches: A headache that is incapacitating, throbbing, and on one side of the head. Nausea and vomiting are often present. Over 70 percent have a family history of similar headaches.

Minimal brain dysfunction (MBD): Twenty years ago, MBD was considered the main cause of attention deficit disorder, dyslexia, and other learning disabilities. Many physicians have discarded this simplistic, unfounded, and harmful label.

Muscular dystrophy: An inherited disease of progressive muscle weakness. Onset at age 2 to 6. In males only.

Myopia: Nearsightedness. Distant objects are difficult to see.

Neuroblastoma: A cancer of the adrenal gland located above each kidney.

Neurofibromatosis: A dominant genetic disorder characterized by 5 or more coffee-colored spots and benign tumors of the nerve sheaths (neurofibromas) or nerves (neuromas). Nervous system complications can occur.

Orthostatic proteinuria: Increased amounts of protein are released into the urine when standing but not when lying down. A harmless condition usually found in adolescent males.

Osgood-Schlatter disease: A disease causing knee pain just below the kneecap on a small normal bump called the tibial tubercle. Occurs in adolescents and lasts 1½ to 2 years. No permanent harm.

Pectus excavatum: A pulled-in or sunken breastbone (sternum). The mild form is common and causes no symptoms. The severe form of this congenital defect may interfere with heart function during exercise and requires surgery.

Peptic ulcer: An ulcer of the stomach or duodenum which causes upper abdominal pain, vomiting, or bleeding.

Phenylketonuria (PKU): An inherited enzyme defect that causes mental retardation, a light complexion, and seizures. Detection by newborn screening permits early treatment with a low-phenylalanine formula, followed by a restricted diet.

Polio: An infection of the spinal cord with serious complications like muscle paralysis and inability to breathe. Practically eliminated from our country by the polio vaccine. Occasionally causes minor epidemics (but great suffering) in religious sects that forbid immunization.

Polydactyly: Extra fingers or toes present at birth. The extra digit is usually adjacent to the little finger or toe. Dominant type of inheritance giving a 50 percent rate in offspring. Surgical removal for cosmetic reasons is fairly simple.

Prematurity: Birth of a newborn weighing less than 2,500 grams (5½ pounds). Occurs in 7 percent of births. The smaller the baby, the higher the complication rate. Neonatal intensive care units have drastically improved survival rates and reduced complications.

Recurrent abdominal pains (RAP): Recurrent stomachaches occur in 10 percent of children. While the causes are legion, over 90 percent are on a nonphysical basis.

Retrolental fibroplasia: Damage to the retina that occurs in small prematures (less than 1,500 grams) with high oxygen therapy requirements. The name comes from overgrowth of fibrous tissue behind the lens. The result is reduced vision or blindness.

Rheumatic fever: A rare complication of an untreated strep throat. The symptoms are migrating joint pains and fever. The heart is involved over half the time and can sustain permanent damage of the valves.

Rheumatoid arthritis: An arthritis that usually involves large joints on both sides of the body. Morning stiffness is common. Joint damage is occasionally seen.

Scoliosis: A sideways curving of the spine. Usually begins at age 10. Predominantly in girls. Screened for in most schools. Bracing is needed if the curve exceeds 20 degrees.

Serous otitis media: Fluid in the middle ear due to blocked Eustachian tubes. A problem of young children, sometimes requiring the insertion of ventilation (tympanostomy) tubes for 1 or 2 years.

Sickle cell anemia: An inherited type of anemia where the normally round red blood cells periodically become sickle-shaped and block off small blood vessels, causing severe pain. Also interferes with growth. Mainly occurs in Blacks at a frequency of 1 in 500.

Sickle cell trait: Children with sickle cell trait carry 1 gene for sickle cell anemia. It takes 2 genes to develop the disease. No symptoms or anemia. Present in 10 percent of Blacks.

Spina bifida: A birth defect of the spinal column and cord that causes paralysis below the level of involvement, as well as poor bladder-bowel control. Also called meningomyelocele. The cause is unknown.

Strabismus: A birth defect of the eye muscles causing crossed eyes (i.e., inward or outward turning of 1 or both eyes). Usually requires surgery. More than 90 percent of children suspected of having this actually have pseudostrabismus due to a broad nasal bridge or folds of tissue (epicanthal folds) over the inner parts of the eye. These decrease the visible sclera (white part) on the inside of the eyes and give an optical illusion of turning in.

Tay-Sachs disease: An inherited disease in which the brain degenerates. Onset at 3 to 6 months of age. Findings are blindness, arrested development, and seizures. Mainly occurs in East European Jews.

Tourette's syndrome: Frequent facial muscle jerks (tics) and irrepressible sounds (such as grunting or profanity). Onset at 2 to 6 years of age. Inherited in 50 percent of cases.

Transvestism: A preference for cross-dressing (i.e., dressing like the opposite sex). More commonly seen in heterosexuals than homosexuals. Occasional cross-dressing in preschoolers means nothing.

Turner's syndrome: In females, a missing X chromosome (i.e., X instead of XX). Features include short stature, abnormal ovaries, lack of sexual development, and infertility. The intelligence is normal.

Ulcerative colitis: Inflammation of the lining of the large bowel, which causes intermittent or continuous loose stools and cramps. Usually the stools contain mucus, pus, or blood.

Von Willebrand's disease: An inherited bleeding tendency due to problems with both platelets and clotting factor 8. Symptoms include severe nosebleeds, excessive menstrual flow, and increased bruising with trauma. Not as severe as hemophilia.

Wilson's disease: An inherited disease in which the liver can't excrete copper. The onset is after age 10, with jaundice, tremors, and deterioration in school performance.

ACUTE ILLNESSES USUALLY REQUIRING ADMISSION TO THE HOSPITAL

Anaphylactoid purpura: A disease consisting of unexplained bruises of the buttocks, hands, and feet; joint pains (70 percent), abdominal pain (30 percent); and blood in the urine (50 percent). The cause is unknown.

Apnea: An episode of cessation of breathing for 20 seconds or more, often associated with cyanosis (a bluish color of the lips). Apnea usually occurs in infants under 6 months of age. The causes are many.

Appendicitis: A blockage and infection of the appendix. The appendix is a blind pouch the size of your little finger that comes off the cecum (first part of the large bowel). Appendicitis gives constant pain in the right lower abdomen and requires surgical intervention.

Arthritis: Inflammation of a joint leading to pain, swelling, and limited motion. The causes are many.

Botulism: The most serious type of food poisoning. First symptoms are double vision, slurred speech, and swallowing problems. The cause is a toxin produced by bacteria in improperly canned vegetables. Contaminated food looks and tastes normal. During the first year of life, botulism can be acquired from swallowing dust or normal honey. Progressive weakness of suck, cry, and neck muscles is the main symptom in these babies.

Cellulitis: A spreading bacterial infection of the skin, often following a wound infection.

Cerebellar ataxia, acute: The abrupt onset of an unsteady gait, shaky hands, and slurred speech. Due to a viral infection of the cerebellum (balance center of the brain). Resolves in 4 to 8 weeks.

Child abuse: The mistreatment of children by adult caretakers (less commonly by strangers). The two most common types are physical abuse (inflicted injuries) and sexual abuse.

Cholecystitis: An infection of the gall bladder, often occurring because the gall bladder is blocked by gallstones. Surgical intervention is usually necessary.

Conversion reaction: The sudden onset of a physical disability (e.g., paralysis or blindness) on an emotional basis. Commonly the youngster shows lack of concern (indifference) for the symptom. Also called a hysterical reaction. Requires psychotherapy.

Diphtheria: A serious bacterial infection of the throat with complications of suffocation, heart disease, and paralysis. Preventable with DPT immunizations.

Diplopia: Double vision. Caused by drug reactions, botulism, eye muscle or brain disease.

Encephalitis: An infection of the brain caused by various viruses. Also called sleeping sickness.

Endocarditis: An infection of the valves and lining of the heart.

Epiglottitis: A life-threatening infection of the tissues surrounding the vocal cords. The cause is the *Hemophilus influenzae* bacterium. The epiglottis is the flap of tissue which normally covers the opening of the windpipe during swallowing and keeps food and drink off the larynx.

Failure-to-thrive: A malnourished, underweight condition usually occurring during the first year of life. While the causes are many, in our country over half the cases are due to underfeeding (i.e., child neglect).

Guillain-Barré syndrome: An acute progressive symmetrical paralysis that starts in the feet and moves up the body over several days. Usually follows a viral infection. Some children need to be placed on a ventilator temporarily.

Hematemesis: Vomiting up blood. The causes are many.

Hematuria: Blood in the urine. The causes are many.

Hemolytic-uremic syndrome: A combination of anemia from red blood cell breakdown (hemolysis) and kidney failure. Often preceded by bloody diarrhea. Occurs in infants. Cause unknown.

Hemoptysis: Coughing up blood. The causes are many.

Hemorrhagic disease of the newborn: A bleeding disorder that occurs on day 2 to day 7 of life. The bleeding usually occurs into the intestines, skin, or circumcision site. Due to vitamin K deficiency and preventable by routine vitamin K administration at birth. This problem is making a resurgence with home deliveries and breast-feeding.

Idiopathic thrombocytopenic purpura (ITP):   The most common bleeding disorder of childhood. Due to a temporary depletion of platelets (which are needed for clotting) following various viral infections.

Intussusception: Obstruction of the bowel due to a telescoping of one segment of intestine into an adjacent one. Cases diagnosed early may become unstuck with a barium enema, but some require surgery. Usually occurs in children less than 2 years old.

Kawasaki's disease: A disease of young children characterized by a red rash, red eyes, red mouth, enlarged nodes, and a fever lasting over 5 days. The cause is unknown. Over 20 percent of the children who get it develop heart disease. Also called mucocutaneous lymph node syndrome.

Malaria: A parasite transmitted by mosquitoes. Causes fever, shaking chills, anemia, convulsions, and coma. Affects over 200 million people worldwide and kills several million annually. The world's greatest cause of human disability. Could be eradicated if funds were provided. (Note: Doesn't occur in the United States.)

Mastoiditis: A bacterial infection of the air cells in the bone behind the ear. A complication of an untreated ear infection. Often requires surgery.

Melena: The passage of tar-colored blood in the stool. Blood darkens only if it comes from the stomach or upper intestines.

Meningitis: An infection of the meninges or thin membranes surrounding the brain and spinal cord. Usually caused by bacteria. Called aseptic meningitis when due to a virus.

Nephritis: Kidney disease where blood is passed in the urine. The causes are many, but strep throat is one of the more common forerunners. Can become chronic.

Nephrosis: Kidney disease where protein is passed in the urine, leading to swelling (edema) of the face and feet. Often becomes chronic.

Omphalitis: An infection of the navel or bellybutton. Can be serious in the first month of life.

Osteomyelitis: A bacterial infection of bone.

Papilledema: Swelling of the optic disc in the back of the eye. Reflects increased spinal-fluid pressure inside the head. Various causes, usually serious.

Pelvic inflammatory disease (PID): A bacterial infection of the Fallopian tubes—often due to gonorrhea or chlamydia. Also called salpingitis.

Pericarditis: An infection of the sac that covers the heart.

Peritonitis: An infection of the lining of the abdomen. Usually caused by a ruptured appendix.

Pertussis: A serious bacterial infection of the windpipe and lungs. Also called whooping cough because coughing spasms often end with a high-pitched whoop. Preventable with DPT immunizations.

Pneumothorax: A blowout of the lung leading to the escape of air into the space between the lung and the chest wall. Symptoms are chest pain and difficult breathing.

Pulmonary embolism: A blood clot carried through the blood stream to the lungs. Causes severe chest pain and difficult breathing.

Pyloric stenosis: An obstruction of the stomach outlet occurring in the first 4 to 8 weeks of life. Causes projectile vomiting and requires surgery.

Reyes syndrome: Abrupt swelling of the brain presenting with confusion, sleepiness, and persistent vomiting. Liver destruction also occurs. Although the cause is unknown, it sometimes follows chicken pox or influenza. Also associated with aspirin ingestion during these illnesses.

Rocky Mountain spotted fever: A life-threatening disease caused by a rickettsia that is carried by ticks. The symptoms include a purple-red rash of the extremities, fever, headache, and delirium. It responds to antibiotics.

Scalded skin syndrome: A bright-red, painful rash in which the skin peels off in sheets like a burn. The rash is caused by a toxin released by staph bacteria, often residing in the nose. The outcome is good.

Septicemia: A bacterial infection of the bloodstream in which the bacteria are actually multiplying there.

Subdural hematoma: A blood clot on the surface of the brain, usually due to direct trauma. Violently shaking a child by the shoulders so the head is snapped forward and back can also cause this life-threatening condition.

Sudden infant death syndrome (SIDS): The sudden unexplained death of a healthy infant under 12 months of age during sleep. The incidence is 2 in 1,000 live births. The cause remains unknown.

Testicular torsion: An unexplained twisting of a testicle that shuts off its blood supply and requires emergency surgical release. Presents with testicular pain and swelling.

Tetanus: A serious bacterial wound infection that progresses from local muscle spasms to total body rigidity and seizures. Preventable by DPT immunizations and tetanus boosters.

Thrombophlebitis: An infection of the lining of a vein, often the deep veins of the calf muscles.

Tonsillar abscess: An abscess deep within the tonsil that causes a severe sore throat, muffled voice, inability to open the mouth fully, and drooling. Requires surgical drainage.

Toxic shock syndrome: Symptoms include shock, fever, diarrhea, and a bright-pink (scarlet-fever like) rash. Caused by a toxin produced by a hidden staph infection. One common source of staph overgrowth is a tampon left in the vagina overnight.

Typhoid fever: A severe form of bacterial diarrhea (often bloody) that can lead to a bloodstream infection or intestinal complications. Treatable with antibiotics.

ACUTE ILLNESSES USUALLY TREATABLE AT HOME BUT REQUIRING A PHYSICIAN FOR DIAGNOSIS

Amenorrhea: The absence of menstrual periods. When regular periods stop, the most common causes are dieting, stress, or pregnancy.

Anemia: A low red-blood-cell count. While the causes are many, iron deficiency ranks first. A blood sample is needed to diagnose anemia.

Ascaris: A roundworm that causes intestinal infections. The main symptom is abdominal pain. In our country, mainly occurs in the Southeast.

Bell's palsy: An abrupt onset of weakness of the facial muscles on one side. Often associated with an ear infection, since the seventh (facial) nerve travels through the middle-ear space. Usually clears in 1 to 4 weeks.

Bronchiolitis: An infection of the bronchioles (small air passages) occurring in the first 2 years of life. The main symptoms are wheezing, rapid breathing, cough, runny nose, and fever. Caused by the respiratory syncytial virus.

Cat scratch fever: A swollen lymph node caused by the scratch of a young cat. Usually lasts several months. A bacterium has recently been identified as the infectious agent.

Chlamydia: A germ that causes urethral or vaginal infections. Spread by sexual contact. Can also cause eye infections or pneumonia in newborns by contact at birth.

Chondromalacia of the patella: A roughening of the underside of the kneecap causing knee pain in adolescents. Often due to excessive deep knee bends or running upstairs. Helped by rest and quadriceps-strengthening exercises.

Cold panniculitis: A lump of frozen fat tissue. Usually occurs in the fatty cheeks of infants less than 1 year of age. Due to prolonged contact with ice, Popsicles, cold metal, or cold weather. The lump can last 2 weeks and occasionally the overlying skin turns red.

Creeping eruption: A localized itchy rash consisting of a wavy red line. Caused by a tunneling young hookworm, from skin contact with dog or cat excrement. Common along the Atlantic coast. Lasts 1 to 2 months without treatment.

Ganglion: A cyst (smooth circular swelling filled with thick fluid) usually occurring on the back of the wrist. These outpouchings of the joint capsule probably result from trauma. Most eventually disappear. Surgery is necessary only if they become very large or painful.

Giardia: A small parasite that causes diarrhea. Without treatment, the diarrhea can last for months.

Goiter: An enlarged thyroid gland, found in the front of the neck. The causes are many.

Gonorrhea: A bacterium that can cause genital infections. Spread by sexual contact. Eye infections of newborns are usually prevented by routine application of silver nitrate or antibiotic eyedrops.

Granuloma annulare: Rings of little bumps, usually found at the ankle. The overlying skin looks normal. The cause is unknown. Clears spontaneously in 2 years.

Gynecomastia: The development of breast tissue in a boy. Usually mild (just breast buds) and a temporary normal condition of 14- to 16-year-old boys. Can be caused by an endocrine problem. Not to be confused with fat deposits in this area, commonly seen in overweight boys.

Heart murmur: A swishing noise heard over the heart. Due to turbulence in blood flow as it goes through the heart. While a murmur can be caused by heart disease, 99 percent are normal sounds (innocent or functional heart murmurs). Your physician can tell the difference. More than 50 percent of normal children have innocent murmurs.

Hepatitis: A viral infection of the liver leading to jaundice (yellow skin), light-colored bowel movements, and dark-colored urine.

Hernia, inguinal: A bulging in the groin due to a hole in the abdominal wall. Requires surgery.

Herpes stomatitis: A viral infection causing multiple small, painful ulcers of the gums and lining of the mouth. Associated fever. Usually occurs in young children and doesn't recur (unlike fever blisters).

Hyperventilation: Rapid, deep-breathing attacks due to emotional stress. The symptoms include a sensation of smothering, dizziness, and tingling of the mouth and fingers. Occasionally proceeds to fainting. Quickly relieved by breathing into a paper bag or deliberately slowing down to 1 breath every 5 seconds.

Hypoglycemia: Low blood sugar with symptoms of hunger, headache, trembling, and sweating. May proceed to convulsions. Commonly overdiagnosed in our country.

Infectious mononucleosis: A viral infection with fever, sore throat, swollen lymph nodes, and an enlarged spleen. Symptoms last 1 to 4 weeks.

Keloids: Overgrowth of scar tissue at sites of surgery or trauma. Some people have a tendency to produce raised scars. Plastic surgery can help.

Kyphosis: An exaggerated posterior curvature of the upper back and shoulders. Usually normal.

Labial adhesions: A fusion of the 2 labia minora by a thin membrane. Caused by irritation of the labia from soaps or a mild infection, followed by healing together. The vagina becomes covered over. Once adhesions have started, the labia are not easy to keep separated. Fortunately, the labia separate spontaneously with the onset of puberty and stay that way.

Lordosis: An exaggerated anterior curvature of the spine at the lower back. Usually normal.

Menorrhagia: Excessive or prolonged menstrual periods, often leading to anemia.

Mittelschmerz: Sharp lower abdominal pain on one side that occurs in menstruating women midway through their cycle. Lasts 1 to 2 days. Caused by small amount of blood or fluid contacting the abdominal lining when the egg is released from the ovary.

Molluscum contagiosum: Small ⅛-inch, skin-colored, waxy-looking bumps with indentations in the center. They contain a hard core. Caused by a virus and last 1 to 2 years, as with warts.

Pityriasis rosea: A rash of the chest, abdomen, and back characterized by matching oval-shaped red spots on both sides of the body. Lasts 4 to 8 weeks. Often preceded by a large scaly patch (herald patch) that resembles ringworm. Harmless and not contagious.

Pneumonia: An infection of the lungs. Generally not contagious.

Popliteal cyst: A smooth firm swelling behind the knee. Over 75 percent disappear spontaneously in 1 to 2 years. Also called a Baker's cyst. Surgery unnecessary unless it becomes painful or very large.

Pyelonephritis: A kidney infection.

Scabies: A very itchy skin rash consisting of small red bumps, pimples, and tunnels. Caused by a mite (small insect) that burrows under the skin to lay eggs. Very contagious.

Sexually transmitted diseases: Infections of the male and female genital tracts. Also called venereal diseases. Chlamydia has passed gonorrhea as the most common organism.

Shigella: A bacterium that causes severe diarrhea, often bloody. Treatable with antibiotics.

Spider nevus: A blood-vessel abnormality of the skin which looks like a spider. When the red spot in the center is pressed with a pen, all the small radiating blood vessels or spokes disappear. Occurs normally from age 6 to 12 in 50 percent of children. Clears spontaneously with puberty. Rarely associated with liver disease.

Strawberry hemangioma: A raised bright-red benign tumor that begins in the first month, grows rapidly during the first year, then slowly shrinks down until it disappears at age 5 to 10. Surgery is unnecessary.

Strep throat: A throat infection caused by streptococcus bacteria. Usually requires a throat culture for diagnosis. Responds to penicillin.

Striae: Stretch marks on the skin occurring in areas of rapid weight gain (e.g., the thighs), rapid muscle expansion (e.g., the shoulders of weight lifters), or on the abdomen during pregnancy. Usually temporary.

Subluxation of the radial head: A partial dislocation of one of the bones of the forearm (the radius) at the elbow. Due to being suddenly lifted or pulled by the hand. An infant with this injury will not use the arm and keeps the hand turned down. Easily remedied by your child's physician.

Swimmer's itch: A widespread itchy, bumpy red rash caused by a snail parasite (schistosome) that penetrates the human skin by mistake. While the parasite quickly dies, it causes a reaction for 1 to 2 weeks. Onset following exposure in freshwater lakes. Partially prevented by toweling off immediately on emerging from the water.

Trench mouth: A bacterial infection causing red, swollen, ulcerated gums and bad breath. Responds to dental hygiene and antibiotics. Not contagious.

Trichinosis: A disease due to a small roundworm sometimes found in pork. Transmitted by undercooking the meat. The symptoms of fever, a swollen face, and muscle pains begin 1 week later.

Trichomonas: An amoebalike organism that can cause vaginal infections and discharge.

Tuberculosis: A bacterial disease of the lungs that can go on for years if not treated. Symptoms include cough, fever, and weight loss. Now rare in the United States except in immigrants.

Urethritis: An infection of the urethra, or tube that drains urine from the bladder to the body's surface.

Urinary tract infection (UTI): An infection of the bladder (cystitis) or kidneys (pyelonephritis).

Vaginitis: An infection of the vagina. At least 6 causes, but not always sexually transmitted (e.g., monilial vaginitis).

Vitiligo: A patchy loss of skin pigment giving milk-white splotches of skin. Inherited as a dominant trait. While occurring in all races, it is a major cosmetic stress for dark-skinned people. Current treatment gives unsatisfactory improvement.

INDEX

Abdomen
  open wounds, first aid for, 26
  pain, 481–83, 537
  swallowed object in, 493–94
  tender, 6
  see also Appendicitis; Colic;
    Constipation; Diarrhea; Gas,
    intestinal; Gastrointestinal tract
    infections; Indigestion; Motion
    sickness; Vomiting
Abrasions, 67–68
Abscess
  skin, 315, 365–67
  tonsils, 464
Accident prevention
  allergic reaction, 12
  burns, 30
  car safety seats, 139–41
  child misbehavior, 215–17
  choking, 11
  drowning, 37
  electric shock, 38
  falls, 60–61
  heat reactions, 42
  infant safety, 139
  poisoning, 44
  sunburn, 400–401
Acetaminophen, 32, 33, 309, 522
Acne, 89, 356–59
Adenoid surgery, 461–64
Adolescents
  acne, 356–59
  aspirin use, 309
  athlete's foot, 359–61
  backache, 521–23
  bibliography, 302
  dandruff, 386–87
  discipline techniques, 196, 199,
    202–203
  and divorce, 281–82

exercise, 472–73
frequent infections in, 317–22
healthy diet, 112–14
jock itch, 372
menstrual cramps, 514–15
overweight, 242–45
pierced ears, 429–31
rebellion, 297–302
skin conditions, 340, 350, 356–59, 402
and smoking, 473
suicide, 7
underarm perspiration, 402
vaginal discomfort, 517–19
Adrenogenital syndrome, 532
Advertising, effect on children, 268,
  271
Aggressive behavior, 216–18, 269, 288,
  291
AIDS, 532
Air travel, 330, 421
Alarms, bed-wetting, 265–67
Alcoholic beverages, 45, 471, 534
Alcohol sponging, avoiding, 32, 311
Allergies
  antihistamines for, 174, 345, 410,
    414, 422, 443
  in breast-fed child, 102, 126
  of eyes, 409–10, 413, 442, 443
  to food, 110, 111, 178, 339
  and immunizations, 177–78, 479
  to medicines, 167, 169, 475
  severe, 12–13, 31
  and skin reactions, 339, 400, 429, 456
  see also Asthma; Eczema; Hay
    fever; Hives; Milk allergy
Alternative caregiver. *See* Babysitter;
  Child care resources, Father
Altitude changes, effect of, 323, 421–22
Alternative caregiver. *See* Babysitter;
  Child care resources, Father

Altitude changes, effect of, 323, 421–22
Amblyopia, 532
Amenorrhea, 544
Ampicillin reaction, 334–35, 483
Anal fissure, 486–87, 500, 501
Anaphylactic reaction, 12–13
Anemia, 112, 115, 396, 544
Anger, 192, 201, 210–11, 213, 281, 301
    see also Temper tantrum
Animal bites, 13–15
Animals. *See* Pets
Ankle, sprained, 50
Anorexia, 236, 532
Antibiotics, 167–68, 169, 171, 173, 370–71, 404, 420, 458
Antihistamines
    adverse reactions, 35
    for allergies, 174, 345, 410, 414, 422, 443
    for coughs, counterindicated, 473
    as first-aid treatment, 12, 174
Antipyretic, 309
Anxiety. *See* Fears and anxiety; Separation anxiety
Apnea, 27, 539
Apologizing, 234
Appendicitis, 481, 539
Appetite, poor, 35–40, 312 *see also* Eating disorders; Food; specific illnesses
Arachnids. *See* Scorpion bites; Spider bites
Arm pain, 50, 523
Armpit temperature, 305, 306
Arterial bleeding, 24–25
Arthritis, 537, 539
Ascaris, 544
Asphyxia. *See* Apnea, 27, 539
Aspirin, 32, 309, 522, 526
Asthma, 339, 532, 534
Astigmatism, 532
Athlete's foot, 359–61
Atopic dermatitis. *See* Eczema, 339–42
Attention deficit disorder, 288–93, 532
Axillary temperature, 305, 306
Baby. *See* Infant
Baby foods. *See* Food
Babysitter, 131, 194, 292, 297.
    see also Child care resources
Backache, 521–23
Backpack, infant, 145, 157, 186
Bad breath. *See* Halitosis, 451–52
Barky cough. *See* Croup
Bath
    for infant, 92, 143
    misbehavior, 233
    for muscle cramps, 523
    for skin irritation, 340–41, 346, 391, 501, 508–509

for vaginal discomfort, 518–19
Bedbug bites, 362, 363
Bedtime refusal, 187–90
Bed-wetting, 258, 261–67
Bee-sting, 12, 173, 361–62
Behavior, 179–302
    see also specific kinds
Bell's palsy, 544
Bifid uvula, 532
Biliary artresia, 532
Bilirubin. *See* Jaundice
Birth. *See* Childbirth preparation classes; Premature birth
Birth defects. *See* specific kinds
Birthmarks, 90–91, 547
Bites. *See* specific kinds, e.g., Human bites
Black eye, 53, 54, 58
Blackheads. *See* Acne, 356–59
Bladder
    abnormalities, 262, 264, 507–508
    control, 254–67
    stretching exercises, 263–64
    see also Toilet training; Urinary tract infections; Urination, painful
Bleeding, easy. *See* Bruises; Nosebleed
Bleeding, severe, 24–25, 55, 57
    see also Hemophilia
Blisters
    blood, 64
    and burns, 29, 399
    and diaper rash, 153
    fever, 320, 342, 401, 454
    foot or hand, 383–84
Blood
    from nose, 437
    Rh incompatibility, 155
    in stool, 499–502
    in urine, 510, 540
    vomiting of, 505–506, 540
Blood poisoning, 394, 406
Blood pressure, abnormal. *See* Hypertension; Shock
Blood sugar. *See* Diabetes; Hypoglycemia
Blowing nose. *See* Nose, clearing
Bluish lips, 6, 384, 468, 539
Body odor, 402
Boils, 315, 365–67
Bonding, parent-infant, 76
Bone and joint trauma, 49–52, 54–57, 69
    see also Fracture; specific body part
Bottle-feeding
    procedures, 99, 105–106
    and sleep problems, 128, 129–30, 182, 184
    supplies, 143
    and weight gain, 81
    see also Formula; Weaning

Botulism, 458, 539
Bowel movement, 254–56, 483–92, 500–502
  see also Constipation; Diarrhea; Fecal smearing; Toilet training
Brain
  illness of, 323–30
  minimal dysfunction, 536
  see also Mental retardation
Bran, 486
Brazelton, T. Berry, 124, 133, 279
Breast-feeding
  advantages, 97–98
  allergies and, 102, 126
  during illness, 155, 160, 491, 505
  medications and, 101
  procedures, 76–77, 97–100
  and sleep problems, 126, 128, 129, 182, 183
  supplemental bottle, 99
  and weight gain, 81–82, 240
  see also Weaning
Breast pumps, 99–100
Breasts, infant, 86
Breath-holding spells, 190–92, 212
Breathing
  noisy, 467–68, 480
  severe difficulty, 6, 26–27
  see also specific conditions
Bribing, 284–85
Broken bone. *See* Fracture, 49–50
Bronchiolitis, 544
Bronchitis, 470, 473
Bronchopulmonary dysplasia, 532
Bronchospasm, 534
Bruises
  muscle, 49
  skin, 64
Bubble bath, 519
Bulimia, 532
Bunions, 384–85
Burns
  chemical, 28
  sun, 398–400
  thermal, 28–30
Burping, 101, 105, 157

Calluses, 384–85
Camping, first-aid supplies, 172–73
Cancer. *See* Leukemia; Lymph nodes, cancer; Skin, cancer
Candida. See Yeast infection
Canker sores, 452–53, 459
Caput, 84
Car
  safety seat, 30, 60, 139–41
  use for emergency, 5, 42, 50
  see also Motion sickness; Seat belts

Cardiac Pulmonary Resuscitation (CPR), 38
Carotenemia, 393
Carrier, infant. *See* Front-carrier, infant
Cat scratch fever, 544
Cavities, *See* Teeth
Cellulitis, 539
Cephalohematoma, 84
Cerebellar ataxia, 539
Cerebral palsy, 533
Chalasia, 156
Chapped lips, 386
Charley horse, 49
Chemical
  allergy, 152, 340
  in eye, 38–39, 411–12
  poisoning by, 43
Chest pain, 468–69
Chicken noodle soup, 439
Chicken pox, 309, 315, 320, 335–37
  see also Shingles
Chigger bites, 362
Child abuse, 8, 201, 540
  see also Sexual abuse
Childbirth preparation classes, 75
Child care resources, 273–76
Child custody. *See* Divorce
Children
  behavior, 127–38
  diet, 112–19
  discipline techniques, 196–235
  frequent infections, 317–21
  growth, 119–21
  immunization, 175–78
  medication, 167–72
Child safety restraint laws, 60, 139–40
Chills, 311
Chlamydia, 544
Chlorpheniramine, 439
Choking, 9–11, 157
Cholecystitis, 540
Cholesterol. *See* Fat, animal
Chondromalacia, 544
Chronic diseases, 532–39
Cigarettes. *See* Smoking
Circumcision, 93–94, 507
Cleft lip/palate, 533
Clubfoot, 533
Coccyx injury, 69
Cognitive development, 122
Colds, 276, 314, 317–21, 327, 435–40, 462
  see also Ear; Eye; Nose
Cold sores. *See* Fever blisters
Colic, 124–27
Colitis, 538
Colon, irritable, 535
Coma, 31

Comedones, 358
Concussion. *See* Head, trauma
Congestion, 469
  ear, 421–22
  lungs, 469–73
  nose, 435–40, 442–44, 445–49,
    471–72
  sinus, 447–49
Conjunctivitis, 315, 411–13
Constipation, 258, 483–88, 495, 509
Contagious disease, 314–16
  see also specific disease
Conversion reaction, 540
Convulsions, 31–34, 308, 311
Cord, 163–65
Corns, 384–85
Corn syrup, 347, 439
Cornstarch, 92, 343
Coronary artery disease, 113
Corporal punishment. *See* Physical
    punishment
Cough
  contagious, 314
  severe, 468–73
  treatment, 174, 347, 439, 471–73
  see also Croup
Cough syrup and suppressants, 174,
    347, 439, 471–72, 473
Crabs. *See* Lice
Cradle cap, 151
Craniosynostosis, 533
Creeping eruption, 544–45
Crib death, 27, 543
Crib safety, 142–43, 228
Croup, 314, 459, 467, 474–77, 480
Crying
  colic, 124–27
  infant, 82, 124–27, 241
  and sleep problems, 185–86
Cryptorchidism, 533
Cuddling, 121, 126
Cup-feeding. *See* Weaning
Custody, child, 282
Cuts, 65–67
Cyanosis. *See* Bluish lips
Cystic fibrosis, 533
Cystitis. *See* Urinary tract infections

Dacryostenosis, 158
Dandruff, 386–87
Daycare. *See* Childcare, 273–76
Decongestants, 422, 438–39
Defecation. *See* Bowel movement;
    Constipation; Diarrhea; Toilet
    training
Dehydration
  from colds in infants, 436
  and overheating, 41–42

prevention of, 488
signs of, 7, 509, 511
treatment, 490, 491
and vomiting, 504
see also Fluid intake
Delirium, 35–36, 41, 311
Dental care. *See* Teeth
Depression, 281
  postpartum, 78–79
Dermatitis. *See* Eczema
Destructive behavior, 221–23
Development, normal, 121–24
Developmental milestones,
    122–24
Dextromethorphan, 472
Diabetes, 533
Diaper changing
  at night, 129, 183, 186
  bed-wetting, 262–63
  procedures, 92, 195, 227
  and strong urine odor, 511
  supplies, 144
Diaper rash, 152–54, 483, 492
Diarrhea
  allergy-related, 441, 483, 501
  causes, 488, 535
  danger signs, 488–89, 492
  infectious, 314, 317, 495
  misconceptions about, 492
  prevention, 320
  symptoms, 488
  treatment, 489–92
Diet. *See* Exercise, diet; Food;
    High-fiber diet; Overweight;
    Weight loss program
Diphtheria, 175, 177, 540
Diplopia, 540
Discharge or drainage. *See* specific
    body part or condition
Discipline
  and adolescents, 300–301
  bibliography, 203–204
  establishing, 192–96
  general techniques, 196–204
  and hyperactive child, 291
  positive reinforcement, 202–03
  punishment techniques, 196–99
  after parents' divorce, 281–82
  rules, 195–96
  and schoolwork, 286–87
  specific recommendations,
    213–35
  see also Physical punishment,
    Timeout
Disease. *See* Contagious disease;
    Infection; specific kinds
Disease glossary, 532–48
Disinfectants, 321–22
Dislocations, 49

Divorce, 280–82
Dizziness, 323–26
Down's syndrome, 534
Dressing misbehavior, 227–28
Drooling, 6, 459, 475
Drowning, 36–37
Drug abuse, 299
Drugs. *See* Medicine; specific kinds
Dysarthria. *See* Stuttering, 248–50
Dysfluency. *See* Stuttering, 248–50
Dysmenorrhea, 514–15
Dysphagia. *See* Swallowing difficulty
Dysuria. *See* Urination, painful

Ear
  congestion, 421–22
  discharge from, 422–23
  fluid in, 420, 421, 433–34, 537
  foreign body in, 425
  infections, 314, 346, 419–20, 429–36,
    462–63
  itchy, 425–26, 431–34
  newborn appearance, 85
  painful, 419–22, 432–34
  pulling at, 431–32
  swimmer's, 432–34
  trauma, 52–53
  travel's effect on, 329, 421
  tubes, 420, 463, 537
  wax in, 423–24
  see also Pierced ears
Earache, 419–22, 537
Eating problems and disorders,
    235–45, 532
Eczema, 339–42
Eel bites, 19
Egg allergy, 178
Electric shock, 37–38
Emergencies, 3–45
  see also specific conditions
Emergency Medical Technicians, 4
Emotional development, 121–24
Employment outside the home, 277–79
Encephalitis, 540
Encopresis. *See* Constipation; Toilet
    training
Endocarditis, 540
Enema, 487
Engorgement, in mother, 98, 99, 109
Enuresis. *See* Bed-wetting
Epiglottitis, 540
Epilepsy, 33, 178, 534
Epinephrine, 12
Epistaxsis. *See* Nosebleed
Erections, 87
Erythema, 98, 331, 353
  see also Fifth disease
Exercise

for constipation, 486
and diet, 116, 245, 268
when to avoid, 472–73, 523, 534
Eye
  allergies of, 409–11, 414, 442, 443
  antibiotic treatment, 78, 174, 415,
    417
  black, 53, 54, 58
  blocked tear duct, 158–59
  chemical in, 38–39, 412
  discharge from, 416–17, 437
  foreign body in, 39–40
  infections, 276, 320, 346, 411–18,
    436, 439
  itchy, 411
  and light sensitivity, 347, 399
  newborn appearance, 84–85
  red or pink, 411–12, 414
  stye, 414–16
  trauma, 53–54
  yellow discharge from, 416–17, 437
  see also Astigmatism; Myopia;
    Vasoconstrictor drops
Eyelids, swollen, 413–14

Failure-to-thrive, 540
Fainting, 326–27
Falls. *See* Head trauma
Family conferences, 300
Fat. *See* Overweight
Fat, animal, 113, 114, 244
Father
  and adolescents, 298–301
  and circumcision, 94
  and colicky baby, 126
  and discipline, 194
  and divorce, 280–82
  role with infant, 77, 78, 80–81, 82–83
  and sibling rivalry, 138
  and working wife, 278–79
Fatigue, in mother, 278
Fears and anxiety, 271, 277, 281, 294,
    295
  see also Separation anxiety
Febrile delirium, 35–36
Febrile seizure, 31–33
Fecal smearing, 234
Feces. *See* Bowel movement; Stools,
    abnormal; Toilet training
Feeding. *See* Breast-feeding; Bottle-
    feeding; Food; Weaning
Fetal alcohol syndrome, 534
Fever
  acetaminophen, 32, 33, 309, 522
  aspirin cautions, 309
  in breast-feeding mother, 101
  causes, 307
  danger signs, 308–309, 311–12

Fever *(continued)*
eating and sleeping with, 312–13
and frequent infections, 317–22
serious symptoms, 7, 31–32, 41, 305, 327
temperature-taking, 305–307, 311
treatment, 31–32, 309–11, 439
Fever blisters, 320, 342, 400, 454
Fiber, high, in diet, 113, 485–86, 501
Fifth disease, 315, 342
Finger injuries, 54–57
Fingernail
infected, 133, 387
newborn, care of, 93
spreading pinworm, 499
torn, treatment of, 56
Fire prevention and drills, 30
Fireworks, 30
First aid
allergic reaction, 12
bites, human, 16
bites, insect, 22–23
bites, marine, 16–19
bites, snake, 19
burns, 28, 29
convulsions, with fever, 32
convulsions, without fever, 34
drowning, 36
electric shock, 37–38
eye, 38–39
fracture, 49–50
heat reactions, 41
poisons, 43, 44
rabies contact, 14
sprain, 50
First-aid kit, 172–73
Fish bites, 16–19
Fit. *See* Convulsions
Flea bites, 362, 364
Flossing, 465
Flu. *See* Hemophilus influenza type B; Influenza
Fluid intake, 311, 476, 488–89, 504
Fluoride, 100, 102, 105, 117–18, 119
Folliculitis. *See* Pimples
Fontanel. *See* Soft spot
Food
advertising's effect on child, 268
choking avoidance, 11, 157
and eating misbehavior, 231–33
healthy diet, 112–17, 237, 484–86
and illness, 313, 439, 483, 489–91, 504
for infants, 107, 110–12, 461
junk, 117
myths, 116–17
refusal of, 108, 235–39, 457
and sleep problems, 182, 184
solid (strained), 110–12

spitting up, 156–58
supplies for infants, 144–45
see also Allergies; Eating disorders
Food poisoning. *See* Botulism
Foot
blisters, 383–84
clubbed, 533
infections, 359–61, 368–69
newborn appearance, 87–88
pain, 523–24
skin conditions, 385–86
Forceps marks, 90
Foreskin, 87, 93, 96–97
Formula, 101–106, 127, 504
see also Soy formula
Fractures, 49–50
Fragile X syndrome, 534
Frankenburg, William K., 122
Freckles, 390
Frequent infections, 317–19
Friends. *See* Peers; Play group
Friman, P.C., 134
Front-carrier, infant, 126, 128, 145, 157, 186
Frostbite, 55, 391

Galactosemia, 534
Ganglion, 545
Gas, intestinal, 133, 494–96
see also Burping; Colic
Gastrocolic reflex. *See* Bowel movement; Constipation
Gastroenteritis, 481, 487
Gastroesophageal reflux (GER), 156–57, 502, 534
Gastrointestinal tract infections, 317, 320, 321
Gates, child safety, 146
Genitals
care of, 509
groin/scrotum swelling, 516–17
menstrual cramps, 514–15
newborn appearance, 86–87
self-stimulation, 246–48
trauma, 57–58
vagina, irritation, 517–19
vagina, foreign body in, 513–14
see also specific body parts
German measles. *See* Rubella
Giardia, 545
Glands. *See* Lymph nodes, Mumps
Glomerulonephritis, 457
Goiter, 545
Gonorrhea, 545
Granuloma, 545
Groin
rash, 371–72
swelling, 516–17

"Growing pains," 523–24
Growth, normal, 119–20 *see also,*
    Height; Weight
Guillain-Barré syndrome, 540
Guilt, 279
Gum massage, 460
Gums, inflamed. *See* Canker sores
Gynecomastia, 545

Hair
    dandruff, 386–87
    loss, 392
    newborn's, 88
    washing, 92
Halitosis, 451–52
Hallucinations, visual, 35
Hand blisters, 383–84
Hand, foot, and mouth disease, 315,
    368–69
Hay fever, 317, 339, 410, 442–45
Head
    newborn's, 84
    trauma, 58–61
Headache, 327–29, 536
Health promotion
    accident prevention, 139–41
    bladder/bowel habits, 253–57
    breast-feeding, 97–102
    cold prevention, 440
    coronary artery disease prevention,
        113
    developmental stimulation, 121–22
    disease prevention, 321–22
    eating habits, 237–39
    exercise, 245, 268
    fluoride, 117–18
    healthy diet, 112–17, 237, 484–86
    immunizations, 175–76
    infection prevention, 320–22
    medical checkups, 82–83
    overweight prevention, 241–45
    parenting skills, 77
    school-refusal prevention, 297
    school responsibility, 283–87
    sleep habits, 127–32, 186
    smoking, avoiding, 30, 321, 472
    spoiling, prevention of, 192
    stuttering, prevention of, 249–50
    sunburn, protection from, 400–401
    tooth decay prevention, 117–19
    TV-addiction prevention, 269–71
    vitamins, 100, 105, 237
Heart failure, 463–64
Heat rash, 343–44
Heat reactions, 41–42
Height, normal, 119–20, 236
Heimlich maneuver, 8, 10
Hemangiomas, 90–91, 547

Hematemesis, 540
Hematoma, subdural, 191, 202, 543
Hematuria, 540
Hemolytic-uremic syndrome, 540
Hemophilia, 534
Hemophilus influenzae type B (H.
    flu), 176, 540
Hemoptysis, 541
Hemorrhagic disease, 541
Hepatitis, 314, 320, 321, 392, 545
Hernia, 164, 516, 545
Herpes, 315, 342, 452, 454
    see also Chicken pox; Fever blisters
Hiccups, 496
High blood pressure, 113, 535
Highchair, 144, 231
High-fiber diet, 113, 485–86, 501
Hip, 87, 534
Hives, 344–45
Hoarseness, 477–78
Home medicine chest, 173–74
Homesickness, 296
Homework, 283–87
Honey, 471
Hospital admission, indications for,
    532, 539–43
Hot tubs, 42
Hot-water heater setting, 30
Housework, 278–79
Human bites, 16
Humidifier, 144, 174, 440, 448, 472, 476
Hydrocele, 87, 516
Hydrocephalus, 535
Hydrocortisone cream, 17, 174, 340,
    376, 399, 518
Hydronephrosis, 535
Hymen, 86
Hyperactivity, 288–93, 532
Hyperopia, 535
Hypertension, 113, 535
Hyperventilation, 546
Hypoglycemia, 546
Hypospadias, 535
Hypothermia, 55, 391
Hypothyroidism, 535

Ibuprofen, 515, 516
Ice, as treatment, 50, 51, 174, 376
Illness. *See* specific types
Immune system disease, 317, 532
Immunizations, 175–78, 320, 348, 479
    see also specific types
Impetigo, 315, 320, 369–71
Incubation period, disease, 314–16
    see also specific diseases
Indigestion, 488
    see also Hiccups; Nausea; Spitting
        up; Vomiting

Infant
appearance, 88–91
development, 121–24
discipline techniques, 195, 204, 233
excessive weight gain, 109, 241–42
foods, 81, 97–106, 110–12
frequent infections, 317–22, 438
growth, 119–21
immunizations, 175–77
night awakening, 181–87
normal behavior, 83, 126–33
physical problems, 149–64
post-delivery, 75–83
safety, 139–41, 145–47
severe illness, 5–6, 149–50
skin care, 91–97, 152–53
sun exposure, 401
supplies, 142–48
Infantile paralysis. *See* Polio
Infant seat, 146, 157
see also Car, safety seat
Infection
contagious, 314–16
frequent, 317–19
incubation period, 314–16
noncontagious, 314
prevention, 320–22
wound, 406–407
see also specific body parts
Influenza, 309, 314, 478
see also Hemophilus influenzae
type B
Ingrown toenail, 403–4
Inguinal hernia, 516
Injuries. *See* body part
Insect bites, 361–65, 413, 475
Intussusception, 541
Ipecac, syrup of, 44, 45, 174
Iron, 102, 105, 115
Iron deficiency anemia. *See* Anemia
Itching
ear, 425–26, 431–34
eczema, 341
eye, 411
jock itch, 372
localized, 355–56
pinworms, 97–98
scabies, 547
swimmer's itch, 547–58
widespread, 323–33
vaginal, 517–18

Jaundice, 154–56, 392–93, 511
Jealousy, 136–38
Jellyfish bites, 17
Jock itch, 372
Joint trauma, 49–52
Junk foods, 117

Juvenile plantar dermatosis, 386

Kawasaki's disease, 541
Keloids, 546
Kidneys, 507, 509
see also Nephritis: Nephrosis
Kindergarten, 297
Klinefelter's syndrome, 535
Knee sprain, 50
Knuckle injury, 56–57
Koplick's spots, 346
Kyphosis, 546

Labia, 86, 509, 546
Lactose, 490, 495, 535
La Leche League, 99
Lancing, 366, 388
Language. *See* Speech development
Lanugo (infant body hair), 88
Laryngitis, 477
Latchkey children, 277
Laxative, 345, 453, 487
Learning disability, 285–87, 288–89,
292, 536
Leg
cramp, 524
injury, 49
limp, 525
newborn's, 87
pain, 523–24
Letdown reflex, 99
Lethargy, 5
Leukemia, 535
Lice, 315, 320, 373–74
Lies, 235
Ligament, pulled, 50
Lightning injury, 37–8
Limb. *See* Arm; Leg
Limp, 525
Lingual frenum, 161
Lip
cleft, 533
cold sores, 454–55
swollen, 456
see also Bluish lips; Chapped lips
Liquor. *See* Alcoholic beverages
Liver. *See* Jaundice; specific condi-
tions; e.g., Hepatitis
Lordosis, 546
Low blood pressure. *See* Shock
Lungs, 467–80
see also Pulmonary embolism
Lymph nodes
abscess, 464
cancer and, 394
function, 394
infections, noncontagious, 314

Lymph nodes *(continued)*
in groin, 516
pierced ears and, 430
swollen, 393–95, 430, 516
tenderness, with wound infection, 406

Malabsorption, 536
Malaria, 541
Maltsupex, 486
Marine animal bites, 16–19
Marriage, 279
see also Divorce; Father
Mastoiditis, 541
Masturbation, 246–48
Maternity leave, 272
Mattery eyes, 416–17
Measles, 176, 177, 315, 346–48
see also Rubella
Meatal ulcer, 153
Medicine chest, 173–74
Medicines
administration, 169–72
adverse reactions, 167, 168, 252, 504, 511
advertising of, 268
while breast-feeding, 101
child's refusal of, 170–72
first-aid kit, 172–73
indications for use, 167–68
medicine chest, 173–74
non-prescription, 167–71, 173–74
poisoning by, 43–44, 168
see also specific types and names
Melena, 541
Meningitis, 541
symptoms, 33, 308, 526
treatment, 314–15, 316, 321
Menorrhagia, 546
Menstruation
absence of, 544
cramps with, 514–15
Mental retardation, 536
Metabolism, diseases of, 535
Metric conversion for fever, 307
Microcephaly, 536
Milia, 90
Miliaria, 343–44
Milk, cow's
allergy, 103, 125, 126, 470, 490, 495, 496, 533, 535
for breast-feeding mother, 101
cleaning up, 157
during illness, 470, 473, 501, 511
low fat, 103, 242
recommended intake, 237
Minerals, 100
see also specific types

Minimal brain dysfunction (MBD), 536
Misbehavior, *See* Discipline
Mittelschmerz, 546
Molding, head, 84
Moles, 395–96
Molluscum contagiosum, 546
Mongolian spots, 90
Mongoloidism. *See* Down's syndrome
Mononucleosis, 316, 546
Mosquito bites, 362
Motion sickness, 329–30
Motor development, 121–24
Mountain sickness, acute, 323–25
Mouth
bad breath, 451–52
blisters, 452–53, 459
breathing, 463
canker sores, 452–54
infections, 159–60, 320, 368–69, 451–59, 548
newborn appearance, 85–86
sore throat, 457–59
thrush, 159–161
trauma, 61–62
ulcers, 452–53, 459
see also Fever blisters; Lip; Teeth; Tongue
Mouth-to-mouth breathing, 8–10, 38
Mucus, 437–38, 467, 472
Mumps, 175, 177, 316, 427–28
Muscles
bruises, 49, 51
pain, 49–52
spasms, 22, 24, 522, 523
strains, 49, 51
twitches, 131, 251–52
Muscular dystrophy, 536
Myopia, 536

Nagging, 284
Nail
infections, 133, 387, 499
ingrown, 403–404
newborn care, 93
trauma, 56
Naps, 132, 183, 186, 228
Nausea, 329, 497, 502
Navel, 163–65
Neck
acute pain, 525–27
stiff, 7, 33, 35, 526
injury, 7, 36, 50, 526
Negativism, 209–10, 229, 236, 256, 298
Nephritis, 541
Nephrosis, 542
Neurofibromatosis, 536
Nevi, 395–96

Newborn, 75–165
Nightmares, 131, 271
Night sweats, 402
Nits. *See* Lice
Noncontagious infections, 314
"No" saying (child). *See* Negativism
"No" saying (parental), 210
Nose
  bleeding, 445–46, 499
  clearing, 144, 174, 437–39, 467–68
  discharge from, 437, 440, 447
  foreign body in, 441
  infections, 314, 320, 329, 367,
    435–41, 461
  newborn appearance, 85
  trauma, 63
  see also Breathing; Colds; Conges-
    tion; Hay fever; Rhinitis; Sinus
Nosebleed, 445–46, 499
Nosedrops, homemade, 437–38
  see also Vasoconstrictor drops
Nursery school. *See* Preschool
Nursing. *See* Breast-feeding
Nutrition. *See* Food, healthy diet

Obesity. *See* Overweight
Omphalitis, 542
Oral hygiene. *See* Fluoride; Gum
  massage; Halitosis; Teeth
Oral rehydration solutions, 490, 504
Oral temperature, 306
Orchitis, 517
Organic foods, 116
Orthostatic proteinuria, 536
Osgood-Schlatter disease, 536
Osteomyelitis, 542
Otitis externa, 432–34
Otitis media. See Earache
Over-the-counter drugs. *See* Medicines,
  non-prescription
Overweight, 109, 113, 120, 241–45

Pacifier, 107, 128, 132, 135, 143, 157
Pain, as emergency symptom, 6
  see also specific types
Paleness, 396
Panniculitis, 544
Papilledema, 542
Parent-teacher conference, 285–86
Parotid gland, 427–29
Parvovirus, 342
Passivity, 267
Paternity leave, 80–81
Pectus excavatum, 536
Pediculosis. *See* Lice
Peers
  early contact, 122, 297

  misbehavior toward, 219–20
  relationships during adolescence,
    297–98, 299
  and school phobia, 296, 297
  see also Play group
Pelvic inflammatory disease, 542
Penis, 153, 510
  see also Circumcision; Erections;
    Foreskin
Peptic ulcer, 536
Pericarditis, 542
Peritonitis, 542
Perspiration, 402–404
Pertussis, 175, 316, 542
Petechiae, 348
Pets
  allergies to, 409–10, 443, 444
  bites from, 15
  as companion, 277
  disease spread and, 321, 373, 377–78
  misbehavior toward, 221
Pharyngitis. *See* Throat, infections
Phenylketonuria (PKU), 535, 537
Phobia, school, 293–97
Phototherapy, 155
Physical punishment, 193, 200–201,
  203, 291, 300
Pierced ears, 429–31, 494
Pimples, 397–98
  see also Acne; Boils
Pink birthmarks, 90–91
Pink eye, 315, 411–13
Pinworms, 314, 497–99
Pityriasis rosea, 546
Plantar wart, 404–405
Plant poisoning, 43, 45
Plastibel ring, 94, 95
Play group, 122, 297
Playmates. *See* Peers; Play group
Playpen, 146
Pneumonia, 314, 346, 436, 547
Pneumothorax, 542
Poisoning
  emergency procedures, 43–44
  from medications, 43–44, 170
  phone hot-line, 4
  prevention, 44–45, 169
Poison ivy, 375–76
Polio, 175, 177, 320, 537
Pollen, 409, 410, 442–44, 471
Polydactyly, 537
Popliteal cyst, 547
Positive reinforcement, 194, 202
Postnasal drip, 447, 470
Postpartum depression, 78–79
Potty chair, 255–56, 259
Premature birth, 537
Preschool, 274, 293, 297
Pressure points, arterial, 24

Prickly heat, 343–44
Psychiatrist/psychologist, 289
Profanity, 214
Public Health Department, 346
Pulled muscle/ligament, 50
Pulling ear, 431–32
Pulmonary embolism, 542
Puncture wounds, 66
Punishment. *See* Discipline; Physical
    punishment
Purple spots, 7, 21, 23, 24, 308, 348
Purpura, 348, 539, 541
Pyelonephritis, 314, 507
Pyloric stenosis, 542

Quality time, 278

Rabies, 13, 14, 15
Ragweed. *See* Pollen
Rash
    allergic, 339, 344, 375, 400, 429, 456
    contagious with skin contact,
        335, 365, 369, 373, 397, 406
    as immunization reaction, 348
    itchy, 332–3, 355–6
    localized, 353–81
    in newborn, 88–91, 153–54
    of unknown cause, 331–32, 343–54
    widespread, 331–52
    with viral infections, 335, 342,
        346, 349, 350, 368
    see also specific kinds
Rattling sounds, throat, 467, 480
Reading, 122, 131, 268, 269, 283, 285
Rebellion, adolescent, 297–99
Rectal itching. *See* Pinworms
Rectal temperature, 306
Red eye, 411–12, 414, 439
Regurgitation. *See* Spitting up;
    Vomiting
Rescue squads, 4
Respiration. *See* Apnea; Breathing;
    Resuscitation
Respiratory illnesses, 467–80
Resuscitation procedure, 8–9, 10, 38
Retardation. *See* Mental retardation
Retrolental fibroplasia, 537
Reyes syndrome, 309–11, 379, 542
Rheumatic fever, 457, 533, 537
Rh factor, 155
Rhinitis, 436, 442–44
R.I.C.E., 50
Ring, caught on finger, 57
Ringworm, 320, 372, 377–78, 380–81
Ritual, bedtime, 131, 188
Rocking to sleep, 126, 182
Rocky Mountain spotted fever, 542

Rooming-in, 76
Roseola, 315, 349
Roundworm. *See* Ascaris, 544
Roughage. *See* High-fiber diet
R-rated movies, 271
Rubella, 175, 177, 315, 350–51
Rubeola. *See* Measles
Rudeness, 214, 224–26, 301
Rule-setting, 195, 210, 283, 300
Running nose. *See* Nose, discharge
    from

Safety. *See* Accident prevention
Safety-related misbehavior, 215–17
Safety seat, car, 60, 139–41
Salt, 115, 492
Salt tablets, 42
Scabies, 315, 547
Scalded skin syndrome, 543
Scalp conditions. *See* Dandruff; Lice;
    Pimples
Scarlet fever, 315, 351–52
School
    for hyperactive children, 293
    homework responsibility, 283–87
    performance in, 268, 270, 281, 299
    return after illness, 318
    see also Preschool; Kindergarten
School refusal, 293–97
Scoliosis, 537
Scorpion bites, 21–22
Scrapes, 67–68
Scratches, 65–66
Scrotum. *See* Testicle/scrotum
Seat belts, 216
    see also Car, safety seat; Child
        safety restraint laws
Sea urchin stings, 18
Security object, 107, 130, 132, 182, 184,
    275
Seizures. *See* Convulsions
Self-esteem, 194, 281, 284, 289, 292,
    298
Separation anxiety, 130, 183, 186, 195,
    295, 297
Sexual abuse, 57, 518, 540
Sexually transmitted diseases, 547
    see also Venereal disease; specific
        types
Shampoo, 92, 151, 373, 381, 386–87, 425
Sharing, 220
Shingles, 315, 378–79
Shin splints, 49
Shock, 24, 26, 41
    see also Electric shock
Shoes, 147–48, 385, 403, 404
Short attention span. *See* Attention
    deficit disorder

Sibling
   and hyperactive child, 290
   misbehavior toward, 218–20
   and newborn, 78
   rivalry, 136–39
Sickle cell, 538
Single-parents, 279
Sinus, 314, 319, 437, 447–49, 471
Skin
   allergic reactions, 339, 344, 375, 400,
      429, 456
   cancer, 399
   care of, 92, 340, 357, 372
   cracked, 386
   dry, 338–39, 340–41
   foreign body in, 389
   itchy, 332–33, 355–56
   non-rash conditions, 383–407, 443
   pale, 396
   trauma, 64–68
   see also Rash; specific conditions
Sleep
   divorce, effect on, 281
   during illness, 313, 471
   misbehavior, 228–30
   position for aches, 522, 527
   problems, 127–32, 181–86
   see also Bedtime refusal; Naps;
      Nightmares; Snoring
Sleepwear, flame-resistant, 30
Sliver, 457–59
Smallpox, 176, 320
Smegma, 97
Smoke detectors, 30
Smoking, 30, 321, 472
Snakebites, 19–21
Sneezing. *See* Hay fever
Snoring, 463, 468
Snorting, 27, 467, 480
Soap, 519
Social development, 121–22
Social interaction, 268
   see also Peers
Soft spot, 7, 84, 330
Soiling. *See* Constipation; Toilet
      training
Sores, 380
Sore throat, 457–59
   see also Throat
Soy formula, 485, 490
Spacing of children, 138
Spanking. *See* Physical punishment
Special education evaluation, 293
Speech
   abnormal, 463
   development, 121–24, 234
   see also Stuttering
Spider bites, 23–24
Spider nevus, 547

Spina bifida, 538
Spinal cord injury, 526
Spitting up, 156–57, 502, 534
Splinters, 389
Spoiled child, 192
Sponging for fever, 32, 309, 311
Sports injury, 50
Sprains, 49–50
Staph infections, 321, 366, 367, 370,
      387, 397
Stealing, 222–23
Steroid cream. *See* Hydrocortisone
      cream
Stitches, 71–72
Stomach. *See* Abdomen
Stomach ache, 481–83
      see also Abdomen; Colic;
         Gastrointestinal tract infections
Stools, abnormal, 499–502
   blood in, 499–501
   unusual color of, 501–02
Stork bites (pink birthmarks), 90–91
Strabismus, 538
Strained muscle, 51
Strawberry hemangioma, 90–91, 547
Strep infections
   skin, 370, 387
   tests, 459
   throat, 315, 352, 457, 462, 547
Stress, 238, 252
Striae, 547
Stridor. *See* Croup
Stroller, 146
Stuffy nose, 144, 437–38
Stuttering, 248–50
Stye, 414–16
Subconjunctival hemorrhage, 54, 85
Subdural hematoma, 191, 202, 543
Subluxed radius, 50, 547
Sucking drive. *See* Bottle-feeding;
      Breast-feeding; Pacifier;
      Thumbsucking
Suction bulb, 144, 174, 437–38
Sudden infant death syndrome (SIDS),
      27, 543
Sugar, 115, 117, 119, 504
Suicide, 7
Sunburn, 398–401
Sunscreens, 174, 401, 455
Sunstroke, 41
Superkids, 122
Surgery, 461–64
Suture removal, 71–72
Swallowed objects, 493–94
Swallowing difficulty, 459, 464, 475
Swearing, 214
Sweating, excessive, 402–404
Swelling. *See* specific body part
Swimmer's ear, 432–34

Swimmer's itch, 547–48
Swing, infant, 145
Swollen glands, 393–95, 430, 516

T & A surgery, 461–64
Tailbone trauma, 69
Talking. *See* Speech development
Tarantula bites, 23
Tay-Sachs disease, 538
Teachers, 285–86
Tear duct, blocked, 158–59
Teenagers. *See* Adolescents
Teeth
  appearance at birth, 86
  brushing, 233, 452
  decay prevention, 100, 105–106, 108,
    113, 117–19
  painful, 464–65
  and thumbsucking, 133, 134–35
  trauma, 69
  see also Fluoride
Teething, 307, 460–61
Telephone, for emergency, 3–4
Television, 267–71, 283
Temperature. *See* Fever; Thermometer
Temperature strips, 307
Temper tantrum, 131, 191, 208–13, 224
Tension, 238, 252
Terrible twos, 208–14
Testicle/scrotum
  jock itch, 372
  swelling, 516–17
  tender, as emergency sign, 6,
    427–28, 516–17
  torsion, 517, 543
  undescended, 87, 533
Tetanus, 71, 175, 177, 543
Thermometer, 144, 174, 305–307
Throat
  infections, 314, 352, 439, 457, 461
  rattling sounds, 467, 480
  sore, 457–59
  strep, 315, 352, 457, 462, 547
  see also Cough; Swallowed objects;
    Swallowing difficulty
Thrombophlebitis, 543
Throwing up. *See* Vomiting
Thrush, 159–61
Thumbsucking, 132–36, 195, 387, 451,
  499
Thyroid. *See* Goiter; Hypothyroidism
Tick bites, 364–65
Tics, 251–53
  see also Tourette's syndrome
Timeout, 197, 202, 205–208, 212, 291,
  300
Tinea corporis. See Ringworm
Tine test, 175

Toe, 54–55, 88
Toenail, ingrown, 403–404
Toilet training, 195, 255–61, 485, 486
  see also Bed-wetting
Tongue, geographic, 455
Tongue-tie, 161
Tonsilitis, 457.
  see also Throat; Tonsils
Tonsils, 457, 461–64, 543
Toothache, 464–66
Tourette's syndrome, 538
Tourniquet, 12, 20, 25
Toxic shock syndrome, 516, 543
Tracheitis. *See* Cough
Transfusion, blood, 155, 462
Transitional object. *See* Security object
Transportation, emergency, 4–5
Transvestism, 538
Trauma. *See part of body*
Travel. *See* Air travel; Motion sickness;
  Water travel
Trench mouth, 548
Trichinosis, 548
Trichomonas, 548
Tuberculosis, 176, 316, 548
Turner's syndrome, 538
Typhoid fever, 543

Ulcer, peptic, 536
Ulcers, mouth. *See* Canker sores
Umbilical ord, 92, 143, 162–65
Umbilical hernia, 164–65
Umbilicus. *See* Navel
Upper respiratory infection. *See* Colds
Urethritis, 507, 548
Urinary tract infections, 314, 507, 548
Urination, painful, 507–508
Urine, blood in, 510
Urine, strong odor, 510–511
Urticaria. *See* Hives
Uterus, 514
UTI. *See* Urinary tract infections

Vaccines. *See* Immunizations
Vagina
  abnormal bleeding from, 57
  discharge, 86–87, 513, 514, 518
  foreign body in, 513
  irritated, 517–18
  newborn's, 86–87
  see also Labia; Vulva
Vaginitis, 548
Vaporizer. *See* Humidifier
Varicella. *See* Chicken pox
Vasoconstrictor drops
  for eyes, 411, 412, 443
  for nose, 174, 435, 439, 446, 448

Venereal disease, 315, 532, 545, 547
Venous bleeding, 24, 25
Ventilation tubes, 420, 463, 537
Violence, 269, 270
Vision. *See* Astigmatism, Eye, Myopia
Vitamin A, 359
Vitamin C, 441
Vitamin K, 78
Vitamins
  and advertising, 268
  for children, 112, 116, 237, 244
  for infants, 100, 105
Vitiligo, 548
Vocal cords, 474
Vomiting, 316, 502–506
  blood, 505–06
  during coughing spasm, 472
  and diarrhea, 489, 502
  inducing, 44
  and nausea, 497, 502
  self-induced, 532
Von Willebrand's disease, 338–39
Vulva, 507, 518

Waking at night. *See* Sleep,
  problems
Walkers, 147, 157
Walking
  painful, 525
  refusal, as emergency sign, 6

  see also Motor development
Warts, 315, 404–406
Water
  and heat reactions, 42
  for infants, 99, 105
  as poisoning antidote, 43
  for weight loss, 243
Water travel, 330
Weaning, 101, 105, 106–110
Weight, 81, 120, 235, 236, 241, 242–45
  see also Anorexia; Bulimia;
    Overweight
Weight-loss program, 242–45
Wheezing, 27, 467, 474, 480
Whining, 211
Whooping cough. *See* Pertussis
Wild animals, bites from. *See* Animal
  bites
Wilson's disease, 539
Working mother, 271–79, 319
Worms. *See* Ascaris; Pinworms;
  Ringworms; Roundworm
Wound infections, 406–07

Yeast infection, 152, 153, 160
Yellow discharge, 416–17, 437, 447, 449
Yellow eyes. *See* Jaundice

Zoster, 315, 378–79